Milan

timeout.com/milan

Published by Time Out Guides Ltd, a wholly owned subsidiary of Time Out Group Ltd.
Time Out and the Time Out logo are trademarks of Time Out Group Ltd.

© Time Out Group Ltd 2009
Previous editions 2002, 2004, 2006.

10 9 8 7 6 5 4 3 2 1

This edition first published in Great Britain in 2009 by Ebury Publishing
A Random House Group Company
20 Vauxhall Bridge Road, London SW1V 2SA

Random House UK Limited Reg. No. 954009

Random House Australia Pty Limited 20 Alfred Street, Milsons Point, Sydney, New South Wales 2061, Australia
Random House New Zealand Limited 18 Poland Road, Glenfield, Auckland 10, New Zealand
Random House South Africa (Pty) Limited Isle of Houghton, Corner Boundary Road & Carse O'Gowrie,
Houghton 2198, South Africa

Distributed in the US by Publishers Group West
Distributed in Canada by Publishers Group Canada

For further distribution details, see www.timeout.com

ISBN: 978-1-84670-059-0

A CIP catalogue record for this book is available from the British Library.

Printed and bound by Firmengruppe APPL, aprinta druck, Wemding, Germany.

The Random House Group Limited supports The Forest Stewardship Council (FSC), the leading international forest
certification organisation. All our titles that are printed on Greenpeace approved FSC certified paper carry the FSC
logo. Our paper procurement policy can be found at www.rbooks.co.uk/environment.

Time Out carbon-offsets all its flights with Trees for Cities (www.treesforcities.org).

Time Out Guides Limited
Universal House
251 Tottenham Court Road
London W1T 7AB
Tel + 44 (0)20 7813 3000
Fax + 44 (0)20 7813 6001
Email guides@timeout.com
www.timeout.com

Editorial

Editors Tristan Rutherford, Kathryn Tomasetti
Deputy Editor Edoardo Albert
Copy Editor Simon Cropper
Proofreader Marion Moisy
Indexer Ismay Atkins

Managing Director Peter Fiennes
Editorial Director Ruth Jarvis
Series Editor Will Fulford-Jones
Business Manager Dan Allen
Editorial Manager Holly Pick
Assistant Management Accountant Ija Krasnikova

Design

Art Director Scott Moore
Art Editor Pinelope Kourmouzoglou
Senior Designer Henry Elphick
Graphic Designers Gemma Doyle, Kei Ishimaru
Advertising Designer Jodi Sher

Picture Desk

Picture Editor Jael Marschner
Deputy Picture Editor Lynn Chambers
Picture Researcher Gemma Walters
Picture Desk Assistant Marzena Zoladz
Picture Librarian Christina Theisen

Advertising

Commercial Director Mark Phillips
International Advertising Manager Kasimir Berger
International Sales Executive Charlie Sokol
Advertising Sales (Milan) Fabio Giannini

Marketing

Marketing Manager Yvonne Poon
Sales & Marketing Director, North America Lisa Levinson
Senior Publishing Brand Manager Luthfa Begum
Marketing Designers Anthony Huggins, Nicola Wilson

Production

Group Production Director Mark Lamond
Production Manager Brendan McKeown
Production Controller Damian Bennett
Production Coordinator Julie Pallot

Time Out Group

Chairman Tony Elliott
Group General Manager/Director Nichola Coulthard
Time Out Communications Ltd MD David Pepper
Time Out International Ltd MD Cathy Runciman
Group IT Director Simon Chappell
Head of Marketing Catherine Demajo

Contributors

Written by Tristan Rutherford and Kathryn Tomasetti, except: **Milan Today** Tim Small. *The wise man of Giardini Pubblici* Tim Small. **Film** Tim Small. **Gay & Lesbian** Gianluca Fratantonio. **Music** Tim Small. **Nightlife** Tim Small. *Filthy rich football face-off* Tim Small. **Monza & Brianza** Tim Small. **Lago di Como** Dan Muirden.

Maps john@jsgraphics.co.uk, except: ATM transport map, used by kind permission of ATM.

Photography by Olivia Rutherford, except: page 14 Getty Images/Bridgeman Art Library; pages 16, 18, 168 Getty Images; page 38 Giampiero Briozzo; pages 143, 169 AFP/Getty Images; pages 149, 160 Gianluca Moggi; page 173 Lara Peviani; pages 178/179, 182/183, 187, 188, 196, 197, 208 Cesare Cicardini; page 190 www.hotelvillacrespi.it; page 194 Distretto Turistico dei Laghi. The following images were provided by the featured establishments/artists: pages 26, 27, 30, 35, 34, 36, 46, 47, 174, 181.

The Editors would like to thank Ornella Bortolato, Gianluca Fratantonio, Raoul de Jong, Ara Tokatyan, William and Myles Howorth, Nancy Di Mauro, Susan Rutherford, Elizabeth Tomasetti, Ann Lomas, Stefano Maranzana, Germana Colombo, Michael Furniss and Alessandra Smith at the Italian Tourist Board in London, and all contributors to previous editions of *Time Out Milan*, whose work forms the basis for parts of this book.

Contents

Introduction

Milan was the Western Roman Empire's capital for a short but significant 109 years. Its position at the top was reconfirmed by Napoleon in 1786, when he declared the city his centre of the Cisalpine Republic. Rome was chosen, some say arbitrarily, as Italy's capital in 1861. But for most northern Italians, Milan is the country's heart.

You won't be dashing from street to street ticking sights off a must-see list, à la Florence, but cultural gems are hardly few and far between. The city is home to Leonardo da Vinci's *Last Supper*, arguably the artist's finest achievement, it was miraculously spared from World War II bombing as the building around it fell. Caravaggio's *Basket of Fruit* hangs in the Pinacoteca Ambrosiana, while his *Supper at Emmaus* graces the Pinacoteca Brera. And the recently restored Duomo is a majestic Gothic folly that took half a millennium to complete. But the city's charms can also be understated: there are pleasures in its dusty churches, on the narrow streets of the Brera district, and in courtyards glimpsed through wrought-iron gates.

Milan is Italy's business capital, home to the country's stock exchange as well as its renowned fashion and design industries. But while people work hard, they play hard too. Whether you're up for eating or drinking, football or shopping, Milan excels at recreation. The so-called Fashion Rectangle is lined with D&G, Versace and Armani boutiques, but you'll delight as much in the stores of local designers. There's not a seat free during the twice-yearly derby at the San Siro Stadium, home for both AC Milan and Inter. And the feast day of Sant'Ambrogio, the city's patron saint, is such a celebration that a massive street fair shuts down a whole neighbourhood. The date also marks the opening night of La Scala's opera season.

On the flip side? The euro has caused the city to become more and more expensive. The pollution can be oppressive: on a good day, you'll see the Alps from the roof of the Duomo, but on a bad day, city driving is restricted according to number plates in an ongoing attempt to lower vehicle emissions. Local politics can be complex and chaotic, with issues so complex that they're often unintelligible even to the Milanese. There are also those who claim that Milan is overly urban and unlike the rest of Italy. There may be some truth in this, but chatty barmen still serve cappuccinos with heart-shaped froth to their female customers, and the markets' vegetable vendors succeed in bringing the countryside to Milan and forcing the city slickers to slow their pace for a moment.

Those who look beyond the glamour will discover a city that strides out in style. Locals look to the future, whether it be the 2015 Expo or next season's catwalks. They just sometimes need tourists to show them what a treasure they have right here, right now.

ABOUT TIME OUT CITY GUIDES

This is the fourth edition of *Time Out Milan*, one of an expanding series of more than 50 guides produced by the people behind the successful listings magazines in London, New York, Chicago, Sydney and many more cities around the world. Our guides are all written and updated by resident experts who have striven to provide you with all the most up-to-date information you'll need to explore Milan, whether you're a local or a first-time visitor.

THE LOWDOWN ON THE LISTINGS

Above all, we've tried to make this book as useful as possible. Addresses, telephone numbers, websites, transport information, opening times, admission prices and credit card details have all been included in the listings, as have details of other selected services and facilities. However, owners and managers can change their arrangements. Also, in Milan, small shops and bars rarely keep precise opening hours, and may close earlier or later than stated. Similarly, arts programmes are often finalised very late. Before you go out of your way, we strongly advise you to call and check opening times and other particulars. While every effort has been made to ensure the accuracy of the information contained in this guide, the publishers cannot accept responsibility for any errors it may contain.

THE LIE OF THE LAND

To make both book and city easier to navigate, we've divided Milan into five areas and assigned each one its own section in the Sightseeing part of the book. These area designations have also been used in addresses

throughout the guide, and are illustrated on the overview map on page 247.

For all addresses given in the book, we've details of the nearest public transport option(s) and a reference to the series of fully indexed colour maps at the back of this guide, which start on page 248. The precise locations of hotels (❶), restaurants (❶), and cafés and bars (❶) have all been pinpointed on these maps; the section also includes a transport map and a street index.

TELEPHONE NUMBERS

The area code for Milan is 02. In Italy, it is necessary to dial provincial area codes with all numbers, even for local calls. Therefore, all normal Milan numbers begin 02, whether you're calling from inside or outside the city. All phone numbers listed in this guide take this code unless stated. We've identified premium-rate and mobile numbers, which will incur extra calling costs.

The country code for Italy is 39. To dial numbers as given in this book from abroad, use your country's exit code (00 in the UK, 011 in the US) or the + symbol (on many mobile phones), followed by the country code, followed by the number as listed. For more on phones, including information on mobiles, *see p232.*

Advertisers

We would like to stress that no establishment has been included in this guide because it has advertised in any of our publications and no payment of any kind has influenced any review. The opinions given in this book are those of Time Out writers and are entirely independent.

PRICES AND PAYMENT

Our listings detail which of the four major credit cards – American Express (AmEx), Diners Club (DC), MasterCard (MC) and Visa (V) – are accepted by individual venues. Some businesses will also accept other cards, such as Maestro and Carte Blanche, as well as travellers' cheques issued by a major financial institution.

The prices we've supplied should be treated as guidelines, not gospel. Fluctuating exchange rates and inflation can cause charges, particularly in shops and restaurants, to change rapidly. If prices vary wildly from those we've quoted, ask whether there's a good reason, then please email to let us know. We aim to give the best and most up-to-date advice, and we always want to know if you've been badly treated or seriously overcharged.

ESSENTIAL INFORMATION

For all the practical information you might need for visiting the city, including customs and immigration information, disabled access, emergency telephone numbers, the lowdown on the local transport network and a list of useful websites, turn to the Directory at the back of this guide. It starts on page 217

LET US KNOW WHAT YOU THINK

We hope you enjoy *Time Out Milan*, and we'd like to know what you think of it. We welcome tips for places that you consider we should include in future editions, and take notice of your criticism of our choices. You can email us at guides@timeout.com.

There is an online version of this guide, along with guides to more than 50 other international cities, at **www.timeout.com**.

In Context

Features

Castello Sforzesco. *See p61*.

Duomo. *See p18.*

History

Beaten at home by the Spanish, French and Germans, resilient Milan is now top of the league.

Italy's strategic gateway to the north has had 2,000 years of two-way traffic: trade out, and occupying armies in. At one stage or another, Celts, Goths, Spaniards, French and Austrians have ruled the city, and at times it seems that the *Milanesi* have taken traits such as style, passion and a prodigious work ethic from each one. For the most part, its Italian overlords – including the Viscontis, the Sforzas, and later Mussolini himself – bequeathed the grandest gifts on the city, although their rule was often as cruel as the rest. But when the going gets really tough, the locals look up from their balance sheets and firmly give their leaders the boot.

EARLY SETTLEMENTS

From prehistoric times up to the Roman conquest, Lombardy's earliest inhabitants, the Camun people, had settlements in the Valcamonica area in the province of Brescia. Down on the marshy plain of the Po river, other tribes, mostly from Liguria, dwelt in stilt-houses by the side of the region's many lakes. The rest of the Italian peninsula was populated by Italic peoples and Etruscans. Gallo-Celtic tribes moved across the Alps and into the fertile plains of the Po Valley some time between the fifth and fourth centuries BC, spreading into territory occupied by Ligurians and Etruscans, and pitching camp in the vicinity of what are now Milan, Brescia, Bergamo and Lombardy's other major cities.

These Celts – particularly the Insubre tribe, whose settlement where Milan now stands was large and dominant by this time – had their hearts set on further expansion towards the south. But it was not to be, though, since it was the Romans who pushed their borders northwards into what they termed Cisalpine Gaul ('Gaul this side of the Alps'). In the 280s BC they began their slow drive across the Po Valley from the east, founding colonies as they went and conquering the town they renamed Mediolanum in 222 BC.

ROMANS AND CHRISTIANS

It was not all plain sailing for the Roman conquerors: during the Second Punic War (218-201 BC), for example, northern Italy's Celts and Ligurians rallied to Hannibal, helping the great Carthaginian general's exhausted troops beat the Romans back across the Po.

It was a temporary hitch, however, and by 42 BC Rome had exerted its hold over Cisalpine Gaul sufficiently to make it officially part of its Italian territories. In his reorganisation of Italy in 15 BC, Emperor Augustus made Mediolanum the capital of the Transpadania region, which included the towns of Como, Bergamo, Pavia and Lodi, and extended as far west as Turin. No longer a mere military garrison, and with its own municipal and judicial structures, Mediolanum began to take on the importance expected of a city placed so strategically between the Italian peninsula and the areas beyond the Alps where Roman interests were so strong.

During the relatively peaceful times that extended from the reign of Augustus, the placid agricultural zone of northern Italy flourished: roads were built and rivers made navigable, to the benefit of communications and trade. And though the area's elite still preferred their country villas to urban residences, towns were endowed with suitably imposing monuments.

When barbarian tribes began baying at the Roman empire's northern borders in the third century AD, Diocletian split the empire into two halves to streamline its military capacities. From AD 292 Mediolanum became the effective capital of the western emperor, Diocletian himself, whereas Byzantium was home to Maximian, his eastern counterpart, leaving Rome to languish.

> ## 'Under Diocletian and his persecuting successors, Milan chalked up nearly as many top-notch martyrs as Rome.'

As Milan's political and military star rose, so did its importance as a centre of Christianity, which – according to local lore – was brought to the city by St Barnabas, a friend of St Paul. Under Diocletian and his persecuting successors, Milan chalked up nearly as many top-notch martyrs as Rome.

Palazzo Reale. *See p20.*

Constantine the Great (306-37), who reunified the two halves of the empire under his sole control and was strongly aware of Mediolanum's strategic importance, diplomatically issued the Edict of Milan (313), putting an end to the persecution of Christians and paving the way for Christianity to become the religion of state. St Ambrose was elected bishop of Milan in 374, remaining in that office until his death in 397. His celebrated piety and charity conferred untold prestige on the local Church, giving his successors in the region unrivalled spiritual and temporal clout for centuries to come.

In 402, Emperor Honorius moved the seat of the empire to Ravenna, which meant that Milan was now pretty much at the mercy of waves of attacking barbarian tribes. When Attila the Hun left the city in 452, Milan was a smouldering wreck. It was partially rebuilt, only to be razed again by the Goths in 489 and 539. Most of the population had taken refuge in the countryside, and the clergy had fled to Genoa. However, by that time, the fate of the beleaguered city was of little interest to anyone. After the death in 476 of the last western emperor, Romulus Augustulus, and the collapse of the empire, Odoacer – the Latinised Goth

A deck of dastardly dictators

Pope or pauper, it didn't pay to get on the wrong side of Milan's strongman leaders. These three tough nuts are the hardest.

Bernabò Visconti (1323-85)

In the Visconti dynasty of hard men, Bernabò was the ace in the pack. He had 20 illegitimate children and a pack of hunting dogs 5,000 strong. While ruling the eastern part of the empire on behalf of his brothers Matteo and Galeazzo, he massacred the animal population in his domains between Bergamo, Brescia and Cremona. Never one to overlook the slightest infraction, he once

had a youth whipped 'because the boy had dreamed of killing a boar'. When not hunting, Bernabò taxed his overburdened populace to pay for wars against Pope Innocent VI, as well as the cities of Florence, Venice and Savoy. Despite taking a bung of 500,000 gold florins in 1364 from pope Urban V to 'maintain the peace in Northern Italy', Milan's odious overlord was back to his bellicose old tricks after a matter of months. Excommunication followed in 1373. In 1385 he was captured and imprisoned by his nephew (and son-in-law, keeping it in the family) Gian Galeazzo Visconti, and probably poisoned.

Iron fist rating 8
Warmongering 10
Nutcase quotient 9
Between the sheets 10
Brainpower 2

Ludovico 'il Moro' Sforza (1452-1508)

The wily fox of the Sforza clan, Ludovico (*pictured*) was a fine manipulator of power. He seized control of the government by preventing the regency going to the 11-year-old son of Bona of Savoy (he was also Ludovico's nephew), Gian Galeazzo in 1480; he kept the young duke a virtual prisoner until his death in 1495. Ruling as regent himself, *il Moro* secured Milan's ducal crown in 1493 by marrying his niece, Bianca, to Holy Roman Emperor Maximilian I. The power games degenerated into farce a year later, when Ludovico invited the French into Italy to regain the Neapolitan throne, only to turn on them, precipitating another 300 years of Gallic invasion. Betrayed by his own mercenaries and captured by a vengeful Louis XII in 1499, he died in the dungeons of a castle in Loches

who wielded the greatest power on the peninsula – had himself crowned king in what had become northern Italy's most important town: not Milan, but Pavia, to the south.

GERMANIC INVASIONS

For decades, Goths and Byzantines alternately colluded and squabbled for control of the Italian peninsula, heedless of the threat swiftly mounting on the other side of the Alps, where the bloodthirsty King Alboin was forging antagonistic tribes of Germanic Lombard peoples into something like a unified front. In 568, the Lombards began their relatively

eight years later. It must be noted, however, that marriage to the beautiful 14-year-old Beatrice d'Este in 1489 did soften Ludovico's heart of stone. Renaissance artists (Bramante and da Vinci among them) and universities were all patronised.
Iron fist rating 8
Warmongering 9
Nutcase quotient 7
Between the sheets 3
Brainpower 5

Joseph Radetzky von Radetz (1766-1858)

A soldier's soldier, this galloping general was immortalised by Johann Strauss's triumphalist *Radetzky March*. Joining the Austrian army at the age of 19, he was in the thick of the action in wars as far afield as Turkey, Germany, Italy, France and the Netherlands before the age of 33. At the pensionable age of 70, he was made Field Marshal, and found himself in the middle of the *Cinque Giornate* (five days) revolt *(see p20)* 12 years later. Forced out of the Porta Tosa city gate by the Milanese rioters on 22 March 1848, he tactfully retreated to Lodi with his 16,000 troops and 400 cannon. It took iron will to wait for reinforcements; he then defeated the Piedmontese at Custoza and Novara and returned to impose an iron rule on Milan. In 1858 he died at the age of 91, and lay in state in the city. The real Risorgimento kicked off a year later.
Iron fist rating 9
Warmongering 9
Nutcase quotient 2
Between the sheets 6
Brainpower 10

challenge-free rampage through northern Italy, setting up their capital in Pavia, which fell to the invaders after a siege in 572. The region they overran was a shadow of its former self, its agriculture and infrastructure in tatters. This seemed to matter little to the Lombards, who taxed and oppressed with glee, only becoming slightly less hostile after wily Pope Gregory the Great (590-604) persuaded the Lombard Queen Theodolinda to convert her people from Arianism (the heretical version of Christianity espoused by the Lombards which taught that Christ was not one with the Father, but rather saw Jesus as a created being, even though pre-eminent) to Roman-style Christianity.

Later popes continued to clash with the ever-expanding Lombards, whose territory now extended from the myriad dukedoms of the Po Valley to the far south of mainland Italy. With the Normans of southern Italy also making life difficult for the occupant of the throne of St Peter's, outside help was sought, in the shape of the Franks. In the second half of the eighth century the head of this Germanic tribe was Charlemagne, a mighty warrior and impressive politician who, although illiterate, had established a glittering court at Aachen, from where he had set out to conquer much of western Europe. In 774 Charlemagne turned his attention to Italy, where he crushed the Lombards – at the time under the leadership of King Desiderius, who was Charlemagne's own father-in-law – and added King of the Lombards to his long list of titles.

Pope Leo III awarded him yet another title – *imperator augustus*, later known as Holy Roman Emperor – in 800. In the short term, it was a sound move on the part of the pontiff, forcing Charlemagne to uphold papal rights against encroaching foes. But after Charlemagne's death in 814, no one could live up to his mighty reputation, and even before his direct family line died out, his empire fell into the hands of bickering minor lords.

Northern Italy was no exception. Already, under Lombard and Carolingian rule, religious orders had established control over large swathes of countryside, building monasteries in the midst of rich agricultural and pastoral holdings. With Magyar invaders harrying them through the ninth and tenth centuries, the locals barricaded themselves into a series of fortified hamlets, each proclaiming its territorial rights over the surrounding countryside and laying the foundations of an extensive feudal system that would later come into conflict with the religious oligarchy.

With the end of the Carolingian line in 888, northern Italy passed into the control of a series of Frankish *reucci* ('little kings'), who

Milan in the early 20th century.

sometimes found themselves in conflict with the questionable characters titled *imperator augustus* by popes kept under the thumbs of Roman nobles. It was the unwise attempt by kinglet Berengar II to force Adelaide, widow of his predecessor Lothar, to marry him (or possibly his son Adalbert; sources are divided) that upset this state of affairs. In 961, the eastern Frankish king Otto I responded to a plea for help from the beautiful Adelaide, who had been locked up in a tower overlooking Lake Garda by her would-be spouse (or, possibly, father-in-law). Otto invaded Italy, carried Adelaide off, and the following year was crowned Holy Roman Emperor in Rome.

Under Otto I, Otto II and, in particular, the devout Otto III, Lombardy's clergy had a field day. The Church was given precedence over the landed nobility, whose uppitiness irked the emperors and whose power was consequently reduced. In Milan a building boom gave the city a succession of new Romanesque landmarks – including the **basilica of Sant'Ambrogio** (*see p89*). Allied with the *cives* – city-dwelling merchants or tradesmen – the clergy became the effective rulers of Lombardy's increasingly wealthy cities from some time around the start of the new millennium.

MERCHANT RANCOUR

By the end of the 11th century, the *cives* were demanding a greater degree of control: in Milan a *consulatus civium* (town council meeting) was recorded in 1097. The towns of Bergamo, Brescia, Como, Cremona and Mantova followed suit in the second decade of the following century. The first of these meetings was held very much under the clergy's auspices, in the *brolo* (garden) of the bishop's palace – hence the abundance of later town halls around Lombardy called palazzo del Broletto.

But increasing civic feistiness also brought the various settlements of the Lombardy region into conflict with each other. Milan, the strongest and wealthiest, imposed its supremacy over Lodi, Cremona, Como and even Pavia, in spite of the latter's imperial connections. This was too much for the Holy Roman Emperor of the time, Frederick Barbarossa, who marched across the Alps to bring Milan to heel. At the end of a seven-month siege in 1162, the emperor had the city's fortifications pulled down and the palaces of leading anti-imperial agitators destroyed. Hated as Milan was by many of its neighbours, Barbarossa's heavy-handed treatment failed to endear him to any of the wary cities of

Lombardy. In 1167, at a meeting of their representatives at Pontida, the *comuni* (towns run by the people) banded together in the Lega Lombarda (Lombard League). Its symbol was a large cart (*carroccio*) with the Lombard standard flying atop it; popular lore has it that the forces of the Lombard League were rallied around this cart when they engaged with and beat back the imperial troops at the Battle of Legnano in 1176. Sentimentalists of the Risorgimento (*see p20*) saw this battle – the subject of the eponymous opera by Giuseppe Verdi – as the beginning of Italian resistance to foreign tyrants; but if truth be told, it was the emperor as tax-imposer, rather than as foreign power, they were fighting against. The moment the Holy Roman Empire ceased to be a threat, the *comuni* returned to their self-interested squabbling.

The Battle of Legnano was followed by further skirmishing against the emperor's forces, but in 1183 the Peace of Konstanz finally awarded Milan the privileges of independence and self-government it had long dreamed of. The city could now settle down to its own internal bickering. Most of the trouble arose from conflicts between the old aristocracy and the pushy ranks of merchants and tradesmen. The city's institutions were powerless to resolve these problems, so solutions were sought from outside, with the aristos lining up with the

pro-empire Ghibelline party, and the parvenus joining the pro-papal Guelphs.

This was yet another indication of Milan's innate inability to free itself from outside interference. Admittedly, geography was against it: Lombardy was inevitably the doorway into Italy for a stream of northern invaders. But the city's habit of wavering between outside powers eventually sealed its fate. In 1266 Pope Clement IV summoned Charles d'Anjou from France to deal with Barbarossa's heirs in Sicily. Forced into a decision, Milan's dominant Guelph (that is, pro-papacy) faction, led by the Torriani family, opted to back the anti-empire movement.

But if there was one thing you could be sure of, it was that popes never backed winners forever: they were unwilling to let anyone get too strong. Charles conquered the south and became king of Sicily, but then the pope switched allegiance, championed a German candidate for the title of emperor, and even backed anti-papal Ghibelline forces in the north.

FAMILY RULE

Among these forces was one Ottone Visconti, an archbishop of Milan who had been ousted by the Torriani family. Ottone seized the initiative, scoring a major victory over the Torrianis in 1277. One year later he was declared *signore* (lord) of the city. The old *comune* system was

Castello Sforzesco. *See p19.*

Milan, 1960.

over: Milan – like many other northern Italian cities – was going the way of one-family rule.

In 1294, on payment of 50,000 florins to Holy Roman Emperor Henry VII, Ottone's great-nephew and designated successor, Matteo, was given the title of *vicario imperiale* (imperial delegate), a rank that also gave him a claim to authority over Milan's neighbours. He was driven out of Milan in 1302 by the Torriani family, but with the emperor's support he made a triumphant return in 1311. From then on, the Viscontis went from strength to strength. In 1330, Azzone Visconti was proclaimed *dominus generalis* (general ruler). Within the space of a generation, the surrounding cities all acknowledged Visconti rule.

> **'There was nothing velvet-gloved about Gian Galeazzo's command. He had a chancellor accused of treachery walled up alive.'**

The family's splendour reached its zenith with the rule of Gian Galeazzo Visconti (1378-1402), who obtained the title of Duke of Milan

in 1395 from Emperor Wenceslas. Two years later he was promoted to Duke of Lombardy: Gian Galeazzo ruled over the second-largest *signoria* in Italy (only the kingdom of Naples was bigger), which included Milan, Pavia, Bergamo, Brescia, Como, Lodi and Cremona, among other cities. Gian Galeazzo was a man of learning and culture, but there was nothing velvet-gloved about his command. Local feudal lords who refused to recognise his authority had their castles razed and were whisked off to prison. One chancellor, accused of treachery, was walled up alive.

It was under this intelligent but ruthless despot that Milan became the largest city in Italy, with a population of around 250,000, at the turn of the 15th century. Major building projects were embarked upon in the region, including the Certosa (charterhouse) in Pavia and the **Duomo** of Milan (*see p52*). When Visconti died of the plague in 1402, the great duchy was divided among his heirs, with his wife Caterina left as regent and tutoress.

Elsewhere in the duchy, Gian Galeazzo's death was the signal for other *signori* to raise their heads; Pandolfo III Malatesta declared himself *signore* of Bergamo and Brescia, and Facino Cane took over the territory in the west.

In Milan, meanwhile, Caterina died – perhaps poisoned – just two years after her husband; and their eldest son, Giovanni Maria, was killed on his way to church. It fell to the younger son, Filippo Maria, to try to regain control of things. He had inherited his father's ambitious spirit and intelligence, along with his bookish habits and suspicious mind. But Milan's further-flung neighbours proved more resilient than they had been in his father's day: despite a number of wars against Florence and Venice, Filippo Maria ruled over a much-reduced duchy, with Bergamo and Brescia ceding to Venice.

A CULTURAL COURT

When Filippo Maria died in 1447, leaving no male heirs, a group of noblemen attempted to re-establish republican life, setting up the *Aurea Repubblica Ambrosiana* (literally, Golden Ambrosian Republic). Never slow to take advantage of a neighbour's weakness, Venice attacked, grabbing Piacenza and Lodi. The new authorities of Milan foolishly entrusted their defence to Francesco Sforza, husband of Filippo Maria Visconti's illegitimate daughter Bianca Maria, and the closest thing there was to a direct Visconti heir. Francesco won back the lost cities, but then did a secret deal with the Venetians, giving them Brescia and other territories in exchange for their recognition of him as the new duke of Lombardy.

After a brief siege, Milan's republican forces capitulated in 1450. Francesco's rule was even more magnificent than that of Gian Galeazzo Visconti. He transformed the city into a powerful metropolis, building among other things the **Castello Sforzesco** (*see p62*) and the Ospedale Maggiore, now **Ca' Granda** (*see p80*). On his death in 1466 he was succeeded by his pleasure-loving son Galeazzo Maria, whose determination to turn the court into a brothel-cum-circus did not endear him to all his subjects. This was made clear in 1476, when he was stabbed to death in church by three young patricians.

As his son was only seven at the time, Galeazzo Maria's wife gave the regency to a trusted minister and two of her husband's brothers. The younger, Ludovico Mauro, known as *il Moro* (the Moor) because of his dark complexion, was clearly the dominant figure, and very soon he had the reins of power securely in his hands. He proved a good ruler, encouraging agricultural development and the silk industry. Under him, the court became one of Italy's great centres of art and culture, with architects like Donato Bramante and polymaths such as Leonardo da Vinci given free scope. Only the court of Mantova could compete for brilliance: there, Ludovico's sister-in-law, the

urbane Isabella d'Este, had married into the Gonzaga family and reigned over a centre of high culture that included court painter Andrea Mantegna.

The life expectancy of these brilliant Renaissance courts was, however, short. On a military level, they hadn't a hope of vying with Europe's great powers. In a fatally flawed attempt to neutralise two birds with one cunningly thrown stone (Naples and France both had a claim on the Duchy of Milan through complicated inter-dynastic marriages), Ludovico suggested that King Charles VIII of France might wish to regain the throne of Naples, which had been seized from the French Anjous by the Spaniards. Charles, who had dreams of becoming a second Charlemagne, was just waiting to be persuaded, and in 1494 he descended into Italy, with encouragement also from Florence and the Pope.

However, after a fairly easy victory in the south, Charles decided upon what was to become a French habit in Italy, and began looting the Kingdom of Naples. At this point he lost the approval of the Neapolitan population and also learned how short-lived papal support could be. Pope Alexander organised a Holy Alliance to drive him out, getting the backing of Ludovico as well. In 1495, Charles was defeated at Fornovo, near Parma, and returned to France.

But four years later, France's new king, Louis XII, took his revenge. When he invaded Italy – determined, among other things, to claim his rights to Milan – Ludovico appealed to the Holy Roman Emperor Maximilian. The ragged army of Swiss and German mercenaries that the emperor drummed up could not match French firepower, and with the help of Mantova's Gonzaga family, the French took *il Moro* prisoner in 1499; he died in France in 1508.

In the same year, French-ruled Milan joined the League of Cambrai, which had been summoned by the great warrior – if not exactly holy – Pope Julius II to counter the threat posed by the expansion of Venice to the Italian mainland. The League scored a major victory against the Venetians at Agnadello (1509), after which the pope – surprise, surprise – switched sides and supported the Venetians. In 1513, the papal armies, Venice and Spain all turned on the French, who were expelled from Lombardy, and Ludovico's son Massimiliano was put in power.

By this time, though, Lombardy's role as rugby ball in the endless scrimmages between the great powers – France, Austria and Spain – was firmly established: for the next three and a half centuries, the region was trampled over by foreign armies and swapped among the great rulers. It was to become a pawn in the Thirty

Years War (1618-48), which pitted Catholic leaders against Protestant, and the Habsburgs against just about everyone else in Europe.

SPANISH SUBORDINATION

The region enjoyed a 14-year semblance of autonomy after France's king Francis I was defeated at Pavia in 1525, his efforts to assert French hereditary rights over Lombardy stymied by imperial forces. Massimiliano Sforza's brother Francesco ruled under the tutelage of the Holy Roman Emperor Charles V (a Habsburg, and King Charles I of Spain); but when Francesco died in 1535, Charles assumed direct power. So began 170 years of Spanish domination. The once-proud independent Duchy of Milan became the neglected capital of a province: administered, guarded and taxed by foreigners.

Milan's population fell from 130,000 to 70,000; industry and agriculture wouldn't recover from the crisis until near the end of the 17th century. When the last Gonzaga died in 1627, another convoluted war of succession ensued, bringing invaders, famine and disease in its wake. The plague of 1630 was especially devastating in Milan, killing thousands.

In the second half of the 17th century, Milan's religious life was given fresh vigour by the imposing Cardinal (later Saint) Carlo Borromeo. He was a leading figure of the Counter-Reformation – the movement that had arisen out of the Council of Trent (1545-63), which was convened to clean up a corrupt Catholic Church so it could hold its own against the spread of Protestantism.

The 18th century began with the impossibly complicated War of Spanish Succession (1701-14), following attempts by the French king Louis XIV – who was married to a Habsburg – to grab for France all the various European possessions of Spain's last Habsburg monarch, Charles II. In 1706, in the course of this war, Milan was occupied by Eugenio von Savoy (whose Italian/German/French name indicates the complexity of his background) on behalf of Emperor Joseph I of Austria; the Peace of Utrecht (1713), and then the Treaty of Rastadt (1714), confirmed the new occupation.

AUSTRIAN ENLIGHTENMENT

Administratively, the Austrians were a step up from the Spaniards, who had made it their business to improve as little and tax as much as possible. They implemented various reforms, one of which was to draw up a land registry for tax purposes. Suddenly, aristocratic land-owners faced an unprecedented need to make their land profitable, which helped get the economy moving.

The Austrians also did their best to alleviate some of the worst judicial abuses, abolishing ecclesiastic tribunals and the use of torture (to the dismay of some conservative Lombards). The intellectual climate brightened as well: a number of lively journals were published in Milan, and Enlightenment ideas began to trickle down through the educated classes. Numerous learned institutions were founded, including the Accademia di Brera, instituted by Empress Maria Teresa in 1776. The **Teatro alla Scala** (*see p59*) was opened in 1778.

'If there is one thing that characterises the Milanese, it's their determination to improve on past records.'

It was in this climate of enlightenment that Napoleon, seen by many optimists at the time as embodying the spirit of democratic reform, was received so enthusiastically when he marched into Milan in May 1796. Milan became the capital of Napoleon's Cisalpine Republic. It was perhaps with rather less enthusiasm, in 1805, that the Milanese watched the French emperor assume the throne of Italy in the Duomo – and the same iron crown that had once sat on the heads of the old Lombard kings.

After Napoleon's fall in 1814, the Congress of Vienna restored Lombardy to Austria. Although the region thrived culturally and economically during the 19th century, the Milanese remained largely hostile to Austrian rule. This hostility found a musical outlet in some of Verdi's early operas, but finally exploded in the heroic *Cinque Giornate* (five days) of 1848, after an initial street protest led to the capture of Austrian seat of power, the Palazzo del Governo (the building now known as the **Palazzo Reale**; *see p55*). Inspired by the spirit of the Risorgimento – the Italy-wide movement to create a united country – the Milanese succeeded in throwing the Austrians out of the city after five days of street fighting. However, owing to the military incompetence of Carlo Emanuele of Piedmont, to whom the generally republican leaders of the insurrection had reluctantly turned for aid, the uprising eventually failed. Austrian forces re-entered the city, which, along with the whole of the Lombardy region, was placed under the iron-fisted control of their commander-in-chief, Count Joseph Radetzky.

UNIFICATION AND FASCISM

Liberation didn't come until the Second War of Independence in 1859. This time, under the pressure of combined military intervention by the French and the Piedmontese – and with the decisive action of Risorgimento hero Giuseppe Garibaldi and his guerrilla troops – the Austrians were forced to cede Lombardy to Vittorio Emanuele II of Savoy, the first king of a united Italy.

Though few doubted that the seat of government had to be Rome, Milan clearly considered itself the new country's cultural and financial capital. In the years immediately after unification, the city celebrated its free status by undertaking a number of grandiose building projects, including the construction of the great **Galleria Vittorio Emanuele II** (*see p55*).

On a more practical level, the opening of the San Gottardo tunnel through the Alps facilitated trade with northern Europe, and gave another boost, if one were needed, to Lombardy's industry. The flip side of this boom was suffering and unrest among the workers. Support for socialism grew; a general strike in 1898 was repressed with extreme brutality, leaving 81 'subversives' dead and 502 injured. Just after World War I, there were 445 strikes within the space of a single year; it was in this

tumultuous climate that the Fascist party began its thuggish activities, with some of its earliest attacks being launched in Milan against the socialist newspaper *Avanti* (previously edited, curiously enough, by Mussolini himself).

'It was in Milan that the fallen Mussolini made his final appearance – strung up in piazzale Loreto.'

With Fascism established, demonstrations of proletarian discontent disappeared. It was not until 1943 that Milanese workers dared manifest their displeasure once again, bringing several factories in Milan and Turin to a halt; these protests contributed to the downfall of Mussolini's regime in July the same year (*see p69* **Mussolini's monolith**). In April 1945 the population of Milan rekindled the old 1848 spirit, rising up against the occupying Nazi forces and liberating the city in just three days. If there's one thing that characterises the

Resurrecting Roman Milan

They came, they saw, they built. Although Milan got its name from the Celts who arrived in about 388 BC – they called it Midlan, meaning 'a place in between' – it was the Romans who left the oldest indelible mark on the city. By the time of Christ, Roman Mediolanum, as it was then known, was a growing provincial capital eager to keep up with the Caesars down south.

As well as various artefacts in several of Milan's museums, including the **Civico Museo Archeologico** (*see p92*) and **Civici Musei del Castello** (*see p62*), evidence of the Romans' presence can be traced in modern-day Milan's basic street layout. In classic Roman city planning, a Decumanus Maximus intersected the Cardo or Cardus Maximus perpendicularly at the forum. In Milan, the Decumanus can be seen in the line that goes from via Santa Maria alla Porta, via Santa Maria Folcorina, via del Bollo, and then towards corso di Porta Romana (and thereafter, of course, Rome). The line of the Cardo goes from via Nerino, via Cantù, via Santa Margherita, piazza della Scala and along via Manzoni. The forum would have been in the area of piazza San Sepolcro, where the Pinacoteca and Biblioteca Ambrosiana are now located.

Rather more evocative of ancient Rome's glory is what remains of the city walls. The best bits are in via Circo, just off via Torino, and in the garden of the Civico Museo Archeologico, where one of the watchtowers is still intact.

Unearthed in 1935 and recently opened to the public is the **amphitheatre** on via de Amicis (*see p82*). Built on an elliptical plan, and not much smaller than Rome's Coliseum, it accommodated 35,000 spectators. The splendour of Roman rule is really brought to life by the Columns of San Lorenzo, which were probably once part of a temple or civic bathhouse – and baths were big business in those days. They stand about ten metres (30 feet) high on corso di Porta Ticinese.

Other Roman finds include the square tower on Corso Magenta's **church of San Maurizio** (*see p91*). A section of the foundations of the San Vittore fort can be found in one of the courtyards at the **Museo Nazionale della Scienza** (*see p88*), as can an octagonal imperial mausoleum thought to be the resting place of Emperor Valentinian II.

Milan remained under Roman domination until 452 AD, when Attila the Hun, culture vulture that he was, left his mark by razing the city to the ground.

Milanese, it's their determination to improve on past records. And it was in Milan that the fallen Mussolini made his grisly final public appearance. Having been captured in Dongo on Lake Como and executed by partisans in 1945, Mussolini and his mistress Clara Petacci were strung up for all to see in piazzale Loreto.

POST-WAR PROSPERITY

At the end of World War II, Lombardy was instrumental in the boom that transformed Italy from an agricultural country to an industrial powerhouse. Over nine million Italians moved from one part of the country to another in search of work between 1955 and 1971, and many ended up in Milan and the larger cities of Lombardy, where work was plentiful. Rich in heavy industry, such as steelworks, car manufacturing and railway construction, the area also provided good opportunities for anyone with a winning idea and plenty of energy to set up their own small concern.

As they expanded to become players on the international stage, these small, often family-run companies found they needed help promoting their businesses. Milan soon developed into the capital of Italy's media industries, including PR and advertising. Long the home of most of the country's book and magazine publishers, the city also provided the base for the birth of commercial television. Silvio Berlusconi caught this wave in the early 1970s when he founded Telemilano.

Despite urban terrorism in the late 1970s and early '80s, Lombardy's new industries continued to gain momentum. In 1975, trying to secure his place in the country's burgeoning fashion industry, which was finding its focus in Milan, Piacenza-born Giorgio Armani sold his Volkswagen to finance his business. Having left his home in Reggio Calabria for Paris, Gianni Versace returned to Italy in 1978 and started plying his trade – in Milan.

By the 1980s, Lombardy – one of Italy's 20 regions – was generating 20 per cent of the country's GDP. The spectacular wealth that Milan had accumulated proved too tempting; in 1992, a scandal blew up: businesses were having to hand kickbacks (*tangenti*) to government officials if they wanted to win contracts. Led by judge Antonio di Pietro, a six-year investigation – dubbed *Tangentopoli* – followed. Arrests were many, but convictions were few, the statute of limitations saving many from jail sentences. Being nothing if not resilient, however, Lombardy as a whole, and Milan in particular, was able to absorb the blow to its reputation as the 'moral capital of Italy'. Economically, a new wave of immigration, the introduction of the euro and a global boom in design, finance and fashion helped the city to grow and prosper through the start of the new millennium. And in 2008, Milan was awarded the hosting of Expo 2015, allowing the city to firmly seize the crown as Italy's economic and soon-to-be cultural capital.

As fashionable on the outside as it is within. **Galleria Vittoria Emanule II**. *See p21.*

Milan Today

Skyscrapers of change.

'Things must change if they are to remain the same.' This phrase, from Giuseppe Tomasi di Lampedusa's classic novel *Il Gattopardo*, is one of the most perceptive statements ever used to describe modern Italy. The nation is Europe's greatest paradox: a traditional culture with a Byzantine bureaucracy at the heart of the EU and the G8; a place where staggering beauty lives alongside the most extraordinary chaos.

In Milan, Italy's most vigorous, affluent, and international city, these contradictions exist at their most extreme. After long years of economic stagnation and general citywide depression, it seems feasible that things may, at last, be on the up – but does this mean they will remain the same? With luck, not exactly.

Italy has one of the world's oldest population averages, and one of the lowest birth rates. In an age of transparency and modernity, the country is still seriously afflicted by the mafia and organised crime – and, contrary to international perception, not merely in Italy's south. It has a lethargic economy, built principally on a mixture of state-subsidised conglomerates and struggling small- to medium-sized family companies. Most economists see the country as ill equipped to face the rising threats from emerging markets, and not dynamic enough to embrace them. It's wedded to traditional safety nets and a conservative religion. And even though these factors stifle meritocracy and progress, promote nepotism and allow rampant intolerance to alternative lifestyles, they are clung to still.

In 2008, the words on Milanese lips have been *la crisi* (the crisis). Economic indicators are so dire that most locals choose to pretend they don't exist. Average economic growth has hovered around one per cent for the past three years, and average inflation has been three per cent per year over the same period. Since the adoption of the euro in 2002, consumer prices have effectively doubled. And how many Milanese shops are cutting their losses with closing-down sales this week?

'There's no doubt that there's less money going around, and thus less opportunities', says *Libero* journalist Francesco Borgonovo, 'but this is true for the whole of Italy, not just

Milan exposed

A century after its first World Fair in 1906, on 31 March 2008, Milan won the bid for Expo 2015. With the first phase under discussion and the press proclaiming a new era for the city, Milan has gone Expo crazy.

The Expo will be spread over 170 hectares (420 acres) in the Rho and Pero areas of north-west Milan. Massimiliano Fuksas, architect of the new Fiera trade centre in Rho, will design the project. Unsurprisingly in such a food-conscious country, the Expo's theme will be 'Feeding the Planet, Energy for Life'. Home to the Slow Food movement (*see p96*) and its spin-off, the University of Gastronomic Sciences in Pollenzo, Italy also has the European Food Safety Authority headquarters in Parma. The non-profit Food Bank was developed in Milan, and provides meals to underprivileged people throughout the country. The Expo plans to explore food-related themes ranging from biodiversity to fish scarcity, and from agricultural techniques to how best to use local produce.

One of the city's most interesting plans, in keeping with the environmentally conscious theme, is to connect the city centre and the Expo via an extension of the *navigli*, the historic canals partly designed by Leonardo da Vinci. Footpaths will line the banks, stemming from the Darsena near piazza XXIV Maggio, adding a much-needed green injection.

In the run-up to 2015, other futuristic plans will come to fruition in the city. The former railway station of Porta Vittoria will see the long-awaited construction of the European Library of Information and Culture, due to be the biggest on the continent. CityLife, a complex of parkland, skyscrapers and a museum, will replace a portion of the old Fiera grounds by 2011. The new City of Fashion (*see p35*) is underway in the Garibaldi district, and a World Jewellery Centre is planned for the zone of Portello.

The Expo promises to be a world-class event, changing the city's skyline and its pace dramatically. But locals have their doubts. With time something of a fluid concept in these Mediterranean climes, there are fears that the big plans may get strangled by the country's red tape. For news of programmes and progress, see the Expo website, www.milanoexpo-2015.com.

---

for Milan.' Indeed, the rising house prices have driven young families out of the city, with access to the property ladder too difficult for most. The real estate market is hardly helped by Italian lenders. Although they may be on a definitive course of improvement, most are still reluctant to hand out loans, particularly in comparison to banks and building societies elsewhere in Europe. Higher home prices means less consumer spending; less consumer spending means that less cash finds its way into shopkeepers' pockets; which in turn results in more lay-offs and more shops closing.

Is Milan at an all time-low? 'If you expect the drinking, partying Milan of the 1980s, or the Milan of the gangsters and cabarets of the '60s, prepare to be disappointed,' says Borgonovo. 'But if you think there's a crisis, the best way to deal with it is to shut up, get busy, and organise something – and many Milanese are doing so.'

Journalist Federico Sarica has a cyclical theory: 'Italy is a country in strong institutional and economic decline. There's an incredible need for reform. But Milan was great in the '60s, culturally and economically. It sunk to darkness in the '70s, but bounced back in the '80s with a golden age for fashion and media. Then it shut itself indoors after the *mani pulite* (clean hands) scandal in the mid '90s. Now we're at the end of a negative cycle. Let's see what happens.'

Although the country's economy is faring fairly badly, there are strong contrasts in Italy's northern capital. Milan's unemployment rate is about half that of the rest of the country. In addition to the food, fashion and fun, the nation's richest city still tops the global charts in many aspects of innovation, from science and engineering to art and design. Be it in luxury goods or sports cars or high-end furniture, Milan is at the pinnacle of its game. It is Italy's star in the fields of finance, media, publishing, music, football, design and advertising; it's even home to Europe's only seven-star hotel.

'Are the wheels of change already creaking beneath the surface?'

Milan teeters on the brink of much-needed change and reform, while retaining its confidence and an enduring capability to pick itself up by its bootstraps. After all, the Milanese are resilient and strong: their city has been rebuilt from scratch at least five times (the last time after the Allies carpet-bombed the area at the end of World War II). History proves its potential for greatness, too. And yet, whether the Milanese are right to feel smugly self-confident remains to be seen. The next few years will be crucial to the city's long-term future, and, indirectly, to Italy as a whole. Everything is based on a simple question: is the city looking at a long slump that may last another decade, or are the wheels of change already creaking beneath the surface?

There are several glimmers of hope. Theoretically, Milan's Expo 2015 World Fair could be revolutionary. A world fair gave Chicago a place on the world map, and another gave Paris its most enduring symbol, the Eiffel Tower. For the next seven years, Milan will be a construction site, with €20 billion of private and public investment pouring in for a much needed urban facelift. And unlike Italy's many 'soft' deadlines, this one is set in stone.

Then there's CityLife, a project to revamp the old Fiera area in the city's north-west, that is gearing itself up as innovative and eco-friendly. Architects Zaha Hadid, Daniel Libeskind and Shota Isozaki are on board, with designs for three steel-and-glass skyscrapers that jut out at improbable angles from a brand new park. Isozaki's skyscraper is the city's tallest building, at 215 metres (705 feet). Eleven square kilometres (4.2 square miles) of parks are also scheduled for development, in a bid to swing the primarily grey leaf-to-concrete ratio.

However, only time will tell whether Milan's Expo endowment will produce an iconic success or a disastrous scandal à la Hanover 2000 (the German bid ended in public ridicule and a €1 billion public deficit). 'Some money will be misdirected, inevitably, but the opportunity is truly epochal,' says Federico Sarica. 'Something great is going to come out of it, perhaps thanks to private investors more than the public administration. I certainly believe Milan will profit from it, ultimately.' One thing the image-conscious Milanese hate is public humiliation, and there's no doubt they will strive for perfection in the world's eyes.

Other projects may swing Milan into a new golden decade. Headlining the improvements are two new metro lines: the M4, running from Lorenteggio in the west, through Parco Vetra and Sant'Ambrogio in the centre, and on until Linate airport in the east; and the M5, linking the San Siro football stadium in the north, Garibaldi and Bicocca to the town of Monza.

The introduction of EcoPass, a project that endeavours to limit pollution by requiring drivers to buy a ticket to enter the town centre, has been controversial. Part of the ticket price will be reinvested in public transport, bike lanes and a proposed new scheme for municipal rental bicycles, similar to that introduced with great success in Paris in 2007.

The number of English-speakers in the city has jumped in the past decade, as has the number of international visitors. With a new trade fair at Rho, Europe's biggest, plus new planned high-speed rail routes to France, Switzerland and Austria, Milan is plying its wares north of the border, rather than aiming southwards to Rome. Although Milan is the country's most multicultural city, it's still light-years away from Amsterdam or London. Its growing Chinese and Albanian populations are often tagged by the Milanese as a leech on the economy, widely blamed for crime or seen as dens of vice. In reality, they are the economic drivers that keep the service trade running.

Conversely, many people believe that the current 'credit crunch' may prove to be a great leveller, letting Milan close the gap on other European cities. Italians are historically distrustful of banks, holidaying in their family's second homes and eating vegetables grown by their relatives. Indeed, the worse aspects of the credit crisis may pass this country by.

Finally, as the covers come off the newly renovated Duomo and Stazione Centrale, the city's symbolic heart and main trade link respectively, even the ever-cynical Milanese have reason to take renewed aesthetic pride in their city. The coming decade could see vibrant Milan emerge as a Berlin or a Barcelona, rather than a Birmingham or a Bremen. In Italy's capital of the north, things really are changing.

Zanotta.

Design in Milan

At home with the style council.

THE BACKGROUND

In the 1940s, Italy's industrial powerhouse rebuilt itself – not for the first time – with all the energy it could muster. Milan put the misery of World War II behind it, and by the early 1950s, the world at large got its first taste of what would become Milan's modernist yet utterly practical trademark: industrial design.

In and around Milan, design firms founded in the 1920s and '30s began to resurface. **Alessi**, creating kitchenware on Lago d'Orta, had been set up in 1921; brothers Cesare and Umberto Cassina had established **Cassina in Meda**, Brianza, in 1927, making high-end furniture for cruise ships and restaurants; and Gio Ponti, Lucio Fontana and Pietro Chiesa had created **FontanaArte** in 1932 while they were still unknown young designers. After the war, these designers and manufacturers sprang back into action, and practical objects were deftly created with a now familiar Italian flair.

The origins of industrial design as a movement are hard to pinpoint. The term defines a blend of function and aesthetics, and the concept was born of an attempt to achieve mass production with a modicum of artistic beauty – or perhaps, more accurately, a creative injection of cleverness and humour. Whether it was the Milanese curiosity or pure and simple passion, the city soon boasted a range of great individual designers and design manufacturers.

THE DESIGNERS

Born in Milan 1918, **Achille Castiglioni** (www.achillecastiglioni.it) would become one of Italy's most renowned industrial designers. After studying architecture, he and his two brothers set up a studio in the city in 1944. Paring down the form of existing items to their very essence, Castiglioni shot to fame during the '50s with his Mezzadro stool, made from the chair of a tractor, and the Sella stool, created from a bicycle seat. **Zanotta** (piazza Tricolore 2, 02 7601 6445, www.zanotta.it, closed Mon am, Sun & Aug), established by manufacturer Aurelio Zanotta in 1954, produced both items.

Through the 1950s, a decade of great post-war reconstruction for Italy, and the '60s, the Castiglioni brothers continued to create experimental home furnishings and lamps.

They developed strong ties with Milan-based manufacturer, **Flos** (corso Monforte 9, 02 7600 3639, closed Mon am, Sun & Aug). Castiglioni designed the company's showroom, and Flos produced Castiglioni's designs. Particularly popular was the Arco, a massive, arched lamp with a marble base that could be stood in a corner and still overhang the centre of a room.

A genius in his field, Castiglioni came up with the revolutionary 'principal design component' theory. Any good design, he believed, must be approached with a clear idea of what will make it work – this component could be its practical function, or the use of a newly developed technology – and not purely aesthetics. (Asking designers about their 'filo conduttore' is a feature of Italian *Elle Décor* even today.) This theory helped to establish a more general understanding of what makes objects in industrial design successful.

In 1961, the **Salone Internazionale del Mobile** (*see p142*) was launched, with 328 exhibitors and as many as 12,000 visitors. This new annual event, paired with the city's thriving design activity, meant the creative world's attention was slowly beginning to focus on Milan. As most of the country's factories had been built shortly after the war, they contained the latest technology, and were able to draw on cheap labour, and from the outset, the fair was notable for its fine, innovative and high-quality products.

The charismatic **Ettore Sottsass**, a fount of big, bold ideas, landed on the Milanese scene at around the same time as Castiglioni, establishing his own studio in the city in 1947. Experimenting in the fields of fine art, journalism and architecture, while curating exhibitions at the city's **Triennale** (Milan's craft and design headquarters since 1933; *see p63*), Sottsass rocketed to fame after his design for Olivetti's ELEA 9003 calculator won the prestigious Compasso d'Oro industrial design award. He also designed the famously sexy red Valentine typewriter for Olivetti in 1970.

Sottsass was a passionate amateur photographer. He was obsessed with the documentation of his own life, and used the world around him – his memory often triggered by his thousands of photos – to inspire his imagination and object development. He designed pieces for most of the big Lombard-based manufacturers, such as Alessi (he helped created their showroom on via Matteotti; *see p137*). FontanaArte produced a range of his glass tabletop containers and vases.

In 1980, Sottsass founded the **Memphis** group, which took its name from the Bob Dylan song 'Stuck Inside of Mobile (With the Memphis Blues Again)' – the song was supposedly stuck on repeat during the group's first gathering. With a group of young designers that included the likes of up-and-coming talents such as **Michele De Lucchi** and **Marco Zanini**, the Memphis group exhibited their first collection of individually designed works at the Arc '74 showroom at the Salone Internazionale del Mobile in 1981. The exhibition rocked the design world, provoking responses that ranged from public incredulity to critical nausea. Their creations were brightly coloured, with a heavy pop art influence; they defiantly took forms to minimalism's polar opposite.

However, well-established Milanese manufacturers, even those who had been previously firmly wedded to a strict template of design sophistication, found they simply couldn't resist the group's playful tug. Lighting giant **Artemide** (via Manzoni 12, 02 7787 12 201, www.artemide.com, closed Mon am, Sun & Aug) picked up Sottsass's Pausania table lamp (and later Michele De Lucchi's iconic Tolomeo table lamp), and Zanini managed the group's designs of office furniture for American company **Knoll** (piazza Bertarelli 2, 02 7222 2932, www.knoll-int.com, closed Mon & Aug).

Sottsass left Memphis on a high in 1985, when the group was still making waves; and although Memphis stopped showcasing as a group in 1988, their influence endures: the current design generation, including **Philippe Starck**, cite the movement as one of its primary inspiration.

The list of local design stars includes Gio Ponti, renowned for his architectural designs, including the Pirelli Tower (Italy's first skyscraper) in the 1950s, and the Denver Art Museum, in the early '70s. However, he also created a range of furniture and lights for some of the city's biggest names, including the Mod Distex and Superleggera chairs for Cassina (via Durini 16, 02 7602 0745, www.cassina.com, closed Sun, Mon am & Aug).

Italy's northern capital nurtured the visionaries above, as well as scores of other hugely influential designers: people like **Vico Magistretti** and **Bruno Munari**, and later **Antonio Citterio** and **Piero Lissoni**. MoMA's 1972 exhibition, 'Italy: the New Domestic Landscape', partially sponsored by Cassina and Pirelli, demonstrated this talent to an American audience. Curated by Emilio Ambasz, the exhibition focused on compact, modular housing: by that time, over 50 per cent of Italy's population lived in tight urban environments. Designs by **Marco Zanuso**, **Gaetano Pesce** and **Gae Aulenti** were typical of the brilliant, multifunctional concepts popular in Milan at the time.

THE MANUFACTURERS

It was not only the designers, but also the manufacturers who helped to solidify Milan's position as the design capital that it is today. Some partnerships, including **Paolo Chiesa** and FontanaArte (via Santa Margherita 4, 02 8646 4551, www.fontanaarte.it, closed Mon am, Sun & Aug), had their origins in the 1930s, whereas other enduring relationships began more recently. Many of Milan's main manufacturers have continued to be prominent forces in the city and within the design world.

De Padova (corso Venezia 14, 02 777 201, www.depadova.it, closed Sun & Aug) has been producing furnishings since the 1950s, as well as household 'extras' like candles and rugs, with an eye to the creation of a functional leisure space. Kitchen and bathroom specialist **Boffi** (via Solferino 11, 02 8901 3217, www.boffi.com, closed Sun, Mon & Aug) is renowned for its natural stone tubs. And Zanotta produced the revolutionary beanbag Sacco in 1968, created by **Franco Teodoro**, **Piero Gatti** and **Cesare Paolini**, as well as manufacturing lines for 1970s Florence-based design group, **Superstudio**.

The affluent 1980s saw Milanese designers make a slight shift in direction. The industry began to focus on businesses and the workplace, which led to an examination of previously overlooked office environments. Architects **Riccardo Sarfatti**, **Sandra Severi** and **Paolo Rizzato** set up **Luceplan**

Take three steps to design heaven at **Triennale**. *See p27.*

Tomorrow's world

For anyone with even a passing interest in aesthetics, the world's biggest design fair, the **Salone Internazionale del Mobile** (*see p142*), is it. The €20 day pass is more enlightening than a year's subscription to *Design Week*. For four days every April, makers of things as diverse as household robotics, airline cutlery and mood lighting ply their pioneering wares at the Fiera in Rho; itself Europe's largest trade ground. From industry leaders such as kitchen stylists Cassina and Bulthaup to cocktail cabinet designers, the fair has it all.

The latest concepts from the 1,400 exhibitors range from the sterile to the wacky. Ergonomically designed bird feeders compete for attention with tent-like garden swings, office putting greens, tin openers that look like light bulbs and the very latest in illusional bathroom tiles, guaranteed to make every shower a 3D sensation. The fair attracted over 350,000 visitors in 2008, 200,000 of them foreign; a shade more than Buckingham Palace. The fillip to Milan's economy is immense: hotels are booked up three months in advance, Malpensa takes on seasonal ground staff, and anyone with a second language and a smile is drafted in to hand out branded water bottles or print out PDFs.

What the festival is to Edinburgh, the Salone is to Milan, with a fringe festival of mammoth proportions. A profusion of mini-

magazines and flyers picked up from bars and galleries promises to guide visitors around the *fuori salone* events – in other words, those taking place outside the official fair. *Interni* magazine (www.internimagazine.it) also lists the city's best spots. Doors are flung open at furniture galleries, each enticing in crowds with free cocktails and free food, hoping to tempt the third of a million potential customers with the latest in plastic chandeliers and aluminium *objets d'art*. The handouts are sometimes so good that there are queues at the door.

Palazzi are taken over by leading designers to promote their work, and are open to the public; shop space is claimed by others. In 2008, John Lobb footwear took over part of the Corso Como 10 store (*see p127*); Panasonic occupied a leather workshop; architect Gio Ponti a place at the Triennale; and the Art Institute of Chicago set up shop in the Palazzina Liberty. The Designersblock exhibition even rented the Piscina Argelati, the city's first open-air lido, for a four-day art party.

But for the ranks of journalists from *Monocle*, *Elle Decoration* and *Wallpaper** magazine, the Salone Satellite exhibition back in Rho is the biggest hitter. It's the chance to mingle with 600 of the finest young designers from as far afield as Malaysia and Turkey, their projects frequently more fantastic than those at the main fair itself.

(via San Damiano 5, 02 7601 5760, www.luceplan.com, closed Mon am, Sun & Aug) in 1978. Winning its first Compasso d'Oro design award in 1981 for the D7 lamp, Luceplan has remained a key exponent of streamlined lighting to this day.

Over the past 20 years, Milanese manufacturers have melded home and office designs, producing furnishings and objects that can be placed according to artistic taste. **Kartell** (via Turati 1, 02 659 7916, www.kartell.it, closed Mon am, Sun & 2wks Aug) produces furniture by design greats such as Philippe Starck, Antonio Citterio, Piero Lissoni and **Patricia Urquiola**, as well as founder **Anna Castelli Ferrieri**. Although originally specialising in car parts, it began in 1963 to create furnishings primarily in plastic. The company now has stores in 96 countries.

Top manfacturer Cassina retains the exclusive right to furniture designed by **Le Corbusier**; it also produces items designed

by **Frank Lloyd Wright**. It is one of the city's most consistently prominent design companies, and a 2008 exhibition at Milan's Triennale was dedicated to Cassina's history, designers and products.

Alessi (*see p137*) continues to forge relationships with big-name designers, including Philippe Starck (he of the iconic long-legged Juicy Salif lemon squeezer), and more recently Zaha Hadid (designer of one of their Tea and Coffee Tower sets). **Dadriade** (via Manzoni 30, 02 7602 3098, www.driade.com, closed Sun & Aug), which is located in the beautifully frescoed Palazzo Gallarati Scotti, creates furniture, objects and lights, with a particular focus on things suitable for the kitchen , and **Danese** (piazza San Nazaro in Brolo 15, 02 5830 4150, www.danesemilano.com, closed Mon, Sun & Aug) has a showroom that's used for design-related events, and shows furnishings by Enzo Mari, James Irvine and Paolo Rizzato.

The centrally located **B&B Italia** (via Durini 14, 02 764 441, www.milano. bebitalia.com, closed Mon am, Sun & Aug) is a capacious venue designed by Antonio Citterio & Partners. B&B produces everything from garden furniture to lighting and textiles, including Patricia Urquiola's Fat Sofa and Fat Fat-Lady Fat tables.

MILAN DESIGN TODAY

Looking for a crash course in Italian design? We've come up with a list of ways to immerse yourself in the city's historical and contemporary design scene.

Easiest of all, hit the town during the Salone Internazionale del Mobile. Now the biggest industrial design-related event in the world, the Salone attracts around 350,000 visitors every year, half of whom are non-Italian. The fair is a haven of futuristic designs, creativity, networking and inspiration. Everyone is eager to get on to the scene: 2008 saw local brewer Nastro Azzuro introducing the first edition of its design award, and Kartell set up seven enormous topiary sculptures in the Triennale gardens, each depicting one of its iconic outdoor designs.

At other times of the year, the Triennale continues to host design-related exhibitions, as well as displaying a permanent collection of some of the city's finest design icons. In late 2007, a portion of the museum became the dedicated **Museo del Design** (www. triennaledesignmuseum.it), its layout devised by Michele De Lucchi to chronicle the history of Italian industrial design.

For a peek into creativity central, visit the **Studio Museo Achille Castiglioni** (piazza Castello 27, 02 805 3606, www.triennale.it, closed Mon, Sun & 3wks Aug, access limited to 20 people per hour, booking advised), Achille Castiglioni's studio for his entire working career, which opened to the public in 2006.

You could also buy a yearly pass (€25) to the **Design Library** (via Savona 11, 02 8942 1225, www.designlibrary.it, closed Sun & Aug), where you can access resources that include floor-to-ceiling archives of multilingual design magazines, use the computers and free Wi-Fi, or leaf through the latest publications in the café.

When it comes to quality souvenirs, there's no shortage of choices. **Post Design** (via della Moscova 27, 02 655 4731, www.memphis-milano.it, closed Mon, Sun & Aug) sells objects designed by '80s superstars, the Memphis group. For crisp new creations, **Dovetusai** (*see p137*) specialises in handmade design objects, with particular emphasis on avant-garde design, accessories and extras, rather than furnishings themselves. Managers Fabio Cocchi and Luigi Rotta look for objects that are beautiful and have 'a soul'. On the other side of town, **Rossana Orlandi**'s courtyard (*see p138*) packs in historical pieces as well as new designs by young creative minds.

Or you could always make it yourself. **Domus Academy** (www.domusacademy.com) and **Istituto Europeo di Design** (www.ied.it) are based in Milan, and offer undergraduate and masters courses in industrial design.

Design Library.

Trattoria Milanese. *See p101.*

Food in Lombardy

An A-Z of Italy's richest cuisine.

A half-millennium of foreign invasion, conspicuous wealth and grinding poverty has left Lombardy with the most varied of all Italy's regional cuisines. Surprisingly, in what is the nation's most dynamic state, the cuisine is still intensely localised. Serious foodies may have to hunt down buckwheat polenta in Bergamo, salted *missoltino* in Bellagio and pigs' cheeks in Lago di Orta. Oh, the hardship!

That said, the Milanese are ever eager to absorb ideas from abroad: words like maki, toast and curry are now common parlance. And despite the nationwide love of olive oil, many high-end dishes are rich and creamy *à la française*. But in times of hardship – and in Lombardy there have been many – locals are quick to fall back on tasty staples.

Think Italy, think pasta, but Lombardy is also justly proud of its paddy fields, dairies and herds. From a fertile plain, the base ingredients of local cuisine would make a supermarket shopper go weak at the knees. So take a deep breath, loosen your belt – and tuck in.

Amaretti

These crisp biscuits made with bitter and sweet almonds, apricot kernels and egg whites become sticky as they melt in the mouth. The name derives from *amaro*, meaning bitter. The most famous amaretti are made by Lazzaroni and sold in a red tin box under the name Amaretti di Saronno – after the Lombard town where they were first made in the 1600s. The popular amaretto liqueur, Disaronno, has been made since 1525 from a secret recipe including burnt sugar, fruit and herb essences soaked in apricot kernel oil.

Arborio

One of the stubby-grain rice varieties grown in Lombardy. Introduced in the 14th century to Lombardy by a wayward member of the ruling Visconti family, rice soon became a local staple. The flatlands of the Po Valley easily flooded and were turned into rice paddies. Along with Carnaroli, Arborio is one of the best varieties for making the beloved risotto, a 19th-century invention whereby rice is sautéed in butter and onions and then cooked slowly in stock.

Bitto

It's the name of a river, a valley, an annual fair and, most famously, a mountain cow's milk cheese from the Valtellina region. Fragrant and slightly sour when young, and bold when aged for up to ten years, the best of *bitto* is a prestigious treat that has a DOP designation, the food equivalent of wine's DOC.

Bollito

This northern version of assorted boiled meats, potatoes, carrots and onion relies on good-quality beef. It's served as a simple dish of broth – normally the strained stock – followed by a platter of slowly cooked meats and vegetables. An entire meal in a dish.

Bresaola della Valtellina

Another delicacy from the mountains, this lean, dried beef is best when sliced thin and splashed with oil, black pepper and lemon.

Campari

Milan is rightly proud of its cochineal-tinted aperitif made with mysterious ingredients. Some call it alcoholic cough syrup; others sip it happily with a spritz of prosecco, soda, a splash of gin or orange juice.

Costoletta alla milanese

Popular lore has it that this breaded veal chop is derived from Austria's wiener schnitzel. Not so. Taken from a different cut of meat and served on the bone, the *costoletta* is fried in butter and not lard. More to the point, Milan's veal chop dates back to at least the 1100s.

Fish

Although many of Lombardy's waterways are polluted – especially the industry-burdened shores of the River Po – they nonetheless teem with excellent freshwater fish.

The Po has pike and perch, whereas the lakes have a range of small and larger varieties, including tiny *alborelle* (bleak) and the elusive and highly prized trout of Lake Como (*persico*).

Franciacorta

This is one of the few winemaking regions of note to be found in Lombardy, its sparkling white made mostly from chardonnay grapes with a little pinot noir and pinot blanc (instead of the pinot meunier of Champagne). Produced in the hills of Lago d'Iseo, these wines were the first Italian bubbly to get a DOCG rating, thanks to the vision of producer Guido Berlucchi.

Gorgonzola

You're on the Milan metro, looking for your stop on the map overhead, and you have a sudden craving for a nice piece of gorgonzola cheese. No wonder: you're looking at the name on the map. Before it became a Milan suburb, this was the town where the creamy blue cheese originated – and it's still where some of the best is made.

Happy hour

A welcome development in recent years. Post-work drinks in most bars are accompanied by complimentary sandwiches, dips, pasta, and even sushi and oysters. Pick the right bar, fill a plate full of freebies, and you might want to skip dinner.

Krapfen

These sweet little doughnuts of leavened pastry, baked or fried and then filled with jam or cream, were imported from Austria and are now made across northern Italy. Despised by some, they're found in most Milan bakeries.

Mascarpone

The main ingredient in *tiramisù* and other rich desserts, this luscious cream cheese is good eaten plain or with a little cocoa and sugar on top. It originally came from Lodi, just south-west of Milan.

Minestrone alla milanese

Rice replaces the usual pasta in the standard Italian veggie soup. Other typical ingredients are greens, pancetta and onion.

Missoltino

More than a tasty little shad from Lake Como, this fish is an object of something close to worship. A festival held each September celebrates it as a symbol of local, traditional foods – complete with souvenir T-shirts featuring the sardine-like image.

Mostarda

A chutney-like preserve of candied fruit, normally peaches, apples and pears, with an added kick of powdered mustard seeds. Nicer than it sounds, and great with cold cuts.

Ossobuco

Ossobuco, the definitive Lombardy dish, reflects the region's love of slowly stewed veal. Thick slices of shank – *ossobuchi* – from milk-fed calves are tied into bundles, browned in butter and then cooked with wine. Some people add tomatoes, but purists disapprove of this. The marrow in the shank makes the dish rich and velvety.

Panettone

Literally, 'big bread'. Milan's own fragrant Christmas fruitcake, notable for its dome shape, is an oversized brioche scented with citrus peel, laced with eggs and butter, and flecked with plump raisins. *Colomba* ('dove') is the Easter edition, crowned with toasted almonds and moulded in the shape of a bird.

Polenta

In Italy, the pejorative term for Lombards is 'polenta eaters'. Once at the bottom of the food chain – you ate polenta if you couldn't afford bread – the pap was a kind of porridge made from spelt, millet and buckwheat (*see p185* **Food fit for a pope**). Polenta rose in status through literature, famously in Manzoni's *I promessi sposi* (*The Betrothed*), and until just a few decades ago most households had a polenta copper pot. Today most polenta is made with cornmeal, and is instant.

Saffron

The yellow spice used in *risotto alla milanese*, one of the city's most famous dishes. The Spanish ruled Milan for nearly two centuries, starting in the 1500s, and left behind saffron (*zafferano*), which provides the risotto's deep golden hue.

San Pellegrino

The salty, mineral-saturated waters of this spa town north of Bergamo have been drawing thirsty travellers by their reputed health-giving properties for centuries. It's the source of the bottled sparkling water of the same name.

Soave

A subtle, crisp white from the balmy microclimate east of Lago di Garda, proudly possessing a DOCG rating. The region's name allegedly derives from the Suevians, a Germanic Lombard tribe that moved south in the sixth century.

Stracchino

This family of typically Lombard cheeses used to be made only in the autumn when tired *stracche* (cows) were milked after their long descent from the mountains to the flatlands. Gorgonzola is a member of the family, as is Crescenza, a super-white, fresh *stracchino*.

Taleggio

Although farmhouse versions are still available in all their nutty glory, this rich cow's milk cheese can also be found in its industrially produced and packaged form in supermarkets. In Bergamo it's often served at the end of a meal with preserved fruit. Eating this makes you an honorary Lombard.

Veal

The Milanese are known for their refined and decadent taste, so it's little wonder that the milk-fed calf is at the centre of the classic meat dishes *ossobuco* and *costoletta alla milanese*.

Weight gain

Milan is undoubtedly a food-lover's paradise, but you must pace yourself if you're trying to watch your figure. Be sure to remember this: three courses are optional, not obligatory!

Zucca

An alcoholic drink made with rhubarb and named after its creator, Ettore Zucca of Milan, former proprietor of the eponymous Zucca café in Galleria Vittorio Emanuele II.

Armani Teatro.

Fashion in Milan

The style city that's going its own way.

It wasn't until the mid 1800s that individual designers began to gain notoriety for their one-off creations. Unsurprisingly, it was the textile industry that gave birth to the first generation of fashion designers: English draper Charles Frederick Worth ('the father of haute couture') opened his private atelier in Paris in 1858. From his nimble sketches, spectacular gowns were made that were soon seen around town on the likes of Empress Eugénie, wife of Napoleon III, and Sarah Bernhardt. Paris remained the world's trendsetting capital for close to a century, with Coco Chanel, Cristobal Balenciaga and Hubert de Givenchy launching international fashion revolutions from here.

Italy was running to a slightly different schedule. During the late 19th century, the country was primarily occupied with matters of national unification. But with struggle against the Austrian empire out of the way, and the republic established, the innately stylish Italians began to elbow their way into the fashion spotlight. In the 1920s and '30s, Salvatore Ferragamo created dazzling hand-made shoes for Hollywood stars (including, in later years, Marilyn Monroe), and innovative knitwear specialist Elsa Schiaparelli set up shop in Paris, collaborating with Surrealist artists, Dalí included.

However, it was in the 1960s and 1970s that Italian designers began to innovate and excel. During these decades of change, psychedelic Emilio Pucci and pop-art Elio Fiorucci flooded the market with funky, fantastical creations; Roman couturier Valentino dressed Elizabeth Taylor and Andy Warhol; Missoni, Krizia and

Versace all received international recognition; dashing Nino Cerruti and dynamic Giorgio Armani burst on to the scene; and suddenly, all eyes were focused firmly on Milan. Its role as a fashion metropolis has been one of the strongest factors contributing to the city's glitzy success, creating a thriving industry and an inimitable international cachet.

In the last three decades, most designers, Italian or otherwise, have pushed fashion's boundaries forward and tried their hand at some form of spin-off. Some have stayed within the strict realm of fashion, including accessories; others have expanded outwards, with forays into art, food or design – such as home furnishings, bars or spas. It has been at this crucial crossroads, and partially based on the success or failure of these ventures, that fashion houses have opted (or been forced) to follow one of two trends: joining a conglomerate and succumbing to multinational pressure of the 1980s and '90s; or forging their own path, strengthening internal company creativity and independently blurring the boundaries between fashion, design and art.

The first trend is exemplified by fashion house Gucci, established in Florence in 1921; Guccio Gucci opened the company's first Milanese boutique on via Montenapoleone in 1951. The brand's popularity peaked during the 1960s, when superstars such as Audrey Hepburn, Maria Callas, Grace Kelly and Jackie Onassis made the label synonymous with chic. However, the 1980s saw Gucci sales plummet, blatant family fighting hit the headlines, and the management descended into chaos. Former creative director Tom Ford is largely credited with turning the company's image around from the mid 1990s onwards: it is now the highest-selling Italian brand in the world. Since 2001, Gucci has been controlled by French luxury conglomerate PPR; Gucci also owns or has partnerships with Yves Saint Laurent, Balenciaga, Alexander McQueen and Stella McCartney. Rival multinational LVMH controls Christian Dior, Givenchy, Marc Jacobs and Fendi brands, among others.

The second trend, going it alone, is the line followed by Milan's big three fashion houses: Armani, Dolce & Gabbana and Prada. Clothes may be their foundation stone, but the threads are no longer the only things they put their names to, and all three firms now dabble with abandon in the worlds of art and design.

Armani was established in Milan in 1976. A former window-dresser at the city's only department store, La Rinascente (see p126), Giorgio Armani has long experimented with different creative outlets. In addition to his famous prêt-à-porter lines, Armani debuted his Giorgio Armani Privé haute couture collection in 2005. He has overseen the design of a number of non-fashion lines, such as Armani Casa (home furnishings), cosmetics, luxury hotels, an airline, cafés and restaurants (in combination with Nobu). In 2001, the company purchased the former Nestlé factory just off via Tortona (a former industrial zone transformed into a hotbed of design), which was renovated by Japanese architect Tadao Ando. It is now used to showcase the latest Armani collections. An Armani retrospective opened at New York's Guggenheim in 2003, before travelling the world and culminating in a final exhibition at Milan's design-focused Triennale (see p63) in 2007. Armani controls the entire company himself.

Domenico Dolce and Stefano Gabbana founded Dolce & Gabbana in Milan in 1986. The pair has produced men's and women's prêt-à-porter lines, lingerie, accessories and perfumes, as well as a spa, old-fashioned barber's, bar and restaurant (see p120). In 2006, late 1940s-cinema Metropol (www.dolce gabbanametropol.com) was renovated, and is now used both for fashion shows and art exhibitions, the latter open to the public.

Fratelli Prada was founded in 1913, originally as a maker of leather goods and seller of imported English luggage. In 1978, Miuccia Prada took over the Milan company, morphing the label into a major international player. Starting with backpacks, nylon totes and shoes, Miuccia launched Prada's first prêt-à-porter line in 1989, to great success. The less-pricey label Miu Miu, aimed at a younger clientele, was launched in 1992. Through the late 1990s, Prada purchased shares in Gucci (sold a year after purchase), Fendi (sold in 2001) and Helmut Lang and Jil Sander (both sold by 2006); but the company has since turned its back on the conglomerate life. Seemingly rested and refreshed, Prada's efforts are now being poured into its non-profit art foundation, Fondazione Prada, with international attention focused on the new office and exhibition space (see p36 **Prada's larder of art**) designed by Rem Koolhaas.

After more than 25 years on the cards, construction of the city's new Città della Moda (city of fashion) near corso Como and corso Garibaldi will soon get under way. The Città will include a fashion museum and a branch of the city's university. While the world waits with bated breath for a comprehensive fashion summary, Armani, Dolce & Gabbana and Prada have shown a refusal to see fashion as solely textiles. By going it alone, Milan's fashion industry has emerged not only as the world's most innovative, but arguably also the world's biggest, and a world-renowned beacon of style.

Prada's larder of art

In April 2008, the Fondazione Prada unveiled plans for the most revolutionary art project to hit Milan in half a century: a new headquarters in Largo Iscaro. Set in an industrial area south of the old Porta Romana railway station, the grand design was drawn up by superstar Dutch architect Rem Koolhaas and his Office of Metropolitan Architecture. When completed in 2011, it will be the most daring building to appear on the city skyline since the Torre Branca tower in 1933 (*see p65*).

The Fondazione Prada is Prada's cultural arm. Under the name Prada Milanoarte in 1993, Miuccia Prada and Patrizio Bertelli began their non-profit foundation with a small collection of sculpture. Artistic director Germano Celant came on board in 1995, and the three have worked together for over a decade to organise contemporary exhibitions, all free to the public. Not only did the Fondazione purchase most of each show, it also commissioned specific installations, and the collection has quickly multiplied: works by Anish Kapoor, Carsten Höller, Steve McQueen, Laurie Anderson, Tom Friedman and Tobias Rehberger included. However, a lack of ample exhibition space in the current venue on via Fogazzaro has meant that most of the pieces have remained boxed up and in storage, hidden from public view.

Largo Iscaro will change all that. Formerly the Società Distillerie Italiane (the city's primary distillery), its late 19th- and early 20th-century buildings will be boosted by new construction to create 17,500 square metres (188,000 square feet) of exhibition space. The Prada fashion offices and the Fondazione will also be housed here, with areas dedicated to a rotating, permanent display of artworks from the hefty collection. The fashion house's archives will have a devoted wing, as will *Luna Rossa*, Prada's sexy sailboat (which, aesthetics aside, was also an America's Cup finalist).

At the west end of the buildings, the Great Hall is an open warehouse area, to be used for exhibiting some of the collection's larger pieces. Individual rooms will house temporary installations, which can be viewed from floor level or overlooked from a small first-floor balcony. In the north-west corner, a wickedly contemporary structure will tower overhead as a temple to art. Partially open, with irregular floors and a coloured exterior, this beacon will be visible from across the city. The centre of the complex will house a subterranean cinema with removable roof, for movies under the stars. The Fondazione also has great plans to restore historic Italian, Chinese, Japanese and Russian films, and future events will be planned in coordination with New York's Tribeca Film Festival and Venice's Fondazione Giorgio Cini.

Some of the Prada offices are already using the site, so keep an eye open for special events.

Where to Stay

Vietnamonamour. *See p45.*

Where to Stay

The lowdown on getting your head down.

Townhouse Galleria is where the serious shopper stays when in Milan. *See p41.*

Well-heeled corporate customers flock from all over Europe to Italy's commercial capital. Whether in textiles, engineering or banking, they nearly all have one thing in common: they're not the ones paying for the room.

What does this mean for the visitor looking for a place to stay at? For one thing, a preponderance of large establishments in the upper price brackets and a shortage of small, inexpensive options. On the up side, though, there's usually plenty of room available on Saturdays and Sundays, often at special rates: you may be surprised just how special if you ask about weekend rates when you book, or check online. Similarly, around Christmas and in summer, rates drop like a stone, with the odd five-star room going for a mere €99 in August.

Since Milan models itself as a design and fashion centre, many of its hotels have been modelled as chic, minimalist establishments. The rise in recent years of the boutique, boundary-crossing and price-busting hotel has been nothing less than staggering (*see p47* **Hip replacement**). Some high-end guestrooms look like NASA space pods; others, like contemporary art showrooms.

Outside the slack summer period, booking in advance is absolutely essential. As well as the constant flow of business travellers, thousands from all over Italy and further afield descend on Milan to attend trade fairs, and prices go up during these periods: the key events are the fashion shows, four times a year (mid February and late September for the women's collections, mid January and late June for men's); and the annual furniture fair, Salone Internazionale del Mobile (mid April).

Milan also suffers from a shortage of parking spaces. Few hotels have their own car park (in this chapter, we have indicated where this is the case), although many have deals with local garages for overnight parking. The price of this service varies considerably, but can be as high as €50 per day. That said, a car is superfluous in compact Milan: there's an efficient public transport system, and your hotel can call you a taxi if you must arrive in style.

STANDARDS AND PRICES

Opting for a three-star or above is likely to reduce the risk of unpleasant surprises – although bear in mind that huge differences exist between the best and worst deals in each category, especially at the cheaper end, and higher prices do not guarantee better service. Shop around. We've listed what we consider to be some of the best budget options below. Some of the worst are not worth thinking about.

There's more than one way to get the best deal. Booking online lets you compare a host of similarly equipped and similarly located hotels. Websites like www.venere.it and www.booking.com have good coverage of Milan, and www.tripadvisor.com has a function that searches for the cheapest rate on all the relevant booking engines. If you're coming for more than a few days, call and ask about long-term rates. Hotels are very open to this in Milan, especially moderately and lower priced ones. Finally, *solo soldi neri sono soldi veri* ('only black money is real money'): cheaper hotels often offer discounts for cash.

Most hotels in the city include breakfast in the price. In a country where a *caffè e brioche* (coffee and a croissant) is the early starter of choice, a hotel breakfast is normally a simple buffet of sliced cheeses, hams and jams. If you're asked to pay extra for breakfast, you may be better off going to a local bar instead.

If you arrive at Malpensa or Linate airports and have nowhere to stay, avoid the travel agency desks. They will book a hotel for you, but the choice is limited to places that pay the agency a commission, and the cost will be passed on to you. The tourist information centre (piazza Duomo 19, 02 7740 4343, www.provincia.milano.it/turismo) by the Galleria Vittorio Emanuele II can no longer provide a list of hotel details, although their website has the name, telephone number and up-to-date price of every one.

Duomo & Centre

Expensive

The Gray
Via San Raffaele 1 (02 720 8951/www.hotelthe gray.it). Metro Duomo/tram 1, 2. **Rates** €520-€680 double. **Rooms** 21. **Credit** AmEx, DC, MC, V. **Map** p252 E6 ❶
The Gray, together with the STRAF (*see p41*), represents one of the latest Milanese trends in high-end hostelry. Despite the name (chosen by architect Guido Ciompi), little is half-tone here: the dominant colour scheme backs neutral colours with splashes

---

❶ Green numbers given in this chapter correspond to the location of each hotel as marked on the street maps. *See pp248-252.*

---

of electrifying vibrancy. The clean-lined rooms – three of which look out on to Galleria Vittorio Emanuele II – are sleek, contemporary and equipped with enormous TVs and jacuzzis. One room has its own Turkish bath, and two have private gyms. The hotel also has its own chic restaurant, Le Noir.
Bar. Concierge. Disabled-adapted rooms. Internet (high speed/wireless). No-smoking rooms. Restaurant. Room service. TV.

Park Hyatt Milan
Via Tommaso Grossi 1 (02 8821 1234/ http://milan.park.hyatt.com). Metro Cordusio or Duomo/tram 1, 2. **Rates** €500-€600 double. **Rooms** 117. **Credit** AmEx, DC, MC, V. **Map** p251 E6/p252 E6 ❷
Carved out of an old bank building, the Park Hyatt is an exercise in serenity and elegant simplicity. The courtyard was covered over with glass to create a splendid top-lit lounge; the warm, beige rooms are equipped with generously proportioned bathrooms (around the same size as the sleeping area) and modern luxuries such as flat-screen TVs and free internet. Relaxing treatments are available in the small

The best Hotels

For celeb-spotting
Four Seasons Hotel Milano (*see p44*).

For your own swimming pool
Principe di Savoia (*see p41*).

For oligarchs
Townhouse Galleria (*see p41*).

For design hounds
3Rooms (*see p43*).

For booze hounds
STRAF (*see p41*).

For eco-warriors
Ariston (*see p46*).

For sheer luxury
Bulgari (*see p41*).

For a home away from home
Foresteria Monforte (*see p45*).

For those not paying
Grand Hotel et de Milan (*see p44*).

For French chic
Petit Palais (*see p46*).

For Asian chic
Vietnamonamour (*see p45*).

For euro-pinchers
Hotel Aspromonte (*see p45*).

spa, which also has separate steam rooms for men and women. The hotel restaurant (entrance for non-residents in via Silvio Pellico 3) serves contemporary Mediterranean cuisine, and the hotel bar is a favourite spot for fashionable Milanese.
Bar. Concierge. Gym. Internet (high speed/wireless). No-smoking floors. Restaurant. Room service. TV.

STRAF

Via San Raffaele 3 (02 805 081/www.straf.it). Metro Duomo/tram 1, 2. **Rates** €308-€465 doubles. **Rooms** 64. **Credit** AmEx, DC, MC, V. **Map** p252 E6 ❸
The STRAF is an upmarket hotel run by the family that manages the Grand Hotel et de Milan (*see p44*). The ultra-modern, minimalist rooms have metallic, industrial overtones, and are equipped with electronic and audio-visual amenities galore. Its central location makes the hotel ideal for shopping, but the weight of the bags won't get you down: the hotel offers an energy boost in the form of in-room mini-spas, Japanese massage chairs, chromotherapy and aromatherapy. Other attractions include the excellent breakfast buffet and cooler-than-thou hotel bar (*see p113*). And for all its chi-chi atmosphere, the STRAF is a remarkably good deal for its category.
Bar. Concierge. Disabled-adapted rooms. Internet (high speed). No-smoking rooms. Restaurant. Room service. TV (free movies).

Townhouse Galleria

Via Silvio Pellico 8 (02 8905 8297/www.townhouse galleria.it). Metro Duomo/tram 1, 2, 20. **Rates** €800-€3,900 suite. **Rooms** 24. **Credit** AmEx, DC, MC, V. **Map** p252 E6 ❹
Queen of the four-hotel Townhouse chain, seven-star Townhouse Galleria is located above the Prada shop in Galleria Vittorio Emanuele. All rooms have a duplex loft, which is kitted out according to the guest's advance request: suggestions include private gym, personal office or children's play area. The two most popular rooms are crowned with ceiling frescoes. Swish touches include a butler per room and a personalised stack of business cards (your name and the hotel's details) on arrival. *Photo p38.*
Bar. Concierge. Internet access (high speed/wireless). No-smoking rooms. Parking (€60 per day). Restaurant. Room service. TV.

Moderate

Hotel Brunelleschi

Via Baracchini 12 (02 88 431/www.milanhotel.it). Metro Cordusio/tram 54/tram 2, 12, 14, 19, 24, 27. **Rates** €110-€450 double. **Rooms** 128. **Credit** AmEx, DC, MC, V. **Map** p252 E7 ❺
A fair-priced business hotel a minute away from the Duomo. Although the Brunelleschi's aesthetics aren't in the same class as the hotels above, the hotel is amenable and completely normal in every way. Book a heavily carpeted and wallpapered room, and get breakfast and a bathrobe thrown in.
Bar. Concierge. No-smoking rooms. Internet (high speed). Restaurant. Room service. TV.

Hotel Gran Duca di York

Via Moneta 1A (02 874 863/www.ducadiyork.com). Metro Cordusio/bus 54/tram 2, 12, 14, 19, 24, 27. **Rates** €208-€248 double. **Rooms** 33. **Credit** AmEx, MC, V. **Map** p252 D7 ❻
Originally built in the 18th century but given an art nouveau makeover in the 1890s, the Gran Duca di York was refurbished in 2004. Situated within easy walking distance of piazza del Duomo, yet away from the traffic, the hotel offers great value – by Milan standards. The peaceful rooms are plain, airy and comfortable; if you want one of the four that have their own outdoor terrace, book well ahead.
Bar. Concierge. No-smoking rooms. Internet (high speed). Room service. TV.

Hotel Star

Via dei Bossi 5 (02 801 501/www.hotelstar.it). Metro Cordusio/bus 61/tram 1, 2, 20. **Rates** €125-€185 double. **Rooms** 30. **Credit** AmEx, DC, MC, V. **Map** p252 D6 ❼
A superb location. The lobby may be 1970s business class airport lounge, but the guest rooms are smart, functional and quiet, albeit a touch on the dated side. Most have parquet floors and a writing desk. The help-yourself buffet breakfast is as completely standard as the rest of the hotel.
Bar. Concierge. No-smoking rooms. Internet (high speed/wireless). TV.

Sforzesco & North

Expensive

Bulgari

Via Privata Fratelli Gabba 7B (02 805 8051/www.bulgarihotels.com). Metro Montenapoleone/bus 61/tram 1, 2, 14, 20. **Rates** €200-€890 double. **Rooms** 58. **Credit** AmEx, DC, MC, V. **Map** p252 E5 ❽
At the end of a private road behind the Pinacoteca di Brera's botanic gardens, the Bulgari oozes the same exclusivity and class as the brand's fine jewellery, with due attention paid to precious materials. The neutral-toned bedrooms are understated yet luxurious, with oak flooring and capacious black marble and travertine bathrooms. Floor-to-ceiling windows open on to teak balconies overlooking the huge private gardens surrounding the hotel. The spa is a study in contemporary calm (*see p170* **Relax to the max**), and the bar is a magnet for style-conscious locals as well as hotel guests; drinks are served on the terrace in summer.
Bar. Concierge. Gym. Internet (wireless). No-smoking rooms. Parking (€50/day). Restaurant. Room service. Spa. TV.

Principe di Savoia

Piazza della Repubblica 17 (02 62 301/www.hotel principedisavoia.com). Metro Repubblica/tram 1, 9, 11, 29, 30. **Rates** €320-€990 double. **Rooms** 401. **Credit** AmEx, DC, MC, V. **Map** p249 F4 ❾
The over-the-top marble foyer and reams of polished oak are a fine antidote to Milan's proliferation of

design hotels. Most of the rooms are stately and traditional, complete with lavish marble bathrooms and Acqua di Parma toiletries. Frank Sinatra, Robert De Niro and Madonna have all stayed in the presidential suite, which has its own pool. Staff are efficient and down to earth, and the gym is one of the best in Milan, with panoramic views of the city. The location isn't the best, but it's an easy stroll from here to the centre of town.

Bar. Business centre. Concierge. Disabled-adapted rooms. Gym. Internet (wireless). No-smoking rooms. Parking (€30-€80/day). Pool (indoor). Restaurant. Room service. Spa. TV (free movies).

3Rooms

Corso Como 10 (02 626 163/www.3rooms-10corso como.com). Metro Garibaldi/tram 11, 29, 30, 33. **Rates** €250-€310 suite. **Rooms** 3. **Credit** AmEx, DC, MC, V. **Map** p248 D3/4 ⑩

You've browsed the boutique, gazed in the gallery and posed at the bar – and now you can even spend the night at Milan's multipurpose style emporium, 10 Corso Como (*see p129*). Describing itself as a 'bed and breakfast', 3Rooms is actually three apartments, each consisting of three rooms: bedroom, bathroom and living room (plus lots of closet space). Each apartment occupies an entire floor, overlooking the internal courtyard and tea garden, and is individually decorated, with furnishings handpicked from the iconic designers of the last century – Arne Jacobson, Eero Saarinen, Charles and Ray Eames, Marcel Breuer and Sebastian Matta, among others. Be warned: there's no lift, and the apartments are on the second, third and fourth floors of the building. Needless to say, you should book far ahead.

Bar. Concierge. Internet (high speed). Restaurant. Room service. TV.

Moderate

Alle Meraviglie

Via San Tomaso 8 (02 805 1023/www.allemeraviglie. it). Metro Cairoli or Cordusio/bus 54, 61/tram 1, 2, 3, 4, 14, 16, 19, 27. **Rates** €165-€225 double. **Rooms** 6. **Credit** AmEx, MC, V. **Map** p252 D6 ⑪

The *meraviglie* – or wonders – that await the guest at this lovely B&B, just off via Dante, are six inviting rooms with bright white beds, lavish silk curtains and fresh flowers. (The bathrooms, on the other hand, are run of the mill, with basic showers and large bottles of everyday unctions.) Despite it being set in a converted townhouse, with plenty of olde-worlde character, there are also up-to-date touches such as free Wi-Fi connection in each room (though not all have a TV). If you're planning to stay in town for a while, you might consider the Milanosuites, also run by Paola Ora and her team. These mini-apartments, complete with cooking facilities, are available by the week or the month. They also own the Antica Locanda dei Mercanti next door, a less expensive, slightly more twee, option.

Bar. Concierge. Internet (wireless). No-smoking rooms. Room service.

Alle Meraviglie has many wonders.

Antica Locanda Solferino

Via Castelfidardo 2 (02 657 0129/www.anticalo candasolferino.it). Metro Moscova/bus 43, 94/tram 11, 33. **Rates** €180-€400 double. **Rooms** 11. **Credit** AmEx, MC, V. **Map** p248 D4 ⑫

This lovely hotel is set in a Napoleonic-era palazzo in the heart of the Brera district. Each of the 11 rooms feature floor-to-ceiling windows, antique furniture and Daumier lithographs on the walls, creating the illusion that you've stepped into a corner of 19th-century Milan. Reserve well in advance and ask for a room at the rear of the building if you're a light sleeper, or one of the five balcony rooms on the front.

Concierge. Internet (wireless). Room service. TV.

The Chedi

Via Villapizzone 24, corner via Console Marceloo (02 363 1888/www.thechedimilan.com). Bus 57/ tram 1, 12, 19. **Rates** €99-€440 double. **Rooms** 250. **Credit** AmEx, DC, MC, V.

An Asia-inspired addition to the burgeoning Bovisa zone. With a business market in mind, service is extremely slick. There are some great innovations in the bathroom department: bathside candles, Laura Tonatto products and slippers. The second-floor pool, one of Milan's largest, is enclosed by an atrium.

Bar. Business centre. Concierge. Disabled-adapted rooms. Gym. Internet (wireless). No-smoking rooms. Pool. Restaurant. Room service. Spa. TV.

Hotel Tocq

Via Tocqueville 7 (02 62 071/www.epoquehotels. com). Metro Garibaldi/tram 11, 29, 30, 33. **Rates** €115-€400 double. **Rooms** 122. **Credit** AmEx, MC, V, DC. **Map** p248 D3 ⑬

This predominantly business hotel is a top locale for Corso Como and the station. Rooms are on the large side, although rather anodyne compared to the other moderate options listed here. There's Wi-Fi (albeit paid) and a big, help-yourself breakfast. Especially good for last-minute rates in summer.

Bar. Business centre. Concierge. Internet (wireless). Restaurant. Room service. TV.

Budget

Hotel Lancaster
Via Abbondio Sangiorgio 16, corner via Niccolò Machiavelli (02 344 705/www.hotellancaster.it). Metro Cadorna/bus 43, 57, 61/tram 1, 29, 30. **Rates** €119-€234 double. **Rooms** 30. **Credit** AmEx, MC, V. **Map** p248 A4/5
The staff at this mellow little hotel are so nice. With just 30 rooms, they can treat guests with an extra bit of care; and nothing seems too much trouble for the respectful old chap who mans the concierge desk much of the time. Considering the price, the rooms – a cross between French *chambre d'hôte* and British Travelodge – are spacious and squeaky clean.
Bar. Concierge. Internet (high speed). No-smoking rooms. Room service. TV.

London
Via Rovello 3, corner via San Tomaso (02 7202 0166/www.hotellondonmilano.com). Metro Cairoli or Cordusio/bus 54, 61/tram 1, 2, 3, 4, 14, 16, 19, 27. **Rates** €150-€170 double. **Rooms** 29. **Credit** MC, V. **Map** p252 D6
Situated on a pretty little side street just round the corner from Castello Sforzesco, the London is great value for money. Its rooms are simply furnished and a bit small, but the lobby and conversation area around the bar are welcoming, and the staff are friendly. There's a ten per cent discount if you pay cash; if you don't ask you don't get.
Bar. Internet (high speed/wireless). Laundry. Room service. TV.

Not suitable for Yorkists. **Hotel Lancaster.**

Expensive

Four Seasons Hotel Milano
Via Gesù 6-8 (02 770 8167/www.fourseasons.com/milan). Metro Montenapoleone or San Babila/bus 61, 94/tram 1, 2, 20. **Rates** €675-€775 double. **Rooms** 118. **Credit** AmEx, DC, MC, V. **Map** p252 E6
Discretion and luxury are the watchwords at this award-winning hotel, which continues to be a favourite with the fashion and film crowd. No doubt they love the location, slap bang in the middle of the Quadrilatero della Moda. The hotel is housed in a 15th-century convent, although – apart from the idyllic, cloistered courtyard that many of the rooms face on to – you would never know it. Each of the spacious guest rooms is individually designed, with Fortuny fabrics and pear and sycamore wood furniture, as well as CD and DVD players. Some suites have parts of the original frescoes, as do the library bar and lobby. The opulent marble bathrooms are kept toasty with underfloor heating, and well stocked with huge towels and plush bathrobes.
Bar. Business centre. Concierge. Disabled-adapted rooms. Gym. Internet (high speed/wireless). No-smoking rooms. Parking (€53/day). Restaurants (2). Room service. TV.

Grand Hotel et de Milan
Via Manzoni 29 (02 723 141/www.grandhoteletde milan.it). Metro Montenapoleone/bus 61, 94/tram 1, 2. **Rates** €561-€665 double. **Rooms** 95. **Credit** AmEx, DC, MC, V. **Map** p252 E6
In an elegant 19th-century palazzo, the five-star Grand is as sumptuous as it gets: all marble, rich draperies and antiques. The gorgeous suites are named after illustrious past guests, such as Luchino Visconti, Maria Callas and Giuseppe Verdi (the composer lived in the hotel on and off for 27 years, and died here in 1901). The efficient service is as discreet as it is friendly. Though the room prices seem shocking at first glance, it's worth asking about weekend rates: you may be pleasantly surprised. The refurbished bar is a relaxed place for a drink (the waiters still wheel in a drinks trolley), and the Don Carlos restaurant next door, run by chef Alfredo Russo, is one of the finest in the city.
Bar. Business centre. Concierge. Disabled-adapted rooms. Gym. Internet (high speed/wireless). No-smoking rooms & floors. Parking (€48/day). Restaurants (2). Room service. TV.

Sheraton Diana Majestic
Viale Piave 42 (02 20 581/www.sheraton.com/dianamajestic). Metro Porta Venezia/tram 9, 29, 30. **Rates** €185-€605 double. **Rooms** 107. **Credit** AmEx, DC, MC, V. **Map** p249 G5
This five-star art nouveau-style hotel is named after Milan's first public swimming pool, which opened on this site in 1842. The pool has since been replaced with a garden and the first of the city's many summertime outdoor cocktail bars (see *p119*). The

Vietnamonamour.

homely 1920s feel, apparent as you push through the revolving door, is period luxury – not faded grandeur. The large bedrooms are elegantly kitted out with antique furniture.

Bar. Business centre. Concierge. Disabled-adapted rooms. Gym. Internet (high speed/wireless). No-smoking rooms. Restaurant. Room service. TV.

Moderate

Foresteria Monforte

Piazza Tricolore 2 (02 7631 8516/www.foresteria monforte.it). Bus 54, 61/tram 9, 23, 29, 30. **Rates** €150-€220 double. **Rooms** 3. **Credit** AmEx, DC, MC, V. **Map** p249 G6 ⑲

A central and super hip addition to Milan's hotel scene. The three colour-coded guest rooms are large and sexy: the cream one is an upmarket suite; the antique-filled brown is more classic; the purple is stylishly modern. Visitors can use the espresso pots and cheeseboards in the petite shared kitchen at any time, although the lack of space means that break-fast in bed is compulsory. The concierge and propri-etor is the English-speaking pharmacist downstairs. *Internet (high speed). TV.*

Vietnamonamour

Via Pestalozzo 7 (02 7063 4614/www.vietnamon amour.com). Bus 62, 90, 91/tram 11, 23. **Rates** €120 double. **Rooms** 4. **Credit** AmEx, DC, MC, V.

An aura of complete calm pervades this Italian-Vietnamese concept B&B. Hardwood floors and heavy furniture imported from South east Asia dec orate the guest rooms, and the walls are pink floral patterns, earthy colour washes or bare brick. Breakfast in the private garden – orange juice, tea, mangos, bananas and cereal – is a delight. *Internet (wireless). No smoking rooms. Restaurant. TV.*

Budget

Hotel Aspromonte

Piazza Aspromonte (02 236 1119/www.hotelaspro monte.it). Metro Loreto or Piola/bus 55, 90, 91, 93/ tram 33. **Rates** €60-€110 double. **Rooms** 19. **Credit** Amex, DC, MC, V.

This place is cheap, friendly, and even has a decent garden in which to sip your morning coffee and laze around. The hotel has a special agreement with a laundry around the corner, and a car park a stone's

Petit Palais.

throw away. And while the rooms may seem like a vision of Ikea, at least they are tidy, and way better than most to be found in this price range.
Bar. Concierge. Internet (wireless). No-smoking rooms. TV.

Hotel Due Giardini
Via Benedetto Marcello 47 (02 2952 1093/www.hotel duegiardini.it). Metro Centrale FS or Lima/bus 60/ tram 1, 5, 11, 20, 33. **Rates** €75-€145 double. **Rooms** 10. **Credit** MC, V. **Map** p249 G4 ⑳
If staying in the vicinity of the Stazione Centrale is essential, the charming old Due Giardini is a convenient and pleasant choice. The staff are cheerful, and the rooms are functional, bright and, best of all, airconditioned. The *due giardini* have been amalgamated into one tree-shaded garden, where breakfast is served in summer. Reservation in advance is a must.
Bar. Concierge. Disabled-adapted rooms. Internet (wireless). No-smoking rooms. Room service. TV.

Hotel Bagliori
Via Boscovich 43 (02 2952 6884/www.hotelbagliori. com). Metro Centrale FS or Lima/bus 60/tram 1, 5, 20, 33. **Rates** €80-€250 double. **Rooms** 14. **Credit** AmEx, DC, MC, V. **Map** p249 G4 ㉑
A train station cheapie in a turn-of-the-century villa. The carefully planted herbs and hanging baskets in the rear garden – a lovely alfresco breakfast spot – shows how hard this budget hotel tries. Rooms are plain but clean, and staff are friendly and helpful.
Bar. Concierge. Internet (wireless). No-smoking rooms. Room service. TV.

Porta Romana & South

Expensive

Petit Palais
Via Molino delle Armi 1 (02 584 891/www.petit palais.it). Metro Crocetta/bus 94/tram 15. **Rates** €320-€1,200 suites only. **Rooms** 18. **Credit** AmEx, DC, MC, V. **Map** p250 D8 ㉒
On one of Milan's most important canals, this sometime 17th-century palazzo was opened as the Petit Palais in September 2007, after more than five years

of restoration. It's a luxurious hotel and no expense has been spared, from the Murano chandeliers to the crystal wine glasses. The exquisite top-floor suites have roof terraces for your own private view of the Duomo; the hotel is a 15-minute walk from the city centre, yet peacefully far from the crowds.
Bar. Concierge. Internet (high speed/wireless). No-smoking rooms. Parking (€30/day). Room service. TV.

Moderate

Ariston
Largo Carrobbio 2 (02 7200 0556/www.ariston hotel.com). Bus 94/tram 2, 3, 14. **Rates** €320 double. **Rooms** 52. **Credit** AmEx, DC, MC, V. **Map** p252 C7 ㉓
The Ariston is an experiment in eco design: the lightbulbs are energy-efficient, the showers are designed to save water, and all the fittings are made from natural or non-toxic materials. Even the water in your tea is purified, and organic food is available at breakfast. The location, between the centre of town and the Navigli district, is excellent, and the hotel offers guests free use of bicycles.
Bar. Business centre. Concierge. Internet (high speed/ wireless). No-smoking rooms. Parking (€18/day). Room service. TV.

NHOW
Via Tortona 35 (02 489 8861/www.nhow-hotels. com). Metro Porta Genova/bus 68. **Rates** €152-€282 double. **Rooms** 246. **Credit** AmEx, DC, MC, V.
On Milan's offbeat via Tortona, around the corner from Teatro Armani and the Fondazione Pomodoro (*see p87*), contemporary NHOW sits in the shell of the city's former General Electrics factory. From the polished concrete lobby up to the fourth floor, the hotel is dotted with a rotating selection of artworks and limited edition furniture, all for sale (check www.artnhow.com for an up-to-date, comprehensive guide). Rooms are decked out with Artemide lights and funky printed wallpaper, and showers are colourful. Exhibitionists should book the penthouse apartment, complete with glass-bottomed bathtub that acts as the living room's ceiling.

Hip replacement

In times past, Milan was swimming in elegant *grande dame* hotels, relics of House of Savoy tastes; but thanks to the conference industry, it gained more nondescript 1970s business hotels than there are pigeons in piazza Duomo. But now (and long overdue), a design hotel tide has been sweeping over Milan's massive accommodation industry. In a business where the word 'hip' is woefully overused, and the term 'boutique' has come to mean a vase of lilies in reception, Milan has injected some of its style capital into a new wave of überhotels. The eagerly awaited launch of the Armani Hotel in 2009 will cap a decade of groundbreaking design.

The first post-millennial attempts to fuse style with necessity came off expensively and starkly. **The Gray** (*see p39*) went bravely forward with neutral tones, combined with hard lines and the odd splash of bold colour – and if it weren't for the playful touches like suspended beds and sexy but trashy white leather partitions, the project could have come off as seriously overdesigned. Then **STRAF** (*see p41*) softened the heavy urban

style with appealingly hippyish aromatherapy seats and personal fitness centres. Both were priced at over €500 a night, which made them as much of an eye-opener for Milan's hotel owners as for the guests.

Then, in 2006, two personalised options took boutique to a new level. The inexpensive **Foresteria Monforte** (*see p45*) launched a suite-only concept, where visitors are served breakfast in bed, and share a petite kitchen in case they want to chill their own champagne rather than pay minibar prices. Guests at the **Townhouse Galleria** (*see p41*), meanwhile, can recast the upper level of their duplex suite as a children's playroom, or as an office with printer and Italian mobile phone waiting on the desk. Prices nudge €1,000 a night, but the location and discreet entry system are cooler than cool (although you do still have to pay for drinks in the minibar).

Perhaps surprisingly, given Milan's ability to cherry-pick the finest international products, **Vietnamonamour** (*see p45*) and the **Petit Palais** (*see p46*), which opened in 2006 and 2007 respectively, were the city's first hotels with a pronounced overseas flavour. The former is a calm fusion of furniture from a Balinese beach hut and Milanese designer fittings; the latter has reinvented Louis XVI chic.

Finally, north and south of the city centre, the conference hotel standard has been smashed by two hotels offering a slicker business trip option. **The Chedi** (*see p43*) near the Triennale Bovisa has been winning awards since 2007. Its staff are bright and well-trained, not bored, narky and dim. The Asian gardens are a delight, and with rooms from €99, it's certainly affordable. The previous year saw the opening of **NHOW** (*see p46*), handy for the fashion crowd by the Prada offices in southern Milan. The entrance features transparent plastic chandeliers and polished concrete floors, guaranteed to appeal to any design aficionado. It's still good to see a bit of good old-fashioned style over substance, however: trendy beanbags have replaced chairs in the foyer's business area.

NHOW.

Bar. Business centre. Concierge. Internet (wireless). No-smoking rooms. Parking. Restaurant. Room service. Spa. TV.

Sant'Ambrogio & West

Expensive

Hotel Pierre Milano
Via De Amicis 32 (02 7200 0581/www.hotelpierre milano.it). Metro Sant'Ambrogio/tram 3. **Rates** €550 double. **Rooms** 51. **Credit** AmEx, DC, MC, V. **Map** p250 C7 ㉔
Leaves rustle outside as you enjoy breakfast in bed, then snuggle back between the pure linen sheets… Hotel Pierre Milano, located between via Torino and the *navigli*, spoils guests with attentive little luxuries, including free Wi-Fi. Tastefully furnished with Italian antiques, this spot definitely appeals to a more mature crowd, but if peace and quiet is what you're after, it can't be beaten.
Bar. Concierge. Internet (wireless). No-smoking rooms. Restaurant. Room service. TV.

Moderate

Antica Locanda Leonardo
Corso Magenta 78 (02 4801 4197/www.anticalocanda leonardo.com). Metro Cadorna or Conciliazione/tram 16. **Rates** €150-€230 double. **Rooms** 16. **Credit** AmEx, DC, MC, V. **Map** p250 B6 ㉕
An immaculate little hotel, set in an internal courtyard off busy corso Magenta and within easy walking distance of Santa Maria delle Grazie and Leonardo's *Last Supper*. The property is in a late 19th-century palazzo, and the rooms are all tastefully decorated with modern or antique wooden furniture (some have a Japanese feel to them, as a nod to one of the owners). There's also a cosy breakfast/bar area where tea and cakes are served. The hotel has been managed by the same courteous and attentive family for more than 40 years, and it shows in the attention to detail. Five rooms overlook the flower-filled back garden.
Bar. Concierge. Internet (wireless). Room service. TV.

Ariosto
Via Ariosto 22 (02 481 7844/www.hotelariosto.com). Metro Conciliazione/bus 61, 68, 169. **Rates** €160-€290 double. **Rooms** 48. **Credit** AmEx, DC, MC, V. **Map** p248 B6 ㉖
Via Ariosto is an elegant residential street, handy for the central sights and the Fiera. The hotel is airy and well lit, with a beautiful art nouveau staircase. All the rooms have double glazing, parquet floors, plus jacuzzis or sauna showers in the bathrooms; a few also have walk-in wardrobes. There's also a small, attractive patio garden. The bar and restaurant area has been recently renovated, and there's free internet access at computers in the lobby.
Bar. Business centre. Concierge. Internet (high speed/wireless). No-smoking rooms. Parking (€30/day). Restaurant. Room service. TV.

King
Corso Magenta 19 (02 874 432/www.hotelking milano.com). Metro Cadorna/tram 16. **Rates** €110-€395 double. **Rooms** 40. **Credit** AmEx, DC, MC, V. **Map** p252 C6 ㉗
This hotel is centrally located in a picturesque part of town. Travellers may find the lobby, which matches Venetian stucco effects with baroque chairs, a bit over the top. But despite the interior design, the welcome is genuine, the rooms are clean, tidy and quiet, and the buffet breakfast is generous.
Bar. Concierge. Internet (high speed/wireless). No-smoking rooms. Room service. TV.

Hotel Palazzo delle Stelline
Corso Magenta 61 (02 481 8431/www.hotelpalazzo stelline.it). Metro Cadorna/bus 94/tram 1, 16, 19, 27. **Rates** €168 double. **Rooms** 105. **Credit** AmEx, DC, MC, V. **Map** p250 B6 ㉘
This hotel and conference centre is housed in a beautiful 15th-century monastery with arched cloisters, overlooking a grass courtyard and a huge magnolia tree. The tastefully furnished rooms offer total privacy, cocooned from the hubbub of the city. Leonardo da Vinci is said to have grown vines on this site while painting *The Last Supper* at the Santa Maria delle Grazie monastery across the road.
Bar. Business centre. Concierge. Disabled-adapted suite. Internet (wireless). No-smoking rooms. TV.

Zurigo
Corso Italia 11A (02 7202 2260/www.hotelzurigo. com). Metro Missori/tram 15. **Rates** €160-€290 double. **Rooms** 41. **Credit** AmEx, DC, MC, V. **Map** p250 D7/8 ㉙
Zurigo's front door opens off a busy street at a major intersection in central Milan, with trams clanking by every few minutes. Still, no need to worry as none of the rooms overlooks the street. Indeed, the entire place is very quiet and peaceful. The rooms are on the small side, but they are cosy, with original mosaic floors. Free bike hire is available for those brave enough to pedal. For everyone else, it's a ten-minute stroll to piazza del Duomo.
Bar. Business centre. Concierge. Internet (high speed). No-smoking rooms. Parking (€28/day). Room service. TV.

Budget

Ostello Piero Rotta
Via Salmoraghi, corner of via Calliano (02 3926 7095/www.ostellomilano.it). Metro Lotto or QT8/ bus 68, 199. **Rates** €19 per person. **Beds** 84 (6 beds per room). **Credit** AmEx, MC, V.
The only official youth hostel in Milan is out in the suburbs near the San Siro football stadium, though the nearby Lotto metro station makes it easy to reach the centre. The garden provides a welcome escape from city traffic; there are also washing machines on site. Staff are sometimes not the friendliest, but that doesn't stop the place being full most of the time, no doubt because of the rates (which include breakfast!).

Sightseeing

Features

Università Catollica del Sacro Cuore.
See p91.

Introduction

Art in parks, historical homes and a stadium full of Italian culture.

Piazza Duomo

Milan is twinned with Birmingham. Perhaps because of this, few people expect much culture from Italy's industrial powerhouse; and the dearth of olive groves and cypress trees means it will never conform to the *bella Italia* stereotype. But in the historic centre, Milan's own blend of old and new is flaunted with wild abandon: architecture from the medieval to the belle époque, and art from the Renaissance to the recklessly modern.

The patronage of the arts by Milan's wealthy (an ever-present class) started with Ludovico Sforza, whose friends included Leonardo da Vinci and Donato Bramante. Later, Napoleon crowned himself king of Italy in the city's cathedral, the Duomo (*see p52*), and rounded up many of northern Italy's finest works, depositing them in Milan's ducal palaces; and the stormy history of the 20th century proved an excellent stimulus for the likes of Giacometti, Boccioni and other avant-garde visitors.

As well as culture, there is beauty in Milan, and that in great abundance. Many of the palazzi that housed the rich and famous are described in the following chapters. Once a year, usually on the third weekend of March, the courtyards of these elegant buildings are opened to the public (*see p142*) by the Fondo per l'Ambiente Italiano.

MILAN ON FOOT

Large sections of the centre have been given over to pedestrians. In addition to the principal shopping thoroughfares – corso Vittorio Emanuele II and piazza del Duomo – via dei Mercanti and via Dante are car-free zones, creating a single pedestrianised corridor that runs from the Castello Sforzesco all the way to San Babila. Via Garibaldi and corso Como have also been pedestrianised.

On many Sundays throughout the year, when pollution levels get too high, the council bans cars from the city. There is no way to predict when these *divieti* will take place; they are usually announced by local news services just a few days in advance. But if you happen to catch one of these car-free days, you'll have all of central Milan to roam through, accompanied only by taxis and local families.

MILAN BY THE BOOK

Paradoxically, the perceived culture gap between Milan and other Italian cities means that most of the main spots are refreshingly quiet. And although you can brush past a Canova statue in relative peace, the only sight that requires advance booking is Da Vinci's *Last Supper* (*see p92*) in the Santa Maria delle Grazie church.

Many of the city's main attractions are grouped around the city's mammoth Duomo (*see p52*) and the elegant Galleria Vittorio Emanuele II (*see p55*). From here you can reach the other main sights – including the Pinacoteca di Brera (*see p61*), the Castello Sforzesco (*see p61*) and the Navigli (*see p86*) – in less than 20 minutes on foot. Many museums and galleries require reservations for, and offer discounts to, groups of seven or more.

MILAN'S CHURCHES

More than 100 smaller churches dot the city, providing pleasant surprises. Many of them are all but lost amid the bustle of central Milan, and are oases for the harried tourist. Almost without exception, these buildings are first and foremost active houses of worship, which means hushed voices and dress codes (bare shoulders and thighs are frowned upon). Some churches have coin-operated lighting systems, audio-visual aids and computerised displays (usually in Italian, sometimes in English). Bring loose change for a donation.

MILAN'S MUSEUMS AND GALLERIES

Milan's major museums and galleries generally stay open throughout the day, and some remain open until 10pm or later one night a week; many are closed on Mondays.

Although many attractions offer free admission, many museums charge a small fee. Most offer discounts for students and over-60s, especially if you can demonstrate EU citizenship. Bring appropriate ID, though it's worth asking for a *sconto* (discount) even if you have forgotten it. Many galleries and museums stop issuing tickets 30 to 45 minutes before closing time: we've tried to include last entry times where relevant.

GUIDED TOURS

Milan's tourist office (piazza Duomo 19, 02 7740 4343, www.visitamilano.it, *see also p288*) sells tour tickets, as well as passes for the hop-on hop-off tourist bus service (*see p219*), which is popular with families. Guided tours include a three-hour visit to Castello Sforzesco, Leonardo da Vinci's *Last Supper* and Duomo (€50 including entry fees), a San Siro stadium visit (€25) and a Milan by night circuit with free *aperitivo* (€50). Ever popular are the coach tours to Milan's out-of-town shopping outlets. Other guided tour options include:
● Centro Guide Milano (at Milan's tourist office, *see above*; www.centroguidemilano.net), a non-profit organisation, offers tours in and around Milan.
● A Friend in Milan (02 2952 0570, www.friendinmilan.co.uk) runs a range of personalised tours of the city.

Milan in a day

For a no-holds-barred shot at the city, follow this programme between 8am and 4am. No taxis or trams are needed – just money and stamina.

8am
Join the joggers and t'ai chi gurus for morning air in **Parco Sempione** (*see p61*).

9am
Opening time at open-air **Bar Bianco** (*see p114*). *Caffè e brioche* is the classic.

10am
Take in Caravaggio and Modigliani in Brera's **Pinacoteca** (*see p61*).

11.30am
Time for a blueberry and banana fruit boost at **Jungle Juice** (*see p113*).

Noon
Take the lift to the top of the **Duomo** (*see p52*) for an overview of your morning.

1pm
A lunch break for grilled eel and sashimi picked from the conveyor belt at **Zen** (*see p109*).

2pm
Sip an espresso at local institution **Zucca** (*see p112*).

3pm
Window-shop your way through **Galleria Vittorio Emanuele II** (*see p55*) to the *haute couture* of the **Quadrilatero d'Oro** (*see p134*); or veer off for high culture at the **Museo della Scala** (*see p56*).

7pm
Power up with an alfresco gin fizz in the **HClub** (Diana Garden; *see p119*).

9pm
Sample some contemporary Tuscan fare at **Lucca** (*see p104*), or classic Milanese at **Antica Trattoria della Pesa** (*see p101*).

11pm
Gear up for the night with a lemon caipiroska at **10 Corso Como** (*see p117*).

12.30am
Sashay with the in crowd at **Tocqueville 13** (*see p165*), or bump and grind in artsy **Hollywood** (*see p165*) around the corner.

Sightseeing

The Duomo & Central Milan

Elevating religion, opera and fashion to the status of art.

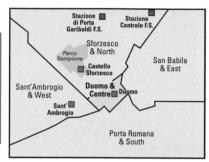

Stazione di Porta Garibaldi F.S.

Stazione Centrale F.S.

Sforzesco & North

Parco Sempione

Castello Sforzesco

San Babila & East

Sant'Ambrogio & West

Duomo & Centre

Duomo

Sant' Ambrogio

Porta Romana & South

Sightseeing

Around the Duomo

In a city centred on a 500-year-old monument, change is normally slow. But in Milan's *centro*, a quiet revolution has spiced up the old and brought in the new. In 2008, the covers were finally lifted off the **Duomo**, Milan's cultural icon, the third largest cathedral in the world. After six years of painstaking restoration, it can flaunt its centuries of unbridled architectural fervour once again.

Across the piazza del Duomo, Milan's vibrant social core, another stalwart is making serious waves in the art world. The **Palazzo Reale** (*see p55*) is challenging the modern art dominance of Paris and London with retrospectives of Kandinsky, Bacon and other crowd-pleasing exhibitions. The grand reopening of the Museo del Duomo next door in 2009, and the inauguration of the adjoining Museo del Presente contemporary art museum in 2011, will make Milan's cultural heart beat still faster.

The glass-roofed **Galleria Vittorio Emanuelle II** (*see p55*), a temple to shopping next to the Duomo, is Milan's main draw for many visitors. Statuesque shop assistants operate the tills, and if you stay at one of the hip hotels around the corner, you can get the bellboy to collect your purchases. A volley of new designer cafés are on hand to serve the Prosecco pick-me-up that pre-lunch shoppers need. Dining right next to the Duomo is seldom done, although a block away, classic Milanese

restaurants still cater to a discerning clientele from the banking HQs around the **Teatro alla Scala** (*see p59*). The pomp attached to what, for many, is the world's finest opera house is still as dazzling as its shows.

In the quieter streets a few steps away from the glitz, it's possible to delve deeper into Milan's illuminating history. The quirkiness of the **Museo Poldi Pezzoli** (*see p57*) and humour in Bramante's trompe l'oeil frescoes in the **Santa Maria** (*see p60*) church are matched by the splendour of **Pinacoteca Ambrosiana**'s fine collections. All in all, a dose of freshness and fun has been injected into the heart of Italy's northern capital.

Duomo

Piazza del Duomo (02 7202 2656). Metro Duomo/ bus 54/tram 1, 2, 3, 12, 20, 23, 24, 27. **Open** *Church* 7am-7pm daily. *Treasury & crypt* 9.30am-12.30pm, 2-6pm Mon-Fri; 9.30am-12.30pm, 2-5pm Sat; 1-3.30pm Sun. *Baptistery & early Christian excavations* 9am-5.30pm daily. *Roof Nov-Feb* 9am-4.15pm daily. *Mar-Oct* 9am-5.45pm daily. **Admission** *Church* free. *Treasury & crypt* €1. *Baptistery & early Christian excavations* €2. *Roof* €7 by lift; €6 on foot. **Map** p251 E7/p252 E7. Standing proudly on the piazza del Duomo, the third largest church in Christendom (outdone only by St Peter's in Rome and Seville's cathedral), the Duomo is truly a joy to behold. Although the key elements were in place by 1391, the Duomo took the best part of 500 years to complete – and indeed, building work continues today: a five-year project to clean the façade started in 2002, and the Duomo's full mind-blowing beauty is now there for all to behold.

The Duomo was begun in brick, but upgraded to marble as its architects understood the grandeur of the project. Over time, it was adorned with Gothic spires and an astonishing wealth of statues, and has been adored by a huge number of art and architecture aficionados. As generations of Lombard builders and architects argued with French and German master stone-cutters about the best way to tackle their mammoth task, an enormous array of styles was employed.

Construction began in 1386 by order of Bishop Antonio da Saluzzo, on a site that had been associated with places of worship since the third century: a Roman temple to the goddess Minerva once stood

The **Duomo** is one of the greatest buildings in the world (and has a pretty good view too).

here. On the orders of Gian Galeazzo Visconti, then ruler of Milan, Lombardian terracotta stone was eschewed in favour of Condoglian marble shipped from Lake Maggiore on the Ticino river, and then along the Navigli, a network of canals in southern Milan built specially for the purpose.

Although consecrated in 1418, the cathedral remained incomplete for centuries. Politics, physical setbacks (a pink granite column sank, in transit, in Lake Maggiore), a lack of money and downright indifference kept the project on permanent standby. Finally, early in the 19th century, the façade was put on the church by order of none other than Napoleon; he kick-started the final stages of construction before crowning himself king of Italy here in 1805.

The exterior

A staggering 3,500 statues adorn the Duomo, about two thirds of them on the exterior. The oldest are at the apse end, which was built from 1386 to 1447; those along the sides were added as the building work progressed, between the late 15th and early 18th centuries. The façade is baroque up to the first order of windows, and neo-Gothic above. Each of the five bronze doors that provide access to the Duomo was sculpted by a different artist between 1840 and 1965, along particular themes.

To appreciate the statues and 135 spires fully, take the lift (which is near the back of the Duomo,

on the left-hand side) to the roof, from where, on clear days, you also get breathtaking views of the Alps. A roof visit brings you closer to an icon dear to the hearts of the Milanese: the Madonnina (1774), the gilded copper figure of Mary on the church's highest spire that was the city's highest point until it was pipped by the Pirelli skyscraper in 1958.

The interior

The 52 pillars of the five-aisled Duomo correspond to the weeks of the year. On their capitals, imposing statues of saints stretch up into the cross vaults of the ceiling, to vertiginous effect. On the floor near the main entrance is a sundial installed in 1768 by astronomers from the Accademia di Brera, placed so that it is struck by a ray of sunlight breaking through a hole in the opposite wall. On the summer solstice (21 June), the ray strikes the tongue of bronze set in the floor; on the winter solstice (21 December), the ray of light stretches out to reach the meridian. The sundial is so precise that it was used in the past to regulate clocks throughout the city.

In the first chapel on the right is the 11th-century sarcophagus of Bishop Ariberto d'Intimiano, and a 17th-century plaque commemorating the founding of the Duomo. The oldest of the stained-glass windows in the next three chapels was made in 1470-75 and is in the fifth bay on the right; it shows scenes from the life of Christ.

Duomo.

In the crossing of the transept, the presbytery floor has been worn by the passage of the many millions of pilgrims who have visited the Duomo over the centuries; Cardinal (later saint) Carlo Borromeo wanted the Duomo to serve as his model Counter-Reformation church. Flanking the 15th-century high altar are two gilded copper pulpits, both 16th-century; the organ is also here, its wooden shutters painted with biblical scenes by Giovanni Ambrogio Figino, Camillo Procaccini and Giuseppe Meda.

A nail allegedly from the Cross hangs at the apex of the apse's vaulted roof. Once a year, on the Saturday closest to 14 September (prior to the beginning of vespers), the archbishop ascends to the apex to retrieve the nail, moving up slowly and solemnly through the air in the Duomo's decorated wooden *nivola* – an angel-studded basket constructed in 1577 under orders by Borromeo, and significantly renovated and redecorated in 1701 (when the *putti*, or angels, were added). The nail is then exhibited at the altar until the following Monday after vespers, when it's lifted back up to the church ceiling.

In the right transept you'll find a funerary monument to Gian Giacomo Medici, long attributed to Michelangelo but now recognised as the work of sculptor and collector Leone Leoni (1560-63).

On a pedestal in the wall opposite the Medici monument stands an arresting and remarkably lifelike statue of a flayed St Bartholomew. This incredibly accurate study of human anatomy was carved in 1562 by Marco d'Agrate, a student of Leonardo da Vinci. Above and to the right, the splendid stained glass showing St Catherine of Alexandria – who died on the original Catherine wheel – is the work of the Arcimboldo brothers (1556).

Completed in 1614, the sculpture that closes the choir – designed by Pellegrino Tibaldi and carved by Paolo de' Gazzi, Virgilio del Conte and the Taurini brothers – is a masterpiece of its time. The three tiers of the sculpture represent (above) the life of St Ambrose, (centre) the martyred saints venerated by the Milanese church, and (below) the Milanese bishops Anatalone and Galdino.

The ambulatory windows blaze with fabulous 19th-century stained glass by the Bertini brothers, and depict scenes from both Testaments. From the ambulatory, stairs lead down to the crypt, where Carlo Borromeo is buried. Entrances to the treasury and the choir are also in the ambulatory.

In the left transept, the fantastic monsters on the bronze Trivulzio Candelabra, an impressive example of medieval goldsmithing, represent the arts, professions and virtues, and were created by the great 12th-century goldsmith Nicolas of Verdun. In the left aisle, the Cappella del Crocifisso (third past the transept) has stunning 16th-century stained glass.

The remains of the earlier churches of Santa Tecla and the Baptistery (where St Ambrose baptised St Augustine in 387) can be reached by descending the stairs just to the left of the main entrance. The stairs to the right lead to a set of early Christian excavations, two storeys below the Duomo's main door.

From 4 November until the Epiphany, the great *Quadroni di San Carlo*, a devotional pictorial cycle with scenes from the life of the saint, are displayed in the naves between the pillars. The works are a compendium of 17th-century Lombard painting.

Galleria Vittorio Emanuele II

Between piazza del Duomo & piazza della Scala.
Metro Duomo/bus 54, 65/tram 1, 2, 12, 19, 20, 24.
Open 24hrs daily. **Map** p251 E6/p252 E6.

The magnificent Galleria Vittorio Emanuele II isn't known as *il salotto di Milano* (Milan's living room) for nothing. It connects piazza del Duomo with piazza della Scala in grand style, and the upper echelons of Milan society all pass through at some point. Suited businessmen will happily pay €10 for a cappuccino on the terrace at Zucca (*see p112*), and elegant grandmothers carry their chihuahuas in Fendi bags. Shopping is, and always has been, the Galleria's main activity, and fashion flagships radiate out from the twin powerhouses of Prada and Louis Vuitton in the centre.

The Galleria's designer, Giuseppe Mengoni, pioneered its complex marriage of iron and glass 20 years before the Eiffel Tower was built. The Galleria was officially opened in 1867 by Vittorio Emanuele II, king of a newly united Italy; but, in a sour twist of fate, Mengoni wasn't present, having fallen to his death from his own creation a few days earlier.

The ceiling vaults are decorated with mosaics representing Asia, Africa, Europe and America. At ground level are mosaics of more local concerns: the coats of arms of Vittorio Emanuele's Savoia family, and the symbols of Milan (a red cross on a white field), Rome (a she-wolf), Florence (an iris) and Turin (a bull). If you can't see Turin's symbol, look out for the tourists spinning on their heels on the bull's privates – it's said to guarantee good luck. *Photo 57.*

Palazzo Reale

Piazza del Duomo 12 (02 875 672/www.artpalazzo reale.it). Metro Duomo/bus 54/tram 1, 2, 3, 12, 20, 23, 24, 27. **Open** for exhibitions only. **Admission** prices vary from free to €9. **No credit cards.**
Map p252 E7/p252 E7.

A mansion of utter opulence, and host to a swath of world class art shows. Recent big hitters have included a Canova exhibition, a Francis Bacon portrait show and a Vivienne Westwood retrospective.

Built in the 1300s, the Palazzo Reale was ordered by the Visconti family, then updated in the 16th century as part of the series of architectural reforms under the Sforzas. Giuseppe Piermarini, the Teatro alla Scala architect, gave the palazzo its neo-classical look when he was commissioned to design a residence for Archduke Ferdinand of Austria in the 1770s. Only a fraction of his stuccos and frescoes survived Allied bombing, but the Sala delle Cariatidi remains in an interesting state of semi-dereliction. Tours of the latter take place at set times of the day.

The palazzo also contains the Museo del Duomo in a neighbouring building. Due to reopen in mid-2009, it delves into the Cathedral's history.

Sightseeing

A walk on the style side

The Duomo took five centuries to build, but rather than looking like a mishmash of styles, it is a harmonious, glorious whole. Similarly, the centre of Milan is home to some interesting, lesser-known buildings whose contrasting styles seem to provide a synopsis of the city's history.

A perfect place to begin is **piazza San Sepolcro**. The square itself was part of the forum in Roman times, and Roman remains can be seen in the crypt of the church of **San Sepolcro** (*see p60*); its façade was renovated in 1717, and then again between 1894 and 1897. More obvious period juxtapositions can be seen opposite the church, on the **Palazzo Castani**, now a police station. The left side is distinctly 1930s, yet slots well into the 18th-century renovation of a late 15th-century façade, the original portal of which has survived. This is decorated with medallions

featuring portraits of Francesco Sforza, as well as (a long way from home) Romulus and Remus.

Next, slip down via Valpetrosa, cross via Torino, and into via della Palla. This leads into **piazza Sant'Alessandro**. If you like baroque excess, step inside the church of the same name; it's the most outrageous example of this style in Milan. The two vast confessionals flanking the altar come close to defying description: marble, inlays, gilt bronze – no expense was spared.

Back to the real world, and, heading east, to **piazza Missori**. Look up and to the right and see a high-rise in a low-rise city: the **Torre Velasca** (*see p79*), inaugurated in 1958. The tower takes its name from the piazza on which it stands, created in 1651 by the city's Spanish governor, Juan Fernandez de Velasco. Some 100 metres (330 feet) high, the 26-storey office building has a protruding, cantilevered upper section reminiscent of a medieval tower – although the architects, Studio BBPR, refuted the similarity at the time.

Next, walk up via Mazzini, named after one of the architects of Italian unification. Turn left up via Speronari and into via Falcone for the church of **Santa Maria presso San Satiro** (*see p60*), with its trompe l'oeil apse.

For some culinary rewards after all that pavement pounding, retrace your steps to via Speronari, then cross over via Torino into via Spadari where you'll find **Peck** (*see p134*), the world-famous deli that will fill the hungriest of bellys.

Around piazza della Scala

The shop-free **piazza della Scala** starts as you surface from the stores at the northern exit of Galleria -- Emanuele II. One of the world's most celebrated opera houses, the **Teatro alla Scala** (*see p59*) stands on the square's northern edge. Even if you can't see one of the performances, listed outside, the neighbouring **Museo Teatrale alla Scala** (*see p59*) offers an ample glimpse of La Scala's majesty. A statue of Leonardo da Vinci separates the theatre from **Palazzo Marino** on the other side of the square. Formerly a Genoese banker's private mansion, it's now the municipal hall.

Nearby, in its eponymous piazza, the Jesuits' baroque church of **San Fedele** (*see p58*) faces a statue of the author Alessandro Manzoni, one of Italy's greatest writers. **Casa del Manzoni** (*see p57*), the novelist's perfectly preserved house, is just around the corner, but you'll first have to pass the curious **Casa degli Omenoni** (via Omenoni 3), with its eight stone sentries of Atlas, sculpted in 1565 by Antonio Abbondio, and **Palazzo Belgioioso** (piazza Belgioioso 2), designed by Giuseppe Piermarini in 1777-81 for Alberico XIII di Belgioioso d'Este; his family's heraldic symbols figure large in the façade's decoration. Adjacent to the palazzo is the classy Boeucc (*see p98*), Milan's oldest restaurant.

West of piazza della Scala, the 18th-century **Palazzo Clerici** (via Clerici 5, 02 863 3131) has marvellous rococo interiors, and frescoes by Giambattista Tiepolo. The palazzo is open by appointment only. In the other direction, on via Manzoni, you'll find two neo-classical buildings overseen by Luigi Canonica around 1830, **Palazzo Anguissola** (no.10) and **Palazzo Brentani** (no.6), a former headquarters of the Piedmontese government. Nestling between similarly impressive façades along the street is the entrance to the **Museo Poldi Pezzoli** (*see below*). This late 19th-century aristocratic residence holds one of the most prestigious collections of European art, furniture and *objets*.

Casa del Manzoni

Via Morone 1 (02 8646 0403/www.casadelmanzoni. mi.it). Metro Montenapoleone/bus 61/tram 1, 2, 20. **Open** 9am-noon, 2-4pm Tue-Fri. **Admission** free. **Map** p251 E6/p252 E6.

A friendly curator will lead you around the wonderfully ornate former home of author and poet Alessandro Manzoni (1785-1873), second in Italian literature only to Dante. Several of the parquet-floored rooms, stocked with Manzoni's personal effects and early editions of his work, overlook what must be an estate agent's dream: a leafy quadrangle that serves as headquarters to Banca Commerciale on Piazza della Scala. The fire alarm is the only addition to the perfectly preserved room where Manzoni died, after falling on the steps of nearby San Fedele (*see p58*) in 1873.

Museo Poldi Pezzoli

Via Manzoni 12 (02 794 889/02 796 334/www. museopoldipezzoli.it). Metro Montenapoleone/ bus 61, 94/tram 1, 2. **Open** 10am-6pm Tue-Sun. **Admission** €8; €5.50 reductions. **Credit** MC, V. **Map** p251 E6/p252 E6.

It's the curious touches that make the Museo Poldi Pezzoli so memorable. The room after room of tasteful collections, collected by notable art enthusiasts Giuseppe and Rosa Poldi Pezzoli, and later expanded by their son Gian Giacomo, was opened to the public in 1881. One room upstairs contains a selection of early gold timepieces, and an armoury downstairs exhibits over 100 coats of flamboyant armour worn by Europe's poorer princes. The paintings are widely admired, and include Pollaiuolo's *Portrait of a Young Woman*, Vincenzo Foppa's *Portrait of Francesco Brivio* and Botticelli's *Virgin with Child*. The collections of attractively displayed jewellery, tapestries, glasswork, porcelain, paintings and books can occupy further hours.

Palazzo Marino

Piazza della Scala 2 (no phone). Metro Duomo or Montenapoleone/bus 61/tram 1, 2, 20. Closed to the public. **Map** p251 E6/p252 E6.

Although you can't enter the Palazzo Marino (it's been the city government HQ since 1861), you can enjoy its interesting history from all four sides. The architect Galeazzo Alessi was commissioned in 1558 by Tommaso Marino, a Genoese banker who collected taxes in Milan. Marino wanted to impress a noble Venetian lady, and Alessi was told, 'When finished, it should be the finest palazzo in Christendom.' The plan seems to have worked, as Marino married

Galleria Vittorio Emanuele II. *See p55.*

Piazza Cordusio looking towards Castello Sforzesco.

her. However, his financial ostentation irritated the locals, who predicted the palazzo, 'built by stealing, would either burn, fall into disrepair, or be stolen by another thief'. Marino died in financial ruin, and the Austrian army took over the palazzo in 1814; but the building stands unburned for now.

San Fedele

Piazza San Fedele (02 863 521/www.gesuiti.it).
Metro Duomo/bus 61/tram 1, 2, 20. **Open** 7.30am-1.15pm, 4-7pm daily. **Admission** free. **Map** p251 E6/p252 E6.

This imposing baroque church is the Milanese headquarters of the Jesuit order. It was designed by Pellegrino Tibaldi in 1569 as an exemplary Counter-Reformation church. Note its single nave, an invention that let the priest keep his eye on the whole congregation. The cupola, crypt and choir were added by Francesco Maria Ricchini between 1633 and 1652. The carved wooden choir stalls in the apse were lifted from Santa Maria della Scala, the church demolished to make way for the Teatro alla Scala.

San Fedele is a veritable hit parade of Milanese baroque and mannerist painting. In the first chapel on the right is Il Cerano's *Vision of St Ignatius* (1622); in a room leading to the sacristy beyond the second chapel on the right are a *Transfiguration* and *Virgin and Child* by Bernardino Campi (1565). The exuberant carvings on the wooden confessionals and the sacristy (designed by Ricchini and executed by Daniele Ferrari in 1569) help liven up the edifice's Counter-Reformation sobriety. The façade's stonework is full of deep-pink hues, thanks to a recent, and much needed, renovation.

Teatro alla Scala & Museo Teatrale alla Scala

Piazza della Scala (02 7200 3744/www.teatroalla scala.org). Metro Duomo/bus 61/tram 1, 2. **Open** *Museum* 9am-12.30pm (last entry noon), 1.30-5.30pm daily (last entry 5pm). **Admission** *Museum* €5; €2.50-€4 reductions. **Credit** AmEx, DC, MC, V. **Map** p251 E6/p252 E6.

If you can get hold of, or afford, a ticket to La Scala, opera-lovers worldwide will hold you in higher esteem. When the new season begins on 7 December (the feast of Sant'Ambrogio, Milan's much-loved patron saint), paparazzi and TV crews descend to catch shots of the fur- and jewel-heavy ladies and their suave male companions.

The opera house takes its name from Santa Maria della Scala, the 1381 church that once stood on the same site. It was commissioned by Regina della Scala, wife of Bernabò Visconti, but torn down in 1776, when the Palazzo Reale (*see p55*) was damaged by a fire, leaving the city with no principal theatre. Giuseppe Piermarini was given the task of building a replacement, and what a fine job he did: La Scala has a massive stage, 2,015 seats and some of the best acoustics in the world, and it draws in some of the very finest performers.

It was inaugurated in 1778 with an opera by Salieri; many of the best-known works of Puccini, Verdi, Bellini and others premièred here. La Scala is also a significant symbol of national pride. Destroyed by heavy bombing during World War II, it was swiftly rebuilt after the war's close and rein-augurated in 1946 with an opera conducted by one of Milan's favourites, Arturo Toscanini. Three years of refurbishments were completed in late 2004, although controversy about the directorship continues (*see p160* **Melodrama at La Scala**).

The museum, created in 1913, gives a taste of La Scala's splendour. Visitors can see a room dedicated to portraits of the greats, from Puccini to Caruso, and stand inside boxes 13, 15 and 18 for a peek at the splendid auditorium itself.

Piazza dei Mercanti and around

West of the Duomo, **piazza dei Mercanti** was once the epicentre of the city's medieval market, and has some of the city's oldest buildings. This fact is also reflected in the various street names alluding to activities that took place in the surrounding lanes: via Spadari (sword-makers), via Cappellari (milliners) and via Armorari (armourers), to name three. Appropriately, the area around via Orefici (goldsmiths) is still lined with jewellery stores.

The square is flanked by **Palazzo Affari ai Giureconsulti**, a magnificent building that was once the headquarters of the Collegio dei Nobili Dottori, which trained Milan's highest-ranking civil servants, and **Palazzo della**

Ragione (*see p60*) – built 1228-33 by Oldrado da Tresseno (then *podestà*, city leader) to symbolise the independence Milan had won from its Germanic rulers in the 12th century.

The coats of arms of patrician families who lived around the piazza are much in evidence (see, for example, the **Loggia degli Osii**, on the south-west side of the square, with Matteo Visconti's shield from 1316), as are portraits of classical scholars and church fathers (for instance, the 1645 **Palazzo delle Scuole Palatine**, with statues of St Augustine and the Latin poet Ausonius).

Piazza Cordusio links to via Dante and the Castello Sforzesco, but if you follow via Meravigli westwards, then take a southerly turn, you'll find yourself in 'Milan's Wall Street' – **piazza Affari**, built between 1928 and 1940. Here, the commanding grandeur of the **Palazzo della Borsa**, home to Milan's *borsa* (stock exchange), will remind you that many locals think of their city, the country's financial heavyweight, as the real capital of Italy. The *borsa* was founded in 1808, but only settled in this, its permanent home, in 1931. The Palazzo della Borsa was designed by local boy Paolo Mezzanotte, and typifies the rationalist style of the late 1920s and '30s. Stand on the opposite side of piazza Affari and feel dominated by the muscular façade.

Further south is the neo-classical **Banca d'Italia** (piazza Edison), built 1907-12, a vast structure that takes up the best part of an entire block. Nearby is **San Sepolcro** (*see p60*) and the unmissable **Biblioteca e Pinacoteca Ambrosiana** (*see below*), which holds a beautiful collection of art and artefacts. It's also notable because it was from a balcony on the piazza San Sepolcro side of the Ambrosiana that Mussolini first explained the wonders of fascism to an attentive crowd.

East of piazza San Sepolcro is **piazza Borromeo**, featuring a baroque statue by Dionigi Bussola of the saint who gave the square its name, and the **Palazzo Borromeo**, with its 15th-century terracotta arches and internal frescoes. Another statue of Borromeo – by Costantino Corti – stands in piazza San Sepolcro. Further south, on the shopping alley of via Torino, are the churches of **San Sebastiano** and **Santa Maria presso San Satiro** (for both, *see p60*).

Biblioteca & Pinacoteca Ambrosiana

Piazza Pio XI 2 (02 806 921/www.ambrosiana.it). Metro Cordusio or Duomo/bus 50, 58/tram 1, 2, 3, 4, 12, 14, 18, 19, 20, 27. **Open** *Pinacoteca* 10am-5.30pm Tue-Sun. *Library* open to scholars only. **Admission** €8; €5 reductions. **Credit** AmEx, DC, MC, V. **Map** p250 D7/p252 D7.

Sightseeing

Founded in 1609 by Cardinal Federico Borromeo, this 400-year-old project began life as one of the first ever public libraries. The world-class paintings on display, the palazzo setting and the scores of untitled statues dotted around reinforce the impression that Milan has more fine art in one city than most other countries have in their national collections.

Borromeo's private art collection of 172 paintings (now in rooms one, four, five, six and seven) were put on display in 1618. There's Titian's *Adoration of the Magi* and a portrait of a man in armour in room one; Jacopo Bassano's *Rest on the Flight from Egypt*, Raphael's cartoon for *The School of Athens* and Caravaggio's *Basket of Fruit* in rooms five and six; and works by Flemish masters, including Jan Brueghel and Paul Bril, in room seven.

Renaissance works from outside the Cardinal's original donation are in rooms two and three, including Sandro Botticelli's *Madonna del Padiglione* and Leonardo da Vinci's *Musician*. The rest of the Pinacoteca contains later works. A lachrymose *Penitent Magdalene* by Guido Reni – darling of the Victorians – is in room 13 on the upper floor. There are two works by Giandomenico Tiepolo in room 17. The De Pecis' donation of 19th-century works, including a self-portrait by sculptor Antonio Canova, can be found in rooms 18 and 19. The Galbiati wing houses objects such as a lock of Lucrezia Borgia's hair (between rooms 8 and 9) and the gloves Napoleon wore at Waterloo (room 9).

The Biblioteca's collection includes Leonardo's original *Codex Atlanticus*, a copy of Virgil with marginalia by Petrarch, an Aristotle with a commentary by Boccaccio, and autograph texts by Aquinas, Machiavelli and Galileo, among others. Pages from da Vinci's ancient work, especially those showing his inventions, are revolved every few months in glass cabinets in rooms one, two and three.

Civico Tempio di San Sebastiano

Via Torino 28 (02 874 263). Metro Duomo/tram 2, 3, 14, 20. **Open** 8am-noon, 3-6.30pm Mon-Sat; 9am-noon, 3.30-6.30pm Sun. **Admission** free. **Map** p250 D7/p252 D7.

When Milan emerged from a bout of the plague in 1576, its residents heaved a sigh of relief and, to express their gratitude to God for their deliverance, built this church on the site where the 14th-century church of San Quilino had stood. They dedicated it to the patron saint of those with contagious diseases. Pellegrino Tibaldi designed the building, though he originally planned a much larger dome; if the heavenly vision of Agostino Comerio's *Evangelists and Church Fathers* (1832) inside the cupola makes your head spin, just imagine the effect Tibaldi was originally aiming for.

Palazzo della Ragione

Piazza Mercanti (02 7200 3358/www.comune. milano.it). Metro Duomo or Cordusio/bus 50, 58/ tram 1, 2, 4, 12, 16, 18, 19, 20, 27. **Open** exhibitions only. **Admission** prices vary. **No credit cards. Map** p250 D6/p252 D6.

The courtyard of the Palazzo della Ragione – also known as Broletto Nuovo (from *brolo*, an old word denoting a place where justice was administered) – is one of the few quiet, sheltered corners of central Milan. The palazzo was erected in 1233 by order of Oldrado da Tresseno, then *podestà* (mayor), to serve as law courts. Oldrado's portrait can be seen in relief on the façade facing piazza del Broletto Nuovo, and he is also the subject of an equestrian statue inside the arches of the *broletto*. Markets and public meetings were once held in the ground-floor porticos; people also flocked here to see hangings.

In 1771, the Holy Roman Empress Maria Theresa decreed the building should become an archive for deeds, and had it enlarged. Today it houses municipal offices and is closed to the public. It's one of the few remaining medieval buildings in the city: restoration work carried out in 1988 uncovered 13th-century frescoes.

San Sepolcro

Piazza San Sepolcro (no phone). Metro Duomo/ tram 2, 3, 14, 20. **Open** noon-2.30pm Mon-Fri. **Admission** free. **Map** p250 D7/p252 D7.

The forum of Roman Mediolanum occupied the area between piazza San Sepolcro and piazza Pio XI. It was here that a church dedicated to the Holy Trinity was built in 1030, only to be rebuilt in 1100 and rededicated to the Holy Sepulchre. The church underwent the usual Counter-Reformation treatment in the early 1600s, and an 18th-century façade was replaced by a neo-Romanesque one in 1894-97. The crypt, which runs the whole length of the church, is all that remains of the original Romanesque structure. A forest of slim columns divides its five aisles, and by the apse is a 14th-century sarcophagus with reliefs of the Resurrection.

Santa Maria presso San Satiro

Via Torino 19 (02 874 683). Metro Duomo/tram 2, 3, 14, 20. **Open** 7.30-11.30am, 3.30-7pm daily. **Admission** free. **Map** p250 D7/p252 D7.

Satiro (or Satirus) was St Ambrose's brother. It was to this lesser-known sibling (who also became a saint) that a certain Archbishop Anspert wanted a church dedicated, and he left funds for the task when he died in 876. All that remains of the early basilica is the Greek-cross Cappella della Pietà. In 1478 Renaissance genius Donato Bramante was called in to remodel the whole church to provide a fitting home for a 13th-century image of the Virgin – said to have bled when attacked by a knife-wielding maniac in 1242 – and to accommodate the pilgrims flocking to see it. The fresco concerned is still visible on the high altar.

Bramante's gift for creating a sense of power and mass – even in a space as limited as the one occupied by this church – emerges in the powerful, barrel-vaulted central nave that ends in a trompe l'oeil niche that simulates the perspective of a deep apse in the space of a mere 97cm (38in). The octagonal baptistery to the right was made by Agostino de' Fondutis in 1483 to Bramante's designs.

Castello Sforzesco, Brera & Northern Milan

Green parks and old streets filled with temples, monuments and marble arches.

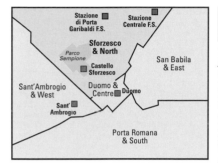

Milan's original overlords, the Viscontis and the Sforzas, made this area their stamping ground. For many, it's Milan at its most authentic and exciting. The winning blend of old and new is best seen in Parco Sempione, Milan's green lung and home of the fairy-tale Castello Sforzesco. The old masters housed in the latter are complemented by the innovation at the Triennale gallery across the park.

The select suburb of Brera is the area's high-class hub, studded with the mansions, churches and (nearby) cemetery of Milan's original upwardly mobile classes. It has the shops and restaurants to match, as well as the must-see **Pinacoteca di Brera** (*see p65*), a 38-room gallery with works by Bramante, Caravaggio, Picasso, de Chirico and more.

But it's not all high-class gloss and glamour: a combination of low rents and investment in the previously blue-collar zones of Garibaldi, Isola and Bovisa has made these surrounding districts shine. Hipsters flock to the relaxed bars and clubs of the former, young professionals have colonised Isola, and the city's latest Triennale outpost changed Bovisa from gritty suburb to urban star, where Milan's surprisingly large industrial legacy meets the effects of immigration: it's here that you'll find the city's best Sicilian, Sri Lankan and Chinese cuisines.

To see Milan's best array of frescoes and fine art, palazzos and former factories, do as the locals do and head north.

Castello Sforzesco & Parco Sempione

The imposing **Castello Sforzesco** (*see p62*)
is a cultural history lesson in itself. Its successive roles as a ducal residence, Visconti prison and barracks for invading Spanish, French and Austrian troops have produced a host of different architectural touches, most of them either ostentatious or plain menacing. Its dozen museums (*see p66* **Museum multitude**), ranging from the bold to the bizarre, lie within the castle's parade grounds and crenellated walls.

Surrounding the Castello is the green expanse of **Parco Sempione** (*see p64*). A legacy of Francesco Sforza's predilection for hunting, the park once teemed with deer, hare

Palazzo d'Arte (Triennale). *See p63.*

Sightseeing

and pheasants imported from nearby Varese and Como. These days, however, you're much more likely to spot some of the thousands of Milanese canines that have been crammed into this dog-loving city.

On one side sit the **Arena** (*see p64*) and the recently refurbished 1906 **Acquario** (*see below*). To the west the Palazzo d'Arte (more commonly known as the **Triennale**; *see p63*) shows art, video and design installations. A walk past the goldfish ponds to the north side of the park takes in the **Arco della Pace** (*see p65*), an unmistakably neo-classical arch begun in 1807 to commemorate Napoleon's victories. It presides pompously over the wide boulevard of **corso Sempione**, strategically located on the road that links Milan to Paris.

In the other direction, the castle overlooks one end of a long pedestrianised corridor that runs from the castle down via Dante, through piazza del Duomo, and all the way along piazza Vittorio Emanuele II to piazza San Babila.

Via Dante is notable for several palazzi, all begun under Napoleonic rule (1796-1814) and continued in the 19th century. All, that is, except Palazzo Carmagnola (no.2, not open to the public), which, despite its neo-classical façade, dates back to the 14th century and retains its original courtyard. Milanese ruler Ludovico 'il Moro' Sforza used this building to house his most illustrious guests, from da Vinci and artist/architect Donato Bramante to his mistress Cecilia Galleriani. Next door is the original **Piccolo Teatro** (*see p174*), founded in 1947 and now called Teatro Grassi.

Piazza Castello is cupped by the curved **foro Buonaparte**, on which stands the 1895 *Hero of Two Worlds* by Ettore Ximenes. The equestrian statue is dedicated to Giuseppe Garibaldi's involvement in the Uruguayan civil war and the Italian unification movement. Walk westwards, and you'll come to Cadorna metro and Stazione Ferrovie Nord; taking foro Buonaparte north-east will take you past the fascinating exploration into phoney art at the **Museo d'Arte e Scienza** (*see p63*).

Acquario

Viale Gadio 2, Parco Sempoine (02 8846 5750/ www.acquariocivico.mi.it). Metro Lanza/bus 57, 61, 70, 94/tram 3, 4, 7, 12, 14, 27. **Open** 9am-1pm, 2-5.30pm Tue-Sun. **Admission** free. **Map** p248 D6/p252 D6.

A whacking great Poseidon guards the goldfish pond in front of this fun Parco Sempoine freebie, which was reopened in 2006. The Aquarium's strong reliance on a handful of river species, most notably trout, becomes amusing after the sixth reconstruction of a River Po or Lake Como underwater scene. The 25 newly installed tanks are large and bright, however, and the collection of bristled Adriatic sturgeon and barracuda-like pike are gloriously ugly.

Castello Sforzesco/ Civici Musei del Castello

Piazza Castello (02 8846 3700/www.milanocastello. it). Metro Cadorna, Cairoli or Lanza/bus 43, 57, 61, 70, 94/tram 1, 3, 4, 12, 14, 18, 19, 27. **Open** *Grounds* 8am-6pm daily. *Museums* 9.30am-5.30pm Tue-Sun. **Admission** *Grounds* free. *Museums* €3; free 4.30-5.30pm Tue-Thur, 2-5.30pm Fri. **Map** p248 C6/p252 C6.

Parco Sempione. *See p64.*

After the Duomo, the Castello Sforzesco is Milan's main attraction – not least because of its 12 mini-museums and archives running all the way from Palaeolithic history through to 1950s furniture. It was home to the noble Visconti family from 1368, and restored to its original splendour by the equally aristocratic Sforzas in the 1450s, and the court gathered here a few decades later by Francesco's son, Ludovico 'il Moro', was regarded as one of Europe's most refined. Castle and court fell into decline in 1499, and Ludovico's game of playing off the French under Charles VIII against Holy Roman Emperor Maximilian I ended in disaster and imprisonment in 1500.

While Milan was bristling under French rule in the early 19th century, the castle's star-shaped bulwarks were knocked down. In the late 1800s there was much talk of demolishing the rest, but luckily for the city, architect Luca Beltrami fought to preserve it, coming up with the idea of headquartering Milan's various art collections here. From 1893 until 1904, Beltrami oversaw the castle's restoration, rearranging and rebuilding unashamedly; but it was his unorthodox efforts that saved the edifice from total oblivion. Coming to a spindly point above the façade is an early 20th-century recreation of a tower originally built by the 15th-century architect Antonio Averlino, dubbed Il Filarete (hence the tower's name, Torre del Filarete).

Visitors enter via the enormous piazza d'Armi; gates lead into the Rocchetta (the oldest part of the castle, on the left), and into the Cortile (courtyard), where sculptures are often displayed, and Palazzo della Corte Ducale (on the right), in Renaissance style. The entrance to the Civici Musei collection of museums (*see p66* **Museum multitude**) is here.

Museo d'Arte e Scienza

Via Quintino Sella 4 (02 7202 2488/www.museoarte scienza.com). Metro Cairoli or Lanza/bus 57, 61, 70, 94/tram 1, 3, 4, 12, 14, 27. **Open** 10am-6pm Mon-Fri. Closed 1wk Aug. **Admission** €4-€8. **Credit** MC, V. **Map** p248 D6/p252 D6.

A unique, mature and fascinating museum, primarily exposing fraudulent works of art – and the scientific techniques involved. With detailed explanations in English, the underground rooms line up fake weapons, icons, paintings and more; the ethnographic collection is superb. Don't miss the secret tunnel to the Castello in Room 14. Upstairs, you're invited into the working research labs, established in 1993 to authenticate international art. There are also permanent exhibitions devoted to da Vinci's life and work.

Palazzo d'Arte (Triennale)

Viale Alemagna 6 (02 724 341/www.triennale.it). Metro Cadorna/bus 57, 61, 94/tram 1, 19, 27. **Open** 10.30am-8.30pm Tue-Sun. **Admission** €8. **Credit** AmEx, DC, MC, V. **Map** p248 C5.

This superb museum was once home to Milan's huge design culture event, held every three years. Now its vast collection of chairs, Olivetti typewriters and other design masterpieces are revolved every six months in a funky, open-plan showroom, flanked by exhibits in an outdoor atrium.

At least two major design-themed temporary exhibitions are held in the Palazzo d'Arte at any one time. At the time of writing, a junk-house building installation, an extravaganza of Australian home design and a show by Cassina, the celebrated Milanese furniture company, were all in full swing. Even non-art lovers will enjoy browsing the books in the excellent

Pinacoteca di Brera. *See p65.*

Big trouble in little China

milanesi, the growth of the local Chinese zone is viewed with suspicion. Rumours abound that valid passports are sent back to relatives in China, who use them a second time to enter Italy – a charge levelled at Italians entering the United States via Ellis Island a century ago. The Chinese minority is regularly accused of tax dodging and profiteering in wholesale imports of trinkets, which are sold on to Milan's sub-Saharan Africans, who ply these wares on the city streets.

In the 1920s, immigrants arriving from China's south-eastern Zhejiang province established an enclave in via Paolo Sarpi. Today, it's the city's Chinatown, packed with wholesalers, restaurants and foreign food stores. A warm mix of colours, dialects and pungent smells, it's the only truly exotic area of this ever more ethnically diverse city.

With little colonial history, Italy is one of Europe's most homogeneous nations. Of the 60 million residents, fewer than five per cent are ethnically non-Italian, and fewer than three per cent are ethnically non-European. A 2007 survey put Milan's Chinese populace at approximately 13,000, although it is estimated that there are roughly double that number living in the city, many waiting in restaurants, working in shops and staffing small leather and textile factories. For many

In April 2007, what had been a delicate balance between Italians and Chinese violently broke down. On the narrow streets of the Paolo Sarpi quarter, Italian police officers started cracking down on the loading and unloading of wholesale goods from private vehicles. Users of large trolleys, tagged as a safety threat to residents, were fined. Italian residents hung flags from their windows, visually contesting the Chinese 'invasion' of the zone. Chinese residents, some of them fourth-generation Italian, took to the streets in response, convinced that they were being targeted for their nationality. In the ensuing mêlée, a handful of police officers and local Chinese were injured, tarnishing the reputation of what is usually a welcoming place in which to shop, eat and drink.

ground-floor bookshop. The DESIGN café next door has a proud jumble of designer chairs, and dishes up tea and cakes to an arty mob, all peering at their purchases through D&G glasses. *Photo p61*.

Parco Sempione

Metro Cadorna, Cairoli or Lanza/bus 43, 57, 61, 70, 94/tram 1, 3, 4, 12, 14, 27, 29, 30. **Open** *Mar-Apr, Oct* 6.30am-9pm daily. *May* 6.30am-10pm daily. *June-Sept* 6.30am-11.30pm daily. *Nov-Feb* 6.30am-8pm daily. **Admission** free. **Map** p248 C5.

Parks are rare in Milan, and this 47-hectare (116-acre) expanse behind Castello Sforzesco is the city's biggest. Since its 1996 clean-up, it has become a firm favourite with everyone from canoodling teenagers to summertime drinkers in the park's outdoor bars.

Milan's French rulers began carving the orchards,

vegetable gardens and a hunting reserve out of the remains of the ducal gardens in the early 1800s. It was only in 1893 that it was landscaped, by Emilio Alemagna. He opted for the then-popular 'English garden' look, with winding paths, lawns, copses and a lake. The Arena Civica, the mini-colosseum designed in 1806 by Luigi Canonica and located at the back of the park, is another addition from the city's Napoleonic period. The rulers of the Roman-inspired French Empire used it for open-air entertainment – chariot races and mock naval battles (for the latter, the arena was flooded with water from nearby canals). Today, it's used for athletic events and the occasional outdoor concert.

There's a handful of museums and galleries in the park, including the Palazzo d'Arte (Triennale, *see p63*); near this palazzo are several abstract sculptures from the 1970s. Be sure to visit Giò Ponti's 1933 Torre Branca, Milan's answer to the Eiffel Tower, which offers visitors a 360° view of the entire city. At the base of the tower is designer drinking spot Just Cavalli Café (02 311 817, www.justcavallicafe. com, closed Sun).

Construction of the Arco della Pace, currently under renovation (until 2010) at the northern end of the park, was begun in 1807 to a design by Luigi Cagnola, to celebrate Napoleon's victories. Work proceeded too slowly, however, and came to an abrupt halt in 1814 when Napoleon fell from power. Construction resumed in 1826 – with a few changes to the faces in the reliefs – and the arch was eventually inaugurated on 10 September 1838 by Austrian Emperor Ferdinand I. Among its decorative sculptures are the *Chariot of Peace* by Abbondio Sangiorgio, and *Four Victories* by Giovanni Putti. *Photo p62.*

Brera

Milan's answer to London's Notting Hill, Brera has been transformed from hip 1980s artists' zone to understatedly wealthy desres. Home to Milan's must-see gallery, the **Pinacoteca di Brera** (*see below*), and a renowned fine arts university, the area brims with exhibition spaces, offbeat boutiques and seriously cool bars.

At via Brera 15, near the corner of via del Carmine, is the 17th-century **Palazzo Cusani** (note that it is not open to the public). If you're wondering about its unusual appearance an anecdote supplies the answer: the Cusani brothers shared the residence in the 18th century, but commissioned separate architects to design their respective entrances. One façade of the palazzo is in *barocchetto* style, by Giovanni Ruggeri, complete with ornate windows and balcony decorations; and the other is in a more traditional neo-classical style, and was designed by Giuseppe Piermarini. The rearing horse sculpture on the via Brera side is Aligi Sassu's 1960 creation, *Cavallo Impennato*.

Further north along via del Carmine, in the piazza of the same name, is **Santa Maria del Carmine** (*see p68*), one of three originally Romanesque churches hidden in this web of streets, that sadly fell prey to 19th-century restoration; the others are **San Marco** (*see p67*) and **San Simpliciano** (*see p68*). Although Santa Maria del Carmine's baroque chapel remains intact, the current brickwork façade was added in 1879.

Back on via Brera is the **Palazzo di Brera**, built by Francesco Maria Ricchini in 1651 on the site of a 14th-century Umiliatian convent and Jesuit school. You don't have to be visiting the palazzo's most famous portion, the

Pinacoteca, to wander around the courtyard's porticoes and statues; you're also free to push on inside through the statue-filled corridors, which house the Istituto Lombardo Accademia di Scienze e Lettere (Lombard Institute of Science and Letters) and the Accademia di Belle Arti (Academy of Fine Arts). If only all universities looked this elegant. The palazzo also houses the **Biblioteca Braidense**, a library with an intriguing collection of volumes, as well as richly decorated interiors, an observatory and botanical garden (*see p67*).

The Franciscan church of **Sant'Angelo** (*see p68*) stands north-east of here. From piazza Sant'Angelo, via della Moscova and largo Donegani lead to via Turati and the Palazzo della Permanente, its façade at the moment in the process of extensive renovation, although it still hosts a solid stock of temporary modern art exhibitions.

Pinacoteca di Brera

Via Brera 28 (02 722 631/reservations 02 8942 1146/www.brera.beniculturali.it). Metro Lanza or Montenapoleone/bus 61, 67/tram 1, 2, 8, 12, 14. **Open** 8.30am-7.30pm Tue-Sun (last entry 6.45pm). **Admission** €5; €2.50 reductions; free under-18s, over-65s. **No credit cards**. **Map** p248 D5.
A stupendous collection of fine art from Caravaggio to Bramante, often considered Lombardy's finest art

Meet Worzel at **Orto Botanico**. *See p67.*

Sightseeing

Museum multitude

The **Castello Sforzesco**'s (*see p62*) vast collections cover everything from Renaissance masterpieces to Egyptian mummies. Its well-presented museums are a fount of knowledge: set aside a whole day to do the place justice, and games of Trivial Pursuit will never be the same again.

The Castello also houses historical and photo archives, a print collection and archaeological and art history libraries, which are not open to the general public. Comprehensive explanations of the works displayed are available in English in most of the rooms.

Civiche Raccolte d'Arte Antica

The sculpture gallery begins on the ground floor with early Christian and medieval works, including a marble head of the Byzantine Empress Theodora. Dominating room two is an equestrian statue (1363) of Bernabò Visconti by Bonino da Campione. Room six contains a bas-relief (1171) from the Porta Romana showing Milanese scenes after one of Barbarossa's rampages. In room eight, the Sala delle Asse, you'll find heavily restored frescoes of exotic botanical scenes attributed to Leonardo da Vinci, which ilusrate the park's former use as a Sforza hunting ground. The Cappella Ducale (duke's chapel, room 12) was built in 1972 and decorated by the leading painters of the day under the direction of Bonifacio Bembo; the room boasts a dizzying frieze of gold leaf, above which a squadron of angels plays. Room 14 has a 15th-century portal from the Milan branch of the Medici bank and a collection of arms. The swords are in true Milanese style: elaborate, showy and expensive-looking.

In room 15, Bambaja's masterpiece, the supine monument to Gaston de Foix, is a tribute to the Lombard classical style of the early 16th century; de Foix, Louis XII's nephew, was a French military commander who died heroically in Ravenna in 1512. The journey through Gothic and early Renaissance works of art ends with a heavily guarded sculpture by Michelangelo, the *Rondanini Pietà*. The piece was first sculpted and subsequently partially destroyed and abandoned in the mid 1550s, but Michelangelo returned to it in the last year of his life, still working to perfect it until his death in 1564.

Civiche Raccolte d'Arte Applicata

This section runs the whole gamut of the so-called minor arts: wrought iron (room 28); ceramics of the world from the 15th to the 19th centuries in rooms 29 and 30 – don't miss the eccentric pieces made by architect Giò Ponti (1920s) for Richard Ginori in room 30; Italian and European porcelain (room 31); liturgical objects, ivories and scientific instruments (room 32); leather objects (room 35); and goldsmith works, enamels, bronzes, textiles and wall coverings. The level of intricacy displayed in some of these objects is breathtaking.

Museo di Arte Applicata

Recently redesigned and very accessible, this furniture museum is a lot more exciting than it might sound. Ducal wardrobes and writing desks are shown off in context, surrounded by objets d'art and classic paintings. The question 'How on earth did they get that up the stairs?' occurs with more than one 18th-century chest of drawers. Contemporary pieces include Ettore Sottsass's ultra sexy Casablanca bookcase (1981).

collection. The Pinacoteca began life as a collection of paintings for students of the Accademia di Belle Arti in the same building; the paintings were harvested from churches and monasteries suppressed by the Napoleonic regime.

Although it can't compete with the Louvre or London's National Gallery, the Pinacoteca is of a size that makes for an easy visit. The collection is modest in breadth, but exquisite in quality, and covers works by major Italian artists from the 13th to the 20th centuries. It has its share of important works of art, including the exercise in foreshortening that is Andrea Mantegna's *Dead Christ*; a mournful *Pietà*

by Giovanni Bellini (both in room VI); Piero della Francesca's *Virgin and Child with Saints* (room XXIV); the disturbingly realistic *Christ at the Column* by Donato Bramante, and Caravaggio's atmospheric *Supper at Emmaus* (room XXIX). Titian, Tintoretto and Veronese are all here, and rooms VIII and IX contain a series of huge pieces.

The palazzo was begun in 1651 by Francesco Maria Richini for the Jesuits, who wanted it to house their college, astronomical observatory and botanical garden. In 1776 part of the building was allocated to the Accademia di Belle Arti, and in 1780 Giuseppe Piermarini completed the main portal. The

Museo Egizio

The highlight of any Egyptian museum is always the mummy, and the Castello's is no exception; although visitors who know their ancient Mesopotamian history will be equally excited by the fragments of writing, the statuettes of various grotesque divinities and reconstructed pottery. The all-important mummy in this pocket-sized museum was brought back from the Orient by a Roman marquis, Carlo Busca. His superstitious son Ludovico disposed of the artefact in the 1850s, and it ended up being used for anatomy study in Milan's Maggiore hospital. When they tried to inter it after years of posthumous abuse, a bureaucratic custodian halted the burial as no official death certificate had been produced, and so it ended up here.

Museo della Preistoria e Protostoria

Digging deep into Milan's history, this space tells the story of Milan's earliest colonisers, from the (neolithic) fourth century BC to the era of the Celts and Gauls, who were beginning to be touched by Roman influence. The artefacts from the 'warrior's tomb' show an early level of globalisation on the plains of Lombardy; the helmet is from Slovenia, short-sword from Switzerland and shin guards from Greece. This is one of two collections housed in the basement beneath the Cortile della Rocchetta; the other is the Museo Egizio (*see above*).

Museo degli Strumenti Musicali

The castle houses one of the largest collections of musical instruments in Europe (rooms 36 and 37), brought together by Natale Gallini. In all, there are 640

instruments, arranged in five sections: string, plucked, keyboard, wind and exotic. The exhibits range from the rare (including violins by Stradivarius) to the bizarre (such as *pochette* – a pocket-sized violins used by dancing instructors).

Pinacoteca di Castello

Reopened in 2005 after a four-year restoration, this is Milan's third major *pinacoteca* (art gallery); the others are the Brera (*see p65*) and the Ambrosiana (*see p59*). The gallery proper begins in room 20, which features a panorama of 15th-century Italian painting, including Mantegna's majestic masterpiece *Madonna and Child with Saints and Angels in Glory* (1497) and Antonello da Messina's *St Benedict* (1470), with his penetrating, suspicious gaze. The Veneto is represented by Giovanni Bellini's *Madonna con Bambino* (1470s). There are also works by the Florentines, including the *Madonna dell'Umiltà* (1430s) by Filippo Lippi.

Room 21 is an extravaganza of Lombard painting from the early to late Renaissance, including Vincenzo Foppa's stoic *St Sebastian* (before 1490) and a *Noli Me Tangere* (c1508) by Bramantino. The 16th-century schools are represented by the languorous male nudes of Cesare da Sesto's *San Rocco* polyptych (1520s), the melting gaze of Correggio's *Madonna and Child with the Infant St John* (1517) and Moretto da Brescia's *St John the Baptist* (c1520).

Rooms 23 and 24, meanwhile, are full of the forced elegance and erudition of the Lombard mannerists. The Pinacoteca closes with 17th- to 18th-century works: Bernardo Strozzi's fleshy *Berenice* (1630) and the inevitable photo-realistic views of Venice by Canaletto and Guardi.

Pinacoteca was established as a study collection, with plaster casts and drawings for the students at the academy. Today, the 38 rooms are arranged in a circuit that begins and ends with 20th-century Italian painting. Two are glass-walled art restoration rooms, open to the public. *Photo p63*.

The Orto Botanico behind the Pinacoteca (open Apr-June 9am-noon, 3-5pm Mon-Fri; July-Mar 9am-noon) is a lovely little spot, stacked with aromatic herbs, climbers and vegetable gardens (for research, not the pot). Europe's oldest ginkgo biloba trees came over from China in the early 1700s and stand 30m (98ft) tall in the south-west corner. *Photo p65*.

San Marco

Piazza San Marco 2 (02 2900 2598). Metro Lanza/ bus 43, 61, 94/tram 1, 2, 3, 4. **Open** 9am-noon, 2-7pm daily. **Admission** free. **Map** p249 E5.

San Marco was built in 1254 by the Augustinian Lanfranco Settala on the site of an earlier church that the Milanese had dedicated to Venice's patron, St Mark. This gesture was to express their thanks to the Venetians for their intervention in the battle against Frederick Barbarossa. The church's façade was redone by Carlo Maciachini, a champion of the neo-Gothic revival; inside, nine chapels provide a survey of 16th- and 17th-century Lombard painting.

San Simpliciano

*Piazza San Simpliciano 7 (02 862 274). Metro Lanza/
bus 43, 61, 94/tram 3, 7, 12, 14.* **Open** 7.30am-
12.30pm, 4-7pm daily. **Admission** free. **Map** p248 D5.
One of the oldest churches in the city, San
Simpliciano was founded in the fourth century by
St Ambrose (and dedicated to his successor), and finished in 401. The original church was called the
Basilica Virginum, and had a porticoed structure
where penitent parishioners and neophytes attend-
ed mass. The present façade was added in 1870 by
Carlo Maciachini in his favoured neo-Gothic style,
and the central entrance was reconstructed in the
11th and 12th centuries. The apse decoration, *The
Coronation of the Virgin*, is by Leonardo da Vinci's
disciple, Il Bergognone.

Santa Maria del Carmine

*Piazza del Carmine 2 (02 8646 3365). Metro
Lanza/bus 43, 61, 94/tram 3, 7, 12, 14, 27.*
Open 7.15am-noon, 4-7.15pm daily. **Admission**
free. **Map** p248 D5.
Little remains of the original Romanesque church
built in 1250 and rebuilt in 1400; the current façade
(1880) is the work of Carlo Maciachini. And yet the
structure contains much Milanese history: the tomb
(1472) of ducal councillor Angelo Simonetta stands
in the right transept, and the body of finance minister Giuseppe Prina was brought to the sacristy after
he had been killed by the mob for raising the tax on
salt in 1814. The wooden choir (1579-85) houses the
plaster models that were used by the artists working in the Duomo in the 19th century.

Sant'Angelo

*Piazza Sant'Angelo 2 (02 632 481). Metro Moscova
or Turati/bus 43, 61, 94/tram 1, 2, 20.* **Open**
6.30am-8pm daily. **Admission** free. **Map** p249 E5.
Built in 1552 to a design by Domenico Giunti, and
intended to take the place of a Franciscan church the
Spanish had destroyed to build defences, Sant'Angelo
is a highly significant example of 16th-century
Milanese architecture. The interior is full of paintings
by noteworthy Milanese and Lombard artists of the
16th and 17th centuries, including Antonio Campi, Il
Morazzone and Camillo Procaccini.

Porta Garibaldi, Isola & beyond

A fabulous array of one-off shops and bars
lines **corso Garibaldi** as it winds up north to
Santa Maria Incoronata (*see p70*) – a rare
example of a double-fronted temple – and the
neo-classical arch of **Porta Garibaldi**, built
in 1826 and renamed in Giuseppe Garibaldi's
honour in 1860. The unemployed from Como
and Brianza would pass under this arch to seek
work in Milan's factories. The residential
districts of Garibaldi and Isola further north
grew to accommodate them and later itinerant
workers from Italy's poorer southern regions.

Linking Porta Garibaldi to the train station
of the same name is **corso Como**, a short,
entirely pedestrianised boulevard with a host of
restaurants, clubs and one-off shops, epitomised
by Carla Sozzani's 10 Corso Como (*see p129*), a
beacon of cool since 1991. A block to the west
are via Bramante and via Paolo Sarpi, the axis
of Milan's **Chinatown**, harbouring restaurants,
silk tailors and wholesale toyshops. This zone is
hemmed in, a block north, by the **Cimitero
Monumentale** (*see p69*), a glory of Milanese
art nouveau architecture.

To the east of Porta Garibaldi, on a 1,000-
square-metre (10,753-square-foot) site that was
once occupied by Pirelli's tyre factory, rises the
Grattacielo Pirelli, or Pirellone (Big Pirelli),
as the locals call it. Erected between 1955 and
1960, the Pirellone is an exemplar of post-World
War II reconstruction, designed by a team of
architects that included Giò Ponti, Pier Luigi
Nervi and Arturo Danusso. The sides of the
building are tapered, a feat that required great
architectural skill. More controversially, it was
the first building in Milan to dare to rise higher
than the golden Madonnina statue on top of the
Duomo, although a mini replica version was
soon placed upon the Pirellone's crown to
appease her. On 18 April 2002, the Pirellone
made headlines again when a small piston-
engined plane collided with it, killing the
pilot and two people in the building.

To the right of the Pirellone is the massive
bulk of Ulisse Stacchini's **Stazione Centrale**
(*see p69* **Mussolini's monolith**), an example
of the heavy end of the Milanese Liberty style,
built between 1912 and 1931. The front aspect
is entirely covered in Aurisina stone, and the
roof was constructed from five huge iron and
glass panels. On the façade, 'Anno IX' refers to
1931, the ninth year of Mussolini's Fascist
regime, when the station opened.

The *quartiere* of **Isola** (Island) was so named
because of its isolation on the 'wrong side of the
tracks' over the via Farini bridge. In the 19th
century, this area was a gathering place for
drunkards and petty criminals. However,
carpenters, blacksmiths, artists and the like
took the opportunity offered by low property
prices, and the area filled with workshops. In
recent years, a new wave of wealthy boho
residents tired of the city centre glitz have
moved in: designers, architects and other young
professionals. The bars and restaurants here
are thus friendlier and more experimental than
their counterparts in central Milan.

From piazza Segrino in the heart of this area,
via Thaon di Revel leads to the church of **Santa
Maria alla Fontana** (*see below*), which has
a sanctuary previously attributed to both
Leonardo da Vinci and Donato Bramante.

Mussolini's monolith

The central station has played a central role in Milan history: the marble, ebony and onyx in the royal waiting room is a reminder of the last days of the monarchy; and platform 21, in 1944, was the departure point for a one-way journey – to Auschwitz. In more recent times, the station has been the scene of mass arrivals. From the mid 1950s to the mid '70s, workers moved from the south to work in the factories in Milan and throughout Lombardy. From the station, the new arrivals fanned out to catch trams and buses to addresses written on scraps of paper, where a relative or friend waited to help them to make their first moves in the 'big city'.

As 'the man who made the trains run on time', Mussolini would probably approve of current plans to make Stazione Centrale Italy's high speed rail hub. A dedicated commuter line between Milan and Bologna, which will reduce the run to 55 minutes when it opens in December 2008, will join the express link inaugurated for the 2006 Winter Olympics in Turin. Upgrades further south should bring the Milan to Florence journey times down to 90 minutes by late 2009, and Rome will be cut to three hours, reducing the need to fly between Italy's two largest cities.

Il Duce's legacy lives on in Milan's imposing Stazione Centrale. Built between 1912 and 1931, it was designed by Florentine architect Ulisse Stacchini and inspired by Union Station in Washington, DC. World War I slowed progress, and it wasn't until 1925 that construction gathered force again. The final project became more elaborate, spurred on by Mussolini's desire for a station that would reflect the might of his Fascist regime.

The result is an exuberant combination of styles: colossal golem-head fountains flank its imposing façade, which is 207 metres (679 feet) long; and inside, the walls of the vast ticketing hall are embellished with bas-relief signs of the zodiac.

The station itself is undergoing a massive upgrade. Although the covers are off in many parts, including the 11.5-metre (38-foot) conservatory roof in the entrance hall, work is likely to last until 2010. The tourist office is moving from the first floor, and may well move again during the lifetime of this guide. As far as buying train tickets is concerned, although it's worthwhile stopping to admire the magnificent ticketing hall, canny travellers get theirs from the yellow, multi-lingual electronic machines lining the entire floor. And bear in mind that Centrale has been fertile ground for pickpockets for the last 75 years: keep your eyes open.

West of here, the previously run-down industrial zone of **Bovisa** is undergoing a major renaissance. New additions such as the Chedi design hotel (*see p43*) and several art workshops have been spurred on by the **Triennale Bovisa** (*see 70*).

Cimitero Monumentale

Piazzale Cimitero Monumentale (02 8846 5600). Metro Garibaldi/bus 43, 70/tram 3, 4, 7, 12, 14, 29, 30, 33. **Open** 8am-noon, 1-4.30pm Tue-Sun. **Admission** free. **Map** p248 C3.

The Egyptians had their pyramids; the Milanese have the Cimitero Monumentale, last resting place of the perpetually ostentatious. The cemetery was begun in 1866 by Carlo Maciachini, the result being 250,000sq m (2,688,000sq ft) of pure eclecticism. It's virtually an open-air museum of art nouveau, though later Italian artists – including Giacomo Manzù, Adolfo Wildt and Lucio Fontana – were also commissioned to produce monuments.

The whole complex is centred on the 'Temple of Fame' (Famedio), where celebrated *milanesi* and other illustrious bodies are buried, including Luca Beltrami (restorer of the Castello Sforzesco and champion of the neo-Gothic movement), conductor Arturo Toscanini, poet Salvatore Quasimodo, and entertainer Giorgio Gaber. The most famous resident is novelist Alessandro Manzoni, author of *I Promessi Sposi* (*The Betrothed*), whose tomb is right in the middle of the Famedio.

Non-Catholics are buried in separate sectors; the Jewish sector, to the south, is notable for its comparative restraint. A free map of the most noteworthy monuments is available from the entrance booth.

Santa Maria alla Fontana

Piazza Santa Maria alla Fontana 11 (02 688 7059). Metro Garibaldi or Zara/bus 70, 82, 91, 92/tram 3, 7. **Open** *Church* 8am-noon, 3-7pm Mon-Fri; 8am-1pm, 4-7pm Sat, Sun. *Sanctuary* 3-5pm Sat; 9.30am-12.30pm Sun. **Admission** free. **Map** p248 D2.

This church is essentially a modern structure in the neo-Renaissance style, with various nondescript additions. The presbytery, however, rests on a much older sanctuary, open at weekends. According to local lore, French governor Charles d'Amboise was miraculously cured at a spring here, and so had an oratory built on the spot in 1506. The design for the building has variously been attributed to Leonardo da Vinci and Donato Bramante, but more rigorous scholarship identifies it as the work of Giovanni Antonio Amedeo. Some emotive Auschwitz-inspired frescoes reside in the church's eastern corner.

Santa Maria Incoronata

Corso Garibaldi 116 (02 654 855). Metro Garibaldi or Moscova/bus 33, 43, 70, 94/tram 3, 11, 29, 30. **Open** 7.30am-1.30pm, 4-7.30pm Mon-Fri; 7.30am-noon, 4-7.30pm Sat; 8am-12.30pm, 4-7.30pm Sun. **Admission** free. **Map** p248 D4.

This essentially Romanesque church is, in fact, two buildings erected by Guiniforte Solari and united in 1468. The one on the left went up in 1451, coinciding with the arrival in Milan of Duke Francesco Sforza; the Augustinian fathers dedicated it to the new duke. Nine years later, Francesco's wife Bianca Maria Visconti decided that another church should be erected, adjoining the first. Frescoes in the chapels of the left nave are attributed variously to the Leonardo-esque painter Bernardo Zenale and da Vinci's *pupillo*, Il Bergognone.

Triennale Bovisa

Via Lambruschini 31 (02 3657 7801/www.triennale bovisa.it). Bus 82, 92/tram 1, 12. **Open** 9.30am-6pm Mon-Fri. **Admission** prices vary. **Map** p248 D2.

The structure may look temporary – scaffolding and sheets of plastic – but this Triennale outpost is here to stay. It was built on the cheap and to adapt to the range of temporary exhibitions it hosts, such as the recent Che Guevara iconography show. Sculptures and large pieces are normally posted outside at the rear; a pink 'junk house' was another recent exhibit. The defunct gasworks opposite often have quirky artworks hanging from them.

Where the best people go to die: **Cimitero Monumentale**. *See p69*.

San Babila & Eastern Milan

Aristocratic addresses, designer dresses and €1,000 handbags at dawn.

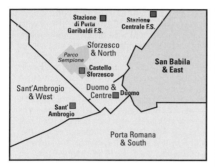

Judging by the high concentration of *palazzi*, this elegant *zona* has always been the district of choice for the extremely rich. It's also home to Milan's high-end fashion district, the so-called Quadrilatero della Moda; the painstakingly dressed windows at ground level are topped by €15,000 per square metre apartments above. The 'wealthier than thou' attitude also applies in San Babila's clutch of fine museums, many of which display the collections of previous high rollers. But if the overt affluence gets overpowering, make for the streets around the leafy Giardini Pubblici, spotted with fine restaurants and upbeat bars.

Via Manzoni & the Quadrilatero della Moda

Via Manzoni is named after the 19th-century author whose house stands just off the Scala end of the street (*see p57*). Before his death in 1873, the thoroughfare was known as corsia del Giardino because it was lined with lush-gardened villas, and because it led to this zone's green public space, the **Giardini Pubblici** (*see p72*). The park remains, but because of the road's elite status, its private gardens have gradually been replaced by private banks and expensive property.

Heading north-east, via Manzoni culminates at the **Archi di Porta Nuova**, a gate that was once part of the fortifications built to protect the city from the attacks of Frederick Barbarossa.

Though the gate was first erected in 1171, it was heavily restored in 1861, using white and black marble, and the more friable sandstone. The arches were then decorated with Roman funerary stones found in the area. Beyond the gate is **piazza Cavour** (*see p72*).

The style and wealth of Milan's fashion quarter, the **Quadrilatero della Moda**, is awe-inspiring; little wonder it's also known as the Quadrilatero d'Oro ('golden rectangle'). This designer heaven is delineated by via Montenapoleone, via Sant'Andrea, via Manzoni and pedestrianised via della Spiga. If you think €750 is a reasonable price for a pair of shoes or your dog just wouldn't be seen dead outside without its Christian Dior coat, then this is the place for you.

But even for the visitor without a gold card, this area is worth a look, on an anthropological level (as a glimpse of how the other half lives) and a cultural one: two eccentric but rewarding museums, the **Museo Bagatti Valsecchi** (*see below*) and the **Museo di Milano e Storia Contemporanea** (*see p72*), are located here, as is one of Milan's prettiest (and least-visited) churches, **San Francesco di Paola** (*see p72*). What with the fashion feeding frenzy nearby, you may well have these all to yourself.

Museo Bagatti Valsecchi

Via Gesù 5 (02 7600 6132/www.museobagatti valsecchi.org). Metro Montenapoleone/bus 61, 94/ tram 1, 2, 20. **Open** 1-5.45pm Tue-Sun. Closed Aug. **Admission** €8; €4 Wed. **Credit** MC, V. **Map** p249 E6/p252 E6.

This late 19th-century neo-Renaissance palazzo – residence of the Bagatti Valsecchi brothers, Fausto and Giuseppe – opened as a museum in 1994, a tribute to the extraordinary tastes of the two collectors. When not messing around on penny-farthings and early hot air balloons, the brothers shared a taste for all things Renaissance, and strove to reproduce 15th-century palazzo life in their own home. Inside are numerous works of Renaissance art, Murano glass, Flemish tapestries and *objets d'art* dating up to the 19th century. Artefacts are not labelled, in order to preserve the feel of a private home; instead, information sheets in English are available in each room, and free English-language audio guides can be borrowed from the ticket desk.

Museo di Milano e Storia Contemporanea

Palazzo Morando Attendolo Bolognini, via Sant'Andrea 6 (02 8846 5933/www.museodistoria contemporanea.it). Metro Montenapoleone/bus 61, 94/tram 1, 2, 20. **Open** *Museum* 2-5.30pm Tue-Sun. *Exhibitions* hours vary. Closed Aug. **Admission** *Museum* free. *Exhibitions* free-€5. **No credit cards.** **Map** p249 F6/p252 F6.

Fully renovated in 2002, the 18th-century Palazzo Morando Attendolo Bolognini is at once a living museum exhibiting the Countess Bolognini's collection of porcelain, sculptures and other objects in what were her private apartments, and home to a section of the city's civic art collections. The bulk of the artwork exhibited here consists of Luigi Beretta's collection, donated in 1935. These paintings have helped historians create a thorough picture of the city as it was during the Napoleonic era and under Austrian rule, and chart its urban development over the years. The ground floor has been remodelled as a space for visiting exhibitions; recent shows have focused on Maria Callas, African photography, wartime resistance and Islamic art.

San Francesco di Paola

Via Manzoni 3 (no phone). Metro Montenapoleone/ bus 61, 94/tram 1, 2, 20. **Open** 7.30am-noon, 3.30-7pm daily. **Admission** free. **Map** p249 E5/p252 E5.

Displaying an almost divine sense of irony, this charming baroque church constructed by the Minimi fathers (a particularly ascetic Franciscan order founded in 1506) lies right in the heart of the wealthiest and most ostentatious part of Milan. Its attractive baroque façade (completed in 1891) plays with concave and convex forms; inside, in addition to the classic marble altars, gilded woodwork and detailed stucco, you'll find a painting in the vault by Carlo Maria Giudici showing the glory of San Francesco di Paola, the church's patron saint.

Piazza Cavour to Giardini Pubblici

A catwalk away from the fashionistas of the Quadrilatero d'Oro is **piazza Cavour**. The statue of the Conte di Cavour, the 19th-century statesman credited with bringing about the unification of Italy, is on the north-east corner of this pretty square. Less attractive is the grey neo-classical Palazzo dell'Informazione (no.2), designed in 1942 as the headquarters for the fascist newspaper *Il Popolo d'Italia*. Mussolini's daily only survived until July 1943, but thanks to its relative proximity to the most newsworthy area of the city (the finance capital of piazza Affari), the building has become the Milanese headquarters for many Italian and international press agencies, among them Reuters and the Associated Press.

The **Giardini Pubblici** leading off piazza Cavour is the best place in which to relax with a paper. Cool and shaded in summer, it features a host of rambling museums that are great come rain or shine, including the **Civico Museo di Storia Naturale** (*see p73*), the **Museo del**

Squares not welcome in the **Quadrilatero della Moda**. *See p71*.

Cinema (*see below*) and the **Planetario Ulrico Hoepli** (*see below*). Over via Palestro is the opulent **Museo dell'Ottocento** (*see below*), now a gallery, formerly home of Napoleon and, later, Radetzky. The attached **PAC** gallery (*see below*) shows some interesting installations. South of the park, on corso Venezia, is Giuseppe Sommaruga's art nouveau **Palazzo Castiglioni** (no.47; 1900-03), which was occupied by the German army during World War II.

Civico Museo di Storia Naturale

Corso Venezia 55 (02 8846 3337/guided tours 02 8846 3289). Metro Palestro/tram 9, 20, 29, 30. **Open** 9am-5.30pm Tue-Sun. **Admission** €3; free Sun and under-18s. **No credit cards. Map** p249 F5.
Giovanni Ceruti's neo-classical building was put up in 1838 to house the collections left to the city by aristocrat Giuseppe de Cristoforis. It's a great rainy day museum: the displays cover botany, mineralogy, geology and palaeontology, with a lifesize triceratops the highlight of the latter. At times it feels like a museum of taxidermy, with diorama after diorama of jungle, prairie and arctic scenes populated with a stuffed cast. English explanations are scattered seemingly at random throughout the museum. *Photo p75.*

Giardini Pubblici

Metro Palestro, Porta Venezia, Repubblica or Turati/bus 43, 61, 94/tram 1, 2, 9, 11, 20, 29, 30. **Open** *Mar, Apr, Oct* 6.30am-9pm daily. *May* 6.30am-10pm daily. *June-Sept* 6.30am-11.30pm daily. *Nov-Feb* 6.30am-8pm daily. **Map** p249 F5.
As corso Venezia takes you away from the built-up areas of the city centre towards the built-up areas of its outskirts, you'll notice the green expanse of the Giardini Pubblici on your left. The gardens were designed in the English style by Giuseppe Piermarini in 1786, and enlarged in 1857 to include the Villa Reale (now renamed Villa Belgiojoso Bonaparte) and the Palazzo Dugnani. The park's present arrangement – complete with natural elements, such as waterfalls and rocky outcrops – was the work of Emilio Alemagna for the 1871 World Fair. In addition to the galleries and museums on its outer edges, the park has a bar with outdoor tables (open 8am-7pm daily) and a small children's train (€1.50 a ride). There are also more dogs than you could throw a stick at.

Museo del Cinema

Via Manin 2B (02 2900 5659/www.cinetecamilano. it). Metro Turati/bus 43, 94/tram 1, 2, 20. **Open** 3-6pm Fri-Sun. Closed July, Aug. **Admission** €3; €2 reductions. **No credit cards. Map** p249 F5.
Reached through a little gate at the side of the late 17th-century Palazzo Dugnani, Milan's cinema museum may be small, but Hitchcock and Capra were reportedly among its fans. Highlights of the collection include early Italian forays into moving pictures, such as the 17th-century Venetian contraption *mondo novo*, which allowed viewers to see images on perforated coloured prints by candlelight,

the Lumière brothers' works and original sketches by Luchino Visconti for his film *Senso*. For information on film screenings, *see p149.*

Museo dell'Ottocento

Villa Belgiojoso Bonaparte, via Palestro 16 (02 7634 0809/www.villabelgiojosobonaparte.it). Metro Palestro/bus 61, 94. **Open** 9am-1pm, 2-5.30pm Tue-Sun. **Admission** free. **Map** p249 F5.
It's little wonder that Napoleon chose to live here in 1802, followed by the Austrian field marshal Count Joseph Radetzky. This recently restored neo-classical villa, formerly known as the Villa Reale, is one big conspicuous display of wealth. The English-style grounds, complete with pond and footpaths, simply add to the majesty.
The building's marble columns were laid down in 1790 by Austrian architect Leopold Pollack, who designed the mansion for Count Ludovico Barbiano di Belgiojoso. After unification, ownership passed to the Italian royal family, who gave it to the city of Milan in 1921. Today it's the home of the Museo dell'Ottocento (museum of the 19th century), formerly the Galleria d'Arte Moderna.
The collection is splendid. Made up of bequests by leading Milanese families, it occupies 35 rooms in the central body and on the first and second floors of the west wing of this U-shaped building. The ground floor is given over to neo-classical paintings, sculpture and bas-reliefs. Spread out over the ballroom and former living areas on the first floor are paintings from the Romantic period, as well as some Futurist works. (Look out for Giuseppe Pellizza da Volpedo's fine example of the socialist arte nuova movement, *The Fourth Estate*.) The second floor showcases the Grassi and Vismara collections, the latter including works by modern Italian and international masters such as Giorgio Morandi, Van Gogh, Gauguin, Cézanne, Matisse and Picasso.

PAC (Padiglione d'Arte Contemporanea)

Via Palestro 14 (02 7600 9085/www.comune.milano. it/pac). Metro Palestro or Turati/bus 61, 94. **Open** times vary. **Admission** €6; €4 reductions; free under-6s. **No credit cards. Map** p249 F5.
The PAC organises international contemporary exhibitions, and generally features a wide range of well-established artists. Designed by Ignazio Gardella (1905-99) in the 1950s, it was rebuilt by the original architect after it was almost destroyed by a deadly mafia bomb in 1993.

Planetario Ulrico Hoepli

Corso Venezia 57 (02 8846 3340/www.comune. milano.it/planetario). Metro Palestro/tram 9, 20, 29, 30. **Open** *Shows* 9pm Tue, Thur; 3pm, 4.30pm Sat, Sun. Closed July, Aug. **Admission** €3; €1.50 reductions. **No credit cards. Map** p249 F5.
A gift to the city from publisher Ulrico Hoepli, this planetarium was built in 1930 by Pietro Portaluppi in faux-classical style. Projections take place in a great domed room, last renovated in 1955.

From piazza San Babila to Porta Venezia

Corso Vittorio Emanuele II, one of Milan's main commercial streets, stretches from piazza del Duomo (*see p52*) to piazza San Babila. For people who can't afford designer prices, the porticoes of this wide thoroughfare are filled with mass-market Italian brands. Halfway down is the late neo-classical church of **San Carlo al Corso** (no.13; *see p76*), its light-filled cupola an inspired, ethereal addition.

The *corso* is stopped at its far end by **piazza San Babila**, an unattractive post-war revamp. The faux-Romanesque brick façade of the church of **San Babila** (*see p76*) stands meekly in the north-east corner of the square, cowed by the surrounding abundance of steel and stone and the racing traffic.

Much more elegant is **Corso Venezia**, shooting straight out of piazza San Babila and north-east to Porta Venezia. The street is notable for a string of classy noble residences, including the late 15th-century **Casa Fontana Silvestri** (no.10) up on your right. It's one of

The wise man of Giardini Pubblici

Milan's Giardini Pubblici (*see p72*) is home to a statue of a thin, balding man, sitting on a stack of newspapers as he hammers away on an old typewriter. Below him, a simple label reads: 'Indro Montanelli, journalist'.

But Montanelli was more than a simple journalist. He was a living legend, a figure whose intellect and experience hovered over the nation's public life for decades. He began his career in the early 1930s. Initially a supporter of Mussolini, he returned to Italy after the disastrous Abyssinian campaign with a radically altered opinion. The public devoured his articles, highly critical of the Axis during the Spanish Civil War and the invasions of Norway, Poland, Estonia and Lithuania. In 1943, he joined a partisan resistance group, but was arrested and sentenced to death.

After escaping and making a dash for Switzerland, where he stayed until the end of the war, Montanelli started writing for the *Corriere della Sera*, the most prestigious

Italian daily. He defined himself as an 'anarco-conservative', and his reporting during the Soviet occupation of Hungary was instrumental in de-romanticising the USSR in post-war Italy. A champion of journalistic integrity, he left the *Corriere* when it took a swing towards radical chic in 1973. Montanelli then founded a successful new daily, *Il Giornale*, aimed at the liberal-conservative middle classes. In 1977, as he walked along via Manin past the Giardini Pubblici, members of the 'Red Brigades', a communist terrorist group, shot him in the legs. Having been sentenced to death by fascists for being anti-fascist, he was now shot at by communists for being anti-communist.

Il Giornale was bought that year by a young Silvio Berlusconi, who agreed that Montanelli could control the paper's editorial line. However, once 'il Cavaliere' entered the political arena and imposed his views, Montanelli quit, and founded *La Voce*. The new venture quickly folded, and he spent the last eight years of his life as letters editor for the *Corriere*. It's said that he gauged public opinion by talking to old-timers on the benches of the Giardini Pubblici.

Montanelli died on 22 July 2001, and was promptly celebrated as Italy's greatest journalist. The next day, the *Corriere* published a full front-page letter of farewell to his readers. The visitors who paid their respects at his wake found no coffin; only a folded copy of the *Corriere* on a chair.

the few remaining examples of a Renaissance residence in the city; the terracotta decoration on the façade is typically Lombard. Across the street, at no.11, is the **Seminario Arcivescovile**, commissioned by Carlo Borromeo in 1565 to implement the Council of Trent's regulations concerning the education of the clergy. The monumental doorway, decorated with allegorical representations of Hope and Charity, was added in 1652.

The neo-classical **Palazzo Serbelloni** (no.16), at the intersection with via San Damiano, was finished in 1793; Napoleon stayed here in 1796, Metternich in 1838, and Vittorio Emanuele II and Napoleon III in 1859. It's now home to the journalists' club, the Circolo della Stampa. Across the road is via Senato, which leads to **Palazzo del Senato** (built 1608-30). Since 1872 the palazzo has housed the Archivio di Stato, but was once used as government offices under Austro-Hungarian Emperor Joseph II and, later, Napoleon. The courtyards were designed by Fabio Mangone and the concave façade, currently being restored, by Francesco Maria Richini. The aforementioned via San Damiano in turn leads to the newly reopened **Villa Necchi Campiglio** museum, a little piece of the 1930s preserved inside and out.

Back on corso Venezia, **Palazzo Rocca Saporiti** (no.40) was built to a plan by La Scala's stage designer Giovanni Perego in 1812; its imposing Ionic columns and cornice surmounted by statues of gods make it a perfect example of neo-Palladian architectural canons. The façade is decorated with a frieze displaying scenes from the history of Milan and was equipped with a loggia on the first floor from which its residents could watch parades. At no.47 is **Palazzo Castiglioni**, with its bronze and wrought iron art nouveau decoration; the façade once featured statues of female nudes, which earned it the nickname Ca' di Ciapp, or 'house of buns'.

Corso Venezia ends in **piazza Oberdan**, where deafening, lung-testing traffic screams across **Porta Venezia**. Originally known as Porta Orientale, this was one of the eight main entrances in the 16th-century Spanish fortifications. It was the first to be redesigned by Giuseppe Piermarini (architect of La Scala) in 1782, when the city's Spanish walls were torn down to make way for tree-lined avenues. In 1828 Piermarini's original neo-classical gate, which he left unfinished, was replaced by the two triumphal arches still standing today; bas-reliefs of Milanese history decorate the two buildings. The one on the left is the **Casa del Pane** (see p74), which gives its three floors to a changing array of contemporary art. To the

north-west of the piazza is the minimalist exhibition space **Spazio Oberdan** (see p76).

Continuing north-east from Porta Venezia, corso Buenos Aires extends all the way up to **piazzale Loreto**. The historically minded visitor might be tempted to visit this square, as it's where Mussolini and his lover Clara Petacci were publicly displayed, hanged by their feet, after their execution in 1945; but gory memories aside, it's a grim square, and the largely mainstream stores of corso Buenos Aires will make you doubt Milan's fashion credentials. Alternatively, take a slight detour to the small but interesting **Casa Museo Boschi-di Stefano** (see below).

Casa Museo Boschi-di Stefano

2nd floor, Via Giorgio Jan 15 (02 2024 0568). Metro Lima/bus 60/tram 5, 9, 11, 29, 30. **Open** 2-6pm Wed-Sun. Closed Aug. **Admission** free. **Map** p249 G4.

Husband and wife Antonio Boschi and Marieda di Stefano took their modern art collection seriously: they once sold their car to buy more paintings, and even hid part of their collection behind a false wall in their country home during the war. So it's no surprise that they left their life's work to the people of Milan. The foundation opened its doors in February 2003, with ten rooms filled with 250 works of 20th-century art up through the 1970s.

Civico Museo di Storia Naturale. *See p73.*

Sightseeing

Casa del Pane

Corsa Venezia 63, piazza Oberdan (02 7428 1344/ www.casadelpane.net). Metro Porta Venezia/tram 9, 11, 29, 30. **Open** 10am-7pm Tue-Sun. **Admission** free. **Map** p249 G5.

A light-filled gallery housed in one half of Porta Venezia's former gatehouse; recent subjects have included Franco Pisani and Russian photography. The top floor has a viewing terrace that overlooks piazza Oberdan and the Giardini Pubblici.

San Babila

Corso Monforte 1 (02 7600 2877). Metro San Babila/ bus 54, 60, 61/tram 23, 27. **Open** 8am-noon, 3.30-6pm daily. **Admission** free. **Map** p249 F6/p252 F6.

Standing out like a sore thumb in the midst of the post-war architecture of piazza San Babila is the church that gives the square its name. The original fourth-century basilica was rebuilt in the 11th century and further modified in the 16th, only to have its Romanesque façade badly 'restored' in 1906 by Paolo Cesa Bianchi, who also did the main altar. It's not the most inspiring church in Milan, but remains notable if only because Alessandro Manzoni was christened here in March 1785.

San Carlo al Corso

Piazza San Carlo, off corso Vittorio Emanuele II (02 773 302). Metro Duomo or San Babila/bus 61/tram 23. **Open** 7am-12.20pm, 4-8pm Mon-Sat; 9am-1pm, 4-10pm Sun. **Admission** free. **Map** p251 F6/p252 F6.

Considered to be the final work of the neo-classical movement in Italy, this church was begun in 1839 and completed in 1847. It stands on the site of Santa Maria de' Servi, built in 1317, which was demolished in order to create corso Vittorio Emanuele II. The present structure, essentially a cylinder covered by a voluminous dome, recalls the pantheons in Rome and Paris. The sunlight shimmering through the cupola in the centre is an enchanting sight.

Spazio Oberdan

Viale Vittorio Veneto 2 (02 7740 6300). Metro Porta Venezia/tram 9, 11, 29, 30. **Open** times vary. **Admission** prices vary. **No credit cards.** **Map** p249 G5.

This exhibition space designed by Gae Aulenti and Carlo Lamperti hosts art and design shows. The schedule at its in-house movie theatre is packed with golden oldies, Italian classics and foreign films.

Villa Necchi Campiglio

Via Mozart 14 (02 7634 0121/www.fondoambiente. it). Metro Palestro/bus 54, 61, 94. **Open** 10am-6pm Wed-Sun. **Admission** €6; €4 reductions. **Map** p251 F6.

Built between 1932 and 1935 to a design by architect Pier Portaluppi, the Villa Necchi Campiglio reopened in 2008 after three years of careful renovation. The beautiful building, which belonged to the Necchi Campiglio industrial family, has been donated to non-profit organisation Fondo per l'Ambiente Italiano. Visits are enhanced by the collection of artworks, including works by Sironi, Martini and de Chirico, and its extensive collection of 18th-century decorative arts. For the moment, all visitors are required to join a small tour (no fixed times) around the house, and commentary is only in Italian.

Casa del Pane.

Corso Monforte & south

Corso Monforte connects piazza San Babila to bustling piazza del Tricolore, a block away from the **Museo dei Beni Culturali Cappuccini** (*see below*) religious art museum. Further south, the Porta Vittoria zone and the city's law courts (*see below*) are linked by **via Conservatorio**. Just past the political science department of the Università di Milano, located in the late baroque Palazzo Resta-Pallavicino at no.7, is a little piazza whose south-east corner is enclosed by the **Santa Maria della Passione** (*see below*), Milan's second largest church.

Directly opposite is **via della Passione**, opened up in 1540 to create a panoramic view of the church and allow access to the canals that once ran through the area. Continue south on via del Conservatorio past the **Conservatorio di Musica Giuseppe Verdi** (*see p162*) – a former monastery – to corso di Porta Vittoria.

Once on this thoroughfare, go west for the church of **San Pietro in Gessate** (*see below*), or east for the **piazza V Giornate**, with its 1895 monument by Giuseppe Grandi in honour of five days in March 1848, when the Milanese ended 33 years of Austrian rule.

Crossing corso di Porta Vittoria brings you to a heavy, travertine-clad building, the **Palazzo di Giustizia** (law courts). This monstrous monument to justice was built between 1932 and 1940 by Marcello Piacentini in the fascist style as a replacement for the old Palazzo dei Tribunali in piazza Beccaria. It has well over 1,000 rooms, and covers a vast area. Hopefully you won't have any reason to see the building's interior (though its enormous atrium, decorated with mosaics, would be worth a look); but a long walk around the outside will give you an idea of its colossal proportions.

Just to the west, at corso di Porta Vittoria 6, the city's library is housed in the splendid 17th-century **Palazzo Sormani**.

Museo dei Beni Culturali Cappuccini

Via Antonio Kramer 5 (02 7712 2321/www.bcc museum.org). Bus 54, 61/tram 9, 20, 23, 29, 30. **Open** 2.30-6.30pm Tue, Wed, Fri-Sun; 10.am-6.30pm Thu. **Admission** free. **Map** p251 F7/p252 F7.

A collection of religious artworks from the Cappuccini order of monks. Talks on iconography, religious art and other subjects take place weekly.

San Pietro in Gessate

Piazza San Pietro in Gessate, at corso di Porta Vittoria (02 5410 7424). Bus 60, 73, 77, 84/tram 9, 12, 20, 29, 30. **Open** 7.30am-6pm Mon-Fri; 8.30am-noon, 4-8pm Sat; 8.30am-1pm, 4.30-8pm Sun. **Admission** free. **Map** p251 F7/p252 F7.

This church was commissioned by Florentine banker Pigello Portinari and built between 1447 and 1475 to a design by Pietro Antonio and Guiniforte Solari. In 1862, frescoes were discovered under a layer of plaster. In the 16th and 17th centuries, even art was affected by the widespread plague paranoia: these frescoes were covered with lime-based plaster in order to disinfect them. The church's eight-stall choir is a reconstruction based on what was left of the one built in 1640 by Carlo Garavaglia: the original was used as firewood during World War II. The façade was put up in 1912 by Diego Brioschi, but the 17th-century entrance has been preserved.

Santa Maria della Passione

Via Bellini 2 (02 7602 1370). Metro San Babila/bus 54, 61/tram 9, 20, 29, 30. **Open** 7.30am noon, 3.30-6.30pm Mon-Fri; 9am-12.30pm, 3.30-6.30pm Sat, Sun. **Admission** free.

Construction of the church of Santa Maria della Passione began in 1486, to a design by Giovanni Battagio. It was originally a Greek-cross church, but one arm was lengthened to form a nave and six semicircular side chapels were added in 1573, making it the second-largest church in Milan after the Duomo. The barrel vault of the church abounds with frescoes of the Evangelists, St Ambrose, St Augustine, angels and allegories of the virtues by Giuseppe Galbesio da Brescia (1583); more intriguing are the paintings lower down in the church's three-aisled interior, a veritable picture gallery of works by many of the leading 16th- and 17th-century Lombard artists, including Crespi, Procaccini and Bramantino; Crespi's masterpiece *San Carlo Borromeo Fasting* is perhaps the most impressive.

Porta Romana, the Navigli & Southern Milan

Cutting-edge contemporary art and a doorway to ancient history.

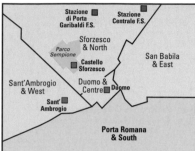

Porta Romana ('Roman door') was one of Milan's six original gateways; now it's a solitary arch standing in piazza Medaglia d'Oro, disconnected from the old city walls that extend westwards, fortifications built by the Spanish during the mid 1500s. The area surrounding it is known throughout the city for its dozens of design studios and some of the trendiest *trattorie*; it's also home to the prestigious Istituto Europeo di Design, and surrounding boutiques and bars are peppered with plenty of laptop-toting creative types year round.

To the west of Porta Romana, Milan's Navigli district is a potent reminder of the city's illustrious past, when a complex series of canals (*navigli*) allowed a network of trade routes to develop. Partially designed by Leonardo da Vinci, the *navigli* helped establish the city as an important economic hub, and also as a major port; not bad for a land-locked metropolis. These days, the waterways operate as cultural arteries, lined with one-off shops and bars – reliable bets even on a Sunday – and lead to inviting side streets packed with a wealth of artists' studios and authentic *trattorie*.

From piazza Fontana to Porta Romana

The central area stretching from via Larga to Porta Romana is largely student territory, which not surprisingly is reflected in its shops, bars and cafés. This means some varied

shopping opportunities and, in general, more modest prices than in other central areas.

Piazza Fontana initially appears to be notable only for its small fountain, an unusual sight in Milan, decked out with hanging foliage and two kneeling nymphs. Look a little closer and you'll see the former home of the Milanese court, the **Palazzo del Capitano di Giustizia**, built between 1578 and the early 17th century by Piero Antonio Barca, and, on the west side of the square, the **Palazzo Arcivescovile** (no.2). This archbishop's palace dates from 1170, when a previous structure was rebuilt after Barbarossa sacked the city; its rectory courtyard was designed in 1565 by Pellegrino Tibaldi.

However, since 12 December 1969, the piazza has been most closely associated with a terrorist blast that killed 17 people; a plaque on the Banca Nazionale dell'Agricoltura commemorates the bomb that went off inside. On the Palazzo del Capitano's lawn opposite the bank, two smaller plaques recall 'Giuseppe Pinelli, anarchist railwayman. An innocent man tragically killed at police headquarters, 16.12.1969'. Pinelli was reported by local police to have jumped from a window while being questioned about the bombing, thus confirming his guilt, but several enquiries have cast this claim into serious doubt. Most people now believe that he was already dead when he was thrown out. The event was dramatised by Dario Fo in the play *Accidental Death of an Anarchist* (1970); the Nobel prize-winning author (unsuccessfully) stood as a candidate for mayor of Milan in 2006.

Across via Larga in **piazza Santo Stefano** you'll find the church of **San Bernardino alle Ossa** (*see p81*). A sanctuary dating from the 13th century, it was built to handle the burial of corpses for the nearby (now defunct) Ospedale del Brolo, Milan's most important hospital prior to the construction of the Ospedale Maggiore (now the Ca' Granda). This way station for the dead is made even more macabre by its ossuary, a sanctum decorated with human bones that dates back to an 18th-century reconstruction; the ossuary had

Sightseeing

been all but destroyed in 1642 when the tower of nearby Santo Stefano collapsed on it.

Via Larga takes you south-west past Milan's largest theatre, the Lirico (no.14; closed for refurbishment until 2009), designed in 1778 by Giuseppe Piermarini and given an internal overhaul in 1939 by Renzo Gerla and Antonio Cassi Ramelli. Continuing down via Larga, you eventually arrive at the 26-storey **Torre Velasca**, inaugurated in 1958. The tower's top-heavy structure, which looks almost medieval, was the architects' response to the need for more office space than the ground space allowed. The tower takes its name from the square on which it stands, itself named after 17th-century Spanish governor Juan Fernandez de Velasco.

Via Chiaravalle, the second left off via Larga before piazza Velasca, loops left around to via Sant'Antonio, where you'll find the church of **Sant'Antonio Abate** halfway down the road on the right. Built in the 14th and 15th centuries, it has several interesting paintings, including a St Cajetan by Cerano. Head back to largo Richini, where you can't miss the magnificent **Ca' Granda** ('big house'; *see p80*), conceived in the 15th century to bring the city's 30-plus minor hospitals under one roof. The building now houses the arts faculties of the Università degli Studi di Milano.

Rosebushes fill the green expanse down to piazza San Nazaro. Cut through the tiny vicolo Santa Caterina in the far left corner of the piazza, which will pop you out on corso di Porta Romana. Heading left, the wide road leads south-east down to **Porta Romana**, a 1598 monumental gate designed by Aurelio Trezzi. It was a customs point for those arriving from or leaving for the south (every major Italian city has a Porta Romana leading in the direction of the capital).

To the north-east is the elegant **Rotonda di via Besana** (via Besana 12, open daylight hours). This circular, porticoed structure was built at the end of the 17th century as a graveyard for the Ca' Granda hospital (*see p80*); the little church in the centre often serves as an exhibition space for contemporary art and design shows.

The Porta Romana district, roughly delineated by the viale Filippetti, corso Lodi and viale Isonzo, and stretching as far west as via Bocconi, is one of the city's most vibrant areas – modern Milan laced with hundreds of years of history. Sixteenth-century residences line the crisscross of elegant boulevards. Fashion houses have snapped up abandoned factories along the area's southernmost streets and set up shop. Tiny galleries crammed with contemporary art compete avidly for the attention of passers by, and the **Fondazione Prada** (*see p81*) is due to open its new museum here in 2011 (*see p36* **Prada's larder of art**). Porta Romana has long been touted as the city's up-and-coming area; it looks very much like it has finally arrived.

Once a cemetery now, apparently, a kindergarten. **Rotonda di via Besana**.

Of course it's stylish. **Ca' Granda (Università degli Studi di Milano).**

Basilica dei Santi Apostoli e Nazaro Maggiore

Piazza San Nazaro 5 (02 5830 7719). Metro Crocetta or Missori/bus 94/tram 16, 24. **Open** 7.30am-noon, 3.30-6.30pm Mon-Sat; 8am-12.30pm, 3.30-7pm Sun & hols. **Admission** free. **Map** p251 E8.

Situated on what was the ancient colonnaded corso di Porta Romana, San Nazaro was one of the four basilicas built during St Ambrose's evangelising drive, between 382 and 386. Constructed to accommodate relics of the apostles Andrew, John and Thomas, the church was given the name Basilica Apostolorum. When Ambrose brought along the remains of local martyr St Nazarus (who died in 396), the church was rededicated. You can see the saintly remains in the two altars of the choir, but their silver container is a copy; the one St Ambrose commissioned is in the treasury of the Duomo.

When it was built, the basilica stood outside the city walls in a Christian burial area established by Ambrose when still a bishop, hence the sarcophagi behind the church. The church was destroyed by fire in 1075 and rebuilt using material from the original structure, including the pilasters holding up the central dome. The *basilichetta* of San Lino, to the right of the altar, dates from the tenth century. The octagonal Cappella Trivulzio, designed by Bramantino – his only known architectural work – was added to the church in 1512. Reworked in the late 16th century and given a neoclassical interior in the 1830s, the basilica suffered considerable damage during World War II. Between 1946 and 1963, it was stripped of many of its post-fourth-century trappings to restore a sense of its early Christian austerity.

Ca' Granda (Università degli Studi di Milano)

Via Festa del Perdono 5 (02 503 111/freephone 800 188 128). Metro Duomo or Missori/bus 54, 60, 65/tram 12, 23, 24, 27. **Open** 8am-6pm Mon-Fri; 8am-12.30pm Sat. Closed Aug. **Admission** free. **Map** p251 E7/p252 E7.

Now home to the arts, history and law faculties of Milan university, Ca' Granda began life as a hospital and hospice. It was Francesco Sforza who set out to consolidate Milan's 30 hospitals into one Casa Granda, or Ospedale Maggiore ('main hospital'), in 1456. The Ca' Granda was also a place to protect the poor and sick (thus ensuring the salvation of its sponsors) – and to keep beggars, lunatics and other social embarrassments out of the public eye.

Francesco's favourite architect, Antonio 'il Filarete' Averlino, incorporated the idea into his grandiose plan to transform Milan into an ideal Renaissance city. The building had one wing for men and another for women, each subdivided into four inner courts and separated by the Cortile Maggiore ('great court'). The façade, with its typically Lombard terracotta decoration, is one of the few in the city to survive from the 1400s. The courtyards, also from the 15th century, contained the women's baths.

Work continued on the project after Filarete's death (around 1469), but ground to a halt with the fall of Ludovico il Moro, picking up again from time to time during the 17th and 18th centuries. In 1942 the hospital was moved to its new headquarters at Niguarda, in the northern suburbs. The university took up residence here in 1958.

The Cortile Maggiore, with its Renaissance portico and baroque loggia, is decorated with busts sculpted from the yellow, rose and grey stone from Angera on Lake Maggiore. It was reconstructed after sustaining heavy damage during World War II. The neo-classical Macchio wing – now home to university offices – once contained an art gallery.

Fondazione Prada

Via Fogazzaro 36, at via Cadore (02 5467 0515/ www.fondazioneprada.org). Bus 62, 84/tram 9, 16, 29, 30. **Open** 11am-8pm Tue-Sun. Closed between exhibitions. **Admission** free. **Map** p251 H8.

Housed in a former bank archive, this massive venue holds international contemporary art exhibitions, including a strong selection of video installations. The majority of artworks have been bought outright by the non-profit Prada Foundation, and will form part of the new Rem Koolhaas-designed permanent museum in largo Isarco, due to open to the public in 2011 (*see p36* **Prada's larder of art**). Featured artists have included Steve McQueen, Anish Kapoor, Marc Quinn and Carsten Höller.

San Bernardino alle Ossa

Piazza Santo Stefano (02 7602 3735). Metro Duomo or Missori/bus 54, 60, 73/tram 12, 15, 23, 27. **Open** 7.30am-noon, 1-6pm Mon-Fri; 7.30am-12.30pm Sat; 9.30am-12.30pm Sun. **Admission** free. **Map** p251 E7/p252 E7.

One of Milan's most bizarre attractions, the San Bernardino alle Ossa's ossuary chapel manages to create a freakish sort of beauty from a bone-chilling template. The chapel (marked 'ossorio') to the right as you enter is decorated in delightfully disturbing fashion, with symbols and patterns picked out in human bones supplied by the nearby Ospedale del Brolo – and the occasional skull, supplied by decapitated criminals. Other, more colourful theories suggest that these are the bones of the illegitimate children of Milanese noblewomen, or martyrs from Arian massacres. The interior gloom is enlivened by the bright colours of the vault painting by Sebastiano Ricci (1659-1734), *Triumph of the Soul Among the Angels*. The chapel itself was built in 1695 on the site of a structure dating from 1210. *Photo p83.*

From via Torino to Porta Ticinese

Whereas the area north of the Duomo has a mature bourgeois feel, via Torino and corso di Porta Ticinese are where the wild kids spend time; consequently, the pavements and trendy shops are packed out during evenings and on Saturday afternoons. Narrow and traffic-heavy via Torino runs down from the south-west corner of piazza Duomo to largo Carrobbio (a name derived from the Latin *quadrivium*, a place where four roads meet), providing the intrepid pedestrian with a wealth of bargain shops and inviting side streets.

South of via Torino, down via Palla, is the often overlooked church of **Sant'Alessandro** (02 8645 3065, open 7am-noon, 4-7pm daily). Begun in 1601 and worked on by various architects including Francesco Maria Richini, it was given a rococo façade in the 18th century. Inside are many interesting works, including Daniele Crespi's *Beheading of John the Baptist*.

Returning to via Torino and heading southwest again, you'll pass piazza San Giorgio and the church of **San Giorgio al Palazzo** (*see p83*) on your right.

Further along via Torino, via Soncino runs off left to the **Palazzo Stampa**, a beautiful Renaissance building that was once home to a traitor. At the beginning of the 16th century, the building's owner, Massimiliano Stampa, was on excellent terms with the city's rulers, the Sforza family. But as the Sforzas' star began to wane, Stampa sold his allegiance to Holy Roman Emperor Charles V. In return, he obtained the title of Count of the Soncino. Stampa was suddenly elevated to Renaissance superstar status, and his palazzo was soon considered the most important salon in the city, attracting nobles from across the region. However, Stampa's time in the limelight was relatively brief, and the palazzo passed to the Casati family within the century. The new owners made various changes to the building, opening, for example, a new entrance on to via Soncino; but they kept the count's 15th-century tower, crowned with the golden globe, eagle, crown and cross escutcheon (look straight up and you can still see it today), used by Charles V to express royal ownership.

Corso di Porta Ticinese shoots south out of largo Carrobbio, passing by via Gian Giacomo Mora on the right; the name of this street commemorates a man falsely accused of spreading plague, and tortured, in 1636. His house was demolished, and a pillar was put up on the site; Manzoni wrote about it in *La Storia della colonna infame* (1842). A plaque and a small Ruggero Menegori sculpture, tucked away next to the main entrance of a brand-new apartment building, have replaced the pillar.

Further down corso di Porta Ticinese, on the left, is the church of **San Lorenzo Maggiore** (*see p83*). Facing the church are 16 massive Roman columns, recovered some time after the third century – most likely from a Roman spa or temple – and erected here in commemoration of St Lawrence, who was martyred in 258.

At the junction of corso di Porta Ticinese with via de Amicis and via Molino delle Armi is the **Antica Porta Ticinese**, which dates from the 12th century. It marks what, in ancient times, was the entry point into the city for travellers coming from Ticinum (modern-day

Pavia, south of Milan), before the city walls were demolished and rebuilt further out to encompass the growing population. Via de Amicis leads west from here to the site of the **Roman Amphitheatre** (no.17, 02 8940 0555, closed Sat pm & all Sun). First uncovered in 1936 but only brought fully to light in the 1970s, the structure has suffered not so much the ravages of time as those of church-builders: much of it was dismantled and used to build San Lorenzo. A small, free museum of coins, tools, shards and other antiquities has recently opened on the site (closed Wed, Fri & Sat pm & all Mon, Tue, Thur & Sun). North-west of here, across corso Genova, the little church of **San Vincenzo in Prato** (*see p86*) stands in what was a pre-Christian necropolis.

Behind San Lorenzo is **piazza della Vetra**, a name that probably derives from *castra vetera* (old barracks), an allusion to the fact that Roman soldiers defending the imperial palace camped here. During the Middle Ages, the piazza was often used as a point from which to defend the city; the Seveso and Nirone rivers converged here and were redirected to feed defensive waterworks around the city walls. All these military associations may have prepared piazza della Vetra for an even bloodier vocation as an execution ground. For a period of nearly 800 years, from 1045 to 1840, the square was the place where commoners condemned to death were beheaded. (The nobility met their gruesome end in the more central, slightly more attractive, piazza Broletto.)

From here you can strike south across via Molino delle Armi to the pretty **Parco delle Basiliche** and along corso di Porta Ticinese to the impressive **Museo Diocesano** (*see below*), a splendid collection of religious art and artefacts. Leave the park and head east along via Banfi, and take via Cosimo del Fante to corso Italia, where you'll see the church of **Santa Maria dei Miracoli** (*see p84*). Alternatively, look just behind the Museo Diocesano at the church of **Sant'Eustorgio** (*see p85*), set on the spot where Milan's first Christians are said to have been baptised by the apostle Barnabus. For a blast of more contemporary culture, head south of piazza XXIV Maggio to **Spazio Forma** (*see p86*), Milan's newest exhibition space, devoted entirely to photography.

Museo Diocesano

Corso di Porta Ticinese 95 (02 8942 0019/www. museodiocesano.it). **Open** *Mid Sept-June* 10am-6pm Tue-Sun. *July-mid Sept* 7pm-midnight Tue-Sat. **Admission** €8; €6 reductions; €4 Tue; €12 combined ticket with Cappella Portinari at Sant'Eustorgio & Cappella di Sant'Aquilino at San Lorenzo Maggiore. **No credit cards. Map** p250 C8.

The Museo Diocesano houses a large collection of religious art treasures taken from churches and private acquisitions throughout Lombardy. The museum, which opened in 2001, occupies three floors of the former Dominican convent of Sant'Eustorgio. A slick entrance leads into a great hall, from where visitors can follow slightly confusing colour-coded placards (occasionally in English) and study computer points scattered around (in Italian only).

On the ground floor are select works from the former Basilica di Sant'Ambrogio museum, including the olive wood frame of St Ambrose's letterpress. These are followed by works from the 14th to 16th centuries, a multimedia room and a collection of 17th- and 18th-century Italian paintings; there's a corner room dedicated to Gaetano Previatis's *Via Crucis*. Liturgical furniture (reliquaries, crucifixes, chalices and the like) is housed in the basement.

The first floor has a space for temporary exhibitions, as well as the collections of several cardinals: that of Federico Visconti (1617-93) is held in one small room, and includes copies of famous drawings, including portraits of Raphael and Titian by an anonymous Lombard painter of the 17th century; the collection of Giuseppe Pozzobonelli (1696-1783) has 17th-century Italian landscapes; that of Cesare Monti (1593-1650) has Lombard and Venetian works of the 16th and 17th centuries (including Tintoretto's *Christ and the Adulteress*, 1545-47). There's also a beautiful selection of 14th- and 15th-century altarpiece paintings with *fondi d'oro* (gold backgrounds), accompanied by a video in Italian explaining the gold-leafing process.

San Bernardino alle Ossa. *See p81.*

As of 2008, the museum is open during the evening only in July and August, and is organising events, including an *aperitivo* hour, for people staying in the city during the summer holidays.

San Giorgio al Palazzo

Piazza San Giorgio 2 (02 860 831). Metro Duomo/ tram 2, 3, 14. **Open** 7.30am-noon, 3.30-6.30pm Mon-Sat; 9.30am-12.30pm, 4-7pm Sun. **Admission** free. **Map** p250 D7/p252 D7.

Founded in 750, San Giorgio was rebuilt in 1129 and heavily reworked in the 17th and early 19th centuries. Among the neo-classical trappings are a baptismal font fashioned out of a Romanesque capital and a couple of pilasters from the original church at the far end of the nave. Don't miss the vivid *Scenes from the Passion of Christ* cycle by Bernardino Luini (1516) in the third chapel on the right. Commissioned to decorate the whole church with frescoes, he fled Milan after killing a clergyman critical of his work.

San Lorenzo Maggiore

Corso di Porta Ticinese 39 (02 8940 4129). Bus 94/ tram 2, 3, 14. **Open** *Church* 7.30am-12.30pm, 2.30-6.45pm Mon-Sat; 9.30am-12.30pm, 2.30-6.45pm Sun. *Cappella di Sant'Aquilino* 9.30am-12.30pm, 2.30-6.30pm daily. **Admission** *Church* free. *Cappella* €2; €1 reductions; €12 combined ticket with Museo Diocesano & Cappella Portinari at Sant'Eustorgio. **No credit cards**. **Map** p250 D8.

Built at the end of the fourth century, San Lorenzo is one of the oldest centrally planned churches, and may have been the chapel of the imperial Roman palace. Fires all but destroyed it in the 11th and 12th centuries, but it was rebuilt on the exact lines of the original model. When the cupola collapsed in 1573, the new dome – the tallest in Milan and a far cry from the original – outraged the locals.

On the backs of the two great arches that flank the main altar, columns were placed upside down to symbolise the Christian religion rising up out of the ruins of paganism. To the right, the octagonal fourth-century Cappella di Sant'Aquilino may have been an imperial mausoleum. Legend has it that a group of porters discovered St Aquiline's corpse in a ditch; taking it to the Duomo, they got lost in the fog and ended up in San Lorenzo. Thus his remains are still here, in a glass coffin on top of the altar; he also became the patron saint of porters. On the walls of the *cappella* are fragments of the late fourth-century mosaics that once covered the entire chapel. Behind the altar, descend the stairs to the passage under the church, where stones from pre-existing Roman structures used in the construction of San Lorenzo can be seen.

Outside the church stand 16 Corinthian columns from the second and third centuries. They were moved here from an unidentified pagan temple some time in the fourth century, and topped with pieces of architrave, only some of which date from the same period. The 17th-century wings flanking the entrance to San Lorenzo were designed to link the columns to the church in a sort of pseudo-ancient atrium. In the centre, a bronze statue of Emperor Constantine is a copy of one in Rome – a reminder of his Edict of Milan (313), which put an end to the state persecution of Christians.

Walk on Channel hopping

With a project that took 200 years to start and another 500 to complete, it's no surprise that Milan's Navigli (canal) district has some of the city's widest architectural variety.

Start your wander with the Roman wonder that is the **Colonne di San Lorenzo**, or San Lorenzo's columns, which date from Roman times. Their original purpose is unknown, although they provide a breathtaking frame for the nearby San Lorenzo church, the oldest in the city. Head south along corso di Porta Ticinese, passing under the **Antica Porta Ticinese**, one of the two remaining medieval gates to the city (the other is Porta Nuova, *see p71*). It was originally a double archway, but in the early 14th century, Azzone Visconti (murderous overlord of Milan, but also one of its great town planners) insisted that the

passageway be narrowed to a single arc for increased security.

Cross over the **Naviglio Interno**, a major waterway until 1932, now covered by via E de Amicis and via Molino delle Armi. (Most of Milan's original canals were concreted over in the late 1920s to make way for trams and traffic). Continuing south along corso di Porta Ticinese, you'll pass the building used as the headquarters for the Catholic Inquisition in the 16th century at **no.98**. On your right at piazza XXIV Maggio is the pool known as the **Darsena**. It's all that remains of the zone's extensive river docks, and was formerly one of the country's biggest ports. In an echo of Leonardo da Vinci, who mapped out a lock-based canal system stretching from Milan to Lagi di Como, plans are afoot to dig a waterway from Darsena to the Expo 2015 site in Rho (*see p24*), in line with the sustainable living ethos of the World Fair.

Back on piazza XXIV Maggio, swing right along viale Gorizia, then left down Strada Alzaia Naviglio Grande until you reach the utterly picturesque **vicolo dei Lavandai**. This was formerly the spot where the neighbourhood's laundrywomen brought their buckets of clothes for some serious scrubbing. These days the shady waterside seats are often occupied by local musicians or couples enjoying a picnic.

Join them, or, if you'd like to explore the *navigli* further, double back until you reach Navigli Lombardi's pier at no.4 (*see p86*). Hop on for a one-hour tour along the canals or, in warm weather, opt for a longer trip out of the city.

Santa Maria dei Miracoli presso San Celso

Corso Italia 37 (02 5831 3187). Metro Missori/ bus 94/tram 15. **Open** 7am-noon, 4-6pm Mon-Sat; 8.30am-12.30pm, 4-7pm Sun. **Admission** free. **Map** p250 D8.

Two little chapels once stood on this site where, according to legend, St Ambrose was led by a vision to the bodies of martyrs Nazaro and Celso. The chapel of San Nazaro fell down long ago, but so great was the flow of pilgrims to the remaining chapel of San Celso – where, in the 15th century, the Blessed Virgin Mary was said to be hard at work perform-ing miracles galore – that in 1493 construction began on something bigger: Santa Maria dei Miracoli (St Mary of Miracles). Preceded by a beautiful early 16th-century *quadriportico*, the lively façade is from

the same era, animated by sculptures by Stoldo Lorenzi and Annibale Fontana. The interior of the church was decorated by the usual cast of Lombard Renaissance, mannerist and baroque artists, with Ambrogio Bergognone's particularly impressive *Madonna tra i santi* in the first chapel on the left. It's referred to locally as the *chiesa degli sposi* (new-lyweds' church), and it's a traditional custome for newly married couples to drop in with a bouquet of flowers, a token offering to the Virgin in hope for a long and happy life together.

Through a gate and across the garden, San Celso was founded in the ninth century and rebuilt in the 11th, and is decorated with frescoes that date from the 11th to 15th centuries. It's now a venue for art exhibitions, theatrical performances and concerts, although it's often closed to the public at other times.

Take a walk on the wet side along Milan's **navigli**. See p86.

Sant'Eustorgio

*Piazza Sant'Eustorgio 1-3 (02 5810 1583/Cappella
Portinari 02 8940 2671). Bus 59/tram 3, 9, 15, 29,
30.* **Open** *Church* 7.30am-noon, 3.30-6.30pm daily.
Cappella Portinari 10am-6pm Tue-Sun. **Admission**
Church free. *Cappella Portinari* €6; €3 reductions;
€12 combined ticket with Museo Diocesano &
Cappella di Sant'Aquilino at San Lorenzo.
No credit cards. **Map** p250 D8.

Sant'Eustorgio, when he was still but a bishop, had
this church built in the fourth century to house the
relics of the Three Kings. The specific site was chosen when animals pulling the relic-laden cart
reached this spot and refused to budge. In 1164,
Frederick Barbarossa absconded with the relics, but
they were returned (in part) in 1903 and are venerated at Epiphany (6 January). The ceremony takes
place at the end of a mass timed to coincide with the
arrival of a procession from piazza del Duomo led
by the 'Three Kings' (played by a trio of *Milanesi*).

The church is filled with works by Milanese and
Lombard artists from the 13th to the 15th centuries:
Giovannino di Grassi, Giovanni da Milano, Giovanni
di Balduccio (see his 1327 Gothic funeral monument
to Stefano Visconti on the left wall of the fifth chapel
on the right), Bernardino Luini and the *maestri cam-
pionesi* all feature. The fourth chapel on the right
contains the 14th-century painted wooden crucifix
that was supposed to cure pregnant women of fever.

The main attraction, however, is the Cappella
Portinari next door, built between 1462 and 1466 by
Florentine banker Pigello Portinari for his own
tomb, and as a repository for the body of St Peter
Martyr, murdered when heretics stuck a knife into
his skull 200 years earlier. Perhaps the earliest truly

Sightseeing

Renaissance work in the city, the chapel unites the classical forms championed by Brunelleschi in Tuscany with typical Lombard fresco decoration by Vincenzo Foppa. Foppa's scenes of the life of the Virgin and of St Peter Martyr's miracles (1466-68) are perhaps the painter's greatest masterpieces. In the centre of the chapel, the intricate, carved Ark of St Peter Martyr, containing most of the saint's remains, is by Giovanni da Balduccio (1336-39); the rest of him (his skull) is in a silver urn in the little chapel to the left of the Cappella Portinari.

The chapel's entry price also allows you access to a room stocked with hundreds of saints' relics, housed in glass cabinets, and an oppressive but interesting Paleochristian cemetery, located under the Sant'Eustorgio Basilica.

San Vincenzo in Prato

Via Daniele Crespi 6 (02 837 3107). Metro Sant'Agostino/bus 94/tram 2, 14. **Open** 7.45-noon, 3.30-7pm daily. **Admission** free. **Map** p250 B8.

Once an expanse of *prati* (fields), the area around this small church was used as a pagan, and subsequently Christian, necropolis. Benedictine monks occupied the adjacent monastery in the ninth century and remained there until 1520; it's uncertain whether the present church dates from the ninth or 11th century. French occupiers turned it into a storehouse and then barracks in 1798. Later it became a chemical factory, belching fumes that earned it the nickname Casa del Mago ('magician's house'). It was restored and reconsecrated in the 1880s.

Spazio Forma

Piazza Tito Lucrezio Caro 1 (02 5811 8067/www. formafoto.it). Bus 59, 79, 90, 91/tram 3, 9, 15, 29, 30. **Open** 11am-9pm Tue, Wed, Sat, Sun; 11am-11pm Thur, Fri. **Admission** €7.50; €6 reductions. **Map** p250 D9.

Founded in 2005, Spazio Forma is the city's only space dedicated to photography. Exhibitions highlight the medium's history and practitioners; there are also occasional shows devoted to fashion and design photography. Housed in a former tram shed, the centre runs courses and workshops (in Italian), and has an excellent bookshop. Subjects of past exhibitions have included Richard Avedon, Elliot Erwitt, Josef Koudelka and Peter Lindbergh.

The Navigli

North-west of piazza Sant'Eustorgio is the Darsena, the confluence of the two canals that connect Milan with the Ticino and Po rivers (the Olona river still flows in underground). Built in 1603, the Darsena was Milan's main port, a hotbed of commercial activity for goods flowing in and out of the city. Today the waters have stilled, but on weekend and summer evenings, the Milanese come for a more sedate trade of riverside shopping, dining and drinking, normally in that order.

The *navigli* (canals), which extend south and west from the Darsena between Porta Ticinese and Porta Genova, are all that remain of a once-vital network that crisscrossed much of the city. Partly the fruit of Leonardo da Vinci's engineering gifts, they are intimately connected to the highest cultural point of Milan's history. By providing an essential link to the rest of Italy, the waterways enabled Milan to become a thriving port by the late 19th century.

Excavations for the Naviglio Grande, Italy's (contested) claim for Europe's first canal – which carries the waters of the diverted Ticino river from Lake Maggiore to the Darsena – were begun in 1177. Canals for Bereguardo, the Martesana and Paderno followed, boosting Milan's already considerable commercial clout. Barges arrived with coal and lumber; they departed with iron, grain, fabric and other goods manufactured in the city.

In 1359 a scheme was launched to build the Naviglio Pavese. The waterway was conceived merely to irrigate Gian Galeazzo Visconti's hunting reserve near Pavia, but in the 15th century Ludovico il Moro called in Leonardo da Vinci to improve the system and create a canal network that extended into the heart of the city. Funding issues hampered a 1597 plan to extend the *navigli* still further, which stalled at the Conca Fallato ('failed lock') in the southern suburbs until the French applied themselves to the task in the 19th century. Not long after its inauguration in 1819, its traffic rates were outstripping those on the Naviglio Grande. Although much of the historic network had been filled in by the 1930s, after World War II, materials for reconstructing the badly bombed city were transported by water. The last working boat moored up on 30 March 1979.

These days, boutiques, antiques restorers, bookshops and plenty of nightspots line the canal banks and side streets. Best of all, bars compete for short-term summer leases along the *navigli* banks, making the area one of the best places at which to while an evening away.

Navigli Lombardi

Alzaia Naviglio Grande 4 (02 667 9131/www.navigli lombardi.it). **Tours** Apr-Sept, mid Oct-Nov 10.15am, 11.20am, 12.20pm, 3pm, 4.05pm, 5.10pm, 6.15 pm Fri-Sun. **Rates** €12; €8 reductions.

If you fancy spending an hour cruising the canals, Navigli Lombardi organises a tour that takes in the ancient washhouses of vicolo dei Lavandai and San Cristoforo, the Scodellino bridge and the old Darsena port. As of summer 2008, Navigli Lombardi also runs full days out in June and July (9.30am-7pm Sat, Sun), with return transport to Gaggiano, lunch and afternoon bike hire (€45). Tickets can be bought at Studio Mitti, an artist's shop opposite the boat's dock, by telephone or on board.

Sant'Ambrogio & Western Milan

From kick off at *The Last Supper* to extra time at San Siro.

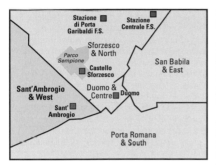

Sant'Ambrogio is home to one of the city's biggest tourist attractions, namely Leonardo's painting of *The Last Supper* (*see p88* **Supper group**), but the streets surrounding it also have much to offer. Lose yourself in the maze of alleys south of the district's main thoroughfare, corso Magenta, and you'll find each turn presents a frescoed church by Bramante or another of da Vinci's designs. Dig deeper and you'll hit Mediolanum, old Roman Milan, as revealed at the Civico Museo Archeologico. Students at the nearby Università Cattolica bring a youthful vibe, and there are chic bars and cheap restaurants to go with all the ancient history. Head west to corso Vercelli, lined with shop after shop; it's easy to find a bargain. And further north is a powerful football fix, the famous San Siro stadium.

Sant'Ambrogio & around

The Duomo may be more famous and more beautiful to look at, but there's a church in Milan that is more important to locals. **Sant'Ambrogio** (*see p89*), named after the city's patron saint, dates from Roman times, and has the stronger claim to be the city's 'true' church. Sant'Ambrogio was built outside the Roman city walls in an area of early Christian cemeteries and imperial buildings. Nine Italian kings were crowned at its altar between the ninth and 15th centuries (four of them are buried here), and Napoleon and Ferdinand of Austria honoured this tradition by paying a

visit immediately after their coronations (1805 and 1838) in the Duomo.

Once a year the streets surrounding the church host the Oh Bej! Oh Bej! festival (*see p144*); the rest of the time you'll find the square out front filled with students from the nearby **Università Cattolica del Sacro Cuore** (*see p91*), a former monastic complex that now houses Milan's private Catholic university.

South-west across the square, the **Pusterla di Sant'Ambrogio** is a 1939 imitation of the medieval gate that once stood here, part of the 1171 defences built after Barbarossa's attacks. Some older materials, including a 14th-century relief showing saints Ambrose, Gervasius and Protasius, have been incorporated. Just to the west of the basilica's main entrance is the Roman *colonna del diavolo*, a column marked by two holes, allegedly made by the Devil's horns: the evil one is said to have suffered a fit of pique at Ambrose's purity and incorruptibility.

To the south, on the corner of corso di Porta Ticinese and via De Amicis, is the crypt of Santa Maria della Vittoria, which houses artefacts from recent archaeological digs around Lombardy. North-west, beyond the Pusterla, the **Museo Nazionale della Scienza e della Tecnologia Leonardo da Vinci** (*see p88*) is a magic box of technological wonders from across the ages.

Next door, the church of **San Vittore al Corpo** (*see p91*) backs onto via degli Olivetani, where San Vittore jail – the temporary home of many of the businessmen and politicians caught up in the *Tangentopoli* scandal (*see p22*) and subsequent *Mani Pulite* investigations of the 1990s – has loomed threateningly since its construction in the 1860s and '70s. The area around the prison is fairly colourless, so skip it and take a leisurely walk south-west from Sant'Agostino metro station down via Modestino, which merges into via Andrea Solari. Passing the church of Santa Maria del Rosario on the right, you come to the **Fondazione Arnaldo Pomodoro** (on the left; *see p88*), a sculpture gallery that opened in 2005 in the former industrial area of Ansaldo, now filling up with smart housing.

Supper group

A wealth of art is dotted around Milan's three *pinacoteche* and many churches, but Leonardo da Vinci's *Il Cenacolo* (1495-97; *see p93*), known in English as *The Last Supper*, remains the biggest art draw of them all.

The work is arguably the greatest painting of the Renaissance. It depicts the dramatic moment immediately after Jesus has revealed that one of his disciples will betray him. Da Vinci portrays the expressions of shock, amazement and hostility with acute psychological acuity.

It won't take you long to realise that the painting is in a seriously deteriorated condition. Da Vinci experimented with a new technique for *The Last Supper*, painting on to dry plaster, rather than mixing his paints with the substance while it was still wet. This enabled him to retain control over tone and nuance, but prevented the paints from impregnating the plaster base.

The work has a history of dereliction. Paint began to peel off even within da Vinci's lifetime. In the early 19th century, invading French soldiers used the monastery refectory as a stable, and the Renaissance masterpiece was used for target practice during their drunken binges.

World War II air raids came close to destroying parts of the church, including one complete wall of the refectory, and portions of two others; *The Last Supper* – a miracle, some might say – remained unscathed. And yet, despite surviving all this, the work still suffers from a wound inflicted early in its life: the door that was cut into the bottom centre, cutting off Christ's feet.

Though the mural has been more or less *in restauro* since it was first painted, the biggest, most definitive restoration got under way in 1977. This removed layers of paint and detritus accumulated over the centuries, and allowed some of the original luminous colours to re-emerge; the fresco was unveiled again in 1999.

It has been necessary to reserve a (timed, 15-minute) visit to see the painting for some years now. Try to book one of the twice-daily guided tours for €3.25; alternatively, hire an audio guide for €2.50. Not surprisingly, visitor numbers shot up after the publication of Dan Brown's bestselling novel *The Da Vinci Code*, followed by the movie of the same name. The book claims that da Vinci hid secret messages in his paintings; and, specifically, that there is no Holy Grail in the painting, that the disciple immediately to Jesus' right ('with flowing red hair, delicate folded hands, and the hint of a bosom') is actually Mary Magdalene, and that 'an enormous, flawlessly formed letter M' is traced by Jesus and the group to his right (signifying Mary, of course). The book has fired the imagination of millions, but it is, for all that, purely a work of fiction. The figure on Christ's immediate right is – as *Cenacolo* staff point out – clearly identified in da Vinci's sketchbooks as John the Apostle, which rather weakens the novel's suggestion that it might be Mary Magdalene; and art historians know that it was common practice to paint John with a feminine aspect in da Vinci's time.

On the opposite wall is Donato da Montorfano's *Crucifixion*, painted in 1495. Da Vinci added the portraits of Ludovico il Moro, his wife Beatrice and their children, but these too have faded beyond recognition.

Fondazione Arnaldo Pomodoro

Via Andrea Solari 35 (02 8907 5394/www. fondazionearnaldopomodoro.it). Metro Porta Genova or Sant'Agostino/bus 58, 61, 90, 91/tram 14. **Open** 11am-6pm Wed, Fri-Sun (last entry 5pm); 11am-10pm (last entry 9pm) Thur. Closed mid July-Sept. **Admission** €7; €4 reductions. **No credit cards. Map** p250 A8.

Housed in a vast metallic warehouse, the Fondazione Pomodoro provides a welcome contrast to Milan's dim and often cavernous church-based sightseeing. As he approached his 80th birthday, the celebrated artist Arnaldo Pomodoro set up this centre, devoted entirely to sculpture, in the former Riva & Calzoni factory (maker of hydraulic turbines, including those used at Niagara Falls). Crisscrossed by suspended walkways that lead to the various levels, the museum contains a permanent collection (including many artworks by Pomodoro), a temporary exhibition space and an area devoted to their yearly young sculptors' competition.

Museo Nazionale della Scienza e della Tecnologia Leonardo da Vinci

Via San Vittore 21 (02 485 551/www.museo scienza.org). Metro Sant'Ambrogio/bus 50, 58, 94. **Open** 9.30am-5pm Tue-Fri; 9.30am-6.30pm Sat, Sun. **Admission** €8; €3-€6 reductions. **No credit cards. Map** p250 B7.

The big tomato. **Fondazione Arnaldo Pomodoro**.

This impressive science and technology museum is a fitting tribute to Milan's revered former resident. One of the most fascinating halls here displays modern models based on da Vinci's sketches, in the fields of military theory, ballistics and aeronautics – but this is just one section of a 10,000-item collection.

Originally a 16th-century monastery, the buildings have had various incarnations – military hospital (Napoleon), barracks (Italian army) and rubble (World War II Allied bombs). Established just after the war, the current museum was finally inaugurated in 1953, and is now the largest of its kind in Italy. Wandering through, it's hard to think of any aspect of industry or technology that isn't covered. There are displays dealing with metallurgy, printing, bell-casting, minting, engines and horology, as well as the sciences of physics, optics, acoustics and astronomy. An exhaustive computing section shows the evolution of calculating techniques from Pascal's abacus of 1642 to the first IBM processor. Exhibits are laid out so you can see the evolution of a cartwheel into a Vespa, or a Morse code transmitter to state-of-the-art mobile phones. The museum's interactive labs, where children can learn, hands on, about the background and application of cutting-edge advancements in science and technology, was expanded for a second time during a temporary closure in 2008, and new galleries were also added.

The museum's biggest draw is the *Enrico Toti*, the first submarine constructed in Italy after World War II. It was launched on 12 March 1967 as an SSK (hunter-killer submarine), primarily as a deterrent against the nuclear-propelled torpedo-launchers of the Soviet Army. It was discharged from service in 1999, and the following year the Italian Navy donated the vessel to the museum. After transport and extensive preparation, it opened to the public in December 2005. Viewing regulations are strict: groups consist of a maximum of six helmeted visitors, led by a museum guide. Tickets (€8, no reductions) can be reserved in advance or on the day, and paid for at the museum's reception.

Sant'Ambrogio

Piazza Sant'Ambrogio 15 (02 8645 0895/www.sant ambrogio-basilica.it). Metro Sant'Ambrogio/bus 50, 54, 58, 94. **Open** *Church* 7.30am-12.30pm, 2.30-7pm Mon-Sat; 7.30am-1pm, 3-8pm Sun. *San Vittore chapel* 7.30am-noon, 3.30-7pm daily. **Admission** free. **Map** p250 C7.

The charismatic Bishop Ambrose (Ambrogio) – who defended orthodox Christianity against Arianism and later became Milan's patron saint – had this Basilica Martyrum built between 379 and 386. The remains of local martyr-saints Gervasius and Protasius still lie in the crypt.

The church was enlarged in the eighth century, when the Benedictines erected the Campanile dei Monaci (monks' bell tower) to the right of the façade. In the ninth century, under Archbishop Anspert, the atrium preceding the church was added; it was here that the populace sought sanctuary in times of trouble. The church's Romanesque appearance stems from ninth- and tenth-century redesigns. Anspert's atrium was remodelled in the 11th century, when a reconstruction of the church got under way. Its capitals feature biblical scenes and mythical beasts symbolising the struggle between Good and Evil.

Sightseeing

Sant'Ambrogio. *See p89.*

The Torre dei Canonici ('canons' tower') to the left of the façade was built between 1128 and 1144. Further changes to the interior of the church were made in 1196 after the dome collapsed.

In 1492 Ludovico 'il Moro' Sforza called on Donato Bramante to remodel the eighth-century Benedictine monastery. The fall of il Moro in 1499 put an end to Bramante's makeover, which as a result was limited to one side of the old cloister (the Portico della Canonica, accessible from the left of the nave). The church had a lucky escape from a remodelling job in the 17th century, but suffered severe air raid damage in 1943; the bombing destroyed Bramante's work, which was subsequently rebuilt using salvaged original materials.

The interior has the sober proportions of the austere Lombard Romanesque style, its three aisles covered with ribbed cross-vaults and false galleries holding up the massive walls. Beneath the pre-Romanesque pulpit, reconstructed from the original pieces after the dome collapsed on it in 1196, lies what is known as the Stilicone Sarcophagus. This fourth-century masterpiece was traditionally believed to have been the burial place of the Roman general Stilicone, who served the Emperor Honorius and died in 408; later research disproved this legend. The 12th-century golden altar, illustrated with scenes from the life of Christ on the front and of St Ambrose on the back, once covered the porphyry casket commissioned to house the remains of Ambrose, Protasius and Gervasius when they were dug up in the ninth century.

To the right of the main altar, a series of chapels leads to the Sacello di San Vittore in Ciel d'Oro. Part of the church's original fourth-century structure, this chapel was clinically reworked in the 1930s, so that only its glowing, golden fifth-century mosaics in the dome remain to remind us of its antique glory. They portray St Ambrose standing between Gervasius and Protasius, with a sprinkling of other minor local martyrs looking on. This section of the church has been converted into a small museum (access is through the 18th-century Cappella di Sant'Ambrogio Morente) consisting of the mosaics and precious church furnishings.

The museum that was once housed in the cloisters has been split up and the exhibits moved to the Museo Diocesano (see p82) and the San Vittore in Ciel d'Oro chapel here. There's also an exhibition space, albeit normally for modern art, in the Antico Oratorio della Passione (piazza Sant'Ambrogio 23A, opening times vary, admission free).

San Vittore al Corpo

Via San Vittore 25 (02 4800 5351). Metro Sant'Ambrogio/bus 50, 54, 58, 94. **Open** 7.30am-noon, 3.30-7pm daily. Closed July, Aug except mass. **Admission** free. **Map** p250 B7.

The church and former monastery of San Vittore al Corpo grew up around the mausoleum of Emperor Valentinian II, who died in 392; parts of this ancient structure are now beneath the Museo Nazionale della Scienza e della Tecnologia Leonardo da Vinci (*see p88*). The complex was taken over in 1010 by Benedictine monks, who got down to some serious rebuilding. It was given another overhaul in 1560, when it became one of Milan's most sumptuously decorated churches. Works by many local names of the late 16th and 17th centuries – Girolamo Quadrio, Camillo Procaccini, Giovanni Ambrogio Figino, Daniele Crespi – are still here. There are also choir stalls with wood-inlay intarsia work from the 1580s.

Università Cattolica del Sacro Cuore

Largo Gemelli 1 (02 72 341/www.unicatt.it). *Metro Sant'Ambrogio/bus 50, 54, 58, 94.* **Open** 8am-6.30pm Mon-Fri; 8am-2.30pm Sat. Closed Aug. **Admission** free. **Map** p250 C7.

In 1497, Ludovico il Moro called upon Donato Bramante to expand what had been – before it was turned over to the Cistercian order in the late 15th century – the most powerful and influential Benedictine monastery in northern Italy. Although Bramante was hired to add four grandiose cloisters, only two were completed (an Ionic one in 1513 and a Doric one in 1630). As a result of an agreement between the Catholic Church and the Fascist government, the ex-monastery became home in 1921 to the Catholic university. Throughout the 1930s and '40s, architect Giovanni Muzio overhauled the complex in his characteristic dry, straightforward style. The student life has proved more colourful than the architecture: the 1968 protests kicked off here. *Photo p93.*

Santa Maria delle Grazie & around

Stylish corso Magenta, running from south of the Castello to more suburban corso Vercelli, links a number of the city's most important sights. With its dazzling floor-to-ceiling frescoes by Bernardino Luini, the 16th-century church of **San Maurizio** (corso Magenta 15, 02 8645 0011, closed Mon, Sun) is chief among them, fresh from a long bout of renovation. Be sure to duck through the small doorway to the left of the altar and visit the massive frescoed Convent Hall, accessible although still under partial restoration. Next door is the **Civico Museo Archeologico** (*see p92*), a less colourful though no less interesting sight. The two both formed part of the Monastero Maggiore, a Benedictine convent that housed the city's most influential order of nuns. Their shared architectural remains (seen from the back) date from the time when Milan was one of the Roman army's key strongholds.

Across the road at no.24, the Palazzo Arese Litta, now home to the **Teatro Litta** (*see p175*) as well as the HQ of the Italian state railways, has a rococo façade with two colossal telamones flanking the entrance. It was designed between

Sightseeing

1642 and 1648 by Francesco Maria Ricchini, and the rococo façade by Bartolomeo Bolli was added in the mid 18th century. A monumental staircase by Francesco Merlo (1740) leads to the Sala Rossa with its red brocaded walls (sadly closed to the public); a pearl set in the floor recalls the tear shed by the awestruck Duchess Litta when she met Napoleon.

This stretch of corso Magenta is home to two additional palazzi of note. Back at no.12 you'll find the **Casa Rossi**, a notable building designed by Giuseppe Pestagalli around 1860 to simulate the superimposed loggias of Renaissance palazzi. The building has a pretty little octagonal courtyard that's worth a look, as well as the organic herbalist Officinali di Montauto (*see p136*). At no.29 is the palazzo given to Lorenzo de' Medici in 1486 by the Sforzas – though today there's nothing more remarkable about the edifice than that fact.

Continuing westwards along corso Magenta, you'll come to **Santa Maria delle Grazie** (*see p93*) and the refectory housing Milan's most precious work of art, *The Last Supper* (*see p88* **Supper group**). While you're here, pay a visit to the church itself, a welcome break from the timetabled tourism around Leonardo's masterpiece. Nearby, on via Carducci, stop for a drink in Bar Magenta (*see p121*), a mainstay of the Milan bar scene.

Across the street from Santa Maria delle Grazie, the **Palazzo delle Stelline**, at no.61, houses a charitable foundation named after the palazzo, as well as a fine hotel (*see p48*). The present **Fondazione Stelline** (*see below*) works to promote the cultural, social and economic development of the city.

Civico Museo Archeologico

Corso Magenta 15 (02 8645 0011). Metro Cadorna/ bus 50, 58, 94, 199/tram 16, 18, 19. **Open** 9am-1pm, 2-5.30pm (last entry 5pm) Tue-Sun. **Admission** €2; €1 reductions; free after 2pm Fri. **No credit cards. Map** p250 C6/p252 C6.
The buildings of the archeological museum are as interesting as the collections within. The initial courtyard was once the entrance to the Monastero Maggiore; and a detailed model, just past the museum's reception, shows Milan's Roman incarnation as Mediolanum.

Indeed, almost the entire ground floor is dedicated to artefacts from the important settlement Mediolanum, including the unique Coppa Trivulzio Diatreta from the late fourth century, a cup created from a single piece of glass, and the wonderful stone Zeus head from the first or second century. The impressive prehistoric section covers the Milan area from the Neolithic period to Roman times.

Downstairs you'll find a stretch of Roman city walls (built under Emperor Maximian in the third century) and an area (newly refurbished in 2008)

containing a small selection of Greek artefacts. There's also a surprisingly extensive collection of Buddhist art from the ancient kingdom of Gandhara (now northern Pakistan and eastern Afghanistan), bought by the museum in the 1980s.

The gardens at the rear hold a polygonal tower, originally part of the city's defence system; later, it was transformed into a chapel for the monastery. The round interior is decorated with 13th-century frescoes, including a vivid image of Jesus beaming his stigmata through the air to St Francis of Assisi.

Fondazione Stelline

Palazzo delle Stelline, Corso Magenta 61 (02 4546 2411/www.stelline.it). Metro Cadorna or Conciliazione/tram 16, 18. **Open** 10am-6pm Tue-Sun. **Admission** varies according to exhibition. **Map** p248 B6.
Built on the site of the original Santa Maria della Stella convent after the latter burned to the ground, Palazzo delle Stelline was designated by the far-famed Carlo Borromeo as an orphanage in 1578 – and continued to function as such until the 1970s. In 1986, the local municipality established the Fondazione Stelline, whose mission is to preserve the 500-year old building and promote cultural events in the Magenta neighbourhood.

Across a pretty internal courtyard is a small temporary exhibition space, the Sala del Collezionista, far from the traffic of corso Magenta. Featured shows range from 18th-century works by Lombard painter Cesare Ligari to sculptures by contemporary light artist, Massimo Uberti.

Università Cattolica del Sacro Cuore. *See p91.*

Santa Maria delle Grazie & The Last Supper

Piazza Santa Maria delle Grazie. Metro Cadorna or Conciliazione/tram 16, 18. **Map** p250 B6. **Church** *(02 4676 1123/www.grazieop.it).* **Open** 7am-noon, 3-7pm Mon-Sat; 7.30am-12.15pm, 3.30-9pm Sun. **Admission** free. **The Last Supper (Il Cenacolo)** *(02 8942 1146/ www.cenacolovinciano.it).* **Open** (reservations obligatory) 8.15am-7.30pm Tue-Sun; guided tours in English 9.30am, 3.30pm Tue-Sun. **Admission** €8; €3.25 reductions; free under-18s, over-65s; €3.25 guided tour. **Credit** AmEx, DC, MC, V.

The church of Santa Maria delle Grazie was begun in 1465 to a plan by Guiniforte Solari. Just two years after it was finished in the 1480s, Ludovico 'il Moro' Sforza commissioned architect Donato Bramante to turn the church into a family mausoleum in the new Renaissance style; this work was never completed. (Some experts doubt Bramante was involved in the project at all, or accord him only a minor, preliminary planning role.) So down came Solari's apse and up went a Renaissance tribune in its place. At the same time, the adjoining Dominican monastery was given the *chiostrino* (small cloister) and a new sacristy. The monks ran an active branch of the Inquisition in their monastery from 1553 to 1778, and continued to endow their church with decorative elements. During Napoleon's suppression of religious congregations during the late 18th century, the complex was turned into barracks and a military warehouse. Control of the church was returned to the Dominican monks in 1905. In 1943, bombing destroyed the great cloister of the monastery but fortuitously spared the three walls of the refectory, including the one with Leonardo's *Last Supper* (*see p88* **Supper group**), and the *chiostrino*.

The terracotta façade of the church is in the best Lombard tradition; the portal is attributed to Bramante. Inside, Solari's Gothic leanings in the three-aisled nave clash with the fresco-covered arches and Bramante's more muscular, massive style. Standing out among works by leading local artists from the 15th to 17th centuries is an altarpiece (in the sixth chapel on the left) showing the Holy Family with St Catherine by 16th-century Venetian painter and student of Titian, Paris Bordone, The carved wooden choir stalls in the apse date from 1470.

The gardens provide a welcome, relaxing atmosphere after the bustle and crowd in the piazza outside the church. During mass the cloisters can be reached through a door in via Caradosso 1 (same opening times as the church).

San Siro & the Fiere

FieraMilanoCity and newish FieraMilano headquarters out in Rho (*see p94*) receive millions of trade-fair-going visitors every year. During some of the most popular events, hotel rooms are booked months in advance, and getting a taxi becomes almost impossible.

The city-based Fiera was formerly one of the largest trade-fair grounds in Europe. For years, discussions about potential expansion were monopolised by various proposals for moving the complex somewhere further away from the centre. In 2005 the proposals came to fruition, and the massive FieraMilano opened in Rho. Although the original complex still hosts minor trade events, the really famous jamborees, such as the annual furniture fair (*see p29* **Tomorrow's world**), are held at the Rho site.

In May 2008, to a mixed local response, demolition engineers blasted FieraMilanoCity's vast pavilion 20 to smithereens. By 2014, the area will be new home to CityLife, a district that will include a skyscraper and contemporary art museum designed by Daniel Libeskind, and two additional skyscrapers by Harata Isozaki and Zaha Hadid.

For the moment, though, if you're not in town for the latest developments in dental tools or wedding dresses, it's unlikely you'll be drawn to the city's far north-west, despite its beautiful, tree-lined neighbourhoods. Slightly closer to the city centre, the **Casa di Riposo per Musicisti** (*see below*), final resting place of Giuseppe Verdi, is a short walk down leafy via Buonarroti from the piazzale Giulio Cesare side of the Fiera. Further south, corso Vercelli's shopping strip heads east from piazza Piemonte.

West of the Fiera is the **San Siro** district, a verdant area notable for its modern apartment buildings, luxury cars and rooftop swimming pools. It's also home to the city's world-famous San Siro soccer stadium (or, to give it its proper name, **Stadio Giuseppe Meazza**; *see below*), which includes a must-see **museum** for football fans. Also in the area are Leonardo da Vinci's enormous bronze **Gran Cavallo** (*see below*) and several parks: Monte Stella (via Cimabue or via Terzaghi), an artificial hill made from World War II rubble; the Parco del Trenno (via Novara or via Cascina Bellaria); and nearby Boscoincittà (via Cascina Bellaria or SS11).

Casa di Riposo per Musicisti – Fondazione Giuseppe Verdi

Piazza Buonarroti 29 (02 499 6009/www.casaverdi. org). Metro Buonarroti/bus 61, 67. **Open** *Crypt* 10am-noon, 2.30-6pm daily. **Admission** free.
A statue of composer Giuseppe Verdi presides over piazza Buonarroti, where a neo-Romanesque palazzo, designed in 1899 by architect Camillo Boito (the top floor is a post-war addition), houses a retirement home for musicians. Across the courtyard – often filled with the sound of retired tenors or sopranos running through a few scales – stairs lead down to the crypt where Verdi and his wife Giuseppina Strepponi are buried.

Cavallo di Leonardo

Piazza dello Sport 16 (02 482 161/www.ippodromi milano.it). Metro Lotto/bus 78/tram 16. **Open** 9am-5.30pm Tue-Sun. **Admission** free.

Commissioned by Ludovico 'il Moro' Sforza in 1482 in honour of his father Francesco, this enormous bronze horse took over 500 years to complete. Leonardo da Vinci made drawings and a colossal clay model, and sketched out a new method for casting bronze on such a large scale. But Charles VIII's 1494 attempt to invade the city meant that the 70 tonnes of bronze went from potential art to working weapons in a blink of the eye. In 1999, American Charles Dent supplied the funds necessary to make the vision a reality, and da Vinci's 7.2m (23.6ft) horse is now the largest equestrian statue in the world.

The 'Gran Cavallo' stands on the grounds of Milan's Hippodrome. Although there are large photos that show the making of the sculpture, there is nothing in the way of additional information.

FieraMilano

Strada Statale del Sempione 28 (02 499 71/ www.fieramilano.it). Metro Rho/shuttle from Linate, Malpensa & Orio al Serio. **Open** times vary. **Admission** prices vary.
The sparkling trade fair hub since 2005, FieraMilano is truly vast, and has an enormous external show area for open-air fairs. Milan's most important fairs, including MiArt, featuring modern and contemporary art, and the Salone Internazionale del Mobile (*see p29* **Tomorrow's world**), take place here.

FieraMilanoCity

Piazzale Carlo Magno 1 (02 499 71/www.fiera milano.it). Metro Amendola-Fiera/bus 48, 78/ shuttle from Linate & Malpensa. **Open** times vary. **Admission** prices vary.
Milan's original trade fair was set up near Porta Venezia in 1920 in an effort to kick-start an economy that was slow to recover from World War I. As fair events grew, the structure was moved to its current address, expanding as permanent pavilions were added over the years. Of the original buildings, only a portion of the Palazzo dello Sport (1925) and a few art nouveau edifices near the beginning of via Domodossola still exist.

Museo & Tour San Siro

Stadio Giuseppe Meazza, Piazzale dello Sport 1, Gate 14 (02 404 2432/www.sansirotour.com). Bus 420/tram 16. **Open** 10am-5pm daily; times may vary on match days. **Admission** *Museum* €7; €5 reductions. *Museum & tour* €12.50; €10 reductions. **Credit** MC, V.
An essential place of pilgrimage for any football fanatic, small but chock-full of AC Milan and FC Inter paraphernalia. Highlights include 1928 Inter cufflinks, documentation on Berlusconi's football club purchase in 1986, and white ceramic busts of AC Milan stars Marco van Basten, Ruud Gullit and Frank Rijkaard. There are also plenty of items of historical interest, including old table football sets, photos from the stadium's first Milan-Inter match and a display of football boots showing how they have developed over the past century. Extend the experience with a tour of the stadium.

Eat, Drink, Shop

Features

Pane e Acqua. *See p110.*

Restaurants

Pinch yourself. You've entered a new culinary world.

L'Incoronata. *See p103.*

The residents of Italy's business capital are wealthy, well travelled and demanding. These traits are matched in Milan's VIP visitors – industry bosses, editors and designers, discerning restaurant judges all. The city's dining scene replies with a nonchalant dose of *sprezzatura*, the Italian art of making the difficult look easy. In most respects you'll find the dining world-class: the finest ingredients melded with the finest culinary traditions.

Innovation is another key. The city's nine Michelin stars have been handed out for creativity and consistency; but almost no address has the foamy faddiness seen in London, or the sometimes archaic traditions seen in Paris. At the other end of the scale, hearty *trattorie* do a roaring trade in Milan's time-honoured staples: ossobucco, *costoletta* and *risotto alla Milanese*. Add to this the regional cuisine imported by Milan's pan-Italian workforce, from Sicilian to Ligurian and Abruzzese, and you'll be hard-pressed to find a similar dining selection in any other city.

SLOWING IT DOWN

The Slow Food movement has done much to make Italy more aware of its culinary heritage. For many years, there was little difference between dishes served at home and those made outside. The restaurant was simply the place to go to when *mamma* was too tired to cook, or during the traditional fortnight at the seaside. The food at most restaurants was homely, and the cook was, more likely than not, a surrogate *mamma* who made sure the family was well fed and content. Once food became serious, though, the rules changed. The chefs are now largely trained and male, and the sense of satisfying abundance has given way to the challenge of boutique quality. The good old plate of mozzarella has become a plate of mozzarella di bufala DOC, and has been priced accordingly.

Is this good or bad? For people looking for pristine ingredients, carefully prepared, the answer is 'good'. For those who look for hidden pleasures and the thrill of hunting out the unknown, it's more ambiguous. Yes, there is more choice these days – but wasn't part of the charm of that little trattoria the fact that the salami was cured by *zio* Tommaso, and a big plate would cost just 3,000 lire? Now Uncle Tommaso has gone 100 per cent *biologica* (organic) – as if he wasn't before – and the same (smaller) plate of salami costs €10.

For the visitor, all this means that tracking down the old-style trattoria with red checked tablecloths is harder than ever – though they do exist if you know where to look (we've listed the best of them below). Despite the introduction of the euro, and the consequent inflation in prices, dining in Milan still represents good value compared to most major European cities.

MAKING A MEAL OF IT

Do Italians still eat an *antipasto* (starter), a *primo* (usually pasta, risotto or soup) and *secondo* (meat or fish course), accompanied by a *contorno* (vegetable side dish), and, finally, cheese, dessert, fruit, coffee – and perhaps a *digestivo* or a grappa? They do, but in practice few Milanese care to put aside the two or three hours necessary to do such a meal justice. Most prefer to choose two out of the three main courses (*antipasto*, *primo* and *secondo*), complementing the meal with a *contorno* here and a slice of cheese there. (And many will still finish with the *digestivo*.) But remember that the full Italian meal is a luxury, not an obligation, so don't feel pressured into eating more than you want.

Fixed-price meals are still seen as something for the tourists (indeed, it's probably a wise move to steer clear of any establishment that has a *menù turistico* written in several languages). Some of the more upmarket and creative restaurants, such as **Joia** (*see p104*) and **Cracco-Peck** (*see p101*), will offer a tasting menu (*menù degustazione*). This can be a good way to sample a bit of everything.

WHAT TO EAT

For years, Milan acted as a magnet for southern Italians looking for work. The result was that pasta became as common as Lombard rice and polenta. Nevertheless, most Milanese still have a soft spot for well-prepared risotto: thick kernels of Arborio or Carnaroli rice, slowly simmered in broth, supplemented with vegetables, seafood or meat, butter and sometimes cheese. True Lombard pasta dishes tend to be based on fresh pasta: *tortelli di zucca* (pumpkin-stuffed pasta) and *pizzoccheri* (buckwheat pasta with cheese, cabbage and potato) are two such Lombard specialities.

Unlike other Italian soups, Lombard versions are so thick they easily constitute a main course. *Zuppa pavese* (broth with bread and eggs) and *zuppa di porri e bietole* (with leeks and Swiss chard) are found in rural restaurants. *Casoeûla* is a soupy cabbage stew with polenta, pork and sausage. Polenta, topped with mushrooms or meat, is a common feature of Lombardy, especially in winter.

❶ Purple numbers given in this chapter correspond to the location of restaurants as marked on the street maps. *See pp248-252.*

When it comes to *secondi*, land-locked Lombardy is a surprisingly good place to dine on freshwater fish and seafood. Milan is Italy's biggest sea fish distribution centre; the morning catch is flown in so quickly that it's served as fresh here as on the coast. Not to be outdone, the area's lakes and rivers yield sturgeon and grey caviar in late November; perch, trout, carp, salmon and eel are also used in the cuisine of the lake regions.

Succulent cuts of meat – veal in particular – are transformed into namesake specialities: *ossobuco alla milanese* (braised veal shanks) and *costoletta alla milanese* (breaded and fried veal chop). Lombardy also produces some excellent cured meats.

The region is a cheese-lover's heaven too, its offerings ranging from ripe gorgonzola to oozing taleggio and spreadable stracchino. In most traditional Lombard dishes, butter is used instead of olive oil, and thick cream is common.

For more information on local cuisine, *see pp31-33* **Food and drink in Lombardy** *and p111* **On the menu**.

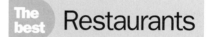

The best Restaurants

For celebrity chic
Da Giacomo. *See p104.*

For celebrity chefs
Bistrot Triennale Bovisa. *See p102.*

For sushi
Poporoya Shiro. *See p105.*

For seafood
13 Giugno. *See p104.*

For pizza
La Piccola Ischia. *See p110.*

For traditionalists
Antica Trattoria della Pesa. *See p101.*

For modernists
Lucca. *See p104.*

For post-modernists
Joia. *See p104.*

For a birthday party
Premiata Pizzeria. *See p110.*

For a first date
L'Incoronata. *See p103.*

For a marriage proposition
Fioraio Bianchi. *See p102.*

Eat, Drink, Shop

WHERE TO EAT

Traditionally, an *osteria* was something like a social club, a place where the working class could get a glass of wine and some nibbles; a trattoria was a cheap restaurant serving basic home fare (*cucina casalinga*); and a *ristorante* was a more refined venue. These old distinctions are now best left to students of historical linguistics, though, particularly since 'osteria' has become a trendy addition to a restaurant name; many creative chefs eschew the 'ristorante' title, and many *trattorie* charge restaurant prices. Their decor might be all exposed brick and plain wood floors, but the owners have probably forked out lavishly for that distressed look.

GLASS CONSCIOUSNESS

Food is not the only thing being taken more seriously these days. Italian wines, particularly regional ones, have finally moved out of the shadows cast by Barolo, Barbaresco and Chianti. Milanese wine lists now include a dazzling range of national wines, from local Nebbiolo to Nero d'Avola from Sicily. The DOC (*denominazione di origine controllata*) seal of quality on the bottle is a reliable pointer to a good wine, but there are some wonderful wines sold under the humble guise of *vini da tavola* (table wines) because they do not conform to stringent DOC regulations. Your sommelier will be able to help in all circumstances, and waiters in the simplest establishments are familiar with their own wine lists.

Lombardy is more wine consumer than wine maker. That said, the Franciacorta area between Bergamo and Brescia produces Champagne-quality sparkling wines, and the Oltrepò wines from the hills on the far side of the Po River provide a variety of good-value reds and whites.

Most *trattorie* and *osterie* (and some *ristorante*) also serve *vino sfuso*, which can be ordered in quarter-, half- or one-litre carafes. Although the quality varies greatly, you might well get a young, quaffable wine, particularly at the better addresses. The traditional accompaniment to pizza is beer or soft drinks.

If you've ordered a full meal, you might be invited to a *digestivo* or a grappa on the house. The choice of *digestivi* is endless; Ramazzotti – a dark, syrupy liqueur made from herbs and spices – is a distinctly Milanese variant.

UP IN SMOKE

The occasional restaurant in Milan has an interior smoking section, complete with ducts and extractor fan. We've listed a few that do below. If not, unlike in the UK or US, there's little stigma attached to popping outside for a postprandial puff. A comfy chair and ashtray (plus heater in winter) will normally be placed outside the restaurant for smokers.

PRACTICALITIES

Most eating establishments charge a *coperto* (cover charge) for providing a tablecloth and bread. This ranges from €1.50 in simple establishments to €6 in classy joints, and is often sweetened by an *amuse-bouche*.

Italians are not big on tips. A euro or two is standard, although more will be left if the food or service was outstanding. Tourists, however, are generally expected to be more generous: five to ten per cent will put a smile on your waiter's face – but bear in mind that you're under no obligation to leave anything.

Italy is still predominantly a cash society, and many establishments will try to dissuade you from using plastic. However, all but the smallest *trattorie* and *pizzerie* accept credit cards. By law you must be given an official receipt (*scontrino fiscale*) upon paying the bill. Hold on to this: in the unlikely event that a policeman catches you leaving a restaurant without one, you (and the restaurateur) could receive a nasty fine.

Italians like to eat at regular times and opening hours are fairly standard. The times listed here refer to those when hot meals can be ordered, though the establishment may stay open much later. Normal eating hours are 12.30-2.30pm and 8-10.30pm.

CLOSE TO THE VEG

Entirely vegetarian restaurants are few and far between in Milan; Joia, a temple to veggie *haute cuisine*, is an honourable exception, as is **Govinda** (*see p110*) in the budget category. However, vegetarians are by no means limited to salads and pizzas. Most Milan restaurants offer at least two or three vegetarian starters and main courses; *contorni* of grilled veg, or a vegetable *antipasto* buffet add yet more variety. And the rising popularity of global grub, from sushi to Sri Lankan, makes this Italy's best city for meat-free dishes. Life will be harder for vegans (Lombard cuisine is heavy on dairy products), but again, there's never any shortage of fresh fruit and vegetables.

Vegetarianism is still considered cranky in Milan, however, and the usual riposte to 'I only eat vegetables' is 'There's only a bit of meat in it' – or 'There's no meat, just ham'. Play the gastro-conscious Italians at their own game by saying 'Non riesco a digerire la carne', which translates as 'I can't digest meat'.

Average restaurant prices given in the listings below are per person, and are based on three courses (two for *pizzerie*), drinks excluded.

A taste of the future

Flat-screen TVs dot the walls: portholes on to puffy clouds and candyfloss-pink skies. Zanotta beanbags, each a classic 1968 'Sacco' design by Cesare Paolini, Franco Teodoro and Piero Gatti, fill the centre of the room. With a mass of art catalogues at the bookshop around the corner and a stream of Milanese trendies flowing in through the door, it would be easy to pigeonhole the **Bistrot Triennale Bovisa** (*see p102*) as a haven designed exclusively for the city's art and fashion gang. But although the cooler-than-cool are definitely present, it's not just the visual fiesta that pulls in the crowds. The magnet is chef Moreno Cedroni and his mind-blowing contemporary dishes.

Cedroni – laden with Michelin stars and Gambero Rosso forks – is Italy's answer to Heston Blumenthal. He's one of the nation's most original cooks, topping tuna with a rich mustard ice-cream, and marrying polenta with octopus, peas and Parmesan shavings. The dishes are based almost entirely around fresh fish and *salumeria ittica*, various sorts of cured salmon, tuna and swordfish. Impressively, over 95 per cent of the ingredients used are Italian. The menus

sport a photo of the current exhibition at the Triennale Bovisa (*see p70*) contemporary art museum next door, and the offerings are revamped with each new inauguration.

What makes the Bistrot refreshingly different from most of Milan's hip locales is its mixed clientele. Mains cost between €15 and €25, but there's always a *piatto del giorno* (dish of the day) for around €5, popular with students from the Bovisa design polytechnic down the road. The menu suggests appropriate wines to go with each dish, and there are 35 types by the glass: that brings in the wine buffs. With live jazz and discounts for children at Sunday's buffet brunch (under-12s half price, under-fours free), the families roll in. And what about those designers? Lounging with a Philippe Starck book, munching on a late lunch (the kitchen stays open all afternoon) and enjoying the atmosphere as much as anyone.

To get to Bovisa, a formerly industrial, now thriving zone in the northern suburbs, take a ten-minute trip on the *ferrovia passante* commuter train (*see p219*). The Bovisa Triennale is a clearly signposted ten-minute walk from Bovisa station.

www.treesforcities.org

Trees for Cities
Charity registration number 1032154

Travelling creates so many lasting memories.

Make your trip mean something for years to come - not just for you but for the environment and for people living in deprived urban areas.

Anyone can offset their flights, but when your plant trees with Trees for Cities, you'll help create a green space for an urban community that really needs it.

Leave Your Mark

Create a green future for cities.

Duomo & Centre

Italian

Boeucc

Piazza Belgioioso 2 (02 7602 0224/www.boeucc.it).
Metro Duomo/bus 61/tram 1, 2, 20. **Meals served**
noon-2.30pm, 7.30-11pm Mon-Fri; 7.30-11pm Sun.
Average €80. **Credit** AmEx, DC, MC, V.
Map p252 E6 **①** **Traditional**
A discreet, 'old money' establishment, a block away
from the HQs of several of Italy's banks. The dark-
suited financiers doing deals over a salver of *fine de
claire* oysters, the fashion crowd and ladies who
lunch all enjoy impeccable service and staunchly traditional Italian fare. Well-presented classics such as
bistecca alla fiorentina per due (T-bone steak for two)
and *scaloppina di vitello con funghi porcini* (veal cutlet with porcini mushrooms) are two key dishes.

Cracco-Peck

*Via Victor Hugo 4 (02 876 774/www.peck.it). Metro
Cordusio or Duomo/bus 199/tram 1, 2, 3, 12, 14,
16, 19, 27.* **Meals served** 7.30-10.30pm Mon, Sat;
12.30-2.30pm, 7.30-10.30pm Tue-Fri. Closed 3wks
Dec-Jan, 3wks Aug. **Average** €100. **Credit** AmEx,
DC, MC, V. **Map** p252 D7 **②** **Contemporary**
Cracco-Peck's creative menu is custom-made for
Milan's expense account diners. The two Michelin
stars and consistently high ratings in the Italian
Gambero Rosso and Veronelli dining guides show
how seriously food is taken here. Although loved
and hated for his controversial ingredients, Carlo
Cracco's best dishes are often the ones that seem
most bizarre. For a showstopper, try the pasta with
sea urchins and coffee, or opt for one of the tasting
menus (€130-€160). Although Cracco-Peck would
raise nary an eyebrow in New York, Paris or
London, Milan tends to equate fine dining with tradition, so you'll find this place frequented primarily
by foreigners or Milanese looking to impress.

Il Marchesino

*Via Filodrammatici 2 (02 7209 4338/www.ilmarche
sino.it). Metro Duomo/bus 61/tram 1, 2, 20.* **Meals
served** 7.30am-1am Mon-Sat; open 1hr before shows
Sun. **Average** €60. **Credit** AmEx, DC, MC, V.
Map p252 E6 **③** **Milanese**
Local superchef Gualtiero Marchesi (knight of the
Italian republic, and the first Italian to win three
Michelin stars) opened this chic little diner next door
to La Scala in May 2008. The bar area, serving
breakfast and post-performance snacks, is sexy in a
1980s NASA HQ kind of way; the restaurant is more
refined, with deep-red upholstery. Although
Marchesi is nearly 80, his dishes smack of innovation: a kebab version of *costoletta Milanese*, for
instance, and a Campari and grapefruit slushy.

Papà Francesco

*Via Marino 7 (02 862 177/www.papafrancesco.
com). Metro Duomo/bus 61/tram 1, 2, 3, 14, 19,
24.* **Meals served** noon-2.30pm Mon, Tue; noon-

2.30pm, 7-10.30pm Wed-Sun. Closed 3wks Aug.
Average €30. **Credit** AmEx, DC, MC, V.
Map p252 E6 **④** **Milanese**
Inexpensive and family-run, with *molto rapido* service – all a stone's throw from the Galleria Vittorio
Emanuele. The seven daily specials include the likes
of *carpaccio di tonno affumicato* (thinly sliced
smoked tuna), or Milanese classics such as *ossobuco con risotto*.

Peck Italian Bar

*Via Cesare Cantù 3 (02 869 3017/www.peck.it).
Metro Cordusio or Duomo/bus 199/tram 1, 2, 3,
12, 14, 16, 19, 27.* **Meals served** 7.30am-7.30pm
Mon-Fri. **Average** €45. **Credit** AmEx, DC, MC, V.
Map p252 D7 **⑤** **Contemporary**
In addition to its food hall and restaurant, the Peck
empire also includes a casual café. The mood is one
of upmarket bustle, with stockbrokers from the nearby Borsa rubbing elbows with Milanese *signore* in
for a morning's shopping. The menu offers a seasonal selection of *primi* and *secondi*, along with a variety of pastries from the cases near the entrance. In
a land where it's next to impossible to sit down for
a meal outside fixed lunch and dinner times, Peck
Italian Bar is unusual: it serves food all day long.

Trattoria Milanese

*Via Santa Marta 11 (02 8645 1991). Metro
Cordusio/tram 2, 3, 14, 20.* **Meals served** noon-
2.30pm, 7.15-10.30pm Mon, Wed-Sun. Closed mid
July-Aug. **Average** €45. **Credit** AmEx, DC, MC, V.
Map p252 D7 **⑥** **Milanese**
Seemingly unchanged in 50 years, this warm trattoria is refined yet inviting. Its fine, traditional
Milanese cuisine is well known, and you'll share dining space with wealthy locals and guidebook-wield-
ing foodies. Saffron-infused risotto (*risotto alla
Milanese*) is the house speciality, dished up fresh
every 30 minutes: catch the waiter's eye and stake a
claim. Ossobucco and *costoletta Milanese* (breaded
veal chops) are ever-popular classics.

Pizza & snacks

Panzerotti Luini

*Via S Radegonda 16 (02 8646 1917/www.luini.it).
Metro Duomo.* **Open** *Jan-Nov* 10am-3pm Mon; 10am-
8pm Tue-Sat. *Dec* 10am-3pm Mon; 10am-8pm Tue-
Sun. Closed Aug. **Average** €8. **No credit cards.**
Map p252 E6 **⑦** **Pizza**
See p107 **Sandwich time**.

Sforzesco & North

Italian

Antica Trattoria della Pesa

*Viale Pasubio 10 (02 655 5741). Metro
Garibaldi/bus 43/tram 3, 4, 11.* **Meals served**
12.30-2pm, 7.30-11pm Mon-Sat. Closed 2wks Aug.
Average €40. **Credit** AmEx, MC, V.
Map p248 D3 **⑧** **Milanese**

Eat, Drink, Shop

Da Claudio is the place to go for fresh fish.

Our top pick for sampling Milanese food, located in a 19th-century weigh station. It has friendly service, a cosy ambiance and some of the finest *funghi porcini* pasta in the city; the generous *costoletta alla Milanese* (breaded veal) barely fits onto its serving plate. Any deviations from tradition will be strongly discouraged, including the sacrilegious squeezing of lemon juice on to your cutlet.

Bistrot Triennale Bovisa

Via Lambruschini 31, Bovisa (02 3657 7828/www. triennalebovisa.it). Bus 82, 92/tram 1, 3. **Meals served** 11am-1am Tue-Sun. **Average** €45. *Brunch* €28; €10 under-12s; free under-4s. **Credit** AmEx, DC, MC, V. **Contemporary**
See p99 **A taste of the future**.

Da Claudio

Via Ponte Vetero 16 (02 805 6857/www.pescheria daclaudio.it). Metro Lanza/bus 57, 61/tram 4, 7, 20. **Meals served** noon-2.30pm, 5-9pm Tue-Sat. Closed Aug. **Average** €25. **Credit** MC, V. **Map** p252 D6 **9** **Seafood**
Da Claudio is a consummate fishmonger with a major sideline in fresh seafood. The weak nautical decor doesn't detract from the lovingly prepared platters of tuna tartare, diced swordfish with spring onions and octopus *carpaccio* flaunted on crushed ice. There's sparkling white wine on draught rather than the normal Peroni beer tap, and sauced-up half lobsters on the shell for a minor blowout. Order from the cashiers, canteen-style, then pick up your order

from the servers. The dining area is a series of angled lecterns; balance your tray of *frutti di mare* on top and proceed towards repletion.

Di Cotte di Crude

Via Porro Lambertenghi 25 (02 668 8455). Metro Gioia or Zara/bus 70, 82/tram 7, 11. **Meals served** 12.30-2pm, 7.30-11pm Tue-Sat. Closed Aug. **Average** €50. **Credit** AmEx, MC, V. **Map** p248 D2 **10** **Seafood**
Squeamish diners should probably give this live lobster specialist a miss. The short menu turns on cooked and raw (*cotte e crude* in Italian) Canadian and Breton crustaceans, served up by owner-chef Paolo Arrigoni. With just five small tables surrounded by lobster tanks, it's a niche dining experience.

Fioraio Bianchi

Via Montobello 7 (02 2901 4390/www.fioraio bianchicaffe.it). Metro Moscova/bus 43, 61, 94/ tram 1, 2, 20. **Meals served** 9am-10pm Mon-Sat. Closed Aug. **Average** €60. **Credit** AmEx, DC, MC, V. **Map** p249 E5 **11** **Contemporary**
Covent Garden florist meets modern Italian cuisine. Each dish is lovingly conceived, although you pay handsomely for that love. But with a typical meal of buckwheat penne with 'pixel' chopped tomatoes for starter, rolled seabass with *gateau di verdura* (vegetable gateau) for main, and tepid chocolate tart with red pear sorbet for pudding, who's counting? The €8 happy hour (6-8pm) can give you an inkling of the previous night's menu.

L'Incoronata

Corso Garibaldi 127 (02 657 0651). Metro Moscova/bus 43, 94/tram 3, 4, 7, 12. **Meals served** 8-10.30pm Mon-Sat. **Average** €30. **Credit** MC, V. **Map** p248 D4 ⓬ **Traditional**
L'Incoronata is simply designed, with a refreshing menu of just five pasta *primi* and five meaty main courses. A pleasing French touch can be discerned in some of the dishes: the mustard glaze on the faux fillets is one example. Keeping it simple, the selection of five wines by the bottle, including a good Nero d'Avola and a Barbera, are €15 each. The assortment of whitewashed tables and chairs lend a calm, uncluttered air. *Photo 96.*

Innocenti Evasioni

Via Privata della Bindellina (02 3300 1882/www. innocentievasioni.com). Bus 48, 57, 69/tram 1, 14, 19. **Meals served** 8-10.30pm Mon-Sat. Closed Aug. **Average** €45. **Credit** AmEx, DC, MC, V. **Contemporary**
Well worth the trek to its unlikely location (tucked away down a narrow private road near piazzale Accursio), this delightful restaurant provides thrillingly inventive food in settings that have a strongly Zen aesthetic. Two softly lit dining rooms look over a pretty Japanese garden, and nice little details make it feel special: a basket of freshly baked breads, complimentary nibbles before the *antipasto*, and the use of silver covers (even though it's not actually a formal sort of place). Desserts, such as the chilled strawberry and lavender mousse with coconut biscuits, are spectacular.

La Latteria

Via San Marco 24 (02 659 7653). Metro Moscova/ bus 41, 94. **Meals served** 12.30-2.30pm, 7.30-11pm Mon-Fri. **Average** €25. **No credit cards.** **Map** p248 D5 ⓭ **Traditional**
La Latteria has been serving clean, creative takes on northern Italian classics since 1988: the dishes are listed on a hand-typed menu that's pinned to front door. *Maccheroni al pomodoro e burro* (pasta with butter and tomatoes) is a typical daily dish, and they do a mean *bollito* (mixed meat stew) too. Note that no reservations are accepted.

Trattoria da Ottimofiore

Via Bramante 26 (02 3310 1224). Metro Moscova/ bus 43, 70/tram 4, 12, 14. **Meals served** 12.30-2.30pm, 7.30-10.30pm Mon-Sat. Closed Aug. **Average** €30. **Credit** MC, V. **Map** p248 C4 ⓮ **Traditional**
Any doubt about the authenticity of this prime Sicilian joint is banished by the *antipasti* buffet. For €10, Trattoria da Ottimofiore's buffet includes Sicily's finest: around eight different platters brim-full of deep-fried baby sardines, *caponata di verdure* (roasted peppers, aubergines and courgettes) and *frittelle alla salvia* (sage and vegetable fritters). The concise menu includes swordfish with capers and lemons, *pasta alla norma* (spaghetti with aubergine and aged ricotta) and *pasta alle sarde* (rigatoni with a sardine-based ragu).

International

Armani/Nobu

Via Pisoni 1 (02 6231 2645/www.giorgioarmani.it). Metro Montenapoleone/tram 1, 2. **Meals served** noon-2pm, 7-11pm daily. **Average** €100. **Credit** AmEx, DC, MC, V. **Map** p252 E5 ⓯ **Japanese**
Raw fish just doesn't get more fashionable than the sushi at the Milan outpost of Nobuyuki Matsuhisa's restaurant empire. Purists will say the food isn't as good here as at his New York or London flagships, although you can try for yourself during the €14 happy hour (7-11pm). *Ceviche* (Latin-style marinated sushi) and bento boxes are on the menu at lunch.

La Felicità

Via Rovello 3 (02 865 235). Metro Cairoli or Cordusio/bus 58/tram 1, 3 14, 16, 19, 20. **Meals served** noon-4pm, 7pm-midnight daily. **Average** €20. **Credit** MC, V. **Map** p252 D6 ⓰ **Chinese**
An open-all-hours, family affair: daughter dishing out the prawn crackers, mum taking orders, and dad in the kitchen. Said family is from Shanghai, and the food is crisp, subtle, tender and unbattered, and includes cheap *prix fixe* lunches of pickled cucumbers, sesame-scented duck and stuffed pork buns.

Tara

Via Cirillo 16 (02 345 1635/www.ristorantetara. com). Metro Cadorna/bus 57/tram 1, 29, 30. **Meals served** noon-2.30pm, 7-11.30pm daily. **Average** €25. **Credit** AmEx, DC, MC, V. **Map** p248 B4 ⓱ **Indian**
A thriving Indian restaurant just north of Parco Sempione. The regular menu is straightforward (rogan josh and tikka masala), but the vegetarian selection is far more experimental: *baingan bharta* based on smoked aubergine, and *alu gobi* that combines cauliflower with spicy spinach and potatoes.

Tomoyoshi Endo

Via Vittor Pisani 13 or Via Fabio Filzi 8 (02 6698 6117/www.tomoyoshi-endo.com). Metro Centrale or Repubblica/bus 169, 200/tram 2, 9, 29, 30. **Meals served** noon-2.30pm, 7.30-11pm Mon-Sat. Closed 3wks Aug. **Average** €45. **Credit** MC, V. **Map** p249 F3 ⓲ **Japanese**
Italy's oldest Japanese restaurant is tucked away on the ground floor of a nondescript office block near Stazione Centrale. As well as the usual selection of sushi and sashimi, specialities include *tonno scottato* (tuna perfectly pan-fried, with crisp edges and a deep red centre) and *guancia di tonno* (giant tuna cheeks baked in a salt crust). The service can be off-hand but the food makes it a must-visit.

Pizza & snacks

Cracco Coffee Design

Triennale, viale Alemagna 6 (02 875 441/www. triennale.it). Metro Cadorna/bus 57, 61, 94/tram 1, 19, 27. **Meals served** 10am-7pm Tue-Sun. **Average** €25. **Credit** AmEx, DC, MC, V. **Map** p248 C5 ⓳

Eat, Drink, Shop

The Triennale's old café has been given a total overhaul by architect Michele De Lucchi, to become the latest feather in chef Cracco's cap. Cracco Coffee Design was launched during Milan's Salone Internazionale del Mobile (*see p29* **Tomorrow's world**) in April 2008. Watch the preparation of sandwiches, salads and other light snacks take place behind the kitchen's glass wall. Rumour has it that an on-site Cracco restaurant is in the pipeline.

OL

Bastioni Porta Nuova 9 (02 655 5560). Metro Moscova or Repubblica/bus 43/tram 11, 29, 30, 33. **Meals served** 12.30-2.30pm, 7.30-11.30pm daily. **Average** €25. **Credit** AmEx, MC, V. **Map** p249 E4 ⑳
The portions of meat at this homely trattoria are medieval, in size and preparation. A skewer of whole sausages, chunks of pork and beef is matched with entire aubergines in the *spiedone di carne misti e verdure alla griglia.* Best of all, OL is totally informal, and a bargain to boot. Candles make a change from the fluorescent lighting in restaurants of this ilk, and the extensive terrace by one of Milan's old river locks comes alive from May to September.

San Babila & East

Italian

Da Giacomo

Via P Sottocorno 6 (02 7602 4305). Bus 169/tram 9, 23. **Meals served** 12.30-2.30pm, 7.30-11pm daily. Closed 3wks Aug. **Average** €60. **Credit** AmEx, DC, MC, V. **Map** p249 G6 ㉑ **Traditional**
It looks unremarkable on the outside: an anonymous trattoria in an anonymous street. But this is one of Milan's most exclusive (though by no means most expensive) restaurants. In a series of bright and chatty rooms decorated by the late Renzo Mongiardino, major players from Milan's fashion and business worlds jostle for elbow room. Service can be uncertain, and the competent Mediterranean cuisine, with the emphasis on fish, might not win any prizes. But this is just what the city's captains of industry want: colour and comfort food in a 'trattoria' that's as hard to get into as the Ivy in London.

Da Giannino L'Angolo d'Abruzzo

Via Rosolino Pilo 20 (02 2940 6526). Tram 5, 23. **Meals served** 12.20-2.30pm, 7.30-11pm Tue-Sun. **Average** €25. **Credit** DC, MC, V. **Map** p249 H5 ㉒ **Traditional**
Barely changed since 1963, Da Giannino L'Angolo d'Abruzzo is, as its name suggests, a typical Abruzzese diner: hot, busy, and redolent of grilled meat. Dishes from the central Italian province are thrown down on the checked red tablecloths with abandon. The *grigliata mista* (mixed grill) is a popular bet: a platter of lamb, *arrosticini* (kebabs), scamorza cheese, sausages and *lonza* (pressed pork). Meals start with grilled bruschetta, and may finish with a home-made *digestivo.*

13 Giugno

Via Goldoni 44 (02 719 654/www.ristorante13 giugno.it). Bus 54, 61, 62, 92. **Meals served** noon-2pm, 7.30-11pm daily. **Average** €65. **Credit** AmEx, DC, MC, V. **Map** p249 H6 ㉓ **Seafood**
This Sicilian seafood specialist feels like a gentleman's club: past the golden doorbell and leather chesterfields lies an extremely elegant dining room (with pianist). At €8, the *coperto* is pricey, but it entitles you to an *amuse-bouche* of seabass carpaccio, tuna tartare and heavenly breadsticks. Better value and more creative than the set menus is the à la carte selection; the *piatto crudo* (platter of raw langoustine, swordfish carpaccio, plump red shrimp and squid) is sublime. There's a pile of lemons and chopping knife on each table: it must be a Sicilian thing.

Joia

Via P Castaldi 18 (02 2952 2124/www.joia.it). Metro Porta Venezia or Repubblica/tram 1, 11, 29, 30. **Meals served** 12.20-2.30pm, 7.30-11pm Mon-Fri; 7.30-11pm Sat. Closed Aug, 2wks Dec-Jan. **Average** €65. **Credit** AmEx, DC, MC, V. **Map** p249 F4 ㉔ **Contemporary**
This calm, minimalist but wood-warm space near the Giardini Pubblici is the domain of Swiss chef Pietro Leemann, whose often inspired and always creative cooking has earned him a Michelin star – a rare achievement for a vegetarian chef. Among the Asian-influenced menus, which also feature a few fish and vegan dishes, the lunchtime four-dish taster (*piatto quadro*) is a snip at €17. There's also a €60 *scoperta* (discovery) menu, and a €70 *enfasi della natura* ('natural emphases'), a whimsical array of the chef's finest creations.

Lucca

Via Panfilo Castaldi 33 (02 2952 6668/www.ristora ntelucca.it). Metro Porta Venezia or Repubblica/tram 1, 11, 29, 30. **Meals served** 12.30-2.30pm, 7.30-11pm daily. Closed Aug. **Average** €35. **Credit** AmEx, DC, MC, V. **Map** p249 G4 ㉕ **Traditional**
A modern Tuscan gem, with traditional trattoria decor, chilled-out tunes and a friendly staff. The menu is scintillating, even if the occasional dish is overly prepared; the broad bean balls with red pepper dip, and cabbage with pine nuts and raisins, are refreshingly different. Watch the chefs at work in the glass-fronted kitchen next to the smokers' room at the rear.

Osteria di Mario

Via Tadino 5 (02 2952 2574). Metro Porta Venezia/ tram 1, 9, 11, 29, 30. **Meals served** 12.30-3pm, 7.30-11.30pm Mon-Sat. Closed 3wks Aug. **Average** €30. **Credit** MC, V. **Map** p249 G4 ㉖ **Tradtional**
Advertised outside as a *tipica osteria pugliese* (typial Pugliese restaurant), Mario dishes up a southern Italian feast that will leave you reeling. Rows of candlelit dark wooden tables line the interior, boarding school refectory style. The *antipasti* buffet is memorable: bowls of grilled fennel tops, pickled garlic cloves, artichokes in oil, breaded sardines and *pomodori secchi al tonno* (tuna-stuffed sun-dried

Giulio Pane e Ojo. *See p108.*

tomatoes) to name but a few. *Horse and Pony* readers can eschew the large equine selection and go for hearty beef stew or grilled lamb chops.

Il Teatro

Four Seasons Hotel, via Gesù 6-8 (02 7708 1435/ www.fourseasons.com/milan). Metro Montenapoleone or San Babila/bus 61/tram 1, 2, 20. **Meals served** 7.30-11pm Mon-Sat; 11.30am-3pm Sun. Closed Aug. **Average** €110. **Credit** AmEx, DC, MC, V. **Map** p252 E6 **㉗ Milanese**
The flagship restaurant of one of Milan's flagship hotels doesn't disappoint. Il Teatro has a formal atmosphere (crisp tablecloths, immaculate table settings and lots of waiters) and looks on to a beautiful courtyard, but Sergio Mei Tomasi's award-winning food is the real star. The recipes are traditionally Milanese – ossobucco, *tagliatta* of beef and *costoletta* – but there's a real touch of class in each dish. More playful are the desserts: the lime tart comes drizzled in balsamic vinegar, and the ginger and mango ice cream has a tangy edge.

International

Nu Cube

Via San Gregorio 6 (02 7428 1341). Metro Porta Venezia or Lima/tram 1, 5, 11, 20. **Meals served** 12.30-2.30pm, 7.30-11.30pm Tue-Sun. Closed 2wks Aug. **Average** €25. **Credit** MC, V. **Map** p249 G4 **㉘ Japanese**
The best of a bunch of new East Asian restaurants, feeding the city's addiction to Japanese culture and

design. The plum and bare brick interior is lit by light bulbs hanging on fishing poles, and we can't even begin to describe the unisex loos. Lunch is a bargain, a selection of six sushi-heavy set menus. For the more adventurous, there's Kobe beef and tuna *tataki* (seared tuna with a ginger, sesame and soy dipping sauce).

Poporoya Shiro

Via Eustachi 17 (02 2951 2635). Bus 60, 91, 92/ tram 5, 11, 33. **Meals served** 7-10pm Mon; noon-3pm, 7-10pm Tue-Sat. Closed Aug. **Average** €20. **Credit** MC, V. **Map** p249 H5 **㉙ Japanese**
This place is set in the back of a minuscule Japanese supermarket. Check out the menu (be ready to place your initial order before you sit down) as you queue among the seaweed and soy sauce. You'll be squeezed in at one of the four tables, or at the bar. The owners are from southern Japan; expect generous dabs of their own spicy sauce in the *maki*. No reservations are taken; call ahead for takeaway.

Warsa

Via Melzo 16 (02 201 673/www.ristorantewarsa.it). Metro Porta Venezia/tram 9, 23, 29, 30. **Meals served** noon-3pm, 7-10.30pm Mon, Tue, Thur-Sun. **Average** €20. **Credit** MC, V. **Map** p249 G5 **㉚ African**
Eritrean cooking was one of the first ethnic cuisines to establish itself in Milan, with many of the restaurants setting up shop in the Porta Venezia area, home to much of Milan's large East African community. Warsa is a tad more sophisticated than the norm here, with a safari-chic interior; its menu

Sandwich time

Business-centric Milan has almost forgotten the good old three-hour *pranzo* (lunch). For better or worse, today's office workers pop out for an hour, and city centre shop assistants take their breaks in sequence, so the phones can be manned and the stores stay open right through the day. However, Italians are nothing if not resourceful as far as food is concerned. So if you decide to

choose shopping or sightseeing over a lingering three-courser, follow the *Milanesi* to their favourite time-efficient pit-stops.

The slogan on the awning at **Bar della Crocetta** (*see p109*) is 'dove il panino è arte' (where the sandwich is art). The menu lists over 100 panini, but you're welcome to peruse the list of ingredients (which range from prosciutto to wild venison) and order exactly what you fancy. The place is very easygoing – which means that you may occasionally be forgotten if you're lurking somewhere out of sight.

Weighing in with over 200 sandwiches, **De Santis** (*see p110*) lists its elaborate concoctions on elegantly handwritten posters, framed in the entrance to this cavernous hole in the wall. Options include basil-flavoured goat's cheese and marinated artichokes, squeezed between thin pieces of their own secret-recipe grilled bread. They don't do takeaway, though they'll wrap your sandwich in a napkin if you need to eat on the go.

And if you fancy an alternative to panini, nip behind the Rinascente department store by the Duomo to **Panzerotti Luini** (*see p101*). A Milan institution since 1940, Luini is famed for its *panzerotti*, rounds of dough stuffed with tomato and mozzarella, then folded and fried. The filling ingredients may vary, but the lunchtime queue out the door doesn't: be prepared to wait.

boasts seafood and meat platters, plus plenty of vegetarian options,which are all eaten with your fingers. Try the *miès*, an aromatic wine.

Porta Romana & South

Italian

Al Merluzzo Felice

Via Lazzaro Papi 6 (02 545 4711). Metro Lodi or Porta Romana/bus 62, 77, 200/tram 9, 29, 30. **Meals served** 8-10.30pm Mon; 12.30-2pm, 8-10.30pm Tue-Sat. Closed Aug. **Average** €40. **Credit** AmEx, DC, MC, V. **Map** p251 G9 ❸ **Traditional**
The 'Happy Cod' is always packed to the gills, so book ahead. Sicilian favourites like *arancini* (fried rice balls) make for tasty first courses, but the speciality is swordfish, prepared in a variety of ways. Other temptations include smoked tuna, octopus and deep-fried breaded sardines. The atmosphere is warm and welcoming, the service friendly and attentive, and the cellar chock-full of good Sicilian wines.

Cozzeria

Via Muratori 6 (02 5410 7164/www.lacozzeria.it). Metro Porta Romana/tram 9, 29, 30. **Meals served** Sept-May 12.30-2.30pm, 8pm-midnight Tue-Fri; 8pm-midnight Sat, Sun. *June, July* 8pm-midnight Tue-Sun. Closed Aug. **Average** €35. **Credit** MC, V. **Map** p251 F9 ❷ **Seafood**
With an ambience that evokes dining in a pal's kitchen, the Cozzeria serves variations on just one basic dish: buckets of mussels, with a side of chips, proof that perfection often comes with specialisation. Patrons choose from 25 different sauces, including classic parsley and white wine, and wilder options like ginger and orange or juniper and gin. Try the outstanding octopus *carpaccio* starter, or crispy grilled mussels, dripping with garlic butter.

Dongiò

Via Corio 3 (02 551 1372). Metro Porta Romana/tram 9, 29, 30. **Meals served** 12.30-2.30pm, 7.30-10.30pm Mon-Fri; 7.30-10.30pm Sat. Closed 3wks Aug. **Average** €30. **Credit** AmEx, DC, MC, V. **Map** p251 G9 ❸ **Traditional**

(side bar) **Eat, Drink, Shop**

Pane e Acqua. *See p110.*

You'll smell this popular Calabrian trattoria from the corner: its slowly simmering pasta sauces, often flavoured with spicy *'nduja* (Calabrian sausage), permeate the entire city block. It does some of the finest steaks in town, grilled *al rosmarino*, with rosemary, or *al finocchio selvatico* (with wild fennel); and if you have room for dessert, try the *brusetti freddi* – dark pistachio chocolates served up with cream.

Giulio Pane e Ojo

Via L Muratori 10 (02 545 6189/www. giuliopaneojo.com). Metro Porta Romana/tram 9, 29, 30. **Meals served** 12.30-2.30pm, 8pm-12.30am Mon-Sat. **Average** €35. **Credit** AmEx, MC, V. **Map** p251 G9 ❹ **Traditional**
Located in a former brothel, this Roman *osteria* is one of the city's cosiest places in which to linger on a winter evening. The menu is short, ensuring fresh seasonal ingredients: favourites dishes include home-made pastas, like the classic *spaghetti cacio e pepe* (with crumbled, aged sheeps' cheese and black pepper) and *abbacchio* (tender spring lamb). For smokers, there's a separate dining room at the back. The restaurant offers just two seatings per evening (8.30pm and 10.30pm); be sure to reserve. *Photo p105.*

Masuelli San Marco

Viale Umbria 80 (02 5518 4138/www.masuelli-trattoria.com). Bus 84, 90, 91, 92. **Meals served** 8-10.30pm Mon; 12.30-2.30pm, 8-10.30pm Tue-Sat. Closed 3wks Aug, 1wk Dec-Jan. **Average** €40. **Credit** AmEx, DC, MC, V. **Map** p251 H8 ❺ **Traditional**

Doing brisk business on these premises since 1921, this Milanese institution lives up to its fine local reputation. The atmosphere is warm, the service attentive, and the kitchen reaches from Piedmont to Lombardy. It's not the place to take a veggie to: the menu includes intense meaty dishes like tripe, lard and veal's tongue; Friday's special is always cod fried up with onions. Order the *risotto alla Milanese* and you'll get a Masuelli souvenir plate to take home.

Osteria delle Vigne

Ripa di porta Ticinese 61 (02 837 5617/www.osteria levigne.it). Metro Porta Genova/bus 59, 169, 325/ tram 9, 29, 30. **Meals served** noon-3pm, 8-11.30pm daily. Closed 1wk Aug. **Average** €40. **Credit** AmEx, MC, V. **Map** p250 B9 ❻ **Traditional**
This cosy *osteria* has been lauded by the Slow Food movement for years, notably for its emphasis on artisanal cheeses. Nibble your way through the €20 cheese tasting menu, served with chutney-like *mostarda* and dried fruits, and try exquisite combinations like the marinated salmon roll on a bed of creamed honey beetroot. The ambience is decidedly laid-back – a boon in a district where the restaurants tend to be noisy and overcrowded.

Rondine

Via Spartaco 11 (02 5518 4533). Metro Porta Romana. **Meals served** noon-3pm, 7.30-11pm Mon-Sat. Closed 3wks Aug. **Average** €35. **Credit** MC, V. **Map** p251 G7 ❼ **Milanese**
Although unobtrusive, this small, unassuming restaurant is one of the zone's top *trattorie*.

Classically Milanese standouts on the menu include *ravioli al burro tartufato*, plump ravioli stuffed with ricotta and spinach, doused with truffle-scented butter, or *polenta* served with a slow-cooked beef stew. The dessert menu is quirky but tasty: try the lip-smacking fluorescent mint mousse. There are several fashion houses nearby, and a glance at the diners' cutting-edge attire is as good as reading *Vogue* with your coffee.

Tano passami l'Olio
Via Villoresi 16 (02 839 4139/www.tanopassami lolio.it). Bus 74, 325/tram 2. **Meals served** 8-11.30pm Mon-Sat. Closed Aug, 2wks Dec/Jan. **Average** €60. **Credit** AmEx, DC, MC, V. **Map** p250 A9 ❸ **Contemporary**
Although quite a hike from the *navigli* action, decadent little 'Tano pass me the oil' is well worth a visit, especially if you like olive oil. Eminently contemporary dishes, like caramelised quail eggs served on a tuna mousse, or duck ravioli perfumed with sage, are paired with one of 40 Italian olive oils, drizzled liberally over the plate to enhance the flavours. The atmosphere is formal, with prices to match.

Trattoria Madonnina
Via Gentilino 6 (02 8940 9089). Bus 59, 71/tram 3. **Meals served** noon-2.30pm Mon-Wed; noon-2.30pm, 8-10.30pm Thur-Sat. Closed Aug, 1wk Dec/Jan. **Average** €30 (lunch €20). **Credit** DC, V. **Map** p250 C9 ❸ **Milanese**
The Madonnina is a down-to-earth place with an appealingly rustic vibe, thanks to the wooden tables,

red and white checked tablecloths, old road signs and posters. The food couldn't be more traditional: four daily *primi*, simple pastas with tomato or meat sauces, and four *secondi*, often meat cutlets with potatoes or veg, and all at low prices. In spring, go out to sit at one of the rear courtyard's tables, boxed in by pots of climbing jasmine.

International

Ali Baba Di Fayoumi
Via Cadore 26 (02 545 0046). Bus 60, 62, 73/tram 12, 27. **Meals served** 7.30pm-midnight Mon-Sat. Closed 3wks Aug. **Average** €40. **Credit** MC, V. **Map** p251 H7 ❹ **Lebanese**
Milan's Middle Eastern restaurants are thin on the ground, but this is good one: Ali Baba has some of the finest *meze* we have tasted. Its set selection for two will leave you with little room or anything else. Round off your meal with a sweet cardamom-infused coffee.

Zen
Via Maddalena 1 (02 8901 3557/www.zenworld.it). Metro Missori/bus 200/tram 15, 16, 24. **Meals served** 12.30-2.30pm, 8-11.30pm Mon-Fri; 8-11.30pm Sat. Closed 3wks Aug. **Average** €40. **Credit** AmEx, MC, V. **Map** p252 E7 ❹ **Japanese**
Near piazza Duomo, this sushi spot offers table service and a dangerously appealing conveyor belt, laden with tiny plates of sushi and sashimi. Prices vary according to the plate's colour: the pricier the colour, the more irresistible the sushi. Green tea and miso soup are topped up for free (unheard of in Milan), and if you're up for something special, order the *barca Zen*, a wooden boat with raw fish on every deck.

Pizza & snacks

Bar della Crocetta
Corso di Porta Romana 67 (02 545 0228). Metro Crocetta/tram 16, 24. **Open** 9.30am-2am daily. Closed 2wks Aug. **Average** €12. **Credit** AmEx, DC, MC, V. **Map** p251 E8 ❹
See p107 **Sandwich time**.

Be Bop
Viale Col di Lana 4 (02 837 6972). Bus 169/tram 9, 29, 30. **Meals served** 12.30-2.30pm, 7.30-11pm daily. **Average** €25. **Credit** AmEx, MC, V. **Map** p250 D9 ❹
A short walk from the Darsena, this art deco-ish pizzeria serves up large, thin-crusted pizzas and a devilishly good assortment of *primi*. Be Bop uses no genetically modified ingredients, and is best known for its ability to cater well to those with dietary restrictions: vegan, gluten allergies *e tutti quanti*.

Ghireria Greca
Ripa di Porta Ticinese 13 (02 5810 7040). Bus 59, 169, 325/tram 3, 9, 29, 30. **Open** noon-2.30pm, 6pm-2am daily. Closed 1wk Aug. **Average** €15. **Credit** AmEx, MC, V. **Map** p250 C9 ❹

Eat, Drink, Shop

With its classic white and turquoise walls and a large counter for serving, this pizzeria makes a great pit-stop for people on the go. For pudding, try the home-made yoghurt with honey and walnuts.

La Piccola Ischia
Viale Umbria 60 (02 5410 7410/www.piccolaischia. it). Bus 84, 90, 91, 92. **Meals served** noon-2.30pm Mon-Fri, 7-11.30 daily. Closed 2wks Aug. **Average** €20. **Credit** AmEx, MC, V. **Map** p251 H8 **45**
The city's finest Neapolitan pizza, made with a slightly thicker crust than northern Italian pizza. Try the *pizza all'ischitana*, heaped with provolone cheese, fresh tomatoes, rocket and shavings of grana. The nautical decor is pretty kitsch, but you'll be too engrossed in your pizza to notice.
Other locations: viale Abruzzi 62, East (02 2941 2420); via Morgagni 7, East (02 204 7613).

Premiata Pizzeria
Via Alzaia Naviglio Grande 2 (02 8940 0648). Metro Porta Genova/bus 169, 325/tram 9, 29, 30. **Meals served** 12.30-2.30pm, 7.30pm-midnight daily. **Average** €25. **Credit** AmEx, MC, V. **Map** p250 C9 **46**
Diners stream through the door at the start of the Naviglio Grande from the moment this joint opens. Pizzas are cooked in the wood-fired oven, and the menu has a satisfying roster of *primi* and *secondi*. An ideal place at which to start a Saturday night.

Sant'Ambrogio & West

Italian

Da Leo
Via Trivulzio 26 (02 4007 1445). Metro Gambara/ bus 72, 80, 91, 92/tram 18. **Meals served** 12.30-2.30pm, 7.30-10.30pm Tue-Sat; 12.30-2.30pm Sun. Closed 3wks Aug, 2wks Dec. **Average** €40. **No credit cards**. **Seafood**
Giuseppe Leo has been going to Milan's fish market at the crack of dawn for the past 30 years to select the freshest produce for his fish-only restaurant. The dishes are simple and wholesome: spaghetti *in bianco* (without tomatoes) with tuna, clams, king prawns or calamari, and a range of main course fish dishes. The interior is unpretentious, the service friendly.

Hostaria Borromei
Via Borromei 4 (02 8645 3760/www.hostaria borromei.com). Bus 50, 58/tram 16, 19. **Meals served** 12.30-2.45pm, 7.30-10.45pm daily. Closed 4wks Aug. **Credit** AmEx, MC, V. **Map** p252 D7 **47 Traditional**
Although the restaurant offers an indoor seating area, Hostaria Borromei is made for summer evenings. The deep-yellow courtyard is hidden within a 15th-century palazzo, off one of the Magenta neighbourhood's back streets; flowers and hanging baskets add to the Italian countryside feel. Owners Alberto and Rosa serve up simple dishes, like Tuscan barley salad, dressed with pesto and olive oil.

Pane e Acqua
Via Bandello 14 (02 4819 8622/www.paneacqua. com). Bus 50, 58/tram 16. **Meals served** *Sept-May* 8-10.30pm Mon; 1-2.30pm, 8-10.30pm Tue-Sat. *June, July* 1-2.30pm, 8-10.30pm Mon-Fri. Closed 3wks Aug, 2wks Dec-Jan. **Credit** MC, V. **Map** p250 B7 **48 Contemporary**
An enchanting, relaxed address with tasty vintage decor and a fine Mediterranean menu. Summer brings *primi* like wild rice salad or gently roasted stuffed onions. One of our top picks in Milan for a romantic night out. *Photo p108.*

International

Govinda
Via Valpetrosa 5 (02 862 417). Metro Duomo or Missori/tram 2, 3, 15. **Meals served** 12.30-2.30pm, 7.30-10pm daily. Closed 4wks Aug. **Set menu** *Lunch* €8-€12 Mon-Fri; €20 Sat, Sun. *Dinner* €20. **No credit cards**. **Map** p252 D7 **49 Indian**
The all-vegetarian Govinda is run by Milan's Hare Krishnas, and dining here is a communal affair. You'll be seated at one of the large tables, and the only choice you'll make is between the *menu completo* (full menu) or *menu ridotto* (four, rather than six dishes; only at weekday lunch). Platters include a salad, carb-based dish, main course and a dessert, and you can help yourself to as much of the home-made bread as you like.

Pizza & snacks

De Santis
Corso Magenta 9 (02 7627 0308/www.paninide santis.it). Bus 50, 58/tram 16, 19. **Open** noon-12.30am Mon-Sat. Closed 3wks Aug, 1wk Dec. **Average** €12. **No credit cards**. **Map** p252 C6 **50**
See p107 **Sandwich time**.

Il Fontanino
Via Torchio 8 (mobile 338 372 8084). Tram 2, 3, 14. **Open** *Sept-June* 9am-7.30pm Mon-Fri. *July* 9am-3pm Mon-Fri. Closed Aug, 2wks Dec. **Average** €10. **No credit cards**. **Map** p252 C7 **51**
Organic ingredients are used in Il Fontanino's pizzas, savoury tarts and delicious desserts, all made daily on the tiny premises. Try the signature tomato and leek pizza, or the chocolate cake stuffed with pears. There's a lunchtime deal for students: a slice of pizza and a beverage for just €3.50.

Pizzeria Meucci
Via Meravigli 18, entrance around corner on via San Giovanni sul Muro (02 8645 0526). Bus 50, 58, 199/tram 16, 18, 19. **Meals served** 11.30am-3.30pm, 7-11pm Mon-Sat; 7-11pm Sun. Closed Aug. **Average** €20. **No credit cards**. **Map** p252 C6 **52**
You'll probably spot the lunchtime queue before you reach Meucci's minuscule entrance. With just six tables, you're encouraged to order while you wait. Unlike anywhere else in the city, Meucci's pizzas are small and deep, perfect for a light meal.

Eat, Drink, Shop

On the menu

Antipasti
Antipasto di mare: assorted fish. Common selections include *alici marinate* (marinated anchovies); *carpaccio* (very thin slices of raw fish, usually *salmone* – salmon), *pesce spada* (swordfish) or *tonno* (tuna); and *insalata di mare* (seafood salad).
Antipasto misto: a selection of starters.
Affettati: cold cuts (which may make up the bulk of *antipasto misto*). Common selections include *bresaola* (cured, air-dried beef); *coppa* (cured pork meat from neck and shoulder); *culatello* (specific cut of Parma ham); *lardo* (bacon fat); *pancetta* (the same cut as bacon, cured, not smoked); *prosciutto cotto* (boiled ham); *prosciutto crudo* (Parma ham).
Nervetti: salad of calf's foot, often served with beans and onions at room temperature.
Sott'aceti: pickles. The most common types are *cipolle* (onions) and *cetrioli* (cucumbers).
Sott'olii: vegetables preserved in olive oil, including *carciofi* (artichokes) and *funghi* (mushrooms).
Verdure ripiene: vegetables stuffed with breadcrumbs, and sometimes cheese; may also be served as a *contorno*.

Pasta
All'arrabbiata: with a spicy tomato sauce.
Al pomodoro: with a simple tomato sauce.
Al ragù: with a meat sauce.
Alle vongole: with a clam sauce.
Casoncelli: meat-stuffed ravioli, often served with *burro sfuso* (brown butter with sage leaves) and pancetta.
Pizzoccheri: buckwheat noodles from the Valtellina area, cooked with potatoes, Swiss chard and bitto cheese.
Tortelli alla zucca: pumpkin-stuffed ravioli, often flavoured with Amaretto; a Mantova speciality.

Risotto
Alla milanese: prepared with saffron and, traditionally, bone marrow.
Con radicchio: made with red *radicchio trevigiano* (chicory).
Con valcalepio: made with red wine, sometimes served with beans or sausages.

Carne (meat)
Al forno: roast (of meat or poultry). Common selections include *agnello* (lamb), *coniglio* (rabbit), *pollo* (chicken) and *tacchino* (turkey).
Alla griglia: grilled (of meat or poultry).

Arrosto: roast meat, most often beef (simply *arrosto*), pork (*maiale*) or veal (*vitello*).
Busecca: a stew of tripe, lard, beef, tomatoes and beans.
Cotoletta (or **costoletta**) **alla milanese**: breaded veal chop, served on the bone.
Cotechino: pork sausage.
Casoeüla: a stew made from of pork cuts, sausage and cabbage.
Involtini: small rolls of beef or aubergine (*melanzane*) stuffed with ham and cheese.
Ossobucco: braised veal shanks.
Polpette: meatballs, or occasionally balls of minced fish.
Polpettone: meat loaf.
Salsicce: sausages, often roasted or grilled.
Stufato: braised meat.

Pesce & frutti di mare (fish & seafood)
Branzino: sea bass.
Fritto misto: mixed fried seafood, most often *calamari* (squid), *pesciolini* (sprats) and sometimes *gamberi* (prawns).
Lavarello: a freshwater fish from Lake Como.
Missoltino: a freshwater fish from Lake Como, the area around Cernobbio, Lake Garda and Lake Iseo.
Orata: sea bream.
Persico: perch.
Pesce spada: swordfish.
Polipo/polpo: octopus.
Salmone: salmon.
Seppie in umido: cuttlefish in a tomato casserole.
Tonno: Tuna
Trota: trout.

Vegetables/contorni (side dishes)
Asparagi: asparagus.
Carciofi: artichokes.
Fagioli: haricot or borlotti beans.
Fagiolini: green beans, often cooked with garlic and lemon.
Funghi: mushrooms, often sautéed with olive oil, garlic and parsley.
Insalata: salad, either *mista* (mixed) or *verde* (green). Usually served without dressing, with olive oil and vinegar offered alongside.
Melanzane: aubergines.
Patate: potatoes.
Polenta: ubiquitous cornmeal mush, often served with roasts and *stufati* (stews).
Pomodori: tomatoes.

Eat, Drink, Shop

Cafés, Bars & *Gelaterie*

Re-tox, gossip and flirt: it's Milan's cocktail hour.

The Milanese practically live in bars. In a city where many reside in the suburbs, in poky apartments or with their extended families, the bar has become a surrogate living room. Every local will have his or her favourite in which to kiss, make up, detox or drink the night away.

The attitude of one-upmanship so prevalent in this competitive city has pushed bar boundaries to another level. The latest locales are owned by fashion houses, are stocked with contemporary art or boast tropical designer gardens, and are often frequented by a young and style-conscious crowd. Drinks menus at these new spots list everything from classic strawberry margharitas to signature cocktails like basil mojitos.

One of the scene's greatest inventions is the *aperitivo* 'happy hour' (*see p118* **Happy days**). This is not a two-for-one drinks hour; the Milanese are far too refined to put quantity before quality. Rather it's a post-work, free buffet slot, normally from around 6pm to 9pm, where platters of prosciutto, mozzarella, and pasta salads, and occasionally even sushi and oysters, are laid out for all to consume.

A decade ago the average Milanese 'bar' was essentially a standard European café: open 7am to 7pm, shut on a Sunday, serving an array of coffee (*see p115* **Coffee counter culture**), sandwiches at lunchtime and Camparis before dinner. These tried-and-tested locals still exist, and are fun to try; indeed, many Milanese prefer to stick to them.

WHERE TO GO

Each of Milan's bars – there are over 40 listed here, but hundreds more waiting to be found – has its own unique character and clientele. Read up, dress up (if necessary), and walk on in. Models from the nearby *Vogue Italia* HQ unwind between shoots in the bars around the Arco della Pace, such as **Deseo** (*see p115*); and the coolest post-work area is Brera, where the suited and booted take the edge off the day in pavement bars like **Radetsky** (*see p117*) and **Princi** (*see p117*). Down south, the staff from Porta Romana's Fondazione Prada and European Design Institute prop up a series of hipper, more experimental bars, including Dolce & Gabbana's **Gold Bar** (*see p121*).

For shoppers there's a clutch of elegant cafés near the Duomo. A more mature crowd rests its Gucci bags at **Trussardi Café** (*see p114*) and **Caffè Miani (aka Zucca)** (*see below*); pre-clubbers take over the pedestrianised corso Como most evenings. And if you plan a boozy night out, you can't go wrong by the canals of the *navigli* in the Porta Ticinese area. **Cuore** (*see p120*) and **Mom** (*see p121*) are recommended for a party-sized drinking bout.

Top ten — Bars

For soaking up the sun
HClub (Diana Garden). See p119.

For free Wi-Fi
Bar Bianco. See p114.

For foodies
Radetzky. See p117.

For pre-club tipples
Bhangrabar. See p114.

For mixmasters
Cuore. See p120.

For mixologists
Nottingham Forest. See p119.

For live bands
Nordest Caffè. See p117.

For exposure
Gold Bar. See p121.

Duomo & Centre

Cafés & bars

Caffè Miani (aka Zucca)

Galleria Vittorio Emanuele II (02 8646 4435/www. caffemiani.it). Metro Duomo/bus 61/tram 1, 2, 19, 20, 24. **Open** 7.30am-8pm Tue-Sun. Closed Aug. **Credit** AmEx, DC, MC, V. **Map** p252 E6 ❶
Most bars in the Galleria are tourist traps, but this place, which has been in the arcade since it opened

❶ Red numbers given in this chapter correspond to the location of cafés as marked on the street maps. See pp248-252.

Bhangrabar. Where the east meets Italy. *See p114.*

in 1867, is an institution, once frequented by Verdi and Toscanini. The interior is spectacular, with an inlaid bar and mosaics by Angelo d'Andrea. Many people who come here order that most Milanese of aperitifs, the rhubarb-based Zucca. You might want to stand and drink at the bar: prices rise sharply once you sit down and have a waiter come to your table.

Caffè Verdi
Via Giuseppe Verdi 6 (02 863 880). Metro Cordusio or Duomo/bus 61/tram 1, 2, 20. **Open** 7am-8.30pm daily. Closed 3wks Aug. **Credit** AmEx, DC, MC, V. **Map** p252 E6 ❷
This quietly dignified *caffè* may be on the touristy side, but it remains a must for opera fans. Situated across the road from La Scala, it's a convenient coffee-break spot for company members. But even if you don't run into Placido Domingo, you can soak up the atmosphere, surrounded by busts and photos of composers. It also serves food, and is popular with bankers at lunchtime.

Jungle Juice
Via Dogana 1 (02 8699 6809/www.junglejuice.it). Metro Duomo/tram 3, 12, 16. **Open** 8.30am-6.30pm Mon-Sat. **No credit cards**. **Map** p252 E7 ❸
Located just off piazza Duomo, this long-established juice bar specialises in smoothies (soya milk optional). Although not your run-of-the-mill Italian spot, it's well worth seeking out when you've had just a few too many plates of pasta.

Straf
Via San Raffaele 3 (02 805 081/www.straf.it). Metro Duomo/tram 1, 2, 20. **Open** 8am-midnight daily. **Credit** AmEx, MC, V. **Map** p252 E6 ❹
Straf is frequented by staff from the Galleria's high-end boutiques. It's a seriously well-dressed crowd who form the smoker's corner outside The Straf's (*see p41*) hotel bar. Wheels of Parmesan and trayloads of *crostini* are wheeled out for the 6-9pm happy hour. Only the passé order a G&T here: instead, try a red berry caipiroska or a champagne mojito.

Trussardi Café

Piazza della Scala 5 (02 806 8829). Metro Cordusio or Duomo/bus 61/tram 1, 2, 20. **Open** 7.30am-11pm Mon-Sat. **Credit** AmEx, MC, V. **Map** p252 E6 ❺

Half of Trussardi is made up of a huge glass cube jutting into via San Dalmazio, so you're sure to be 'seen' here. This very upmarket café is popular with the area's young banking and fashion set. Salads and Aberdeen Angus burgers grace the short lunch menu.

Gelaterie

Grom

Via Pergolesi 3 (02 4351 1942/www.grom.it). Metro Cordusio or Duomo/bus 61/tram 1, 2, 20. **Open** noon-11pm Mon-Sat; 7.30-11pm Sun. **No credit cards. Map** p252 E6 ❻

Ice-cream goes boutique a stone's throw from La Scala. The seasonal *gelato* ingredients include Syrian pistachios, Venezualan cocoa beans from Lake Maracaibo, and other ethically sourced produce. It's a registered Slow Food establishment.

Sforzesco, Brera & North

Cafés & bars

Bhangrabar

Corso Sempione 1 (02 3493 4469/www.bhangra bamilano.com). Tram 1, 29, 30. **Open** 7am-3pm, 6.30pm-2am daily. Closed 3wks Aug. **Credit** AmEx, MC, V. **Map** p248 B5 ❼

Go for a drink at this Indian lounge bar, and you could quite feasibly skip having dinner afterwards. The cocktails (€6 during happy hour, 6.30-9.30pm) entitle you to as many trips as you like to the platters of mini samosas, fragrant pakoras, bhajis and nans. Handmade screens imported from India are used to create cosy alcoves, and a DJ keeps the warm and friendly atmosphere buzzing with soul, jazz, fusion and rare groove sounds. On Sunday nights €20 gets you a cocktail and a 20-minute shiatsu massage as well. *Photo p113.*

Bottiglia Moscatelli

Corso Garibaldi 93 (02 655 4602). Metro Moscova/ bus 43, 94/tram 3, 14, 12. **Open** 8am-2am Mon-Sat. Closed 2wks Aug. **Credit** MC, V. **Map** p248 D4 ❽

Bottiglia Moscatelli is a pretty bar and its *tavola calda* is almost as attractive. Happy hour (6-9pm) is more classic than the many upmarket bars nearby, with Cuba Libre, Campari soda and glasses of good *riserva* on the short drinks menu, and free snacks. The charm extends to the bathroom, which has an art deco sink, a Singer sewing machine and antique bathroom scales (which don't work).

Bar Bianco

Viale Enrico Ibsen 4, Parco Sempione (02 8699 2026/www.bar-bianco.com). Bus 57, 61/tram 1, 4, 7, 19. **Open** *June-Aug* 9am-11.30pm Mon-Wed; 9am-1am Thur, Sun; 9am-2am Fri, Sat. *Sept-May* 9am-11.30pm daily. **Credit** MC, V. **Map** p248 C5 ❾

Bar Bianco is an island of fine drinking and free *aperitivo* snacks, shipwrecked in the middle of Parco

Cucchi is a good place to watch the world go by. *See p120.*

Coffee counter culture

With Starbucks operating in over 40 countries, it seems no nation is immune to the all-consuming charms of America's biggest coffee chain. Even Brazil, the world's largest coffee producer, has seven branches in São Paulo; and the number of outposts in France, home of the *café au lait*, has jumped from a handful five years ago to around 30 in 2008.

But can Seattle's finest ever get a foothold in Milan, the city where Starbucks CEO Howard Schultz first formulated the idea of launching espresso bars on the American public?

Schultz see Starbucks as a 'third place', where people can work, meet and relax outside the office. But Italy's cafés already fulfil this role with zeal: your local *barista* will know your name and will start preparing your usual beverage the moment you walk in. Although Starbucks may claim that it is 'more out of humility and respect that we're not in Italy,' profit is another consideration. The average Italian espresso sells for less than a euro, which suggests that this market might not bear a five-dollar skinny latté. Also, it's unlikely that the fast-food version of coffee would be fast enough for the locals. They expect their *caffè lungo macchiato* or *cappuccino scuro* to be ready at the bar 30 seconds after they come in; and the thought of ordering a 16oz cup to drink on the road… would be too *stupido* to contemplate.

So forget the frappuccino, and dive in to Milan's coffee rituals with our useful primer to Milan's coffee culture:

Americano: an espresso served with a jug of hot water, in case you can't drink it neat like the locals.

Cappuccino: a froth-topped blend of milk and espresso, known locally as a *cappuccio*. Can be ordered *decaffeinato*, *scuro* (with less milk) or *senza schiuma* (without foam).

Caffè macchiato: an espresso with a splash of *latté caldo* or *freddo* (hot or cold milk).

Corretto: a 'corrected' espresso – in other words, given a dash of grappa. A popular breakfast boost and good for blunting a hangover.

Decaffeinato: an espresso without the kick.

Espresso: or more simply *un caffè*. A steamed round of ground coffee. Can be ordered as a *doppio* (double) or *lungo* (with extra water).

Latte: a glass of milk. Order a *latte macchiato* if you'd like the Anglo-Saxon equivalent.

Marocchino: a petite glass of espresso, cocoa powder and milk froth.

Orzo: a popular coffee substitute made with barley. Beware its laxative powers.

Ristretto: a more bitter, concentrated espresso, if you can imagine such a thing.

Shakerato: a chilled espresso *lungo* that is flavoured with vanilla, then shaken over ice. It's all the rage in summer.

Sempione. Although popular for its *caffè macchiato* on a sunny weekend in winter, Bianco comes into its own in June, July and August when its freestanding structure is shaken to the rafters by a late-night, clubby crowd. There's also free Wi-Fi.

Deseo

Corso Sempione 2 (02 315 164). Tram 1, 29, 30. **Open** 6pm-2am daily. Closed Aug. **Credit** AmEx, DC, MC, V. **Map** p248 B4 ❿
'Design' is the byword at this cocktail bar: white pouffes and sofas, dark furniture, mirrors and big columns. It's popular with an older, more refined generation: think local lawyers and dentists, not students on a happy hour challenge. The glorious outdoor terrace overlooks the Arco della Pace.

Jamaica

Via Brera 32 (02 876 723/www.jamaicabar.it). Metro Lanza or Montenapoleone/bus 41, 61/tram 1, 2, 20. **Open** June-Sept 8am-2am Mon-Sat. Oct-May 8am-2am Mon-Sat; 10am-11pm Sun. Closed 1wk Aug. **Credit** AmEx, DC, MC, V. **Map** p248 D5 ⓫

According to local lore, Mussolini had an unpaid tab here when he became prime minister in 1922. In the 1950s Jamaica became a favoured hangout of journalists and artists (Giacometti included), and it started holding art and photography shows long before anybody else thought of combining the arts with alcohol. A Milan institution through and through, with a fine terrace on bustling via Brera.

Luminal

Via Monte Grappa 14 (02 3652 4405/www.luminal-milano.it). Metro Garibaldi/bus 43/tram 11, 29, 30. **Open** 6.30pm-5am daily. Closed Aug. **Admission** €10-€20 Thur-Sun. **Credit** AmEx, DC, MC, V. **Map** p249 D4 ⓬
Be brave, dress to the max and push through the velvet curtains into this super-chic nightspot. The cocktails are not the cheapest you'll find, but the well-heeled clientele (including VIPs from the fashion world) don't mind shelling out – or dressing to kill, for that matter. The upstairs dancefloor is presided over by international DJs.

Airline flights are one of the biggest producers of the global warming gas CO_2. But with **The CarbonNeutral Company** you can make your travel a little greener.

Go to **www.carbonneutral.com** to calculate your flight emissions then 'neutralise' them through international projects which save exactly the same amount of carbon dioxide.

Contact us at **shop@carbonneutral.com** or call into the office on **0870 199 99 88** for more details.

CarbonNeutral®flights

If only every mother cooked like this. **Mom Café**. *See p121.*

Nordest Caffè

Via Borsieri 35 (02 6900 1910/www.nordestcaffe.it).
Metro Garibaldi or Zara/bus 82/tram 7, 11. **Open**
8am-4pm Mon; 8am-1am Tue-Fri; 8.30am-midnight
Sat; 8.30am-10pm Sun. *Brunch* noon-3.30pm Sun.
Closed 1wk Aug. **No credit cards. Map** p249 E2 **⑬**
This Isola hotspot is a neighbourhood drinking den,
with people aged 17 to 70 tucking into the €5 glass
of wine and prosciutto platter deal. It's relaxed and
the Sunday brunch alone is worth a visit. Nordest is
a great place to start at before heading to the Blue
Note Jazz Club (*see p161*).

Princi

Largo La Foppa 2 (02 659 9013/www.princi.it).
Metro Moscova/bus 43, 94/tram 3, 7, 12, 14. **Open**
7am-midnight daily. Closed 2-3wks Aug. **Credit** MC,
V. **Map** p248 D4 **⑭**
Princi is renowned for its industrial-strength cocktails and large terrace, though its interior is none too
inspired. There's no table service, so drinkers walk
up to the accomplished barman (be sure to pay at
the till first) and order whatever they fancy. Princi
also has its own busy bakery, so expect the freebies
dished out to the post-work crowd to include *focca-
cia*, cheesy breadsticks and olive bread.

Radetzky

Largo La Foppa 5 (02 657 2645). Metro Moscova/
bus 43, 94/tram 3, 7, 12, 14. **Open** 8am-1.30am
daily. Closed 1-2wks Aug. **Credit** AmEx, DC, MC, V.
Map p248 D4 **⑮**

Named after the despised Austrian field marshal
who suppressed the 1848 uprising, this is a hip hang
out throughout the week, but it's particularly useful
on Sundays, when Milan can be pretty lifeless.
Famous for its brunches, Radetzky caters to a trendy
crowd from the *zona*'s fashion and advertising
industries, which translates to unbuttoned shirts in
summer, head-to-toe black in winter.

Roialto

Via Piero della Francesca 55 (02 3493 6616).
Bus 43, 57/tram 1, 33. **Open** 6pm-2am Tue-Sun.
Closed mid July-mid Sept. **Credit** MC, V.
Map p248 A3 **⑯**
A church stands opposite Roialto's bright red
façade, a perfect juxtaposition of salvation and
temptation. Inside, it's all white leather sofas, sun-
tans and piña coladas all round, a *Miami Vice* vibe
for the new millennium. Smokers and sunworship-
pers can lounge on the massive roof terrace.

10 Corso Como

Corso Como 10 (02 2901 3581/www.10corso
como.com). Metro Garibaldi/tram 11, 29, 30, 33.
Open 3pm-1am Mon; 10am-1am Tue-Sun. Closed
1wk Aug. **Credit** AmEx, DC, MC, V. **Map**
p248 D4 **⑰**
Designed by American artist Kris Ruhs, this courtyard café is part of Carla Sozzani's multifunctional
arts complex, which includes a hotel (*see p43*), shop
(*see p129*) and restaurant. A favourite with fashion
folk and celebrities (Giorgio Armani is said to be a

Happy days

Competition and pride are watchwords during Milan's daily happy hour (6-9pm). With cocktail prices fixed between €6 and €8, the city's hippest bars all attempt to out-chic the others: DJs are hired for the early evening slot, seasonal concoctions are chalked up on the wall, and mountains of free food are set up to pull in the punters.

We're not talking crisps and nuts here: a growing number of establishments lay on generous and imaginative buffets, with Asian salads, mozzarella kebabs and salami platters dished up for the post-work drinkers. **Bhangrabar** (*see p114*) does a spread of Indian specialities, and **Radetzky** (*see p117*) ups the stakes further with piles of marinated artichokes and oysters on ice. **Fresco Art** (*see p120*) has one of the tastiest displays: its revolving 20-platter selection includes *frittata*, smoked salmon pasta, celery and walnut salads, and crudités.

Carefully tended gardens have been added to the *aperitivo* hour mix, as bars align with office workers in need of a fresh-air boost. **Volo** (*see p121*) has an English-style walled garden, with gravel and wrought iron furniture shaded by trees. The garden at **HClub (Diana Garden)** (*see p119*) is re-landscaped seasonally: a great place in which to lap up their free salvers of Russian salad and queen olives.

In the cocktail stakes, **Nottingham Forest** (*see p119*) and **Cuore** (*see p120*) are in the premier league. Their creations of secret spirits and frozen fruit border on the crass – and as the cocktail list you'll be given on entry will confirm, many of the drinks are one-off house specials, or new for the season.

Volo.

regular, and the whole place was sealed off when Madonna paid a visit), it occupies an old *casa a ringhiera* (working-class apartment building). Try the excellent No.1 cocktail.

San Babila & East

Cafés & bars

Baglioni Caffé
Via Senato 5 (02 7600 9883). Metro San Babila or Turati /bus 61, 94/tram 1, 2, 20. **Open** *Breakfast* 7-11.30am daily. *Bar* 9am-1am daily. **Credit** AmEx, DC, MC, V. **Map** p252 F6 ⑱
The best feature in this elegant café inside the Hotel Baglioni is its private exit, which brings you out by Armani on via della Spiga. The place is laid out in drawing room style, and frequented by ladies who lunch. Cold cuts, Campari sodas and Marlboro Lights (the café is a ventilated smoking zone) are a popular lunchtime combination.

Bar Basso
Via Plinio 39 (02 2940 0580/www.barbasso.com). Metro Lima or Piola/bus 60, 92/tram 5, 11, 23. **Open** 9am-1am Mon, Wed-Sun. Closed 3wks Aug. **Credit** AmEx, MC, V. **Map** p249 H4 ⑲
Mirko Stocchetto, Bar Basso's owner since 1967, is credited with introducing cocktails to bars in Milan (before then, they were available only in hotels). Stocchetto and his son Maurizio still enjoy coming up with interesting concoctions. The house special is the Negroni Sbagliato ('Incorrect Negroni'), made with *spumante* (sparkling white wine) instead of gin.

La Belle Aurore
Via Abamonti 1, at via Castel Morrone (02 2940 6212). Bus 60, 62/tram 5, 11, 23. **Open** 8.30am-2am Mon-Sat. Closed 3wks Aug. **No credit cards**. **Map** p249 H5 ⑳
This Paris-style joint has been a favourite haunt of local writers and artists for over 15 years. Students and intellectuals come at all times of the day to sip coffee or a dry Martini, read the newspapers or add to their *oeuvre*. A gem of a bar.

Lelephant
Via Melzo 22 (02 2951 8768/www.lelephant.it). Metro Porta Venezia/tram 9, 29, 30. **Open** 6.30pm-2am Tue-Sun. Closed 3wks Aug. **No credit cards**. **Map** p249 G5 ㉑
Although first and foremost a gay and lesbian bar (*see p155*), this establishment caters to all. The dirty chairs and peeling paint are worn as a badge of maturity and longevity. Cocktail prices drop to €5 during happy hour (6.30-9.30pm).

Frank
Via Lecco 1 (02 2953 2587). Metro Porta Venezia/ tram 9, 20, 29, 30. **Open** noon-11pm Tue-Sun. Closed 3wks Aug. **Credit** MC, V. **Map** p249 F4/5 ㉒
A cute black and red Porta Venezia outpost with tons of outdoor seating. It's a raw seafood special-ist: tuna tartare, seabass carpaccio and sesame-mar-inated salmon feature on the light lunchtime menu. Post-work drinkers pile in for a glass of *prosecco* and either an oyster, clam or scallop – all €3 each.

HClub (Diana Garden)
Sheraton Diana Majestic Hotel, viale Piave 42 (02 2058 2081/www.sheraton.com/dianamajestic). Metro Porta Venezia/tram 9, 20, 29, 30. **Open** 10am-1am daily. **Credit** AmEx, DC, MC, V. **Map** p249 G5 ㉓
The celebrated bar of the Sheraton Diana Majestic (*see p44*) is something of a hotspot for the Milanese fashion elite, who get to sip aperitifs while gazing at the catwalk shows that are staged inside during Fashion Week. In summer you can sit in the garden (its themed decor changes each season); the white cowhide rocking chairs for two are the seat of choice in winter. Cocktails are €10 or over, so not cheap.

Nottingham Forest
Viale Piave1 (02 798 311/www.nottingham-forest. com). Metro Palestro/bus 54, 61/tram 9, 20, 29, 30. **Open** 7pm-2am Tue-Sat; 6pm-1am Sun. Closed Aug. **No credit cards**. **Map** p249 G6 ㉔
This joint is very proud to be included in a recent selection of the world's 50 best bars. Barman Dario Comino is a master mixologist, whose creations may embarrass a non-Italian palate not used to the ritu-al cocktail hour. Tiny, kooky, and a rite of passage for any serious cocktail enthusiast.

Gelaterie

La Bottega del Gelato
Via Giovan Battista Pergolesi 3 (02 2940 0076). Metro Caiazzo or Loreto/bus 91, 92, 93. **Open** 9am-midnight Tue, Thur-Sun. Closed 3wks Aug. **No credit cards**. **Map** p249 H3 ㉕
In the up-and-coming zone between corso Buenos Aires and Stazione Centrale, this slightly scruffy place serves some of the tastiest ice-cream in the city. Portions from €3 include pink grapefruit, avocado and creamy pine nut.

Porta Romana & South

Cafés & bars

Le Biciclette
Via Torti, at via Conca del Naviglio (02 839 4177/ www.lebiciclette.com). Metro Sant'Ambrogio/bus 94/ tram 2, 3, 14. **Open** 6pm-2am Mon-Sat; 12.30-4pm, 6pm-2am Sun. Closed 3wks Aug. **Credit** AmEx, DC, MC, V. **Map** p250 C8 ㉖
This vibrant bar and restaurant, which opened in a former bike shop in 1998, is one of the core nightlife spots between the *navigli* and *centro*. Le Biciclette prides itself particularly on its art shows and its renowned Sunday brunch. The happy hour buffet (6-9.30pm) is abundant, the Wi-Fi is free and should you get into a creative mood; there's a vending machine selling Lomo cameras near the entrance.

Eat, Drink, Shop

Caffè della Pusterla

Via De Amicis 22 (02 8940 2146). Metro Sant'Ambrogio/bus 94/tram 2, 3, 14. **Open** 7am-2am Mon-Sat; 9am-2am Sun. **Credit** AmEx, MC, V. **Map** p250 C8 ㉗

Known for its excellent wine list, this establishment caters to an assorted clientele throughout the day, with families and locals giving way to a younger crowd in the evening. Happy hour (6-9pm) is a steal: €5.50 gets you a drink and unlimited trips to the tasty buffet bar.

Cucchi

Corso Genova 1 (02 8940 9793). Bus 94/tram 2, 14. **Open** 7am-10pm Tue-Sun. Closed 3wks Aug. **Credit** MC, V. **Map** p250 C8 ㉘

Cucchi has been family-run since 1936, and its bowtie-clad waiters serve up elegant fruit-filled tartlets, *cannoncini* (little pastry 'cannons' stuffed with custard), and savoury snippets like *pizzette* (tiny pizzas). A favourite stop for Milanese post-Sunday mass, it's a lovely spot at which to grab a table in the shade and watch the world go by. *Photo p114.*

Cuore

Via G Mora 3 (02 5810 5126/www.cuore.it). Bus 94/tram 2, 3, 14. **Open** 6pm-2am daily. Closed 2wks Aug. **No credit cards**. **Map** p250 C8 ㉙

Cuore (heart) is tucked away in a quiet little street near the *colonne di San Lorenzo* on Porta Ticinese, with a giant stencil of Roberta Indiana's 'Love' gracing the bar's façade. It features ever-changing decor based around unusual artworks, and an entertainment programme including international DJs and bands. The atmosphere is fun and friendly, and it's a popular spot with students and professionals.

Fitzcarraldo

Via Filippetti 41 (02 5843 0665/www.spazio fitzcarraldo.com). Metro Porta Romana/tram 9, 29, 30. **Open** 6pm-2am Tue-Sun (gallery 11am-7.30pm Tue-Sat). Closed Aug. **Credit** MC, V. **Map** p251 F9 ㉚

Fitzcarraldo is housed in a beautiful old furniture shop, and most of the colonial-style pieces and accessories you see are still for sale. The huge space is full of comfortable velour sofas and low tables, and there's a gorgeous 1960s wooden bar. Since it's in a semi-subterranean space, Fitzcarraldo is a good pick if you're looking to find some shelter from Milan's more extreme weather.

Fresco Art

Viale Monte Nero 23 (02 5412 4675). Metro Porta Romana/tram 9, 16, 29, 30. **Open** 8am-2am Tue-Sun. Closed 1wk Aug. **Credit** MC, V. **Map** p251 G8 ㉛

Fresco Art is a favourite of trendy young lawyers and students from the nearby European Design Institute. It's a good place for a coffee in the morning – their *brioche* are outstanding, and you'll have enough space to check out the temporary artworks on the walls; but the best time to visit is during evening *aperitivo* (6-9pm).

Coffee & Ice Cream.

Gold Bar

Piazza Risorgimento (02 757 777/www.
dolcegabbanagold.it). Bus 54, 61/tram 9, 29, 30.
Open 8am-2am daily. Closed Aug. **Credit** AmEx,
DC, MC, V. **Map** p251 G6 ❷
Dolce & Gabbana's latest flamboyant flourish, Gold
lives up to its name with a vengeance. Mirrored and
metallic surfaces dominate the whole place: take a
trip to the loos if you've ever wondered what bamboo looks like plated with gold. With D&G HQ
around the corner, models and aftershow parties
abound. This is the sort of bar where you can't be
too over the top: dress to impress.

Mom Café

Viale Monte Nero 51 (02 5990 1562). Metro
Porta Romana/tram 9, 16, 29, 30. **Open** 7am-
2am Mon-Sat. Closed 2wks Aug. **Credit** MC, V.
Map p251 G7 ❸
If you lived in Milan, this would be your local: Mom
is a perfectly balanced bar. Great drinks, hearty food,
lively tunes and unique decor means it's packed out
night after night. Prices are reasonable, and most of
the customers prefer to spill out into the nearby park,
making it easy to snag a table. *Photo p117.*

Volo

Viale Beatrice d'Este, corner of via Patellani (02
5832 5543/www.volo-milano.com). Metro Porta
Romana/tram 9, 24, 29, 30. **Open** noon-2.45pm,
6pm-2am Mon-Fri; 6pm-2am Sat, Sun. **Credit**
AmEx, DC, MC, V.
Volo is a restaurant as well as a busy bar. Its main
claim to fame is the abundant *aperitivo*, served every
day between 6pm and 9.30pm in the walled garden.
Sip a caipirinha beneath the canopy of trees, or, on
a cooler eve, opt for a bloody mary in the giant glass
gazebo. Free Wi-Fi. *See p118* **Happy days.**

Gelaterie

Umberto

Piazza Cinque Giornate (02 545 8113). Bus 60, 73/
tram 9, 12, 23, 29, 30. **Open** No fixed hours. No
credit cards. Map p251 G7 ❹
This place opens entirely at whim, and is not particularly friendly; but if you're lucky enough to catch
it with the door ajar, be sure to pop inside.
Unchanged for decades – the wood and leather décor
has been carefully preserved – Umberto serves a
maximum of seven traditional flavours, including
two types of cream and a sumptuous dark chocolate.

Sant'Ambrogio & West

Cafés & bars

Bar Magenta

Via Carducci 13 (02 4229 2194/www.bar
magenta.it). Metro Cadorna/bus 58, 94/tram
16, 18, 19. **Open** 8am-2am Mon-Fri; 9am-2am
Sat, Sun. **Credit** MC, V. **Map** p250 C6 ❺

Surprisingly un-Italian, Bar Magenta's wooden interior is more Edwardian London than modern Milan.
Nevertheless, the place is an institution, and one
much loved by young Milanese as well as the expat
community. It has a huge range of beers on tap, and
makes excellent sandwiches.

Biffi

Corso Magenta 87, at piazza Baracco (02 4800 6702/
www.biffipasticceria.it). Metro Conciliazione/bus 67,
68/tram 16, 18. **Open** 6.30am-8.30pm daily. Closed
1wk Aug. **Credit** MC, V. **Map** p250 A6 ❻
One of Milan's historic cafés, Biffi is set in the ritzy
Magenta/Vercelli neighbourhood. The counter is
cosy but never overcrowded, and the tearoom has a
handful of tables for chatting and resting. It's particularly famed for its *panettone*, the Milanese
Christmas cake it has been producing since 1847.

Morgan's

Via Novati 2 (02 867 694). Metro Sant'Ambrogio/
bus 50, 58, 94/tram 2, 14. **Open** 6pm-2am Mon-Sat.
Closed Aug. **Credit** AmEx, DC, MC, V. **Map**
p250 C7 ❼
This is a friendly bar popular with a laid-back thir-
tysomething crowd for its warm, pub-on-a-winter's-
evening interior, and general lack of pretence.
Morgan's is set in one of the more agreeable areas
of the city: the quiet, residential (and very affluent)
backstreets south of piazza Sant'Ambrogio.

Gelaterie

Chocolat

Via Boccaccio 9 (02 4810 0597/www.chocolat
milano.it). Metro Cadorna/bus 199/tram 1, 19,
27. **Open** 7.30am-1am daily. **Credit** AmEx, DC,
MC, V. **Map** p250 C6 ❽
This gorgeous café excels in all things chocolate.
From the huge, sensual mounds of ice-cream in
flavours like chilli chocolate, ginger chocolate,
orange chocolate and amaretto chocolate, to the
tarts, brownies and slabs of chocolate flavoured with
figs, hazelnuts or weirder options including balsamic vinegar, everything is utterly irresistible.

Coffee & Ice Cream

Via Meravigli 16 (02 862 432). Bus 50, 58, 199/
tram 16, 18, 19. **Open** 9am-8pm Mon-Fri; 11.30am-
7.30pm Sat. **No credit cards. Map** p252 C6 ❾
Frequented mainly by brokers from Milan's nearby
stock exchange, this little hole in the wall is known
for its divine pistachio ice-cream. At lunchtime, it's
packed with figure-conscious Milanese crowding in
for pints of fresh fruit topped with yoghurt.

Gelateria Marghera

Via Marghera 33 (02 468 641). Tram 16, 18. **Open**
10am-1am daily. Closed 2wks Jan. **No credit cards.**
One of Milan's best ice-cream parlours, Marghera
offers a mind-boggling array of flavours (the rum
chocolate is one to die for). The high quality of the
product on sale ensures queues and staff too
harassed to offer the most common of courtesies.

Eat, Drink, Shop

Shops & Services

For art school try Florence, for a shopping masterclass hit Milan.

Eat, Drink, Shop

Along with design and finance, fashion is the city's biggest draw. Its influence spreads to the worlds of publishing, dining, partying and commerce, so you'll be hard pressed to avoid it. What's more, people do actually wear the wacky garments you see paraded at the city's twice-yearly fashion weeks: many a Milan street looks like a photo shoot for Italian *Vogue*.

But what's *di moda* in the fashion capital one month becomes 'so last season' the next, which means a wealth of cast-offs at the many outlets and seconds stores; and because styles generally reach London and New York around a year after launch in Italy, if you fly home laden with shopping bags, you'll be up to date for a while yet. Guilds as diverse as jewellers, *pasticcerie* (speciality bakers) and milliners (who derive their name from the city) have catered to a discerning elite for half a millennium, so quality and choice are superb.

FAMOUS NAMES

Today the streets surrounding via Montenapoleone are mostly lined with big-league fashion boutiques. Among others, you'll find renowned home-grown labels such as Armani, Prada, Versace, Dolce & Gabbana, Krizia and Gianfranco Ferré (*see p134* **Rectangle of gold... cards**). Although locals complain that globalisation has made the area bland, the big labels have tried hard to make their Milan flagships memorable: Armani's superstore in via Manzoni (with its café and Nobu restaurant) is their largest in the world, and Gianfranco Ferré's boutique on via Sant'Andrea boasts a spa.

Another historic shopping spot is the **Galleria Vittorio Emanuele II** (*see p55*), the glass-roofed arcade near the Duomo. It opened in 1867, which makes it one of the oldest shopping malls in the world. Prada's flagship store has been in business here since 1913, joined more recently by Louis Vuitton and Gucci.

There are many ways to bag a bargain throughout the city, if you know where to look. Shops selling end-of-season returns, catwalk cast-offs and seconds abound (see p126 **Insider outlets**), as do second-hand and vintage clothes boutiques. You'll also find heart-stopping deals in the markets, from Gucci shoes to cashmere jumpers (*see p139* **The *mercati*'s whiskers**).

Anyone with a big-brand allergy should head to the smaller, more alternative stores on corso di Porta Ticinese or in Brera. Other zones worth a look are corso Vercelli (the western extension of corso Magenta) and the Isola area, behind Stazione Garibaldi. For the Italian version of high-street shopping, try corso Buenos Aires, via Torino or corso Vittorio Emanuele; many of the shoppers on these streets may still look intimidatingly smart, but head-to-toe Versace is not obligatory.

OPENING HOURS

Traditionally, Tuesday to Saturday retail hours are 9.30am-12.30pm and 3.30-7.30pm, with a half day on Monday (3.30-7.30pm). The majority of shops still close on Sundays, though fashion stores stay open during the major fairs, and, in these cash-starved times, at other times throughout the year. Few shops in central Milan still close for lunch, but much of the city shuts down in August. Sales take place at state-appointed times in January and July.

TAX REFUNDS

Non-EU residents can claim back the value added tax ('IVA' in Italian) on purchases totalling over €154.94 from a single store that displays a 'Tax-Free Shopping' sign. To do so, ask for a 'VAT back' form at the moment of purchase, keep your receipts, and pack your unworn new goods at the top of your suitcase (you may have to show them). Then have the receipts stamped at customs when you leave Italy, and hand over your 'VAT back' paperwork. Next, head for a refund centre (those at Malpensa and Linate airports are open 7am-11pm and 6am-10pm daily, respectively); or post the paperwork when you get back home. There's also a tax-free centre on the basement level of **La Rinascente** department store (*see p126*), where you can get your cash back before leaving the country (9am-10pm Mon-Sat, 10am-10pm Sun). However, you'll still have to queue to clear documents at the airport. For more details, go to www.globalrefund.com.

Antiques

Via Pisacane (metro Porta Venezia) is home to more than 30 antiques shops, selling everything from ceramics to timepieces. Shops dealing in furnishings from the 16th to the 19th centuries

Quadrilatero d'Oro. *See p134.*

AREA MARONCELLI DISTRICT
Galleries/stores • Design • Art • Modernism • Fashion • Jewellery

GALLERIA M. K.
via P. Maroncelli, 2 - 20154 Milano
tel/fax +39 02 655 1035
email: info@galleriamk.com
Mon - Sat 14.30 - 19.00 Closed August
Specialised in 20th century art and design - particularly
from the 40s to the 80s.

GALLERIA ANNA PATRASSI
via P. Maroncelli, 3 - 20154 Milano
tel/fax: + 39 02 4547 2889
e-mail: anna_patrassi@fastwebnet.it
Mon - Sat 14.30 - 19.00 Closed August
Unique collections of 20th Century Interiors.

ISABELLA TONCHI
via P. Maroncelli, 5 - 20154 Milano
tel: +39 02 2900 8589 fax: +39 02 659 7958
email: info@isabellatonchi.com
www.isabellatonchi.com
Mon - Sat 9.00 - 13.00/14.00 - 18.00 Closed August
Women Collections.

AMALGAMA DESIGN GALLERY
via T. Speri, 1 corner via Maroncelli - 20154 Milano
tel: +39 02 3651 4665 fax: +39 02 937 3346
email: info@amalgama.net www.amalgama.net
Mon 15.00 - 19.00 Tue - Sat 11.00 - 19.00
Closed August
Eclectic accessories, lights and furnishing components,
hand made by Italian Designers.

AGATHA RUIZ DE LA PRADA
via P. Maroncelli, 5 - 20154 Milano
tel: +39 02 2901 4456 fax: +39 02 2900 8590
e-mail: milano@agatharuizdelaprada.com
www.agatharuizdelaprada.com
Tues - Sat 11.00 - 19.00 Closed August
Agatha's colourful collections for women and kids.

EDIZIONI GALLERIA PAOLA COLOMBARI
via P. Maroncelli, 10 - 20154 Milano
tel: +39 02 2900 1551 fax: +39 02 2900 2533
email: edizionigalleriacolombari@gmail.com
www.artnet.com/edizionigalleriacolombari.html
Mon - Fri 10.00 - 19.00 Sat by appointment only
Closed August
Specialised in contemporary avantgarde design and art.

GALLERIA ROSSELLA COLOMBARI
via P. Maroncelli, 10 - 20154 Milano
tel: +39 02 2900 1189 fax: +39 02 2900 2533
email: galleria.colombari@libero.it
www.artnet.com/galleriacolombari.html
Mon - Fri 10.00 - 19.00 Sat 10.00 - 13.00
Closed August
Specialised in Modernism and 20th Century
Italian Designers.

STEFANIA CARRERA
via P. Maroncelli 10 - 20154 Milano
tel: +39 02 3453 5021 fax: +39 02 3453 4263
email: ufficiostile@stefaniacarrera.com
www.stefaniacarrera.com
Mon - Fri 9.30 - 18.30 Closed August
Showroom sells exclusive clothing from the Stefania
Carrera collections.

WUNDERKAMMER STUDIO INTERIOR DESIGN
via P. Maroncelli 12 - 20154 Milano
Tel: +39 02 4549 6229
email: info@wunderkammerstudio.it
www.wunderkammerstudio.it
Mon - Fri 10.30 - 13.00/15.00 - 18.30 Sat by
appointment only Closed August
Exclusive contemporary design by Claudia and
Mattia Frignani.

TALLULAH STUDIO INTERIORS
via P. Maroncelli 12 - 20154 Milano
tel: +39 02 3657 9955
www.tallulahstudio.it
Mon 15.30 - 19.30 Tues - Sat 10.30 - 19.30
August Closed
The gallery exhibits an unexpected contemporary
design collection.

ARZIGOGOLO
via P. Maroncelli, 11 - 20154 Milano
tel: +39 347 435 5301
www.arzigogolo.it
Tues - Sat 10:30 - 13:30 / 15:00 - 19:00 Closed August
Jewellery, bracelets, leather bags and an exclusive
collection of skirts.

GALLERIA VINCIANA
via P. Maroncelli, 13 - 20154 Milano
tel/fax: +39 02 2900 1116 +39 02 659 9177
e-mail: vinciana@tin.it
Mon - Fri 10.00 - 12.30/16.00 - 19.00 Closed August
The Gallery specialises in modern and
contemporary art.

LABO.ART
via P. Maroncelli, 14 - 20154 Milano
tel: +39 02 3652 3461
email: milano@laboart.com
www.laboart.com
Mon 15.00 - 19.30 Thurs - Sat 11.00 - 19.30
Closed August

LABO.ART GERMANY
Linienstrasse 113 - 10115 Berlin - Mitte
tel: +49 30 2198 0663
Mon - Sat 15.00 - 19.00
Fashionable stylist designs by Ludovica Diligu
combining cotton and jersey.

are located in several ancient streets that lie to the west of the Duomo: via Lanzone, via Caminadella, via San Giovanni sul Muro and via Santa Marta. The most prestigious (and expensive) antiques dealers have stores in the centre (try via Manzoni) and in the Brera area. For bargains (as well as the occasional rip-off), check out the canalside antiques market along the Naviglio Grande (*see p139* **The** *mercati***'s whiskers**).

Books & stationery

American Bookstore

Via Camperio 16, Largo Cairoli, North (02 878 920). Metro Cairoli/bus 50, 58, 61/tram 1, 4, 27. **Open** 1.30-7pm Mon; 10.30am-7pm Tue-Sat. **Credit** AmEx, MC, V. **Map** p252 D6.

This little store supplies a good range of popular English-language novels. Even better is its used book section, sold at €2.90 apiece.

Feltrinelli International

Piazza Cavour 1, North (02 659 5644/www.la feltrinelli.it). Metro Turati/bus 61, 94, 200/tram 1, 2. **Open** 9am-7.30pm Mon-Fri; 10am-7.30pm Sat. **Credit** AmEx, DC, MC, V. **Map** p249 E5.

This central outpost of one of Italy's leading book chains is one of the city's best stores for titles in English, including an excellent pick of travel books. It also stocks books in Spanish, French, German, Portuguese and Russian, and a large range of international magazines and DVDs.
Other locations throughout the city.

Libreria Babele

Via San Nicolao 10, West (02 3656 1149/www. libreriababele.it). Metro Cadorna/bus 50, 58, 94/ tram 1, 16, 27. **Open** 11.30am-7.30pm Tue-Sat. Closed 2wks Aug. **Credit** MC, V. **Map** p250 C6.

Milan's leading gay and lesbian bookshop stocks thousands of titles, plus magazines, postcards and DVDs in Italian and English. It hosts exhibitions and cultural events, and is a great place at which to learn about club nights and activities throughout the city.

Messaggerie Musicali

Corso Vittorio Emanuele, at Galleria del Corso 4, Centre (02 760 551/www.messaggeriemusicali.it). Metro Duomo/bus 54, 60, 61, 73/tram 12, 23, 27. **Open** 1-8.30pm Mon; 10am-11pm Tue-Sun. **Credit** AmEx, DC, MC, V. **Map** p251 E6/p252 E6.

This large, four-level book and music store has a range of English-language volumes on the first floor, plus CDs and DVDs. There's also a ticket office for concerts and other events, and a vast selection of international press.

Milano Libri

Via Verdi 2, at piazza della Scala, Centre (02 875 871/www.milanolibri.net). Metro Duomo or Montenapoleone/tram 1, 2. **Open** 3-7.30pm Mon; 10.30am-7.30pm Tue-Sat. Closed 2wks Aug. **Credit** AmEx, DC, MC, V. **Map** p252 E6.

Fashion fiends: head upstairs to browse Milan's finest selection of design and textile tomes. Rumour has it that Milan fashion's finest come here for inspiration. There's also an extensive range of photography and fine art catalogues.

Mondadori

Piazza del Duomo 1, Centre (02 454 4110/www. negozimondadori.it). Metro Duomo/tram 12, 16, 24. **Open** 9am-11pm daily. **Credit** AmEx, DC, MC, V. **Map** p252 E7.

Opened in April 2007, this massive complex includes a café (open from 7am), internet points (€3/hr) and a tiny but fabulous corner reading room on the third floor. Great for design and architecture books and international press.

Panton's English Bookshop

Via Mascheroni 12 (entrance in via Ariosto), West (02 469 4468/www.englishbookshop.it). Metro Conciliazione/bus 61, 169. **Open** 9.30am-7.30pm Mon-Sat. Closed 3wks Aug. **Credit** MC, V. **Map** p248 A5.

Founded in 1979, this shop boasts one of the city's widest choices of English-language fiction and non-fiction. There are also English-language DVDs, audiobooks, rare antiquarian history and travel books, and an extensive children's section, as well as a noticeboard for expat community postings.

Papier

Via San Maurilio 4, off piazza Borromeo, West (02 865 221). Metro Duomo or Missori/tram 2, 3, 15. **Open** 2.30-7pm Mon; 10.30am-1.30pm, 2.30-7pm Tue-Fri; 10am-1pm, 3-7pm Sat. Closed 3wks Aug. **Credit** MC, V. **Map** p252 D7.

From handmade papers to coloured envelopes, Papier stocks the gamut of stationery delights, as well as stone vases, soft leather bags and a selection of odd gadgets such as wind thermometers. The store also supplies card for wedding invitations, and all sorts of material for tiny bomboniere sacks (sugar-coated almonds handed out at weddings).

White Star Adventure

Piazza Meda, on the corner of Piazza Belgioioso, Centre (02 8905 1500/www.wsadventure.it). Metro Duomo/bus 54, 61/tram 12, 23, 27. **Open** 9am-9pm Mon-Fri; 9am-10pm Sat. Closed 2wks Aug. **Credit** AmEx, DC, MC, V. **Map** p252 E6.

This travel agency, café and shop stocks the city's finest range of travel books, the bulk of them in English. A portion of the basement is also devoted to travel accessories and gadgets, including luggage, lightweight clothes, maps and miniature napkins that expand when you add water.

Department stores

Coin

Piazza V Giornate 1A, East (02 5519 2083/www. coin.it). Bus 60, 73, 169/tram 9, 12, 23, 27, 29, 30. **Open** 10am-8pm Mon-Fri, Sun; 10am-8.30pm Sat. **Credit** AmEx, DC, MC, V. **Map** p251 G7.

Eat, Drink, Shop

Insider outlets

The Milanese joke that only tourists shop at the Prada flagship store (*see p55*) in the Galleria Vittorio Emanuele II. Locals, on the other hand, prefer the city's many outlet stores, and are prepared to elbow their way through rack after rack of cut-price catwalk fashions to find the best bargains.

Such treasure troves are packed full of end-of-season shop and warehouse returns, stock from boutiques that have closed down, and some factory seconds. There's one drawback: even at discounts of 50-70 per cent, the price tags can still provoke the occasional 'Ouch!' Also, bear in mind that refunds are pretty much unheard of, so try before you buy.

Try the outlets around the corso Vittorio Emanuele II. They employ none too subtle marketing gimmicks to ratchet up the thrill of the hunt, like letting a queue form outside the store, or sealing your handbag inside a special security bag so you're not tempted to snaffle any of the awesome bargains. Serious shopaholics should invest in a copy of the factory outlets bible *Scoprioccasioni* (www.scoprioccasioni.it; also available in English at Milan's major bookstores), which lists over 1,000 reputable establishments.

Among Milan's best known and longest established outlets is **Il Salvagente** ('the lifesaver'; *see p130*), which has three floors of top stuff for men and women, all carefully arranged by size and colour; for children there's a separate location called **Salvagente Bimbi** (*see p130*). Equally worthwhile bargains can be found at discount outlets with more convenient, central locations – places like **Dmagazine Outlet** (*see p130*), wedged between the full-price stores on the city's main shopping drag. It's small, hot and hectic, with some pricey women's lines (€500 per item for the likes of Miu Miu and Marni) for as little as 20 per cent of their original value. Be prepared to dig deep; for men's lines it's best to try elsewhere.

Basement (*see p130*) – housed, as the name suggests, in a cellar – is for women's fashion only. It caters to a more upmarket shopper, and is more boutique, less snakepit. Come here for price slashes of 50-70 per cent on brands including Dolce & Gabbana, Prada and YSL.

Vogue readers on a budget should visit the **10 Corso Como Outlet** (*see p130*), a slightly shabbier version of the übercool original store (*see p129*), with endless racks of mostly black clothes by Helmut Lang, Chloé, Comme des Garçons et al. But even with prices slashed by half, it's expensive.

Many tourist offices around the lakes keep flyers handy for the big out-of-town outlets. These have many more discounted brand shops under one roof: one example is the mega 250-store **Fox Town** (+41 (0)848 828 888, www.foxtown.ch) in Mendrisio, just across the Swiss border from Lago di Como.

One final tip: Milan's end-of-season sales, strictly sanctioned by the local government for a few weeks each January and July, are a bargain hunter's heaven.

This eight-storey department store caters to the refined Milanese taste for classic, reasonable quality, good value clothing and accessories for men, women and children, with most of the big-name brands represented. It also sells homewares, which is where you'll find the food hall from Eataly, the doyens of the Slow Food movement (*see p96*), cosmetics and shoes. There's the recently renovated Globe restaurant on the top floor, as well as two bars, should you start to flag.

Other locations piazza Loreto 16, East (02 2611 6131); piazzale Cantore 12, South (02 5810 4385); corso Vercelli 30-32, West (02 4399 0001).

La Rinascente

Piazza Duomo, Centre (02 88 521/www.rinascente. it). Metro Duomo/bus 54, 60, 65/tram 12, 23, 27. **Open** 10am-9pm daily. **Credit** AmEx, DC, MC, V. **Map** p251 E7/p252 E7.

This eight-floor colossus (part of a nationwide chain) sells nearly everything you can think of, from lingerie to colourful ceramics. The top floor has a tax-free shopping information point, a branch of chic hairdresser's Aldo Coppola (*see p136*), a branch of mozzarella 'sushi bar' Obika, a brand-new 'wellness lounge', and an indoor-outdoor café where you can sip hot chocolate while admiring the gargoyles on

the Duomo's roof. Most of the store was renovated during the summer of 2008; its former mall vibe has been replaced by a boutique feel. There's a passageway on the first floor to La Rinascente's trendy teenage department around the corner.
Other locations viale Certosa, North (02 326 7051).

Dry-cleaning & laundry

Ondablu
Via delle Rimembranze di Lambrate 13, East (no phone/www.ondablu.com). Bus 54, 73/tram 23. **Open** 8am-10pm daily. **No credit cards.**
Coin-operated launderette with washers and dryers.
Other locations throughout the city.

Tintoria Alberti
Piazza Castello 2, Centre (02 8901 7677/www. tintoriaalberti.it). Metro Cairoli or Lanza/bus 50, 57, 58, 61/tram 1, 3, 4, 7, 14, 19, 27. **Open** 8.30am-12.30pm, 3-7pm Mon-Fri; 8.30am-12.30pm Sat. Closed 3wks Aug. **No credit cards. Map** p250 C6/p252 C6.
Big-name designers and well-dressed Milanese all rely on this spot. It was one of the city's first dry-cleaners, and has been in business since 1945.

Fashion

Bags & leather goods

Coccinelle
Via Bigli 28, at via Manzoni, Centre (02 7602 8161/ www.coccinelle.it). Metro Montenapoleone/tram 1, 2. **Open** 10am-7pm Mon-Sat; 11am-7pm Sun. **Credit** AmEx, DC, MC, V. **Map** p251 E6/p252 E6.
This outpost of the Parma-based leather goods chain is one of the best stocked in Milan. Dive in for everything from classic wallets in pretty pastels to handbags with fringes, studs and whatever bits and bobs the fashion crowd demands this season – all at prices that won't make you blanch.
Other locations corso Buenos Aires 16, East (02 2040 4755); corso Genova 6, South (02 8942 1347).

Cut
Corso di Porta Ticinese 58, South (02 839 4135). Metro Porta Genova/tram 2, 3, 14. **Open** 3-7.30pm Mon; 10.30am-1.30pm, 3-7.30pm Tue-Sat. Closed Aug. **Credit** AmEx, DC, MC, V. **Map** p250 C8.
Cut sells high-quality artisan-made leather garments for men and women (no tacky leather thongs); you can also have items made to measure.

Furla
Corso Vittorio Emanuele, corner of Via San Paolo, Centre (02 796 943/www.furla.com). Metro Montenapoleone/tram 1, 2. **Open** 10.30am-7.30pm Mon-Sat; 10.30am-2pm, 3-7.30pm Sun. **Credit** AmEx, DC, MC, V. **Map** p252 E6.
High-end leather bags, soft sacks, wallets and luggage by the famous Bologna-based leather goods company. Furla also stacks a good range of affordable trinkets, including scarves and umbrellas.

Other locations corso Buenos Aires, corner via Omboni 2, East (02 204 3319); corso Vercelli 11, West (02 4801 4189).

Luisa Cevese Riedizioni
Via San Maurilio 3, off piazza Borromeo, West (02 801 088/www.riedizioni.com). Metro Duomo or Missori/tram 2, 3, 15. **Open** 10am-2pm, 3-7pm Tue-Sat. Closed Aug. **Credit** MC, V. **Map** p252 D7.
This tiny store stocks gorgeous and unusual bags, wallets and poufs, created by pressing fabrics and metallic threads between layers of translucent plastic. All items are made from recycled textiles.

Mandarina Duck
Corso Vercelli 20, West (02 4800 7264/www. mandarinaduck.com). Tram 16, 18. **Open** 10am-7.30pm Mon-Sat. Closed 2wks Aug. **Credit** AmEx, DC, MC, V. **Map** p250 A6.
Another world-class Italian brand from Bologna, Mandarina Duck makes all sorts of bags and backpacks in leather and unusual fabrics.

Boutiques

Abside
Vicolo Santa Caterina 1, South (02 5831 5234/ www.ab-side.it). Metro Missori or Crocetta/tram 16, 24. **Open** 10am-7pm Mon-Sat. Closed 3wks Aug. **Credit** MC, V. **Map** p251 E8.
Tucked round a corner just off corso di Porta Romana, Abside stocks a cool mix of own-brand clothes and jewellery, as well as unique pieces by other Italian and European designers. Pick up patchwork belts, felt bags and funky earrings made from old French francs; prices are very reasonable.

Antonioli
Via Pasquale Paoli 1, at ripa di Porta Ticinese, South (02 3656 6494/www.antonioli.eu). Metro Porta Genova/bus 47, 74/tram 2. **Open** 3-7.30pm Mon; 11am-7.30pm Tue-Sun. Closed 1wk Aug. **Credit** AmEx, DC, MC, V. **Map** p250 B9.
This place is a hit with the international fashion crowd. Many of the clothes for men and women are offbeat and deconstructed, and the decor in this former cinema – polished concrete floors and scraped-down walls – has been designed to match. Labels include Dries Van Noten, Dsquared2 and Ring, with retro helmets by Ruby.

Biffi
Corso Genova 6, South (02 8311 6052/www.biffi. com). Metro Sant'Ambrogio/bus 94/tram 2, 14. **Open** 3-7.30pm Mon; 9.30am-1.30pm, 3-7.30pm Tue-Sat. Closed 2wks Aug. **Credit** AmEx, DC, MC, V. **Map** p250 C8.
A Milanese institution for men's and women's classic designer labels, Biffi also stocks the mildly wild trend pieces of the season. Among the designers represented here are Gucci, Fendi, Stella McCartney, Marc Jacobs and John Galliano. Biffi has also opened a slightly more casual sportswear store just across the street (same opening hours).

The best guides to enjoying London life

(but don't just take our word for it)

'More than 700 places where you can eat out for less than £20 a head... a mass of useful information in a genuinely pocket–sized guide'

Mail on Sunday

'Armed with a tube map and this guide there is no excuse to find yourself in a duff bar again'

Evening Standard

'I'm always asked how I keep up to date with shopping and services in a city as big as London. This guide is the answer'

Red Magazine

'Get the inside track on the capital's neighbourhoods'

Independent on Sunday

'A treasure trove of treats that lists the best the capital has to offer'

The People

Rated
'Best Restaurant Guide'

Sunday Times

TIME OUT GUIDES
WRITTEN BY
LOCAL EXPERTS
timeout.com/shop

10 Corso Como

Corso Como 10, North (02 2900 2674/www. 10corsocomo.com). Metro Garibaldi/bus 52, 70, 94. **Open** *3.30-7.30pm Mon; 10.30am-7.30pm Tue, Fri-Sun; 10.30am-9pm Wed, Thur.* **Credit** *AmEx, DC, MC, V.* **Map** *p248 D3.*

This emporium is owned by former Italian *Vogue* editor Carla Sozzani. Prices are not for the faint-hearted, but the design overload is certainly a sight to behold. The merchandise includes men's and women's lines, accessories, shoes, bags, homeware, books and CDs. There's a café/restaurant (*see p117*), photography gallery (*see p152*) and a slick B&B (*see p43*). Shoppers on a budget take note: a nearby outlet store sells previous season's stock at much reduced prices (*see p126* **Insider outlets**).

Zap!

Via Solferino 2, North (02 653 362). Bus 61, 94/tram 3, 4. **Open** *3-7pm Mon; 10am-1pm, 3-7pm Tue-Sat. Closed Aug.* **Credit** *AmEx, DC, MC, V.* **Map** *p248 D4.*

This new city centre address is much smaller than its previous incarnation, although 'mini Zap' still stocks a good range of trendy labels, including Blumarine, Kookai and Moschino lingerie, as well as glittery jewellery by Tarina Tarantino, diamanté tiaras and tableware by Hello Kitty. **Other locations** via Quintiliano 33, South (02 5801 6368).

Independent designers

Anybody who's somebody in the fashion world has a retail foothold in Milan's fashion heartland (*see p134* **Rectangle of gold... cards**). There are the global names, of course, but the Milan-based designers below have their own following.

Anna Fabiano

Corso di Porta Ticinese 40, South (02 5811 2348/ www.annafabiano.com). Metro Sant'Ambrogio/ bus 94/tram 3. **Open** *3.30-7.30pm Mon; 10.30am 1.30pm, 2.30-7.30pm Tue-Fri; 10.30am-7.30pm Sat. Closed 3wks Aug.* **Credit** *AmEx, DC, MC, V.* **Map** *p250 C8.*

This is the sole outlet for clothes and accessories by Fabiano, whose quirky lines include hand-painted, full 1950s-style skirts and beautifully tailored jackets with patchwork inserts on the collar turn-ups. She was formerly a designer for Fiorucci, and her creations have a similar playful flair.

Apolide by Stephan Janson

Via Goldoni 21, East (02 752 6171/www.stephan janson.com). Bus 54, 60, 61, 62. **Open** *10am-7pm Mon-Fri. Closed Aug.* **Credit** *AmEx, DC, MC, V.* **Map** *p249 H6.*

A French designer based in Milan for over 20 years, Janson sells his flowing evening dresses, swirling capes, maxi-dresses and loose leggings at this out-of-the-way shop, set in a garden. It's worth the hike.

Isabella Tonchi

Via Maroncelli 5, North (02 2900 8589/www.isabella tonchi.com). Bus 52, 70, 94/tram 3, 4, 7, 11. **Open** *10am-7pm Mon-Sat. Closed Aug.* **Credit** *AmEx, DC, MC, V.* **Map** *p248 D3.*

A former designer for Miu Miu, Isabella Tonchi opened this elegant shop to showcase her linear, elegant – but never dull – pieces (pink pea jackets, pleated skirts and 1960s-inspired printed fabrics). In summertime, it's a good place to pick up cut-price swimming costumes and sandals.

Love Therapy by Elio Fiorucci

Galleria Passarella 1, at corso Europa, East (02 7639 0631/www.lovetherapy.it). Metro San Babila/bus 54, 60, 61, 73/tram 12, 27. **Open** *10am-8pm Mon-Sat; 1-8pm Sun.* **Credit** *AmEx, DC, MC, V.* **Map** *p251 F6/p252 F6.*

When Milan's famed Fiorucci store closed down in 2003 (its premises taken over by the city's first H&M), it seemed like the end of an era. But the label immortalised (with Halston and Gucci) in a Sister Sledge song lives on at this small shop. The kitsch-cool pieces – T-shirts adorned with Fiorucci's famous angel motifs, dwarf-themed snow globes, fluorescent litter bins, fuchsia feather handcuffs – remind you why Fiorucci was a hit in the first place.

Jewellery

Anaconda

Via Bergamini 7, South (02 5830 3668). Bus 54, 199, 200/tram 12, 15, 27. **Open** *11am-7pm Tue-Sat. Closed Aug, 2wks Dec-Jan.* **Credit** *AmEx, DC, MC, V.* **Map** *p252 E7.*

Want to wow? Follow those in the know to the city's jewellery show-stopper. Monica Rossi mixes antique gems and modern techniques, with ethereal results.

Bliss

Piazza Duomo 25, Centre (02 805 4565/www.bliss. it). Metro Duomo/tram 1, 2, 3, 12, 14, 16, 24, 27. **Open** *10am-7pm daily.* **Credit** *AmEx, DC, MC, V.* **Map** *p251 E7/p252 E7.*

Bliss is fine jeweller Damiani's lower-priced line. Pieces for men and women range from subtle classics to fashion-led items like starburst earrings and Italian flag pendants, flecked with diamond chips.

DoDo

Corso Venezia 8, Centre (02 7631 7581/www.parla condodo.com). Metro San Babila/bus 54, 60, 65/ tram 12, 27. **Open** *3-7pm Mon; 10am-7pm Tue-Sat. Closed 2wks Aug.* **Credit** *AmEx, DC, MC, V.* **Map** *p251 F6/p252 F6.*

In 1995, Milan-based jeweller Pomellato launched DoDo, a range of whimsical yellow-gold charms shaped like animals, birds and flowers. A staunch supporter of the WWF, DoDo donates a portion of its profits to protecting endangered species. The range is sold in other jewellery and department stores, including Coin and La Rinascente. **Other locations** corso Genova 12, South (02 5810 0015).

Eat, Drink, Shop

Donatella Pellini

Via Manzoni 20, Centre (02 7600 8084). Metro Montenapoleone/tram 1, 2. **Open** 3.30-7.30pm Mon; 9.30am-7.30pm Tue-Sat. Closed Aug. **Credit** AmEx, DC, MC, V. **Map** p249 E6/p252 E6.

Granddaughter of Emma Pellini, the famous costume jewellery designer, Donatella augments her signature glass and synthetic resin pieces with striking baubles and bangles that she has collected on her travels. She also designs hats, scarves and bags.

Granievaghi

Via Lomazzo 11, North (02 3310 6748/www.granievaghi.com). Bus 43, 57, 169/tram 11. **Open** 10.30am-7.30pm Mon-Sat. Closed 2wks Aug. **Credit** AmEx, DC, MC, V. **Map** p248 B3.

For over 15 years, Silvia Corti has been making her necklaces and bracelets at this tiny indigo lab and shop. Her designs are magically simple: raffia thread and coloured beads, often with the addition of bells and fabric flowers. Pricey but unique.

Pianegonda

Via Montenapoleone 6, Centre (02 7600 3038/www.pianegonda.com). Metro San Babila/bus 54, 61. **Open** 10am-7pm Mon-Sat. Closed 1wk Aug. **Credit** AmEx, DC, MC, V. **Map** p251 E6/p252 E6.

These silver and yellow-gold baubles – for men and women – by Franco Pianegonda are out to make a statement. Designs include outsized silver crosses, rings with big hunks of quartz or aquamarine, and chunky silver chains. Pianegonda's fans include Britney Spears and Jennifer Lopez.

Lingerie

How can something so small cost so much? It's worth visiting some of the stores listed below to try and figure out the answer.

Kristina Ti

Via Solferino 18, North (02 653 379/www.kristinati.com). Metro Moscova/bus 43, 61. **Open** 3-7pm Mon; 10am-7pm Tue-Sat. Closed 3wks Aug. **Credit** AmEx, DC, MC, V. **Map** p248 D5.

The best thing to come out of Turin since the Fiat Cinquecento, Kristina Ti's lingerie is delicate almost to the point of fragility. Apart from the almost vanishing lingerie, there's also a super-feminine clothing line and the company's signature 'boudoir bag', as well as a new children's line.

La Perla

Via Montenapoleone 1, East (02 7600 0460/www.laperla.com). Metro San Babila/bus 54, 61. **Open** 3-7pm Mon; 10am-7pm Tue-Sat. **Credit** AmEx, DC, MC, V. **Map** p249 E6/p252 E6.

La Perla's sophisticated lingerie, manufactured in Bologna from the finest fabrics, is flattering and of outstanding quality. The label also makes swimming costumes and glamorous nightwear.

Other locations corso Vercelli 35, West (02 498 7770); Showroom via Tortona 27, West (02 805 3092); Men's via Manzoni 17, Centre (02 805 3092).

Mid-range clothing

Chains such as H&M and Zara have branches throughout the city, but the following Italian brands are far more interesting and often similarly priced.

L'Altramoda

Corso Venezia 5, Centre (02 7602 1117/www.laltramoda.it). Metro San Babila/bus 54, 61. **Open** 10am-7pm Mon-Sat. Closed 3wks Aug. **Credit** AmEx, DC, MC, V. **Map** p249 F6/p252 F6.

This Roman womenswear chain is good for a glam outfit at an affordable price. The label hasn't expanded much beyond the Mediterranean yet, so it's a good one to flaunt back home.

Other locations corso Vercelli 20, West (02 469 9248).

Ethic

Corso di Porta Ticinese 50, South (02 5810 5669/www.ethic.it). Bus 3, 94. **Open** 3.30-7.30pm Mon; 10.30am-2pm, 3-7.30pm Tue-Sat. Closed 3wks Aug. **Credit** AmEx, DC, MC, V. **Map** p250 C8.

Sexy Italian style, created in – yes – an ethically sound way. The label makes almost all stock in Italy (no child labour or sweatshops involved), and any leather used comes from animals destined for eating. It sometimes stocks clothes made by local artist-designer teams.

Other locations corso Garibaldi 34, North (02 805 2284).

Outlet stores

For last season's lines, look no further; *see also p126* **Insider outlets**.

Basement

Via Senato 15, Centre (02 7631 7913). Metro Palestro or Turati/bus 61, 94. **Open** 3-7pm Mon; 10am-7pm Tue-Sat. Closed Aug. **Credit** AmEx, DC, MC, V. **Map** p252 F5.

Dmagazine Outlet

Via Montenapoleone 26, Centre (02 7600 6027/www.dmagazine.it). Metro Montenapoleone/tram 1, 2, 20. **Open** 9.30am-7.45pm daily. **Credit** AmEx, DC, MC, V. **Map** p252 E6.

Il Salvagente

Via Fratelli Bronzetti 16, East (02 7611 0328/www.salvagentemilano.it). Metro Porta Venezia/bus 54, 60, 61, 62, 92/tram 12, 27. **Open** 3-7pm Mon; 10am-12.30pm, 3-7pm Tue, Thur, Fri; 10am-7pm Wed, Sat. Closed Aug. **Credit** AmEx, DC, MC, V. **Map** p251 H7.

Other locations Il Salvagente Bimbi, Via Balzaretti 28, East (02 2668 0764).

10 Corso Como Outlet

Via Tazzoli 3, North (02 2901 5130). Metro Garibaldi/bus 43, 70/tram 11, 29, 30, 33. **Open** 1-7pm Fri; 11am-7pm Sat, Sun. Closed 2wks Aug. **Credit** AmEx, DC, MC, V. **Map** p248 D3.

Eat, Drink, Shop

Where old is best. **Cavelli e Nastri**.

Eat, Drink, Shop

Second-hand & vintage

Cavalli e Nastri
*Via Brera 2, North (02 7200 0449/www.cavallie
nastri.com). Tram 1, 3, 27.* **Open** 3-7.30pm Mon;
10.30am-7.30pm Tue-Sat. Closed 2wks Aug.
Credit AmEx, DC, MC, V. **Map** p252 D5.
Vintage clothing from experts. Each piece in this
tidy collection is in mint condition and selected with
a razor-sharp eye: this is the crème de la crème of
vintage chic. The two via Giacomo Mora branches
stock vintage women's lines, and vintage men's lines
and furniture, respectively.
Other locations via Giacomo Mora 3 & 12, North
(02 8940 9452).

Elizabeth the First
*Alzaia Naviglio Grande 44, South (02 8907 7927/
www.elizabethefirst.com). Metro Porta Genova/bus
47, 74, 169/tram 2, 9.* **Open** 11am-8pm Tue-Sat
(later in summer). Closed Aug. **Credit** AmEx, DC,
MC, V. **Map** p250 C9/10/11.
This tiny shop is stocked with fabulous finds, from
Prada heels and Chinese silk tops to loose Indian
tunics and Gautier blazers.

Franco Jacassi
*Via Sacchi 3, North (02 8646 2076). Metro Lanza/
bus 61/tram 1, 3, 4, 27.* **Open** 10am-1pm, 2-7pm
Mon-Fri. Closed Aug. **Credit** AmEx, MC, V.
Map p252 D6.
A treasure trove of antique clothing, bags, shoes,
hats, buttons, trimmings and rare fashion publications. This is where Milan's big-name designers
come when they need inspiration.

Miss Ghinting
*Via Borsieri, opposite no.16, North (02 668 7112/
www.missghinting.it). Metro Garibaldi/bus 82/tram
4, 7, 11.* **Open** 10am-1pm, 3-7.30pm Tue-Sat. Closed
Aug. **Credit** AmEx, DC, MC, V. **Map** p249 E2.
For that fabulous 1950s look, come to this shop run
by two stylish Milanese 'misses' in the Isola district.
The stock at Miss Ghinting is a well-edited mix of
tailored pieces from that favoured decade, and a few
from the '60s and '70s.

Superfly
*Ripa di Porta Ticinese 27, South (339 579 2838).
Metro Porta Genova/tram 2, 3, 29, 30.* **Open** 11am-
9pm Tue-Sat; 3-7pm Sun. Closed Aug. **Credit** MC, V.
Map p250 A9/B9/C9.
Clubbers will think they've died and gone to disco
diva heaven at Superfly: bell-bottoms, hot pants and
minidresses. On the last Sunday of the month,
there's a Superfly stall at the Mercatone dell'
Antiquariato (11am-7pm). *Photo p133.*

Shoes

Amarena Chic
*Corso di Porta Ticinese 46, South (02 8941 5647/
www.amarenachic.it). Metro Sant'Ambrogio/bus
94/tram 3.* **Open** 3-7.30pm Mon; 11am-7.30pm Tue-
Sat; 4-8pm Sun. Closed 2wks Aug. **Credit** AmEx,
DC, MC, V. **Map** p250 C7/8.
A line of brightly coloured, alternative shoes first
launched in Rome in 2004; the Milan branch opened
in spring 2008. Designs include chunky wedges and
strong but feminine strappy sandals.

Wanted. Jumpers, coats and people with their knickers in a twist.

From the people who feel moved to bring us their old books and CDs, to the people fed up to the back teeth with our politicians' track record on climate change, Oxfam supporters have one thing in common. They're passionate. If you've got a little fire in your belly, we'd love to hear from you. Visit us at **oxfam.org.uk**

Be Humankind  **Oxfam**

Registered charity No. 202918

Les Chaussures Mon Amour

Via Cherubini 3, North (02 4800 0535/www.les chaussures.it). Metro Pagano/bus 61/tram 16, 18. **Open** 3-8pm Mon; 10.30am-8pm Tue-Sat. Closed 3wks Aug. **Credit** AmEx, MC, V. **Map** p248 A6.

This colourful shop sells women's shoes by offbeat brands like Fornarina and Irregular Choice, but the best bargains are the shop's own-label shoes, made in nearby Vigevano – a range that runs from suede pixie boots to patent leather pumps.
Other locations via Nino Bixio, East (02 2953 2226).

Mauro Leone

Corso di Porta Ticinese 60, South (02 8942 9167). Bus 94, 169/tram 2, 3, 9, 14. **Open** 3-7.30pm Mon; 10am-7.30pm Tue-Sat; 2.30-7pm Sun. **No credit cards. Map** p250 C8.

Stocking everything from basic black knee-high boots to rainbow suede ballerine, this tiny shop is always packed with Milanese fashionistas fighting over the latest own-brand styles, all made in Italy. There's also a new, larger store at no.103.

Le Solferine

Via Solferino 3, North (02 655 5352). Metro Moscova/bus 43, 61 **Open** 10am-7.30pm Mon-Sat; 10am-1pm, 2.30-7.30pm Sun. **Credit** AmEx, DC, MC, V. **Map** p248 D5.

Le Solferine has a fine selection of uncommon designer footwear for men and women by the likes of René Caovilla, Ungaro and Emilio Pucci. A good source of special-occasion, super-sexy shoes.

Florists

Foglie, Fiori e Fantasia

Via Brisa 15, West (02 8699 8433). Bus 50, 58/ tram 16, 19. **Open** 9am-1.30pm, 3.30-7.45pm Mon-Fri; 10am-1.30pm, 3.30-7pm Sat. Closed Aug. **Credit** MC, V. **Map** p252 C6/7.

Using chilli peppers, apple apples and hollowed-out coconut shells, this mini-florist puts together some of the most imaginative floral creations in the city.

Food & drink

See also p138 Markets.

Confectionery & cakes

L'Antica Arte del Dolce

Via Anfossi 10, South (02 5519 4448/www.ernst knam.eu). Bus 84, 168/tram 9, 29, 30. **Open** 10am-1pm, 4-8pm Tue-Sat; 10am-1pm Sun. Closed 3wks Aug. **Credit** AmEx, MC, V. **Map** p251 H7.

This is where the fashion crowd comes for a sweet fix. Gourmet cakes, chocolates, biscuits, jams and desserts are whisked up in the kitchens by pastry chef Ernst Knam (who trained under renowned restaurateur Gualtiero Marchesi) and his able team. Among the more daring concoctions are apple and rosemary tart and aubergine and chocolate mousse.

Mercatone dell'Antiquariato. *See p131.*

Giovanni Galli Pasticceria

Corso di Porta Romana 2, South (02 8645 3112/ www.giovannigalli.com). Metro Porta Romana/bus 54, 199, 200/tram 12, 15, 16, 24, 27. **Open** 8.30am-1pm, 2-8pm Mon-Sat; 8.30am-1pm Sun. Closed 3wks Aug. **Credit** AmEx, DC, MC, V. **Map** p251 E7.

Milan's best address for marrons glacés, made daily with fresh chestnuts in Galli's own kitchens, according to its own 1898 recipe. The *alchechengi* (Cape gooseberries dipped in chocolate), and the pralines filled with mint, nougat or orange, are just as good.
Other locations via Victor Hugo 2, Centre (02 8646 4833).

Pasticceria Marchesi

Via Santa Maria alla Porta 11A, West (02 876 730/ www.pasticceriamarchesi.it). Bus 50, 58/tram 16, 19. **Open** 8am-8pm Tue-Sat; 8am-1pm Sun. Closed Aug. **Credit** MC, V. **Map** p250 D6/p252 D6.

In one of Milan's most beautiful buildings, this historic *pasticceria* and bar serves up wonderful old-fashioned cakes filled with chocolate and custard cream. It also sells prettily packaged own-brand chocolates. In the run-up to Christmas, its sought-after panettone are ordered weeks in advance.

Delicatessens

Chiu

Via Pontaccio 5, North (02 805 2296/www.chiusrl.it). Bus 61/tram 3. **Open** 10.30am-3pm, 4.30-6.30pm Mon, Sat; 10.30am-3pm, 4.30-8pm Tue-Fri. Closed Aug. **Credit** MC, V. **Map** p248 D5.

Rectangle of gold... cards

Milan is a haute couture powerhouse, where fashions jump from catwalk to clothes rail in weeks. But unlike the sprawling fashion district in Paris, Milan's boutiques fit into a square: via della Spiga, via Manzoni, via Sant'Andrea, via Montenapoleone (*see map p252*), the so-called Quadrilatero d'Oro ('rectangle of gold').

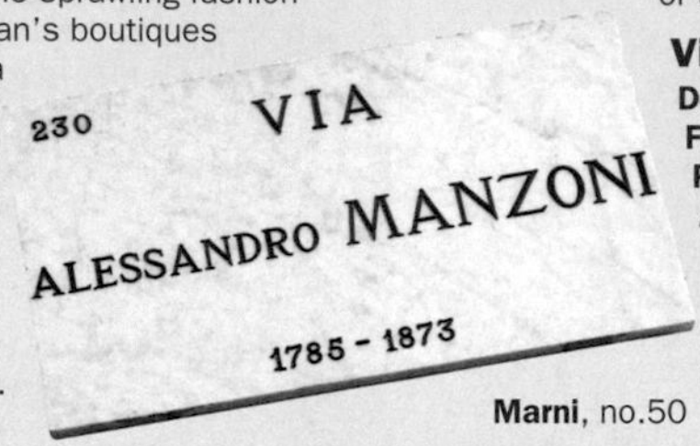

Even if the price tags are larger than your budget, you can spend many a happy hour admiring the window displays. And if you can only just afford €500 on a pair of Miu Miu boots, rest assured: the shopkeepers will happily accept plastic.

Listed below is the crème de la crème of Milan shopping. All are open 3-7pm on Monday and 10am-7pm from Tuesday to Saturday; some open for longer. And when you've shopped your heart out, **Caffè Baglioni**, with its private entrance at via della Spiga 6, is a chic spot to

stop. The area is best reached from metro Montenapoleone or San Babila, by bus 61 or 94, or tram 1, 2 or 20.

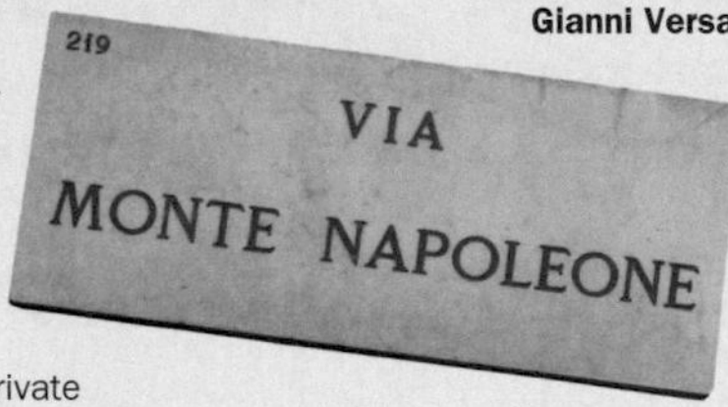

Via della Spiga
D&G accessories, no.2
Fendi, no.9
Prada accessories, no.18
Armani accessories, no.19
D&G woman, no.26
Just Cavalli, no.30
Byblos, no.33
Roberto Cavalli, no.42
Marni, no.50

Via Sant'Andrea
Missoni, no.2
Trussardi, no.5
Kenzo, no.9
Giorgio Armani, no.9
Chanel, no.10
Moschino, no.12
Gianni Versace, no.14
Gianfranco Ferré, no.15
Barbara Bui, no.17
Miu Miu, no.21
Hermès, no.21
Prada sport, no.21

Via Montenapoleone
La Perla, no.1
Louis Vuitton, no.2

The city's top stop for mozzarella di bufala, made from the Campania region's finest buffalo milk. If you're not sure what you want, staff will let you sample different types before you buy.

Pastificcio Pellegrini
Via Cadore 48, South (02 5518 4207). Bus 62/ tram 16. **Open** 3.30-7.30pm Mon; 10.30am-12.30pm, 3.30-7.30pm Tue-Sat. **Credit** MC, V. **Map** p251 H7/8.
This family-run shop has been making delectable pasta for years. Ravioli fillings are seasonal – anything from artichokes to porcini mushrooms – and there's usually a fresh cake or two on the counter.

Peck
Via Spadari 9, Centre (02 802 3161/www.peck.it). Metro Duomo/bus 54, 60, 65/tram 12, 27. **Open** 3-7.30pm Mon; 9.15am-7.30pm Tue-Fri; 8.45am-7.30pm Sat, last 2 Sun in Dec. **Credit** AmEx, DC, MC, V. **Map** p250 D7/p252 D7.
A temple of fine food and wine for more than 120 years, Peck was founded in 1883 by a humble pork butcher from Prague. The three-floor flagship on via

Spadari has a butcher's, bakery, delicatessen, a vast selection of wines from all over the world, prepared foods, oils and bottled sauces, and a delightful tearoom. Its sit-down gourmet restaurant, Cracco-Peck, and café, Peck Italian Bar, are at other addresses; for both, *see p101*.

Health food

Centro Botanico
Piazza San Marco 1, North (02 2901 3254/www. centrobotanico.it). Metro Moscova/bus 43, 61. **Open** Sept-June 10am-7.45pm Mon-Sat; 3-7.30pm Sun. July 10am-7.45pm Mon-Sat. Aug 11.30am-7pm Mon-Sat. Closed 1wk Aug. **Credit** AmEx, DC, MC, V. **Map** p248 D5.
This major centre for health and natural products stocks organically grown produce, groceries and baked goods, vitamins, pure-fibre clothing and more. There's also a juice bar and lunchtime café. **Other locations** via Vincenzo Monti 32, North (02 463 807); via Cesare Correnti 10, West (02 7202 3525).

Eat, Drink, Shop

The groaning shelves of Milan's oldest enoteca hold over 1,000 wines, and grappas, whiskies, rums, cognacs, and gourmet delights like foie gras. Staff wrap up gift baskets as ornate as they are delicious.

N'Ombra de Vin
Via San Marco 2, North (02 659 9650/www.nombra devin.it). Metro Moscova/bus 61, 94/tram 1, 3, 4. **Open** 9am-midnight Tue-Sat. Closed 3wks Aug. **Credit** AmEx, DC, MC, V. **Map** p248 D5.
Owner and wine expert Cristian Corà will help you choose from among the 3,000 bottles in the atmospheric vaulted cellars of this 15th-century monastic refectory. There's a small wine bar at the entrance, serving soups, cold cuts, cheese and pan-fried risotto, as well as wines by the glass.

Health & beauty

State-of-the-art gym **Downtown Palestre** (*see p169*) offers beauty treatments for men and women. For all-organic scrubs and luxury hair treatments, *see also p170* **Relax to the max**.

Cosmetics & perfumes

Calé Fragranze d'Autore
Via Santa Maria alla Porta 5, West (02 8050 9449/www.cale.it). Bus 50, 58/tram 16, 18, 19. **Open** 3-7pm Mon; 10am-7pm Tue-Fri; 10am-7.30pm Sat. Closed Aug. **Credit** AmEx, DC, MC, V. **Map** p250 D6/p252 D6.
Silvio Levi, grandson of the founder, sniffs out rare, artisanal perfumes (and shaving creams and hair products) for this family-run firm. Finds include Creed's historical Fantasia de Fleurs, created in 1862, and Pantelleria's musky Tanit. The wood-beamed room upstairs houses a collection of historic bottles and packaging – not to be missed.

Madina
Via Meravigli 17, Centre (02 8691 5438/www.madina.it). Metro Cairoli/bus 50, 58/tram 16, 18, 19. **Open** 3.30-7.30pm Mon; 10am-7.30pm Tue-Sat. Closed 3wks Aug. **Credit** AmEx, DC, MC, V. **Map** p248 D6/p252 D6.
Products that carry the name Madina Milano become coveted souvenirs not only for their high quality, but also for their international cachet. The make-up line has a strong following in the beauty trade, no doubt attracted partly by the sheer number of shades: 120 lipsticks, 50 lip glosses, 250 eyeshadows and 300 tones of foundation, blusher, bronzer and face powder.
Other locations via Tivoli 8, North (02 860 746); corso Venezia 23, East (02 7601 1692).

Profumo
Via Brera 6, North (02 7202 3334). Tram 1, 3, 12, 14, 27. **Open** 10am-7pm Mon-Sat. Closed 2wks Aug. **Credit** AmEx, DC, MC, V. **Map** p248 D5.
Housed in the 16th-century Palazzo Beccaria, this enticing shop has a selection of rare Italian and inter-

Ralph
Lauren, no.4
Bottega Venezia, no.5
Sergio Rossi, no.6
Gucci, no.7
Prada women, no.8
Armani Junior, no.10
Gianni Versace, no.11
Valentino, no.20
Alberta Ferretti, no.21
Christian Dior, no.21

Via Manzoni
Armani Superstore, no.31
Paul Smith, no.32
Armani Casa, no.37

Wine

As well as **Peck** (*see p134*), the establishments listed below have extensive selections of fine wine, ideal for presents.

L'Altro Vino
Viale Piave 9, East (02 780 147). Metro Porta Venezia/bus 169/tram 9, 23, 29, 30. **Open** 11.30am-7.45pm Tue-Sat. Closed Aug. **Credit** AmEx, DC, MC, V. **Map** p249 G6.
Thanks to the knowledgeable and approachable proprietors, you can wander around this well-stocked shop without feeling intimidated. L'Altro Vino offers a vast selection of Italian and international vintages, and holds regular tastings on the first and third Thursdays of the month.

Enoteca Cotti
Via Solferino 42, North (02 2900 1096/www.enoteca cotti.it). Metro Moscova/bus 70, 94. **Open** 8.30am-1pm, 3-7.30pm Tue-Sat. Closed Aug. **Credit** MC, V. **Map** p248 D5.

national candles and perfumes, including delicate Claus soaps, Dr Sebargh's skin products and Lorenzo Villoresi's powdery Teint de Neige.

Hairdressers

Aldo Coppola

8th Floor, La Rinascente, piazza Duomo, Centre (02 8905 9712/www.aldocoppola.it). Metro Duomo/bus 54, 60, 65/tram 12, 23, 27. **Open** 10am-9pm Mon-Sat; 10am-7pm Sun. Closed Mon & Sun in Aug. **Credit** MC, V. **Map** p251 E7/p252 E7.

Coppola, who opened his first salon in Milan in 1965, now has nine across town, including this funky outpost on the top floor of La Rinascente department store. The salon is overseen by Coppola's right-hand man Roberto Castelli, and the master himself puts in an appearance on Tuesdays and Saturdays. **Other locations** throughout the city.

Anadema

Corso Lodi 1, South (02 545 4449/www. anadema.com). Metro Porta Romana/tram 9, 29, 30. **Open** 10am-6pm, 6-10pm (by appointment only) Tue, Wed; 10am-7pm Thur, Fri; 9am-6pm Sat. Closed 2wks Aug. **Credit** MC, V. **Map** p251 G9/H10.

Anadema is part salon, part exhibition venue, with occasional literary and film events thrown in to the mix as well: it's a relaxing, open space more reminiscent of a cool living room than a traditional hairdresser's. Staff have plenty of experience prepping models for shoots and TV, and it shows.

Antica Barbieria Colla

Via Gerolamo Morone 3, Centre (02 874 312). Metro Montenapoleone/tram 1, 2. **Open** 8.30am-12.30pm, 2.30-7pm Tue-Sat. Closed 3wks Aug. **No credit cards. Map** p249 E6/p252 E6.

This barber shop more than lives up to its name, as it has been in business since Dino Colla opened its door in 1904, and proudly displays the brush that was used on Puccini. A totally traditional shave starts with pore-opening hot towels and closes with splashes of soothing aftershave.

Herbalists

For pharmacies, *see p227.*

Erboristeria Officinale Mediolanum

Via Volta 7, North (02 657 2882/www.erboristeria mediolanum.it). Metro Moscova/bus 70, 94. **Open** 3.30-7.30pm Mon; 9.30am-1pm, 3.30-7.30pm Tue-Sat. Closed Sat pm June & July, all Aug. **Credit** AmEx, MC, V. **Map** p248 D4.

Expert Gabriella Fiumani presides over this intriguing shop, mixing tisanes, cosmetics and medicinal concoctions from more than 400 herbs stored in drawers and cupboards at the back. Other products include organic herbal cosmetics, as well as spices and seasonings – from myrrh granules to blue poppy seeds – displayed in huge glass jars.

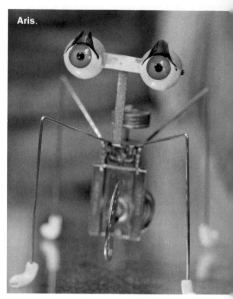

Aris.

Officinali di Montauto

Corso Magenta 12, North (02 3652 2069/www. officinalidimontauto.it). Bus 50, 58/tram 16, 19. **Open** 3.30-7.30pm Mon; 10.30am-1pm, 3.30-7.30pm Tue-Sat. Closed Aug. **Credit** MC, V. **Map** p252 C6.

Hints of rosemary and mint waft through corso Magenta 12's unusual octagonal courtyard. Breeze into OM's all-white interior and take your pick from the shelves of own-brand organic products; or book a night at their agriturismo in Tuscany, surrounded by their lavender fields.

Officina Profumo Farmaceutica di Santa Maria Novella

Corso Magenta 22, North (02 805 3695/www.sm novella.it). Bus 50, 58/tram 16, 19. **Open** 3.30-7.30pm Mon; 10am-1pm, 3.30-7.30pm Tue-Fri; 10am-1pm, 3.30-6pm Sat. Closed 3wks Aug, 2wks Dec-Jan. **Credit** AmEx, DC, MC, V. **Map** p250 B6.

This small outpost of the famous herbalist and apothecary may not have the history of the original 16th-century Florentine store – but it does have most of the products, from skin-whitening cream to hand-moulded mint and olive oil soaps. They make cute gifts in their old-fashioned packaging.

Home design & accessories

As the home of Europe's largest annual furniture fair, the Salone Internazionale del Mobile (*see p29* **Tomorrow's world**), it's hardly surprising that Milan is a great source of designer furniture and household goodies. The best place to start from is via Durini (home to

B&B Italia and Cassina, among others). From there, walk up via Manzoni for several more design stores. There's also a growing number of interesting design gallery-cum-shops in the area between Brera and corso Como. *See also pp26-30* **Design in Milan.**

Alessi

Corso Matteotti 9, Centre (02 795 726/www.alessi. com). Metro San Babila/bus 54, 61, 73. **Open** 3-7pm Mon; 10am-7pm Tue-Sat. Closed 3wks Aug. **Credit** AmEx, DC, MC, V. **Map** p249 E6/p252 E6.

Alessi's Milan flagship store – not far from the main household designer street, via Durini – has everything the company has ever done in bright plastic and polished steel, from toothpick holders to the Merdolino loo brush. For the outlet store on Lago d'Iseo, *see p189* **Alessi's cave.**

Aris

Via Spartaco 11, South (02 5518 1389). Bus 84/ tram 9, 16, 29, 30. **Open** 9.30am-12.30pm, 4.30-7.30pm Mon-Sat. Closed Aug. **Credit** MC, V. **Map** p251 G7/8.

Model planes, microphones, wooden vegetables and a giant tooth hung from the ceiling: Aris stocks some bizarre items (some of which are for rental only).

Armani Casa

Via Manzoni 37, East (02 657 2401/www.armani-viamanzoni31.it). Metro Montenapoleone/tram 1, 2. **Open** 10.30am-7.30pm Mon-Sat; 2.30-7.30pm Sun. **Credit** AmEx, DC, MC, V. **Map** p249 E5/p252 E6.

Oozing the same sophistication as the brand's clothes, this black lacquer store stocks furniture and cushions in Giorgio's favourite greys, beiges, creams and blacks. Portable purchases include streamlined hip flasks, leather-bound notebooks, and candles on metal stands shaped like Armani table lamps.

B&B Italia

Via Durini 14, Centre (02 764 441/www.milano. bebitalia.com). Metro San Babila/bus 60, 73, 84, 94. **Open** 3-7pm Mon; 10am-7pm Tue-Sat. Closed Aug. **Credit** AmEx, MC, V. **Map** p251 F7/p252 F7.

The list of designers who have worked for minimalist kings B&B Italia is like a hit parade of international design: you'll find geometric vases by Ettore Sottsass, salad bowls by Arne Jacobsen and Antonio Citterio's famed Otto chairs, all displayed on museum-like plinths around this massive store. Additional B&B designs by Italian heroes are also on show at the Triennale (*see p63*).

Dovetusai

Via Sigeri 24, South (02 5990 2432/www.dovetusai. it). Metro Lodi/bus 92. **Open** 10am-1pm, 2.30-7pm Mon-Fri; 10am-1pm, 2.30-7pm Sat (Oct-Dec only). Closed Aug. **Credit** MC, V. **Map** p251 G9/H9.

A wild collection of young, cutting-edge designs from all over the world, with particular emphasis on pieces created using unexpected materials, such as Gilles Miller's cardboard grandfather clock, or Change Design's soft vases.

High-Tech

Piazza XXV Aprile 12, North (02 624 1101/www. high-techmilano.com). Metro Garibaldi/bus 70, 94. **Open** 10.30am-7.30pm Tue-Sun. **Credit** AmEx, DC, MC, V. **Map** p248 D4.

Technicoloured dream coats and more at **Rossana Orlandi**.

A labyrinth packed to the rafters with everything for the design-conscious home-owner, from office accessories to incense. Hours can evaporate as you wander from room to room – or simply try to locate the exit. Its offshoot Cargo High-Tech (via Meucci 39, East, 02 272 2131) sells cut-price merchandise; it also has a bar and bakery.

Rossana Orlandi

Via Bandello 14, North (02 4674 47224/www. rossanaorlandi.com). Bus 50, 58, 68. **Open** 3-7pm Mon; 10am-7pm Tue-Sat. Closed Aug. **Credit** AmEx, DC, MC, V. **Map** p250 B6.

Milanese design guru Rossana Orlandi has created a magical space in this courtyard and shop. The stock includes pieces by big-name inventors, as well as items by up-and-coming international designers.

Markets

For the lowdown on Milan's best markets, *see p139* **The *mercati*'s whiskers**.

Antiquariato sul Naviglio Grande

Strada Alzaia Naviglio Grande/Ripa di Porta Ticinese, South (02 8940 9971/www.navigliogrande. mi.it). Metro Porta Genova/bus 59, 74, 169/tram 2, 3, 9, 14, 15, 29, 30. **Open** Jan-June, Aug-Nov 9am-5pm last Sun of mth. Dec 9am-5pm last Sun before Christmas. **Map** p250 C9.

Fauché

Via Fauché/via Losana, North. Bus 57, 94/tram 1, 12, 14, 19, 33. **Open** 7.30am-1pm Tue; 7.30am-5pm Sat. **Map** p248 A3.

Fiera di Senigallia

Strada Alzaia Naviglio Grande/via Valenza, South. Metro Porta Genova/bus 59, 74, 169/ tram 2, 3, 9, 14, 15, 29, 30. **Open** 9am-7pm Sat. **Map** p250 C9.

Isola

Via Garigliano/via Sebenico/via Volturno, North. Metro Garibaldi or Zara/bus 43, 82/tram 2, 7, 11. **Open** 8.30am-1pm Tue; 8.30am-5pm Sat. **Map** p249 E2.

Isola was in the process of moving in 2008 as the guide went to press; its new location may be on the streets listed above or nearby. *Photo p140.*

Mercato Comunale

Piazza Wagner, West. Metro Wagner/bus 67, 199. **Open** 8.30am-1pm Mon; 8.30am-1pm, 4-7.30pm Tue-Sat.

Other locations piazzale Lagosta, North; viale Umbria 60-61, South.

Papiniano

Viale Papiniano, West. Metro Sant'Agostino/bus 50, 58, 68, 169. **Open** 7.30am-1pm Tue; 7.30am-5pm Sat. **Map** p250 B8.

Music

See also p125 Messaggerie Musicali.

La Bottega Discantica

Via Nirone 5, West (02 862 966/www.discantica.it). Bus 50, 58/tram 16, 19. **Open** 3-7pm Mon; 9.30am-1pm, 3-7pm Tue-Sat. Closed Aug. **Credit** MC, V. **Map** p250 C6/p252 C6.

The *mercati*'s whiskers

Shopping heaven though it is, there are days when trawling through *centro Milano* in search of the latest Prada pantsuit can lose its appeal. So pick a sunny day, leave the heels at home and hit the city's best markets.

Relocated to the Alzaia Naviglio Grande while its former home, viale d'Annunzio, is under snail-paced renovation, the **Fiera di Senigallia** (*see p138*) has long been the city's top flea market. Pick through piles of used clothes (often between €2 and €5 per piece) or peruse the '70s vintage disco gear; this is also a top spot for compilation CDs, Peruvian baby clothes or old comic books. Over a canal or two, ever-popular **Papiniano** (*see p138*) starts at piazzale Cantore and runs as far as Sant'Agostino metro station. The mix of goods includes plants, shoes, homewares and linens, with the odd food stall thrown in. Expect to use your elbows if you want to get near the cut-price clothes. Head up north to check out underrated **Isola** (*see p138*), a bargain hunter's delight that has ceramics, end-of-season clothes by Miss Sixty and other labels, and the occasional

offcut of brightly coloured Como silk. It's also good for fresh fruits and vegetables, and ultra-cheap, à la mode fashions. **Fauché** (*see p138*) is the fashionistas' favourite for cut-price designer shoes. Alongside discounted footwear and samples by brands like Gucci and Prada, there are smaller, more interesting labels like Alessandro dell'Acqua and Les Tropeziennes.

For tasty souvenirs like dried porcini mushrooms, each of Milan's zones has its own daily **mercato comunale** (*see p138*), and the one on piazza Wagner is one of the city's best outlets for gourmet food: the cornucopia includes fruit, fish, meat, cheese and flowers.

On the last Sunday of each month, around 400 antiques dealers display their wares at the **Antiquariato sul Naviglio Grande** (*see p138*). Running for two kilometres (1.2 miles) alongside the city's oldest canal, the market pulls in close to 150,000 people, and is a good source of design classics, ranging from furniture and silverware to vintage watches. Nearby bars and restaurants stay open all day, contributing to the buzzy atmosphere.

Eat, Drink, Shop

La Bottega Discantia is a meeting point for classical music lovers and musicians, selling everything from the latest CDs to rare LPs. La Bottega also has its own recording label, specialising in vintage and modern Italian classical music. There's also plenty of folk and ethnic music, as well as an extensive section of opera on DVD.

Buscemi Dischi

Corso Magenta 31, West (02 804 103/www. buscemi.com). Metro Cadorna/bus 50, 58, 94/ tram 16, 19. **Open** 3-7.30pm Mon; 9.30am-2pm, 3-7.30pm Tue-Sat. Closed Aug. **Credit** MC, V. **Map** p252 C6.

One of the city's best stops for alternative tunes, particularly reggae, ska and jazz. In a transitory business it's been trading since 1965.

La Feltrinelli – Ricordi Media Store

Galleria Vittorio Emanuele II, Centre (02 8646 0272/www.lafeltrinelli.it). Metro Duomo/bus 54, 60, 65/tram 12, 23, 27. **Open** 10am-11pm Mon-Sat; 10am-8pm Sun. **Credit** AmEx, DC, MC, V. **Map** p251 E6/p252 E6.

A media emporium under the glass-covered Galleria, Ricordi stocks a varied selection of CDs in all genres, plus instruments, sheet music, games and concert and theatre tickets.

Opticians

Salmoiraghi & Viganò

Corso Matteotti 22, East (02 7600 0100/www. salmoiraghievigano.it). Metro San Babila/bus 54, 61. **Open** 3-7.30pm Mon; 10am-7.30pm Tue-Sat. **Credit** AmEx, DC, MC, V. **Map** p249 E6/p252 E6.

A solid optician that's well known throughout Italy for its professionalism and choice of frames.
Other locations throughout the city.

Photocopying & photo developers

Almost any stationery store (cartoleria) will offer a photocopy and fax service; just ask. **Esselunga** supermarket (viale Papiniano 27, West, 02 498 7674, www.esselunga.it, branches throughout the city) does traditional one-day photo processing, and its rates are cheaper than the 30-minute photo specialists. It will also print digital photos in three to four days.

Mail Boxes Etc

Via Moscova 13, North (02 2900 2245/www.mbe.it). Metro Moscova/bus 43, 94. **Open** 8.30am-7.30pm Mon-Fri; 8.30am-1pm Sat. **Credit** AmEx, DC, MC, V. **Map** p249 E4.

Photocopying and fax facilities, UPS courier pick-up, business card printing, Western Union point, postbox rental, packaging and office supplies sales.
Other locations throughout the city.

Isola. See p138.

Arts & Entertainment

Features

Giò Marconi. *See p153.*

Festivals & Events

From fashion week to partying on the fringe.

Commerce is king in show-me-the-money Milan. Many of its leading art, design and fashion shows are actually trade fairs; often it's their fringe events and parties that take the city by storm. Touring bands and DJs often hit Milan before Rome or Naples, with outdoor revelry the theme of the finest summer festivals. Spring is the time to peek into palazzi, and there are three dedicated open-house events between March and May. Come the winter, there's Christmas shopping around the feast of Sant'Ambrogio, Milan's patron saint: it's the biggest street party – craft stalls included – of the year.

The more traditional festivals tend to be located around the city's prominent churches, particularly the Duomo, or in residential neighbourhoods. Commercial events take place mainly at the massive Fieramilano site in Rho, in the north-western outskirts of the city. Built in record time to plans by Italian architect Massimiliano Fuksas, the Rho complex is an avant-garde glass and steel affair, and – for students of architecture – well worth a visit in its own right. Take a look at the Fiera's website (www.fieramilano.it) for a detailed programme. In addition, the Fiera's old space, Fieramilanocity, still hosts a handful of events, many of them fashion- or art-related.

Before visiting Milan, it's worth finding out what's going on in the city: the buzz generated by international events can be exciting, but hotels and taxis are harder to find. The tourist information office (*see p233*) publishes *Milano Mese*, a monthly guide to events throughout the city (also on their website). For information on disabled access to special events, contact the Associazione Italiana Assistenza Spastici (02 330 2021, www.milanopertutti.it).

Spring

Settimana dei Beni Culturali

Various locations (information 800 991 199/www. beniculturali.it). **Date** early spring.
During cultural heritage week, entry to all of Italy's publicly owned museums and galleries, and to some privately owned sites, is free. Events include special openings, guided tours, concerts and tastings.

Giornata FAI di Primavera

Various locations (information 0141 720 850/ www.fondoambiente.it). **Date** last wknd Mar or 1st wknd Apr.

During this weekend many of Milan's historic palazzi and monuments that are closed for the rest of the year open up to the public, thanks to the sponsorship of the Fondo Ambiente Italiano, Italy's version of the National Trust.

Mercato dei Fiori

Along the Naviglio Grande, South (02 8940 9971/ www.navigliogrande.mi.it). Metro Porta Genova/ bus 59, 68, 74/tram 2, 3, 9, 29, 30. **Map** p250 B9.
Date Apr.
This flower fair creates a spectacular splash of colour along the canal. Over 200 nurseries and horticultural schools from all around Italy take part.

Stramilano

www.stramilano.it. **Date** 1st or 2nd Sun Apr.
Central Milan is closed to traffic as locals and athletes from all over the world take to the streets and race over two distances: the Stramilano (15km/9.3 miles) or the half-marathon (21km/13 miles). The Stramilano starts and finishes at the Arena Civica in Parco Sempione, encircling the whole city. Corso Sempione is a good point from which to watch.

MiArt

Fieramilanocity, via Varesina 76, North (02 485 501/www.miart.it). Metro Amendola/bus 48, 68, 78/ tram 19, 27. **Date** early Apr.
One of Europe's biggest contemporary and modern art shows, held largely at Fieramilanocity. It brings together critics, collectors, artists and dealers; cultural and fringe events kick off all over the city.

Salone Internazionale del Mobile (Furniture Fair)

Fieramilano, Rho (information 800 820 029/02 725 941/www.fieramilano.it/www.cosmit.it). Metro Rho.
Date mid Apr.
Milan goes into party mode for one of the world's largest exhibitions of furniture and fittings from top global designers (*see p29* **Tomorrow's world**). The event's main base is in Rho, but the fringe of exhibitions, events and parties back in town are what really make it. Many galleries and smaller designers install themselves in palazzi, workshops and even open-air swimming pools. On the Sunday the event is open to the public.

Pittori del Naviglio Grande

Along the Naviglio Grande, South (02 8940 9971/ www.navigliogrande.mi.it). Metro Porta Genova/ bus 59, 68, 74/tram 2, 3, 9, 29, 30. **Map** p250 B9.
Date 2nd wknd May.
This open-air art exhibition showcases work by more than 300 artists from all over Italy.

Arts & Entertainment

Orticola ai Giardini Pubblici

*Giardini Pubblici, East (02 7600 1496/www.
orticola.org). Metro Palestro or Turati/bus 61,
94.* **Map** *p249 F5.* **Date** *mid May.*
It's not quite the Chelsea Flower Show, but this
growing exhibition/market does take over the entire
park. It's organised by the Associazione Orticola di
Lombardia, one of the first Italian institutions to
encourage public interest in gardens and plants.

Cortili Aperti

*Various locations (02 7631 8634/www.cortili
aperti.it).* **Date** *late May.*
Some ten private residences open their splendid
courtyards to the public for one Sunday each year.
In previous years, art nouveau buildings on corso
Venezia including Casa Fontana Silvestri, Palazzo
Serbelloni and Palazzo Greppi have taken part.

Idroscalo in Festa

*Idropark Fila, Circonvallazione Idroscalo Est 51,
Segrate (02 7020 0902/www.provincia.milano.it/
idroscalo).* **Date** *late May-Sept.*
The summer season of sporting events, concerts,
nightlife and picnics gets under way at the Idroscalo
Park (*see p147* **Milan's beach resort**), on the eastern outskirts of town.

Summer

Milano Moda Uomo Primavera/Estate

Information www.cameramoda.it. **Date** *late June.*
Men's fashion week for spring and summer: not the
most important event in Milan's fashion calendar,
but it does bring some of the world's best-looking
men to the city. Shows, events, special presentations
and catwalks take place all over town.

Milano d'Estate

*Castello Sforzesco, North (www.visitamilano.it).
Metro Cadorna, Cairoli or Lanza/bus 43, 57, 70,
94/tram 3, 4, 7, 12, 14.* **Map** *p248 C6/p252 C6.*
Date *June-Aug.*
Open-air concerts and performances by the likes of
REM and Radiohead are organised to entertain those
unfortunate *milanesi* who can't leave the city in the
heat of the summer. The action takes place in and
around the grounds of the Castello Sforzesco (*see p61*).

Navigli summer season

*Around the Navigli, South. Metro Porta Genova/
bus 59, 68, 74/tram 2, 3, 9, 29, 30.* **Map** *p250 B9.*
Date *June-Sept.*

Someone give that girl a doughnut. **Milano Moda Donna Primavera/Estate**. *See p144.*

Arts & Entertainment

The traffic-choked streets around the Navigli take a breather for the summer, letting bars and restaurants spill out into the pavements between 8pm and 2am every day.

Festa dei Navigli

Along the Navigli, South. Metro Porta Genova/ bus 59, 68, 74/tram 2, 3, 9, 29, 30. **Map** p250 B9. **Date** 1st to 3rd Sun June.

An eventful fortnight in the canal area, with street artists, concerts, sporting events, antiques markets, cooking demonstrations and more.

La Notte Bianca

Information www.comune.milano.it. **Date** mid June. In Italian, a 'white night' is a sleepless one. For one night each year, bars, restaurants, shops, cinemas et al whoop it up from early evening to 6am.

Notturni in Villa

Information 02 8912 2383/www.amicidellamusica milano.it. **Date** mid June-Aug.

A series of jazz and classical music concerts in patrician villas around the city, such as Villa Simonetta at the end of corso Sempione. Performances start at 10pm and entry is free. See the tourist office (*see p233*) and local press for details.

Sagra di San Cristoforo

In front of San Cristoforo, Navigli, South (02 4895 1413/www.visitamilano.it). Metro Porta Genova/bus 59, 68, 74/tram 2, 3, 9, 29, 30. **Date** 3rd Sun June.

The feast of the patron saint of travellers takes place in the square in front of the little church of San Cristoforo. Decorated boats float down the Naviglio and vehicles are duly blessed.

Festival Latino Americando

Forum di Assago, via D Vittorio 6, Assago (02 4570 9915/www.latinoamericando.it). Metro Famagosta, then bus to Assago. **Date** mid June-mid Aug.

Milan celebrates all things Latino with this festival on the outskirts of the city. Over 60 concerts, events and exhibitions celebrate aspects of Latin music, arts, dance, food, crafts and cinema. Top Latin musicians fly in to give performances.

Autumn

Milano Moda Donna Primavera/Estate

Information www.cameramoda.it. **Date** late Sept.

Yet another fashion week. On this occasion, leading Italian designers present their women's collections for spring and summer. Events galore are held at shops, theatres and galleries. *Photo p143.*

Milano Marathon

www.milanocitymarathon.it. **Date** early Nov.

Nearly 7,000 competitors take part in Milan's annual marathon, held on a Sunday at around 9.30am, when most civilised people are still in bed. The race starts and finishes at the Arena Civico in Parco Sempione.

Winter

Oh Bej! Oh Bej!

Piazza Sant'Ambrogio, West. Metro Sant'Ambrogio/ bus 50, 58, 94. **Map** p250 C7. **Date** 7 Dec.

This street market is one of Milan's top festivals, held on the feast of the city's patron saint, Ambrogio. The streets around piazza Sant'Ambrogio throng with crowds sampling traditional food such as pancakes, roast meat, chestnuts and mulled wine; and there are stalls selling crafts and antiques. Goldsmiths made a gift to the city of a silver statue of the saint, exhibited on this day in the Duomo cathedral; there's also a special morning service in the Sant'Ambrogio basilica.

La Scala opening night

Teatro alla Scala, via Filodrammatici 2, Centre (02 88 791/www.teatroallascala.org). Metro Montenapoleone/bus 61/tram 1, 2, 20. **Date** 7 Dec. **Map** p248 D5.

Piazza della Scala fills with feather boas and black ties as the great and good assemble for La Scala's (*see p59*) first night of the season.

Epiphany

Various locations. **Date** 6 Jan.

Epiphany is also known as La Befana, after a kind-hearted witch who is said to bring presents to well-behaved children and coal to naughty ones. Crowds turn out for the morning procession of the Three Wise Men from the Duomo to the church of Sant'Eustorgio, where their relics are said to be kept.

Milano Moda Uomo Autunno/Inverno

Information www.cameramoda.it. **Date** mid Jan.

Men's fashion week for autumn and winter: a bit of a sideshow to the women's event (*see below*). Still, the talent it attracts is first rate.

Carnevale

Various locations. **Date** Feb/early Mar.

Milan's Carnevale takes place in the days after Shrove Tuesday, later than in the rest of Italy. The celebrations are largely for children, who roam the streets in costumes spraying confetti and foam at passers-by. A fancy dress parade takes place around the Duomo on the first Saturday of Lent.

Milano Moda Donna Autunno/Inverno

Information www.cameramoda.it. **Date** late Feb.

Milan's moment in the fashion spotlight, as 80-odd designers unveil their autumn and winter collections. Catwalks are assembled at venues in Milan from shops to private spaces, though entry to the shows is by invitation only. Metropol, Dolce & Gabbana's renovated cinema (viale Piave 24, www.dolcegabbanametropol.com), hosts exhibitions as well as providing a venue for shows; Armani's catwalk is at the former Nestlé factory he has converted into a theatre (via Bergognone 59).

Children

Milan with kids is a walk in the park.

Welcome to Europe's most child-friendly country. Although Milan has few activities aimed directly at children, you can take kids anywhere: most restaurants and museums will welcome your *bambino* with a friendly smile. The city's two main parks, Parco Sempione (*see p61*) and Giardini Pubblici (*see p71*), are stuffed with outdoor activities, including the fairy-tale Castello Sforzesco, an arena and children's play areas; and when it rains, they have two or three museums either on site or around the corner. What's more, the central Duomo area is filled with churches, children's stores and even more museums, and is easy to navigate by tram, subway or on foot. Milan can be a little polluted at times, not to mention hectic at rush hour; but with a *gelato* in hand, you'll find this fascinating city is also great fun.

GETTING AROUND
Although public transport is one of the many things that the Milanese complain about, it can actually be enjoyable if you're in no great hurry. Tickets are cheap: all journeys are €1 per person (valid for 75 minutes); a 24-hour pass is €3. Children up to five years old travel free; and two children up to ten years old can travel free with every adult. Keep a public transport map, which are available from newsstands, near to hand. The subway is quick but crowded (*see p256* for a map); buses are slow and crowded; and the trams are a great way to hop around. There are three types: the small, yellow 1920s ones, which have period interiors (with wooden benches and cute lampshades); the larger, orange 1950s ones; and the even larger futuristic green ones, known locally as 'caterpillars'. The two hop-on-hop-off bus routes are also a good way to see the city (*see p219*).

A few words of caution: in Italy people park anywhere and everywhere, so it can be hard to negotiate kerbs with a pushchair. Also, the two older metro lines (red and green) do not have lifts in every station, so you may have to lug your buggy down the stairs or escalators; although Italians, being as they are, will often offer to help. Line 3 (yellow) and the Passante are fitted with somewhat unreliable lifts.

INFORMATION
Children's events are listed in Wednesday's *ViviMilano* supplement of the *Corriere della Sera*, and in Thursday's *Tutto Milano* supplement of *La Repubblica*.

Milan's **Giardini Pubblici** has more than just grass to offer children. *See p146.*

Sightseeing

Around the Duomo

One of the advantages of Milan's compact, Duomo-centric layout is that many of the must-see attractions are within walking distance of each other. A good bet is to head to the **Duomo** (*see p52*). It's on most tram routes (take the subway if you're pressed for time), and, as well as having lots to see and do, it's in the middle of a large, mostly pedestrianised zone from piazza San Babila to the Castello Sforzesco.

Piazza del Duomo and the nearby **Galleria Vittorio Emanuele II** (*see p55*) are good places for watching the world go by, but the best attraction for families is the cathedral roof. It's a 150-step climb to the top (there's also a lift): once you're up there, you get a wonderful view of the city and, on a good day, the surrounding countryside and the Alps.

Less well known are the acoustics of the colonnades in nearby **piazza dei Mercanti** (*see p59*) next to via dei Mercanti, a medieval street with buskers, clowns and other interesting characters, especially at weekends. Climb the steps and make for the covered courtyard furthest from the Duomo; stand in one of the corners, and get your child to stand in the opposite one. You can then talk to each other by whispering into the corner. Don't feel embarrassed: if people stare at you, they're merely admiring your insider knowledge.

Museums & attractions

Among child-friendly museums, the leader of the pack is the **Museo Nazionale della Scienza e della Tecnologia Leonardo da Vinci** (*see p87*), which is not too far from *The Last Supper* (*see p92*). The museum's large collection of fossils and models of da Vinci's inventions might not be every child's idea of fun, but its 'railway pavilion' (*padiglione ferroviario*) is outstanding. This large shed contains real trains and trams dating back to the 19th century, and they can be clambered on. The area outside the pavilion has a science park where kids can run around, as well as a couple of fighter planes; the next building houses an impressive collection of boats (models and full size), plus the cross-section of a passenger cruiser; the museum's main section contains vintage cars, bikes and motorbikes. The museum's star is its submarine, the *Enrico Toti*, although guided tours cost an additional €8 per person, children included.

A trip to the **Civico Museo di Storia Naturale** (*see p72*) can also be fun for young visitors, thanks to its model dinosaurs and other goodies. The museum is in the **Giardini Pubblici** (*see p71*), Milan's best park for kids, which also contains the **Planetario Ulrico Hoepli** (*see p73*) planetarium, a children's play park and a mini train.

Another fun place to take children to is the **Castello Sforzesco** (*see p61*), a short walk from the Duomo. Of particular interest here is the armoury hall (room 14), which features a knight on horseback and some vicious-looking swords. The expanse of the Parco Sempione beyond is kiddie heaven, and there are cafés and poolside walkways aplenty. The park's best free activity is the newly renovated **Acquario Civico** (*see p62*), with its indoor and outdoor fish tanks.

Babysitting

In addition to the listings below, Play Planet (*see below*) also has a daily babysitting service.

Il Nano Gigante

Via Lambrate 18, East (02 2682 6650/www.ilnano gigante.it). Metro Loreto or Pasteur/bus 55, 56, 62/ tram 33. **Open** *Free play* 3-7pm Mon-Fri. *Baby parking* 8am-6pm Mon-Fri; by reservation Sat, Sun. Closed Aug. **Rates** *Free play* from €10. *Baby parking* €45 per day; price per hour varies. **Credit** MC, V.
As well as being a fun place for kids to play in, this centre also runs a 'baby parking' system, which lets you drop off your child here (book at least two days in advance). It opens two Saturday evenings per month, from 7.30pm to 10.30pm, giving footloose parents a chance to hit the city's nightlife.

ProntoBaby

Via Lario 16, North (02 6900 2201/www.infanzia. com). Metro Zara/bus 82, 83/tram 4, 90, 91. **Open** *Office* 9am-5pm Mon-Fri. Closed July & Aug. **Rates** from €8 per hr. **No credit cards. Map** p249 E2.
This school for childcare professionals runs a baby-sitting service (they come to you). The sitters are students at the school and most speak some English.

Fun & games

See also above **Il Nano Gigante.**

Fun & Fun

Via Beroldo 2, East (02 2851 0671/www.fun-and-fun.com). Metro Loreto or Pasteur/bus 55, 56, 62/ tram 33. **Open** 3-7pm Mon-Fri; 10am-8pm Sat, Sun. Closed Aug. **Admission** €7.50 Mon-Sat; €10.90 Sun. **No credit cards. Map** p249 H2.
Many local kids have birthday parties at this indoor play centre, which has a giant climbing frame.

Play Planet

Via Veglia 59, North (02 668 8838/www. playplanet.it). Metro Maciachini/bus 51/tram 5, 7, 11. **Open** 3.30-7.30pm Mon-Fri; 10am-11pm Sat; 10am-8.30pm Sun. Closed July & Aug. **Admission** €7 Mon-Wed, Fri; €4 Thur; €6 Sat from 7pm; €9 Sat, Sun. **Credit** MC, V.

Arts & Entertainment

Another good indoor soft play centre with tunnels, ball pools, obstacle courses and in fact most things you'd need to exercise the children on a wet day.

Pottery Café
Via Solferino 3, North (02 8901 3660). Metro Lanza or Moscova/bus 43, 94. **Open** 10am-4pm Mon; 9am-7.30pm Tue-Sun. Closed 3wks Aug. **Credit** MC, V. **Map** p248 D5.
Kids aged four and over can create colourful and cheerful ceramics in this café-cum-art lab while mum and dad relax over a cappuccino.

Teatro del Buratto al Pime
Via Mosè Bianchi 94, West (02 2700 2476/www. teatrodelburatto.it). Metro Amendola or Lotto/bus 90, 91/tram 16. **Open** mostly Sun pm, times vary. **Admission** €6 children; €7 adults. **No credit cards.**
The season at this puppet theatre runs from October to March. Shows are in Italian.

Shopping

It may not have a Hamleys or an FAO Schwartz, but Milan has some fine toy shops on a smaller scale. If you're in the Duomo area, visit **La Città del Sole** on via Orefici (no.13, 02 8646 1683, closed Sun & 2wks Aug): it's packed with children's goodies, has a wooden Brio train set, with which kids are welcome to play, and a large selection of educational toys and puzzles. Alternatively, **Tofy Toys** in via Ruffini (no.9, 02 469 4776, closed Sun & Aug), near *The Last Supper*, is a small but well-stocked shop run by a friendly couple.

Milan's larger book/media stores, such as **Feltrinelli International** (*see p125*) on piazza Cavour and **Mondadori** (*see p125*) on piazza Duomo, are good sources of children's books in English or Italian. **Libreria dei Ragazzi** (via Tadino 53, East, 02 2953 3555,

closed Sun) is a children's bookstore with a good pick of Italian titles, and a few in English.

If it's kids' clothes you're after, Milan has plenty to offer. **Salvagente Bimbi** (*see p130*) has designer returns by top labels, and there's also a selection of children's shops in the centre. The via Dante area has at least three: **L'Angelo** (no.18, 02 866 151, closed Sun), **Petit Bateau** (no.12, 02 8699 8098, closed 1wk Aug) and, around the corner, **Du Pareil au Même** (via Pozzone 5, 02 7209 4971, closed Sun).

When to go

Milan is at its best in spring and early summer, although early autumn can also be pleasant. In July it starts to get unbearably hot, and everything grinds to a halt in August, when most families flee to the seaside. There is, however, some consolation for those left behind. In recent years the city council has organised a summer beach around the Arco della Pace, at the northern end of Parco Sempione (*see p61*). It's not a patch on the Paris version, but if you're stuck in Milan in the summer months, it's worth bearing in mind, as are the city's many outdoor lidos (*see p172*). The man-made lake at the **Idroscalo** (*see below* **Milan's beach resort**) makes for a great day out.

One of the best times for small kids in Milan is Carnevale (*see p144*), the traditional end-of-winter festival that takes place at the start of Lent: it's a sort of Italian Halloween. Youngsters dress up, and in the weeks running up to Carnevale, you'll often see toddlers in Zorro outfits walking with their parents (or grandparents). Piazza Duomo is a highly entertaining place during Carnevale itself – but don't be surprised to be sprayed with shaving foam by merry pranksters.

Milan's beach resort

Idroscalo is Milan's man-made lake. Now an eight-square-kilometre (three-square-mile) zone of water, forest and parkland, it was originally carved out as a watery landing strip by Mussolini, who thought seaplanes would be the future transport of choice.

It's a resort in many ways comparable to Italy's Mediterranean coastline, with beach clubs, waterside dining, barbecue areas and topless sunbathing; the shore is lined with pedalos. A big attraction for children are the two large open-air swimming pools and the children's pool on the eastern shore (€5 weekdays, €7 weekends).

Energetic families can tour the six-kilometre (four-mile) hiking and cycle path around the lake, or kids can try the jungle gyms and skateboard ramps by Idroscalo's western Ingresso Villetta entrance; there are teepees, swings and climbing frames for tots nearby. Longer-term residents can sign up for weekly summer sessions on the climbing wall, badminton courts and archery targets.

Bus number 73 plies the five-kilometre (three-miles) route to Linate airport, from which free buses run the additional half a kilometre (500 yards) to the lake all summer – or you can walk. A taxi from Milan is €20.

Arts & Entertainment

Film

Movies, movies everywhere – and not a line in English.

Cinema isn't one of Milan's strong suits. Among Italy's players, it's outgunned by Rome, with its Cinecittà studios, by Venice, with its international film festival, and by Turin, with its astounding film museum. Yet for all that, it's obvious that the *Milanesi* still love going to the flicks: the city boasts more than 100 screens, an outdoor cinema season, film festivals (*see p150*) for sports, gay and indie movies, and a number of opening nights that's comparable to London.

Bear in mind, though, that only a paltry number of first-release movies are screened in their original language: pretty much everything in Italy, from art-house docs to *South Park*, is dubbed. For visitors keen to hear their favourite actor's own voice, the only viable option is the Sound & Motion programme, which lines up one original language film on Mondays at the **Anteospazio**, on Tuesdays at the **Arcobaleno**, and on Thursdays at the **Mexico** cinema. Their respective websites list forthcoming showings, and the €35 ten-visit ticket is interchangeable between the three picture houses.

Sadly, Milan scores another blank for second-run, repertory and art-house cinema. If you want to see a classic Antonioni or Fellini, you'll be better off in London than in the city of *panettone*. But you can still shop your heart out for rare Italian DVDs, which generally have subtitles: try the bookshops attached to the Anteo cinema or the **Cineteca Italiana**; **La Bottega Discantica** (*see p140*) stocks an excellent selection of obscure opera DVDs. **Bloodbuster** (via Panfilo Castaldi 21, 02 2940 4304), in the Porta Venezia area, is legendary for Italian horror and B-movies.

TICKETS AND INFORMATION

The best way to find out what's on and where to see is to consult the listings in daily papers such as *Corriere della Sera* or *La Repubblica*. Free dailies *Metro*, *Leggo*, *City* or *Dnews*, distributed on public transport and in some bars, can also be of use.

At most cinemas, tickets cost between €4.50 and €5.50 for matinée and afternoon screenings, and from €6 to €7.50 for evening shows. Wednesday nights cost less – but book in advance, especially if the film is in the first week of its run. In most cinemas, the last show starts at around 10.30pm.

First-run cinemas

Arcobaleno Film Center
Viale Tunisia 11, East (02 2940 6054/reservations 199 199 166/information 02 2953 7621/www.cine nauta.it). Metro Porta Venezia/tram 1, 5, 29, 30. **Tickets** €4.50-€7.50; €4.50 reductions; €35 10-film pass; €30 non-Italian students. **Credit** (phone or web bookings only) AmEx, DC, MC, V. **Map** p249 G4.
Arcobaleno takes part in the popular Sound & Motion scheme, which brings the best foreign language titles to the city, albeit a few months behind their British or US releases. The ten-film card, if you plan to stay more than a month, is a good bargain.

Odeon
Via Santa Radegonda 8, Centre (02 875 283/www. medusacinema.it). Metro Duomo/bus 54, 60/tram 1, 2, 3, 12, 14, 27. **Tickets** €4.50-€7.50. **Credit** MC, V. **Map** p251 E6/p252 E6.
The days when Odeon's largest screens featured original language films are sadly missed, but it remains the place to go to if you understand Italian. Its main screen is eye-poppingly large, and the whole palazzo drips with sumptuous, decadent art deco.

Art-house cinemas

Anteospazio Cinema
Via Milazzo 9, North (02 659 7732/www.spazio cinema.info). Metro Moscova/bus 43, 94/tram 11, 29, 30, 33. **Tickets** €4.50-€7.50. **Credit** MC, V. **Map** p248 D4.
With a restaurant, bookshop, exhibition space and film courses – not to mention three screens showing everything – the Anteo is one of Milan's best cinemas. Original language films are shown on Monday as part of the Sound & Motion scheme.

Ariosto
Via L Ariosto 16, West (02 4800 3901). Metro Conciliazione/bus 61, 66, 67/tram 1, 19, 27, 29, 30. **Tickets** €6; €4 reductions. **No credit cards**. **Map** p248 A6.
This is the place for first- or second-run Spanish and French films. Recent international and independent films are screened from Tuesday to Sunday, and in *lingua originale* on Monday.

Il Cineforum Mr Arkadin
Locations vary (mobile 348 756 8859/www.cine arkadin.org). **Tickets** prices vary. **No credit cards**. **Map** p249 F6/p252 F6.
And now for something completely different: Cineforum Mr Arkadin is an 'alternative space' that

screens movies and hosts film-related talks and events in a new venue every few months. It's a good way to catch avant-garde films or those that aren't shown elsewhere. Check online for the location.

Cinema Gnomo

Via Lanzone 30A, West (02 804 125/www.comune milano.it). Metro Sant'Ambrogio/bus 50, 58, 94. **Tickets** *€4.10, plus €2.60 one-off membership fee.* **No credit cards.** **Map** p250 C7.

One of the few venerable art-house institutions in Milan, Gnomo is a cinephile's dream. It is run in close collaboration with Milan's municipality, and offers a varied, off-the-beaten-track selection of films.

Cinema Mexico

Via Savona 57, South (02 4895 1802/www.cinema mexico.it). Metro Porta Genova or Sant'Agostino/bus 61, 68, 90, 91/tram 14. **Tickets** *€4-€6.* **No credit cards.** **Map** p250 A8.

An interesting choice of recently released original language films is shown here all day on Thursdays as part of the Sound & Motion scheme. The Mexico also gives space to local independent productions, and to workshops on various film-related subjects.

Cineteatro San Lorenzo alle Colonne

Corso di Porta Ticinese 45, South (02 5811 3161/ www.teatroallecolonne.it). Metro Sant'Ambrogio/bus 59, 71, 94/tram 3. **Tickets** *€4.* **No credit cards.** **Map** p250 C8.

This experimental art-house cinema and theatre shows independent films in a stunning location.

Cineteca Italiana

Spazio Oberdan, viale Vittorio Veneto 2, East (02 7740 6300/www.cinetecamilano.it). Metro Porta Venezia/tram 5, 9, 20, 29, 30. **Tickets** *€5, plus €3 one-off membership fee; €32 8-film pass.* **No credit cards.** **Map** p249 F5.

Together with Gnomo, this is Milan's top cinema for ardent movie buffs. With a rich and varied programme, the Cineteca Italiana is the place to come to for Bergman retrospectives, Israeli mini festivals, forgotten flicks and silent cinema. *Photo p150.*

Museo del Cinema

Palazzo Dugnani, via D Manin 2B, East (information 02 655 4977/office 02 2900 5659/www.cineteca milano.it). Metro Turati/bus 61, 94/tram 1, 2, 20. **Tickets** *Museum (incl film ticket) €3; €2 reductions.* **No credit cards.** **Map** p249 F5.

The Museo del Cinema offers screenings of obscure classics on Friday afternoons, as well as a permanent exhibition of cinematographic curios and film-related displays. Call in advance if you'd like to arrange a guided tour.

Open-air cinemas

Most of the city grinds to a halt in August, cinemas included; but one of the great things about summer in Milan is its open-air cinema season: the locations, including the three listed, are all splendidly atmospheric. Look for listings under the heading 'Cinema all'aperto' in daily papers *Corriere della Sera* and *La Repubblica*.

Find out the 'truth... 24 times a second' at **Museo del Cinema.**

Conservatorio di Musica Giuseppe Verdi

Via Conservatorio 12, East (02 762 1101/www. consmilano.it). Metro San Babila/bus 56, 61/ tram 9, 20, 29, 30. **Map** p251 F6.

Teatro Litta

Corso Magenta 24, West (02 8645 4546/www. teatrolitta.it). Metro Cadorna/bus 18, 50, 54/ tram 19, 24. **Map** p250 C6/p252 C6.

Umanitaria

Via Daverio 7, Centre (02 579 6831/www. umanitaria.it). Metro Crocetta/bus 60, 79/ tram 4, 12, 27. **Map** p251 F7.

Festivals

A selection of 70-odd films shown at major festivals across Europe comes to Milan cinemas shortly after the awards. In June, **Cannes e dintorni** serves up the Côte d'Azur's finest; in September comes **Panoramica** (films shown at Venice) and **Frontiere** (films shown at Locarno). A weekly pass costs €40; see www. lombardiaspettacolo.com for more details.

Festival del Cinema Africano a Milano

Various locations (02 6671 2077/02 669 6258/ www.festivalcinemaafricano.org). Date late Mar. **Tickets** prices vary. **No credit cards.**

For film buffs. **Cineteca Italiana**. *See p149.*

One of the longest running independent film festivals in Milan, this week-long selection of works by African film-makers has been expanded to include Latin American and Asian movies: it celebrates its 19th edition in 2009.

Festival Internazionale di Cinema Gaylesbico e Queer Culture

Cinema Manzoni, via Manzoni 40, Centre (02 7602 0650/www.cinemagaylesbico.com). Metro Montenapoleone/bus 61/tram 1, 2, 20. Date late May-early June. **Tickets** prices vary. **No credit cards.** **Map** p249 E5.

Founded in 1986, this gay film festival has become an institution on the Milan arts landscape. The line-up offers international previews of major films with gay topics; shorts, documentaries and television programmes also get a look-in.

Film Festival Internazionale di Milano

Various locations (02 8918 1179/www.miff.it). Date late Mar-early Apr. **Tickets** prices vary. **No credit cards.**

Como resident George Clooney is a big fan of FFIM's dedication to 'bring to light the excellence in independent cinema and the film-makers behind it'. With each new edition, Milan's international film festival edges closer to its aim to be the European Sundance.

Invideo

Spazio Oberdan, viale Vittorio Veneto 2, East (02 7740 6300/www.mostrainvideo.com). Metro Porta Venezia/tram 5, 9, 20, 29, 30. Date early-mid Nov. **Tickets** prices vary. **Map** p249 F5.

Established in 1990, the international festival of 'outsider' video art and cinema focuses on experimental non-fiction works, and is Italy's most important festival for electronic arts and new technologies. So if it's non-mainstream cinema, video documentaries, art and animation you're after, this one's for you.

Milano Film Festival (MFF)

Teatro Strehler (Nuovo Piccolo), largo Greppi, North (02 7233 3222/www.milanofilmfestival.it). Metro Lanza/bus 57, 58/tram 3, 4, 7, 12, 14. Date mid-late Sept. **Tickets** €6 daily pass; €20 weekly pass. **No credit cards.** **Map** p248 D5.

The Milano Film Festival started in 1995 as a showcase for shorts by young local film-makers; it only opened to international contributors and feature films in 2000. The festival is an interdisciplinary affair that also covers art exhibitions, live music, performances and workshops.

Sport Movies & TV International Festival

Via de Amicis 17, West (02 8940 9076/www.sport moviestv.com). Metro Sant'Ambrogio/bus 94/tram 2, 14, 20. Date late Oct-early Nov. **Map** p250 C8.

Celebrating 27 years in 2009, this important festival is dedicated to sports films, documentaries and television programmes. Featuring more than 200 films and videos, it's a must-see for sports enthusiasts.

Galleries

Contemporary space exploration.

As you'd expect in Italy's capital of design and fashion, Milan's art scene is as vibrant, dynamic and ready to embrace outside influences as ever. Non-Italians exhibit with growing impact and frequency, but there's no shortage of home-grown talent.

Milan has no contemporary art fair of the scope of Venice's Biennale, nor a dedicated exhibition space like Bolzano's new Museum of Modern and Contemporary Art. In Milan, the latest artists and trends are to be found in gallery spaces. Long-established addresses are present in high concentration in the chic neighbourhood of Brera, and newer ones sprout all over the city, especially around Porta Romana and Porta Garibaldi, and in the studenty area around Lambrate train station. The scene is fairly close-knit: get involved at one opening and you'll be invited to another the following week.

Design features heavily in many galleries; others are fond of showing work influenced by the city's design heritage. The annual week-long Salone Internazionale del Mobile, the world's largest design fair, influences the scene further, not least as it has a ready market of 350,000 potential buyers (*see p29*).

Apart from August, when much of the city shuts down for holidays, there are plenty of shows to attend. For a list, pick up a copy of the *Artshow* booklet (www.artshow.it) from the tourist information centre near the Duomo, or from any of the spaces listed in these pages. Note that a handful of Milan's galleries are housed in apartment buildings: ring the bell and you'll be buzzed in.

Annarumma 404

Via Felice Casati 26, San Babila and East (02 3943 0655/annarumma404.com). Metro Porto Venezia/ tram 5, 9, 11, 29, 30, 33. **Open** 4-7pm Tue-Sat. Closed Aug. **Map** p249 F4.
Photography, oil on canvas and avant-garde sculpture predominate at Milan's outpost of the gallery founded in Naples in 2002 (it's still there). This space revolves between international exhibitors and young Neapolitan artists.

Antonio Colombo Arte Contemporanea

Via Solferino 44, North (02 2906 0171/www. colomboarte.com). Metro Moscova/bus 43, 94/ tram 11, 29, 30, 33. **Open** 3-7pm Tue-Sat. Closed Aug, 2wks Dec-Jan. **Map** p248 D5.

Antonio Colombo's gallery focuses on young Italian artists. The emphasis is on figurative art and media, including painting, sculpture and photography.

Assab One

Via Assab 1, East (02 282 8546/www.assab-one.org). Metro Udine/bus 53, 56, 62. **Open** 3-7pm Tue-Sat. Closed Aug, 2wks Dec-Jan. **Map** p248 D5.
The three floors of this former industrial site host a variety of installations: previous incumbents include a mock planetarium and acoustic shows.

B&D Renoldi Arte Contemporanea

Via Calvi 18, East (02 5412 2563/www.bnd.it). Bus 60, 73/tram 11, 12, 29, 30. **Open** 10.30am-7.30pm Tue-Sat. Closed Aug, 2wks Dec-Jan. **Map** p251 G7.
This cool space provides a backdrop for an international mix of technological media, including digital photography, video and lighting.

Cannaviello

Via Stoppani 15, East (02 2024 0428/www. cannaviello.net). Metro Porta Venezia/bus 60, 92/tram 5, 11, 23. **Open** 3-7pm Tue-Sat. Closed Aug. **Map** p248 D5.
Evocative oil on canvas from the 1980s and '90s is the thing here: the European artists who have exhibited include Nobert Brisky and Günter Brus.

Civati Arte

Via Mercato 3, North (02 3966 1129/www.civati arte.it). Metro Lanza/tram 3, 14. **Open** varies. Closed Aug. **Map** p252 D5.
This small, new gallery is the brainchild of the dynamic Stefano Civati. Exhibition subjects range from global stars like Warhol to contemporary Italian painting or international photography.

Clio Calvi/Rudy Volpi

Via Pontaccio 17, North (02 8691 5009/www. cliocalvirudyvolpi.it). Metro Lanza/bus 61/tram 3, 12, 20. **Open** 3.30-7pm Tue-Sat. Closed Aug. **Map** p248 D5.
A solid selection of recent pieces by Ettore Sottsass and Andrea Branzi: limited-edition shelving, tables, chairs and knick-knacks.

C/O (Care Of)

Fabbrica del Vapore, via Procaccini 4, North (02 331 5800/www.careof.org). Bus 43/tram 12, 14, 29, 30, 33. **Open** 3-7pm Tue-Sat. Closed Aug, 2wks Dec-Jan. **Map** p248 C3.
A non-profit gallery that punches above its weight. This white space inside the Fabbrica del Vapore, a former tram factory, has a hectic schedule. There's room for small installations, and video projects and multimedia are increasingly shown. *Photo p152.*

Take **C/O (Care Of)** your artistic needs at this buzzing little gallery. *See p151.*

Dilmos

Piazza San Marco 1, North (02 2900 2437/www.
dilmos.com). Metro Lanza/bus 61/tram 20. **Open**
2.30-7pm Mon; 10am-1.30pm, 2.30-7pm Tue-Sat.
Closed Aug & 2wks Dec-Jan. **Map** p249 E5.
This gallery is party central during the furniture
fair. A mix of glass, iron and soft fabrics goes into
the creations, which cross the line between furniture
design and visual art.

Galleria Blu

Via Senato 18, East (02 7602 2404/www.galleria
blu.com). Metro Montenapoleone or Turati/bus
61, 94. **Open** 10am-12.30pm, 3.30-7pm Mon-Fri;
3.30-7.30pm Sat. Closed Aug, 2wks Dec-Jan.
Map p249 F5.
Galleria Blu is Milan's oldest and arguably its most
prestigious art gallery, having been founded as long
ago as 1957 to promote promising post-war avant-
garde artists; it was the first gallery in the world to
showcase Lucio Fontana, Alberto Burri and Emilio
Vedova. The list of prominent names whose work is
or has been exhibited here includes Braque,
Basquiat, Chagall, Giacometti, Kandinsky, Klee,
Matisse, Tancredi and Warhol.

Galleria Carla Sozzani

Corso Como 10, North (02 653 531/www.galleria
carlasozzani.org). Metro Garibaldi/tram 11, 29, 30,
33. **Open** 3.30-7.30pm Mon; 10.30am-7.30pm Tue,
Fri-Sun; 10.30am-9pm Wed, Thur. **Map** p248 D3.
Part of Carla Sozzani's Corso Como style/culture/
café complex (*see p43 and p114*), this gallery is big
on black and white photography, digital imagery and
montage. Non-Italians predominate in the line-up of
artists: past exhibitors have included Bruce Weber,
Edward S Curtis, Rodman Wanamaker, Herb Ritts
and Mary Ellen Mark.

Galleria Emi Fontana

Viale Bligny 42, South (02 5832 2237/www.galleria
emifontana.com). Metro Porta Romana, then tram 9,
29, 30/bus 79. **Open** 11am-7.30pm Tue-Sat. Closed
2wks Aug, 2wks Dec-Jan. **Map** p251 E9.
Galleria Emi Fontana has been showing the hottest
international contemporary artists in all the artistic
media – including Turner Prize winner Gillian
Wearing – since 1992.

Galleria Massimo De Carlo

Via Giovanni Ventura 5, North (02 7000 3987/www.
massimodecarlo.it). Metro Lambrate/bus 54, 75/tram
11, 33. **Open** 11.30am-2pm, 2.30-7.30pm Tue-Sat.
This establishment exhibits global contemporary
art: canvases and light sculptures from the likes of
Aernout Mik, Yan Pei-Ming and Diego Perrone.

Galleria Pack

Foro Buonaparte 60, North (02 8699 6395/www.
galleriapack.com). Metro Cairoli or Lanza/bus 50,
58/tram 1, 3, 4, 12, 27. **Open** am by appointment,
1-7.30pm Tue-Sat. Closed Aug, 2wks Dec-Jan. **Map**
p248 D5.
This astoundingly handsome venue showcases
artists such as MM Campos Pons, Pietro Finelli,
Robert Gligorov, Miriam Cabessa and Ofri Cnaani.
Inspired photography and gallery-size installations
are the order of the day. Note: the street numbering
in foro Buonaparte is misleading – number 60 is
closest to the corso Garibaldi end.

Arts & Entertainment

Galleria Ponte Rosso

*Via Brera 2, North (02 8646 1053/www.ponterosso.
com). Metro Lanza/bus 61/tram 3, 4, 12.* **Open**
10am-12.30pm, 3.30-7pm Tue-Sat. Closed July-mid
Sept. **Map** p248 D6.

Founded in 1973, the Ponte Rosso has long given
space to Lombardy painters and the movements
they started, from the early 1900s to the present day.
Among the extensive list of artists who have been
exhibited here are Giuseppe Novello, Cristoforo De
Amicis and Carlo Dalla Zorza.

Galleria Post Design

*Via della Moscova 27, North (02 655 4731/www.
memphis-milano.it). Metro Moscova/bus 43, 94.*
Open 3-7pm Mon-Sat. Closed Aug. **Map** p248 D4.

The gallery hosts frequent themed design exhibitions of objects for the home: porcelain, carpets, lighting, silverware and so on. All around it, in the area
between Brera and corso Como, a number of similar
'design galleries' have sprung up: it's hard to tell a
store from a gallery in this city, as the fields of art
and commerce have become inseparably fused.

Galleria Santa Marta

*Via Santa Marta 19, Centre (02 805 2643/www.
galleriasantamarta.it). Metro Moscova/bus 43, 94.*
Open 10am-1pm, 4-7pm Tue-Sat. Closed Aug.
Map p252 D7.

Modern art meets the odd master at this fine gallery,
where the likes of Hartung and Grosz are hung
alongside younger artists who experiment with different styles and materials.

Giò Marconi

*Via Tadino 15, East (02 2940 4373/www.gio
marconi.com). Metro Lima or Porta Venezia/bus
60/tram 5, 9, 11, 20, 29, 30, 33.* **Open** varies.
Closed Aug, late Dec-early Jan. **Map** p249 G4.

This three-level space caters to all tastes, exhibiting
everything from Italian post-war art to the latest
video installations.

Italhome Sedie Collezioni

*Largo Treves 2, North (02 655 1787/www.pianeta
sedia.com). Metro Moscova/bus 43, 94.* **Open** 3-7pm
Mon-Sat. Closed Aug. **Map** p248 D5.

A homage to sofas, stools and armchairs: they claim
to have sold over 100,000 in the last 20 years. The
collection includes classic designs by luminaries such
as Giò Ponti, Frank Lloyd Wright and Le Corbusier.

Luceplan

*Via San Damiano 5, via Senato, East (02 7601
5760/www.luceplan.it). Bus 54, 61/tram 9, 20, 29,
30, 33.* **Open** 10am-1.30pm, 2.30-7pm Mon-Sat.
Closed 2wks Aug, 1wk Jan. **Map** p252 F6.

Browsing at this branch of Brescia lighting company Luceplan is to take a tour through the best in
lighting design, including works by Luciano
Baldessari and Luciano Balestrini. The firm has
opened further offshoots in London and Paris, and
its designs now grace hip hotels and cruise ships –
but it hasn't betrayed its boutique roots.

Nuages

*Via del Lauro 10, North (02 7200 4482/www.
nuages.net). Metro Cairoli or Lanza/tram 1, 3, 4, 12,
14, 27.* **Open** 2-7pm Tue-Fri; 10am-1pm, 2-7pm Sat.
Closed 2wks Aug. **Map** p248 D6/p252 D6.

Lorenzo Mattotti, Tullio Pericoli and Gianluigi
Toccafondo are among the Italian artists exhibited
here; international stars have included Milton
Glaser, Sempé, Folon and Art Spiegelman.

Photology

*Via della Moscova 25, North (02 659 5285/www.
photology.com). Metro Moscova/bus 43, 94.* **Open**
11am-7pm Tue-Sat. Closed Aug. **Map** p249 E4.

Shows at this long-established photo gallery tend to
be split 50/50 between Italian and other artists.
Among the photographers represented are Mario
Giacomelli and Gian Paolo Barbieri; shows by Luigi
Ghirri and Giacomo Costa have also been held.

Pianissimo Contemporary Art

*Via Lambrate 24, East (02 215 4514/www.
pianissimo.it). Metro Lambrate/bus 60, 62.* **Open**
3-7pm Tue-Sat. Closed Aug.

This ultra-contemporary spot is one of a group of
galleries in the somewhat seedy neighbourhood near
Lambrate station. Focusing on sculpture and installations, it hosts one artist at a time: recently Tobias
Collier and Ingo Gerken.

Studio Guenzani

*Via Eustachi 10, East (02 2940 9251/www.studio
guenzani.it). Metro Lima/bus 60, 62/tram 5, 11, 23.*
Open am by appointment, 3-7.30pm Tue-Sat. Closed
Aug. **Map** p249 H5.

Claudio Guenzani has exhibited the likes of US
painter Laura Owens and Japanese photographer
Hiroshi Sugimoto, and has strong links with Milan
artists, including painter Margherita Manzelli and
photographer Gabriele Basilico.
Other locations: via Melzo 5, East (02 2940 9251).

Viafarini

*Via Farini 35, North (02 6680 4473/www.viafarini.
org). Metro Porta Garibaldi/bus 41, 51, 70/tram 3,
4, 7, 11, 29, 30.* **Open** by appointment only. Closed
Aug. **Map** p248 D2.

More than just a gallery for far-out photography and
other disciplines, this space – run in conjunction
with the city council – provides facilities for
researching contemporary art in Milan. There's an
art library and an archive on young working artists.

Zonca & Zonca

*Via Ciovasso 4, North (02 7200 3377/www.
zoncaezonca.com). Metro Cairoli or Lanza/bus
61/tram 3, 4, 12.* **Open** 10am-1pm, 3.30-7.30pm
Mon-Fri; Sat by appointment. Closed Aug. **Map**
p248 D6/p252 D6.

This space mixes Italian modernism with super-con-
temporary art. Selections by Gianfranco Zonca,
which have included work by Lucio Fontana and
Mimmo Rotella, are offset by his daughter Elena's
taste for cutting-edge installation and photography.

Arts & Entertainment

Gay & Lesbian

Same-sex, but different.

Welcome to the most glamorous and gay-friendly of all Italian cities: style and fun are not options here, they're guaranteed. Milan has no Greenwich Village to speak of, so apart from via Sammartini, a tiny street next to Centrale station, walking through the door of each venue is a voyage of discovery.

Gay-friendly fashionistas visiting from all over the world add a cosmopolitan sparkle to a community of attractive Italians. The Milanese are cool but reserved people, and sometimes unadventurous with new venues – so finding the latest hot address can be tricky, even for them. Persevere, though, and bear in mind that many local trendsetters join the sexy, arty crowds at the city's many gay-friendly theme nights, which are sometimes livelier than the established gay venues. *Pride* and *Clubbing* with *Zerodue,* free magazines found in many of Milan's bars, clubs and stores, will help you find the highlights of the month. Keep 'em peeled and, as they say here, *Divertiti!* – Enjoy!

PRACTICALITIES

Milan is about fashion, and Milanese gays love drama and posing; but the city is not merely fashion-oriented. As in other cosmopolitan cities, there are underground venues aplenty, and there's also scope for visitors who crave harder action, or have a penchant for leather and dark rooms. To get into many gay clubs, bars and saunas, you'll need a membership card issued by Arcigay (Italy's gay and lesbian organisation; *see p226*): the card costs €15, and can be bought at most venues that require it; it's valid for a year. If you're in Milan for a short visit, you can opt for the one-month visitor's card (€8).

While you're in Milan, be sure to stop into the gay bookstore Libreria Babele. There, along with *Pride* and other magazines, you can pick up a handy, comprehensive and free map of Milan's gay scene (*see p125*).

Bars, clubs & discos

For other top gay-friendly nights, *see p163* **Magazzini Generali**.

Afterline

Via Sammartini 25, North (02 669 4476/www.gay street.it). Metro Centrale/bus 41, 82/tram 2, 5, 9.
Open 9pm-2am Mon-Wed, Sun; 9pm-3am Thur-Sat. **Admission** free Mon-Wed, Sun; €6 (incl drink) Thur-Sat. **No credit cards**. **Map** p249 G2.
This kitsch, baroque disco pub is a major meeting point on via Sammartini. It runs themed evenings for the boys, like striptease contests on Friday nights. It's a nice, friendly place in which to relax and drink before heading into the night.

Atomic Bar

*Via Felice Casati 24, East (mobile 333 689 8446/
www.atomicbar.it). Metro Porta Venezia/tram 1, 5,
9, 29, 30.* **Open** *9.30pm-2am daily. Closed Aug.*
Admission *free (drinks €10).* **No credit cards.**
Map *p249 F4.*
Betty Page-style disco decor furnished with 1970s
wallpaper and chairs: this three-room bar has lot of
authentic charm, and the music is a good mix of
indie, electro and rock. A good pre-club bar frequented by local trendies and creative types.

Billy

*Amnesia, via Gatto, at viale Forlanini, East (mobile
335 832 7777/www.billyclub.it).* *Bus 38.* **Open** *noon-
5am Sat. Closed Aug.* **Admission** *€16-€20 (incl
drink).* **Credit** *AmEx, MC, V.*
Frequented by the international crowd with hosts of
foreign DJs to boot, Billy hosts wild outdoor summer parties in June near the Idroscalo leisure park.

Glitter Pagliaccia

*HD, via Caruso 11, at via Tajani, East (02 718 990/
www.glitterdiary.com).* *Tram 5.* **Open** *noon-4am Sat.
Closed July, Aug.* **Admission** *€12 (incl drink).* **No
credit cards.**
The ninth season of Glitter is now at HD until further notice; the club also runs a low-key gay night
on Tuesdays. A mixed gay/lesbian/straight/arty
crowd dances to 1980s sounds, electronica, Britpop
and trash; staff keep things lively with amusing performances. Fun and unpretentious.

G Lounge

*Via Larga 8, Centre (02 805 3042/www.glounge.it).
Metro Duomo or Missori/bus 54/tram 12, 15, 20 23,
27.* **Open** *7am-9pm Mon; 7am-2am Tue-Fri; 6pm-
2am Sat, Sun. Closed 3wks Aug.* **Admission** *free.*
Credit *AmEx, DC, MC, V.* **Map** *p251 E7/p252 E7.*

G Lounge.

This gay-friendly place very close to the Duomo has
been a former Fascist HQ, a billiard hall and a ciga-
rette store, and was transformed recently into a stylish lounge; it's gay-friendly rather than exclusively
gay. The downstairs is minimal and exotic, with
great tunes and delicious cocktails. Saturday is the
best time to meet the like-minded.

Join the Gap

*Borgo del Tempo Perso, via Fabio Massimo 36, East
(02 569 4755). Metro Corvetto or Porto di Mare.*
Open *7pm-2am Sun. Closed July, Aug.* **Admission**
€12-€15 (incl drink) **Credit** *AmEx, DC, MC, V.*
Run by CIG (Centro di Iniziativa Gay), this very popular club is a Sunday-night follow-up to Billy, with
a similar, slightly younger, crowd. The club offers
aperitivo (early evening buffet) and a drag queen
show before the music (hip hop, '70s, R&B) kicks off.

Lelephant

*Via Melzo 22, San Babila & East (02 2951 8768/
www.lelephant.it). Metro Porta Venezia/tram 9, 29,
30.* **Open** *6.30pm-2am Tue-Sun. Closed 3wks Aug.*
No credit cards. Map *p249 G5.*
With its eclectic arty-crafty decor, Lelephant suc-
ceeds well in mixing cocktails for an appreciative
mixed gay, straight and arty crowd. The early
evening *aperitivo* (buffet and drink for €5) is
renowned, particularly on Sundays. The lights go
down after 9.30pm to create a great atmosphere for
a drink and a chat. *See also p119.*

Nuova Idea

*Via de Castillia 30, North (mobile 333 481 6780/
www.lanuovaidea.it). Metro Gioia/bus 82/tram
30, 33.* **Open** *10.30pm-4am Thur-Sat. Closed July,
Aug.* **Admission** *€10-€18.* **No credit cards.**
Map *p249 E3.*
This is a piece of gay Milan history: it has been
pulling them in for over 30 years. The two dancefloors – one for ballroom dancing with a live orchestra, one for the disco – are as surreal and
entertaining as watching a Fellini movie. It's popular with the area's transvestite crowd.

Pervert Gold

*Rolling Stone, Corso XXII Marzo 32, East (02
733 172/www.mondopervert.com). Bus 45, 73, 92/
tram 12, 27.* **Open** *11pm-5am 2nd & 4th Sun of
mth.* **Admission** *€30.* **Credit** *AmEx, MC, V.*
Map *p251 H7.*
An unmissable party extravaganza. Inspired by
opera, theatre and cinema, these events are a hurri-
cane of visual stimulation, feathers, glitter and
make-up. Music is spun by regular DJs Obi Baby,
Lorenzo Lsp and international guests such as
Fischerspooner. The location changes frequently:
check the website or call 338 105 1232 for updates.

Plastic

*Viale Umbria 120, South (02 733 996/www.
thisisplastic.com). Bus 84, 92/tram 16.* **Open**
11pm-4am Thur-Sun. Closed mid June-Aug.
Admission *€15-€25 (incl drink); free Sun.*
No credit cards.

Arts & Entertainment

This gay-friendly club is the Studio 54 of Milan – a den for supermodels, electro music gurus and an arty-glam crowd for more than 20 years. Sunday night (Match à Paris) is the best: great electro music, sexy people and free admission.

Popstarz

Gasoline Club, via Bonnet 11A, North (mobile 339 774 5797/www.discogasoline.it). Metro Garibaldi/bus 70/tram 3, 4, 7, 11, 29, 30. **Open** 10.30pm-5am Thur. Closed mid June-Aug. **Admission** €15 (incl drink). **Credit** MC, V. **Map** p248 D3.

A club night that dreams are made of: strobe lights, beautiful people, bisexuals, transvestites, muscle men and lesbians all getting wild on the dancefloor, while resident DJs Nancy Posh and Tommy Boys play electro, '80s and contemporary pop. One of the best gay-oriented nights in Milan.

Rocket

Via Pezzotti 52, South (02 8950 3509/www.the rocket.it). Bus 79, 90, 91/tram 15. **Open** 10am-2am Mon-Sat. Closed Aug. **Admission** free (drink €10). **No credit cards.**

Milan's coolest gay-friendly bar: a disco joint with a large dancefloor that gets packed out every night. Good DJs man the console, the drinks are great, the crowd is interesting, and it's a stop-off point for visitors: all the ingredients for a memorable night.

Sodoma

Hollywood, corso Como 15, North (02 659 8996/ www.discotecahollywood.com/mondopervert.com). Metro Garibaldi/tram 11, 29, 30, 33. **Open** 10.30pm-4am Wed. Closed July, Aug. **Admission** €20 (incl drink). **Credit** AmEx, DC, MC, V. **Map** p248 D3.

Organised by Pervert, Sodoma is the best night at Hollywood, and the only one where people are not there to see and to be seen. Resident DJs Obi Baby and Nino Lopez keep the dancefloor packed with young boys in sunglasses and cheerful transvestites.

Studio Know How

Via Antonio da Recanate 7, North (02 6739 1224). Metro Centrale FS/bus 42, 81/tram 2, 5, 9, 33. **Open** 9.30am-7.30pm Mon-Sat. Closed 2wks Aug. **Credit** AmEx, DC, MC, V. **Map** p249 F3.

Billing itself as Italy's only entirely gay shop, Studio Know How has a magnificent choice of videos and DVDs. For those who like things a bit harder, there's also large selection of games and sex toys.

Zip After Hour

Zip Club, corso Sempione 76, North (02 331 4904). Bus 43, 57/tram 1, 19, 29, 30, 33. **Open** 4am-11am Sat. Closed June-Aug. **Admission** €25. **No credit cards. Map** p248 A3.

It's hard to find somewhere for dancing in Milan after 5am. One of the few options is Zip, a wacky club near Bullona Station. Most of the people here are transvestites, but gay and hetero night owls also love the place. Music is techno and hard electro, and the dark room is famous. It's a private club; bring an ID card or passport to secure entry.

Cruising bars

Cruising bars are becoming increasingly popular in Milan. Often housed in anonymous blocks (sometimes the only clue is a tiny plaque at the entrance), these establishments offer total discretion, and you can relax in the knowledge that you're among like-minded people.

Cruising Canyon

Via Paisello 4, East (02 2040 4201/www. cruisingcanyon.com). Metro Loreto/bus 90, 91, 92. **Open** 24hrs daily. **Admission** €8-€10. **Credit** AmEx, MC, V.

Cruising at its simplest: this round-the-clock bar has an erotic cinema, labyrinth, dark rooms and cubicles, and a witty mock-up of the 'fossa' cruising area outside Parco Sempione. The lack of a bar is a bit offputting, but there's plenty of space in which to move around, chill out and see who's there.

Depot

Via dei Valtorta 19, North (02 289 2920/www.depot milano.com). Metro Turro/bus 56. **Open** 10pm-3am Mon, Wed, Thur; 10pm-6am Fri, Sat; 3pm-1am Sun. Closed Aug. **Admission** €30. **No credit cards.**

This dark, cosy cruising/fetish bar on three floors is for people looking for hard and raw encounters – from leather to sportswear fetish and naked parties. The venue attracts a slightly older crowd; discounts are often available for under-30s.

Flexo

Via Oropa 3, East (02 2682 6709/www.flexoclub.it). Metro Cimiano. **Open** 10pm-3.30am Mon-Thur; 10pm-6am Fri, Sat. **Admission** €5 Mon-Wed; €10 Fri, Sat (incl drink; €5 after 4am). **Credit** AmEx, DC, MC, V.

A two-floor cruising bar in the north-east suburbs, with cubicles, glory holes, a chill-out area and a labyrinth. There's a large bar area in which to meet friends and mingle, and a leather tower upstairs for harder action. At the weekend, Flexo teams up with Metro Cimiano sauna (*see below*) to offer joint entry tickets. There are naked parties on Tuesday, Thursday and Saturday, plus other themed nights.

Saunas

Metro Centrale

Via Schiapparelli 1, North (02 6671 9089/www. metroclub.it). Metro Centrale FS/bus 42, 53, 90, 91/ tram 2, 5, 9, 33. **Open** noon-2am daily. **Admission** €15 (€12.50 after 8pm). **Credit** MC, V. **Map** 249 G2.

Metro Centrale occupies three floors, with jacuzzis, a steam bath, a massage room and a Finnish sauna. For your private viewing pleasure, there are videos in the chill-out rooms, as well as an internet terminal. It's frequented by a young crowd taking advantage of discounts for under-26s; on the first and second Sunday of the month, a huge buffet is served. **Other locations:** Metro Cimiano, Via Oropa 3, East (02 2851 0528).

Thermas

Via Bezzecca 9, East (02 545 0355/www.thermas club.com). Bus 60, 84/tram 27, 29, 30. **Open** noon-midnight Mon-Wed, Sat, Sun; noon-2am Thur, Fri. Closed 2wks Aug. **Admission** €15; €13 under-25s; €10 Tue & after 8pm daily. **No credit cards.** **Map** p251 G7.

Honest and clean, Thermas is a two-floor sauna relatively close to the centre with friendly staff, a bar, steam bath, small weights room, cooling-off area with porn, small darkroom, and recliners.

Lesbian Milan

Although gay Milan stands proud, facilities for lesbian travellers and residents are fewer. That said, the Gaia360 website (www.gaia360.com) is a good starting point. Then there's Kick-off (www.kickoff.biz), which co-ordinates events and parties at a variety of bars and clubs. Bi-monthly lesbian mag *Towanda* is a good guide that includes book reviews, political commentary and art critiques, as well as news on lesbian holiday spots and events organised by Arcilesbica (*see p226*). Finally, www.listalesbica.it is a good resource for everything from events and chatrooms to jobs.

Bars, clubs & discos

Cicip & Ciciap

Via Gorani 9, Centre (02 8699 5410/www.ricicip. org). Metro Cordusio/bus 54, 58/tram 2, 14, 16, 18, 19, 20. **Open** 7pm-1am Wed-Sun. **No credit cards.** **Map** p250 C7/p252 C7.

This centre for the politically and non-politically minded has recently reopened, hosting discussion groups for women of all ages. The centre also has a bar and a reasonably priced restaurant.

Kick-off at Black Hole

Via Cena 1, East (02 7104 0220/www.kickoff.biz). Bus 90, 91, 92/tram 12. **Open** 11.30pm-4am Fri. Closed July & Aug. **Admission** €12-€14 (incl drink). **No credit cards.**

This disco in an area well served by gay venues hosts a popular lesbian disco on Friday nights. The sleek, modern space has two dancefloors, plus an outdoor garden that's open in summer. Live music and shows are hosted before the disco starts; the music is a mix of commercial R&B, house and pop.

Rhabar

Alzaia Naviglio Grande 150, South (mobile 393 904 5796/www.rhabar.it). Tram 2. **Open** 7pm-2am Wed-Sun. Closed 10 days-2wks Aug.

This bar/disco on the canal is decorated in minimal-Moroccan style; live music and themed nights add to the cosy atmosphere. It appeals to younger, style-conscious women; check out the singles party night, normally on Wednesdays.

Sottomarino Giallo

Via Donatello 2, East (339 545 4127/www.sotto marinogiallo.it). Metro Loreto, Lima or Piola/bus 62, 90, 91, 92/tram 33. **Open** 11pm-4am Tue-Sat; Closed June-Aug. **Admission** €10 (incl drink). **No credit cards.**

This disco used to be a key venue for the lesbian crowd. In the last few years it has become a more generally gay-friendly place, hosting international DJs and a lively crowd, especially on Fridays.

It's positively fantastic at **Plastic**. *See p155.*

Music

Opera, rock and pop raise the roof.

Say 'Milan' and 'music', and the next word rolling off your tongue is likely to be 'opera' – or maybe even 'La Scala'. Milan's original importance in the music world can be attributed largely to its famed opera house, and the growth of academies and industries that have sprung up around it. At one point, most of the world's sheet music was produced in Milan, with Ricordi (the biggest Italian record label before it was bought by BMG in the 1990s) putting out the bulk of it.

Milan is now Italy's pan-musical hub, and Italian recording outfits, the majority of national radio stations and local headquarters for international labels are based in the city. Because of this, artists from all over Italy are often obliged to live here, occasionally against their will. Like many people living in Milan, such musicians seem to suffer from a chronic disposition to moan about their adoptive city. And although it's true that Milan doesn't offer the romantic charm of other Italian cities, it's also true that Italy's provinces don't have

enough to offer to musicians and artists, which is why they came to Milan in the first place.

At the very least, this complex love-hate relationship has served as inspiration for a fair number of Italian songs. In 2001, a Roman artist, Alex Britti, recorded the melancholic 'Milano', which describes a lonely Sunday spent wandering around in search of something to do. In 2002, rap group Articolo 31 recorded 'Milano Milano', which sums up the ambiguous feelings of many residents: 'Whenever I go away, I want to come back,' the group sang, 'but as soon as I come back, I want to escape.'

But don't listen to the self-pitying *Milanesi*: the truth of the matter is that Milan has one of Italy's liveliest music scenes, from rock and pop to jazz and classical. And although it can't match the range of London or New York, there will generally be something musical going on that suits you, whatever your taste. Most major Italian artists perform in Milan at some stage, and the city is also on the concert circuit for most international acts.

A home from home for musicans and fans. **La Casa 139**. *See p160*.

INFORMATION AND TICKETS

When it comes to upcoming concerts, the best source is *Zerodue* (www.zero.eu), the free listings magazine issued every fortnight. Look for it in venues, bars and record stores. Also, there are five free daily newspapers, *Dnews*, *EPolis*, *Metro*, *City* and *Leggo*, all of which can be found stacked in metro stations and at major tram stops in the morning, and publishing details of shows taking place that evening.

For tickets, it's often simpler to use central booking agencies like **Ticketone** (www.ticketone.it). You can also purchase concert tickets in large bookshops and music stores like **Mondadori** (*see p125*), **Ricordi Media Store** (galleria Vittorio Emanuele II, 02 8646 3235), **La Feltrinelli** (*see p125*) and **FNAC** (via della Palla 2, 02 869 541).

OPENING TIMES AND TRANSPORT

In the listings below, we have tried to give fixed box office opening times where possible, as well as performance times and regular opening times (for bars and clubs). Note, however, that the main act may not kick off until an hour or two after the performance is billed to start. Some venues are in out-of-the-way districts, and the chances are that public transport will have stopped running by the time the concert ends. Make sure you've got a cab number in your pocket (*see p221*), just in case; in smaller venues, staff will be happy to book one for you.

Mega venues

DatchForum

Via G di Vittorio 6, Assago, South (199 128 800/ www.forumnet.it). Metro Famagosta, then bus to Assago. **Open** times vary. **Tickets** prices vary. **No credit cards.**
This sports and music venue was built for the 1990 World Cup, and is one of the most love-it-or-hate-it cement structures in the city. It's very hard to get to by public transport, and the acoustics aren't the best, but the auditorium is huge – the sort of place where acts that favour bombast over sound quality can be expected to gig (Céline Dion, KISS and Coldplay). As there's no numbered seating, it's a good idea to arrive as early as possible. Next door (part of the same complex) is the cosier Teatro della Luna.

PalaSharp

Via Sant'Elia 33, West (02 3340 0551/www. palasharp.it). Metro Lampugnano/bus 68, 199. **Open** *Box office* 9.30am-6pm Mon-Fri. **Tickets** prices vary. **No credit cards.**
In 1985, Milan was hit by a freak snowfall, which destroyed the city's indoor sports arena. The 9,000-seat PalaSharp (originally called the Palatrussardi) was rapidly built to replace it. Frank Sinatra was the first to play here, in 1986, and he has been followed by the likes of Bob Dylan and Elton John.

Nordest Caffè. *See p161.*

Stadio Meazza (San Siro)

Viale Piccolomini 5, West (02 4871 3713/www. sansiro.net). Metro Lotto/bus 78, 90, 91/tram 16. **Open** times vary. **Tickets** prices vary. **No credit cards.**
This iconic city-owned soccer stadium (known as San Siro throughout the football world) is shared by the city's two, fiercely competitive soccer clubs, Milan and Inter, throughout the year (*see p168* **Filthy rich football face off**). During the summer months, however, it takes time off from the serious business of *il calcio* to host the occasional megaconcert. Previous performers have included world-renowned acts such as Bruce Springsteen, Madonna and the Rolling Stones, as well as Italian stars Vasco Rossi, Laura Pausini and Ligabue.

Medium to large

Alcatraz

Via Valtellina 25, North (02 6901 6352/ www.alcatrazmilano.com). Bus 72, 90, 91, 92/ tram 3, 4. **Open** times vary. Closed July, Aug. **Tickets** prices vary. **No credit cards.**
This largish site doubles as a disco (*see p164*) and concert venue (mainly on Monday and Thursday nights). It's in a converted industrial space away from the city centre, but is still reasonably accessible. It hosts Italian and international acts, including the Hives and Kanye West.

Melodrama at La Scala

The last few years at La Scala have been eventful, to say the least. In 2002 the company left the theatre it had called home since 1778, taking up temporary residence at the modern Teatro degli Arcimboldi in the north of the city, so that vital restoration work could be done. As the €61-million revamp drew to a finish, the company made a triumphant return on the opening night of the 2004-2005 season, presided over by Giorgio Armani and Sophia Loren.

What planners hadn't been able to foresee was the dramatic upheaval that would take place in 2005, when the company's music director and chief conductor of 20 years, Riccardo Muti, resigned. Muti's official reason for leaving was 'the vulgar show of hostility' by his colleagues. Opponents of Muti had

criticised him for being dictatorial. Film and opera director Franco Zeffirelli described La Scala's programme under Muti as 'one horrendous production after another; constipated, anal and with no explosion of vitality on stage'. Defenders of Muti, on the other hand, saw him as a misunderstood genius and a victim of La Scala's highly unionised, 800-strong workforce.

What was striking about the story was how, in true Italian style, even a dispute at an opera house could become a political issue: generally speaking, left-wingers joined the 'Muti Out' campaign, whereas right-wingers, including Silvio Berlusconi's Forza Italia party and the city's then mayor (and president of La Scala's board of directors), Gabriele Albertini, took up the maestro's defence. A few days after Muti's resignation, two of his presumed political allies followed suit. Fedele Confalonieri, president of Silvio Berlusconi's Mediaset media empire, resigned from La Scala's board of directors, as did Marco Tronchetti Provera, boss of the powerful Pirelli tyre company and Telecom Italia.

Although supporters of Muti thought he was irreplaceable, many opera aficionados feel that his departure, along with the return to the old premises, has led to some much-needed improvements. In purely practical terms, the renovation work has created considerably more storage space, thanks to a controversial new concrete 'fly tower', visible from piazza della Scala. Scene changes are now easier: the tower allows a stage set to slide up and down as well as sideways. Another high-tech addition is the airline-style seat-back screens, which offer an instant translation of the lyrics. But when it comes to the traditional complaint that you get a pretty poor view of the stage from many of La Scala's seats, not much appears to have changed.

Rolling Stone

Corso XXII Marzo 32, East (02 733 172/www.rolling stone.it). Bus 45, 66, 73/tram 12, 27. **Open** times vary. **Tickets** prices vary. **Credit** AmEx, MC, V. This three-floor club hosts several concerts a month. With a top capacity of 2,000 and the ability to close off different floors depending on the size of the act, it bridges the gap between the huge venues and cosier places in the centre. It's also one of the few venues in Milan that has an indoor smoking area (with an air purification system).

Small

La Casa 139

Via Ripamonti 139, South (no telephone/www. lacasa139.com). Bus 90, 91/tram 24. **Open** Mon-Sat. **Tickets** prices vary, entrance with ARCI membership (€5 to join on the door). **No credit cards**.
This multifunctional place seems to play host to just about everything: concerts, DJ sets, exhibitions, conferences and private parties. Its music selection

In artistic terms, the departure of Muti has marked the dawning of a new, more innovative, era. In May 2005, Stéphane Lissner, formerly of the Aix-en-Provence Festival, was appointed as general manager and artistic director. He recently announced that he plans to stage an operatic version of Al Gore's *An Inconvenient Truth* at La Scala in 2011. The company is also on a mission to broaden its appeal by marketing itself more vigorously abroad. A six-date tour of Asia in October 2008 took in Beijing and Shanghai for the first time.

Scandal and disruption still mar La Scala's grand plans, however. Lissner called a walk-out by staff in November 2007 'serious and unacceptable', and several performances of Puccini's *La Bohème* were cancelled in July 2008 as unions demanded a €13m wage hike over the coming four years. And grand theatre well and truly descended into farce in 2006, when leading tenor Roberto Alagna was booed off stage. Although the opening night's performance of Verdi's *Aida* was cheered for 15 minutes by a VIP crowd that included the then prime minister Romano Prodi and German chancellor Angela Merkel, the following evening's act was jeered. Apparently, the *loggionisti*, the hardened opera buffs who occupy the cheap seats in the gods, picked on Alagna for spending too much time on the stages of London and New York and ignoring Milan's famed opera house. The video of him waving his fist at the crowd, then being replaced by understudy Antonello Palombi, casually dressed in jeans and a shirt, is a YouTube hit. 'They literally took me and threw me on stage,' claimed Palombi, 'It was a good test and I passed it.'

features up-and-coming Italian acts and a good selection of underground-ish, 'soft' international acts such as Electrelane, Au Revoir Simone and Gonzales. The cosy atmosphere and feeling that the artists are within arm's reach make it one of Milan's best small venues for live music. *Photo p158.*

Musicdrome
Via Paravia 59, West (348 866 9266 mobile/www. musicdrome.it). Bus 49, 72, 80. **Open** 9pm-3am daily. **Tickets** prices vary. **No credit cards**.

Once known as Transilvania (probably Milan's only death metal bar), this venue has recently been recast as a Swinging London-style place. A pretty weird choice, if you consider that most acts that play there are still mostly metal or punk. Most mid-level rock acts that come to Milan play here, from punk to indie and metal: the likes of the Raveonettes, the Black Lips and Converge.

Jazz

Italian jazz generally enjoys an enthusiastic local reception. In addition to old timers like Paolo Conte and Enrico Rava (another, pianist/painter Romano Mussolini, son of *il Duce*, died in 2006), there's an exciting new generation that includes trumpeter Paolo Fresu, and pianists Stefano Bollani and Giovanni Allevi. Milan's clubs provide a perfect setting for sitting back, relaxing and enjoying the music.

Blue Note
Via Borsieri 37, North (premium rate info line 899 700 022/www.bluenotemilano.com). Metro Porta Garibaldi or Zara/bus 82, 83/tram 4, 7, 11. **Open** 8.30pm-1am Tue-Sat; 8.30-11pm Sun. *Box office* 2-7pm Mon; 2pm-midnight Tue-Sat; 7-11pm Sun. Closed mid June-Aug. **Tickets** prices vary. **Credit** AmEx, DC, MC, V.
The Blue Note club, restaurant and bar is the largest and most prestigious of the Milan jazz venues, and part of a venerable international franchise. The range of music is broad, although it focuses mostly on jazz, soul, world music and blues. Recent guests have also included more widely known stars, such as Suzanne Vega.

Nordest Caffè
Via Borsieri 35, North (02 6900 1910/www.nordest caffe.it). Metro Porta Garibaldi or Zara/bus 82/tram 7, 11. **Open** 8am-1am Mon-Sat; 8.30am-8.30pm Sun. Closed 2wks Aug. **Admission** free. **No credit cards**.
This pleasant wine bar hosts local and international jazz artists on Wednesday and Thursday (from 10pm in winter and from 7.30pm in summer). Entrance is free, although the first drink costs €7.50. *Photo p159.*

La Salumeria della Musica
Via Pasinetti 4, South (02 5680 7350/www. lasalumeriadellamusica.com). Tram 24. **Open** 9pm-2am Mon-Sat. Closed July & Aug. **Tickets** prices vary. **Credit** MC, V.
This venue, whose name means 'the delicatessen of music', prides itself on having been listed by *Down Beat* magazine among the world's 100 best jazz clubs from 2003 to 2006. It's also used for literary and cultural events. Shows start at around 10.30pm, but you might want to get there early to grab a platter of cheese and cold cuts or a glass of wine.

Le Scimmie
Via Ascanio Sforza 49, South (02 8940 2874/ www.scimmie.it). Metro Porta Genova/bus 55, 71/tram 3. **Open** *Club* 7pm-3am Tue-Sat. Closed

Mon or Sun. (*Restaurant* 8pm-2am Mon-Sat.)
Admission varies; usually free with one drink
(€8-€15). **Credit** AmEx, DC, MC, V.

This cosy club and restaurant in the Navigli area
rightfully describes itself as 'the temple of Milan
jazz', although, in a generous ecumenical gesture, it
recently started hosting other types of music as well
– mostly rock, blues, and reggae. It also has a boat
moored on the canal, which makes a perfect location
for wooing that new date.

Opera & classical

Auditorium di Milano

*Largo Mahler 1, South (02 8338 9401/www.
laverdi.org). Bus 55, 71/tram 3, 15.* **Open** times
vary. *Box office* 2.30-7pm Tue-Sun. Closed mid
June-early Sept **Tickets** €13-€50. **Credit**
AmEx, DC, MC, V.

This relatively new addition to Milan's classical
music scene was built in Largo Mahler, which was
appropriately enough named after composer Gustav
Mahler, near the Navigli. Open since 1999, it has
gone on to earn the approval of the city's music critics. The 1,400-seat auditorium is the home of the
city's highly respected Orchestra La Verdi.
Performances usually take place Monday, Thursday
and some Tuesday nights, with big events on
Saturdays and matinées on Sunday.

Conservatorio di Musica Giuseppe Verdi.

Conservatorio di Musica Giuseppe Verdi

*Via Conservatorio 12, East (02 762 1101/
www.consmilano.it). Metro San Babila/bus 56, 61,
94/tram 12.* **Open** *Box office* 8am-8pm Mon-Fri.
Library 8am-7.30pm Mon-Fri; 8am-1pm Sat. Closed
Aug. *Performances* times vary; usually 6.30pm, 8pm
or 9pm Mon-Fri, 11.30am Sun. **Tickets** prices vary.
No credit cards.

This prestigious institution was founded in 1808 in
a former Lateran convent. Many key figures in
Italian music studied here – although, funnily
enough, the young Giuseppe Verdi was rejected –
and it still plays a fundamental role in Italian musical life today. There are two concert halls: the smaller Sala Puccini for chamber music, and the bigger
Sala Verdi for symphonic and choral music, both
with reasonably varied programmes. The library
(free entry) houses over 35,000 volumes and 460,000
musical works, including manuscripts by Mozart,
Donizetti, Bellini and Verdi. Rare string instruments
are housed in glass cases along the corridor.

Teatro alla Scala

*Piazza della Scala, Centre (02 860 775/www.teatro
allascala.org). Metro Duomo/tram 1, 2, 20.* **Open**
times vary. **Tickets** prices vary. **Credit** AmEx, DC,
MC, V. **Map** p251 E6/p252 E6.

The world-famous opera house is still coming to
terms with the return to its old home (and other
changes – *see p160* **Melodrama at La Scala**).
Getting tickets for Italian opera here is extremely
difficult, but if you're prepared to watch the non-
Italian stuff or attend concerts, it isn't quite so tricky.

Teatro dal Verme

*Via Giovanni sul Muro 2, North (02 87 905/www.
dalverme.org). Metro Cairoli/bus 50, 58/tram 1, 4
16, 18, 19, 20.* **Open** *Box office* 10am-8pm Tue-Sat;
10am-1pm Sun. *Performances* normally 9pm Mon,
Wed-Sun. Closed mid July-mid Oct. **Tickets** prices
vary. **Credit** AmEx, MC, V.

Built in 1872, this theatre became a cinema after
World War II. It finally reopened as a music venue
in 2001, after a slow but steady, Italian-style 20-year
renovation, by which time another concert hall (the
Auditorium, *see above*) had already opened. There
are afternoon concerts (I Pomeriggi Musicali) at 5pm
on Saturdays or Sundays.

Teatro degli Arcimboldi

*Viale dell'Innovazione 20, North (02 6411 42 200/
Box office 02 6411 42 212/www.teatroarcimboldi.it).
Metro Precotto/bus 40/tram 7.* **Open** *Box office*
10am-6pm Mon-Fri. *Performances* times vary. Closed
Aug, Sept. **Tickets** prices vary. **Credit** AmEx, DC,
MC, V.

Since fulfilling its original role as the temporary
home of La Scala (while the real thing was undergoing renovation), the Teatro degli Arcimboldi di
Milano has been suffering from an identity crisis. It
continues to host dance and orchestral events, but
also does high-brow pop concerts by the likes of
Tom Waits and Dave Gilmour.

Nightlife

Poseurs, *privés* and disco divas.

They actually want you to dance on the bar at **Loolapaloosa**. *See p165.*

Arts & Entertainment

Add a 'work hard, party hard' ethic to a young, upwardly mobile set, and what do you get? An incessant demand for places in which to party like there's no alarm clock.

Much of Milan's nightlife is concentrated in three areas: the industrial north, the swanky Corso Como area, and hipster-ish Navigli in the south. Pay attention in the summer season, as most clubs either close or move their operations to beach resorts: three of the best are in the eastern suburbs at Idroscalo, the man-made lake beside Linate airport (*see p147* **Milan's beach resort**). The massive, three-floored **Magazzini Generali**, on the city's south side, runs various themed nights; you'll be hemmed in by 19-year-old students on a Wednesday, and media types in tight jeans will flock in on a Friday. As trends shift, classic clubs like **Hollywood**, in the corso Como area, are undergoing radical transformations. Once home from home to the champagne-swilling pinstriped crowd, the club is now embracing the artsy, hip and gay communities with enthusiasm. Other clubs of note are also gay-friendly, such as the ever-popular **Rocket** and beautiful, airy **Old Fashion Café** in Parco Sempione.

Many of the more chi-chi clubs, looking to get the punters in early, also serve dinner before the night begins in earnest: the food is unlikely to be great (except at **Le Banque**, where the top-notch food is as good as the clubbing), but it will definitely be more than palatable. Reserving a table in advance usually ensures access to the *privé* (VIP area) and a bottle of champagne. Although most clubs are legally bound to close the bar at 2am, many of them have secured a semi-legal special licence, and will continue to serve alcohol and stay open as they see fit. And if you crave one last 4am nightcap, Milan is rich in *baracchini*, open-air mobile bars that serve drinks and *panini* until dawn; they're often set up in convenient proximity to Milan's nightlife hotspots.

INFORMATION

Zerodue (www.zero.eu) is a small, free fortnightly magazine that's indispensable for finding out what's on. Look for it at venues around town. Other useful websites are www.2night.it and www.milano.tonight.eu. As most Milanese clubs operate on a six-month season, opening dates and admission details may vary, so check before setting out.

Sounds of the underground

In mid 1980s depression, factories and disused churches were taken over as meeting places for the nation's disaffected youth. Thus, *centri sociali* (social centres) were born. Now, two decades later, they've risen to become a key part of the local music, arts and party scene, described by *Le Monde* as 'the Italian cultural jewel'.

Of the 100 or so still in existence, the oldest is **Leoncavallo** (*see p166*), in its present location since 1994. The vast space is like an indoors Glastonbury, buzzing with bars, restaurants, bookshops and gardens. The likes of Public Enemy have played here, and there's a good calendar of evening classes, language courses and jam sessions.

Typically, *centri sociali* were places small enough to experiment with new musical styles: punk and ska in the '80s, hip hop and drum 'n' bass in the '90s. **Conchetta** (*see p166*) is a small, lively option with a solid schedule of live music and electronica. Cheap drinks are the rule in these strictly not-for-profit centres.

DJs and film screenings are popular at **Pergola** (*see p166*), one of the city's most politically active *centri*. Cooler than most, it's little different from a great local bar with live bands, and gives visitors a good taster of Milan's sub-Armani underground.

Duomo & Centre

Armani Privé
Via Pisoni 1 (02 6231 2655). Metro Montenapoleone/bus 61/tram 1, 12, 20. **Open** 10.30pm-2am Tue-Sat. Closed July, Aug. **Admission** free (1st drink €20). **Credit** AmEx, DC, MC, V. **Map** p249 E5.
Giorgio Armani knows how to accessorise. The latest addition to his sprawling empire is this club in the Armani mega-complex. Drinks are €20, and it's difficult to get in; but if you manage to swing it, your efforts will be rewarded tenfold. Models abound, and the older guests ooze class. If you aren't catwalk material, get there early or blag your way past the bouncers. Smart dress required.

Le Banque
Via Porrone 6 (02 8699 6565/www.lebanque.it). Metro Cordusio/tram 1, 2, 14, 16, 19, 20. **Open** 6pm-5am daily. Closed July, Aug. **Admission** €15-€20 (incl drink). **Credit** AmEx, MC, V. **Map** p248 D6/p252 D6.
This sleekly decorated club is in a former bank with an internal courtyard. The real highlights are the *aperitivo* munchies, which are well above average, and a great wine cellar; in keeping with a certain old-school elegance, patrons who get too blotto to drive are offered a lift to their home or hotel. Music is mostly house and pop; you'll be turned away if you're not decked out appropriately.

Sforzesco & North

Alcatraz
Via Valtellina 25 (02 6901 6352/www.alcatraz milano.com). Bus 70/tram 3, 4, 7, 11. **Open** 10.30pm-4am Fri, Sat. Closed July, Aug. **Admission** €12 (incl drink). **Credit** MC, V. **Map** p248 D1.
During the week, this large, ex-industrial building hosts live gigs; at weekends it turns into a dance club. Friday nights feature house, latino and 'revival' music; Saturdays veer towards classic rock 'n' roll.

Black Hole
Viale Umbria 118 (02 7104 0220/www.black holemilano.com). Bus 90, 91, 92/tram 16. **Open** 10pm-5am Wed, Fri, Sat. Closed Aug. **Admission** €7-€15 (incl drink). **Credit** AmEx, MC, V. **Map** p251 H9.
This huge club was recently renovated, and sports a pleasantly decorated open-air dancefloor and cool chill-out area. Wednesday is 'dark night', with live music followed by clubbing until dawn. Fridays serve up the standard Milanese combo of pop and house; Saturdays are the popular revival night, So-80s.

The Club
Corso Garibaldi 97 (02 655 5318/www.theclub milano.it). Metro Moscova/bus 43, 94/tram 3, 12, 14. **Open** 10pm-4am Tue-Sat. Closed mid Aug. **Admission** €18 (incl drink). **No credit cards.** **Map** p248 D4.

The Club has been recently overhauled, with black walls and iron decoration that give it a very 'Berlin techno' feel. Tuesday's Fidelio is a must for house fans; Thursday is student night, with free entrance for those with student ID; and Saturday is the extravagant 'fashion night', where Milan's yuppies and models can be spotted in droves.

De Sade

Via Valtellina 21/23 (02 607 1255/www.desade.it).
Bus 70/tram 3, 4, 7, 11. **Open** 11pm-5am Fri, Sat.
Admission €10-€15 Fri (free in summer); €25 Sat (incl drink). **Credit** MC, V. **Map** p248 D1.
Its name betrays this club's alternative origins. Once one of Milan's gayest clubs, De Sade now draws a largely hetero crowd, though it's still gay-friendly. Friday nights are hip hop, Saturdays are electro.

Gasoline Club

Via Bonnet 11A (mobile 339 774 5797/www.disco gasoline.it). Metro Garibaldi/bus 70/tram 7, 11, 33. **Open** 11pm-5am Wed-Sun. Closed June-Aug.
Admission €12-€20 (incl drink). **Credit** AmEx, MC, V. **Map** p248 D3.
Situated near hip corso Como, this small club features everything from 1980s pop to deep house. Don't miss brilliant electro night Popstarz, on Thursday; gay night Paté Satan is on Sunday.

HD

Via Tajani 11 (02 7189 990). Metro Piola/bus 62, 90, 91, 93/tram 11, 23. **Open** 8.30pm-2am Mon, Tue, Fri, Sun; noon-4am Sat. **Admission** free; €15 (incl drink) Sat. **No credit cards.**
The HD, in the Lambrate quarter, is a very drab gay club on most nights of the week. On Saturdays, though, it lights up for Glitter, one of the most flamboyant nights in Milan. The music is an eclectic and humorous compilation of electro, indie, cheesy pop and trashy Italian songs. Great fun, gay or not.

Hollywood

Corso Como 15 (www.discotecahollywood.com).
Metro Garibaldi/bus 70/tram 7, 11, 29, 30, 33.
Open 10.30pm-4am Wed-Sun. Closed June-Aug.
Admission €18-€25 (incl drink). **Credit** AmEx, DC, MC, V. **Map** p248 D3.
There's always been a high model to mortal ratio in this place, but recently the club has been pitching for a trendier, more artsy crowd. At the time of writing, Hollywood was closed for renovation; check the website for updates.

Loolapaloosa

Corso Como 15 (02 655 5693/www.loolapaloosa. com). Metro Garibaldi. **Open** 11.30am-3pm, 7pm-3am Mon, Tue, Thur, Fri; 11.30am-3pm Wed; 7pm-3am Sat, Sun. Closed July, Aug. **Admission** €10 (incl drink) after 10pm. **No credit cards.**
Map p248 D3.
Famous for its late nights and the wild dancing on the bar and tables (watch out or the bartenders will scoop you up), Loolapaloosa is now just as popular for its evening *aperitivo*. Book a table – obligatory if you'd like to sit down – and your €8 gets you a

cocktail and heaps of food from the buffet. The outdoor terrace is small but comfy, and the tunes tend to stick to big commercial hits. *Photo p163.*

Old Fashion Café

Viale Alemagna 6 (02 805 6231/www.oldfashion.it).
Metro Cadorna/bus 57, 61, 91/tram 1, 27. **Open** 9pm-4am Mon, Tue, Thur-Sat; 8pm-4am Wed; 7.30pm-1am Sun. Closed Tue in winter. **Admission** €20 (incl drink). **Credit** AmEx, MC, V. **Map** p248 D5.
Central, hip and recently renovated, the Old Fashion Café draws crowds throughout the week, especially during the hot summer months, when its open-air bars and heaving dancefloor are especially inviting. If beautiful people are what you're after, Mondays and Saturdays are best; Wednesday is student night.

Sottomarino Giallo

Via Donatello 2 (mobile 339 545 4127/www.sotto marinogiallo.it). Metro Lima, Loreto or Piola/bus 62, 90, 91, 92/tram 33. **Open** 11pm-4am Tue-Sat. Closed June-Aug. **Admission** €10-€15 (incl drink). **No credit cards.**
Sottomarino Giallo has recently expanded, and has a wide variety of themes, from disco to electro and indie. Formerly the venue for Milan's only lesbian-only night, it's now touting for straight trade with the city's best, and has become one of the hotspots for in-the-know twentysomethings. *Photo 166.*

Tocqueville 13

Via Tocqueville 13 (02 2900 2973/www.tocqueville 13.it). Metro Garibaldi/bus 70/tram 7, 11, 29, 30, 33.
Open 9.30pm-4am Tue-Sat. Closed Aug. **Admission** €10-€20 (incl drink). **Credit** AmEx, MC, V.
Map p248 D4.
Tocqueville 13 attracts footballers, models and local VIPs, though they're likely to be hidden away in the *privé*, a small private room on the first floor. Dinner is served in the evening from 9.30pm; if you dine, you can ask for a pass to the *privé* (free with table booking if requested in advance).

San Babila & East

Rolling Stone

Corso XXII Marzo 32 (02 733 172/www.rollingstone. it). Bus 45, 73/tram 12, 27. **Open** 11pm-5am Fri, Sat. Closed July, Aug. **Admission** €12-€20 (incl drink). **Credit** AmEx, MC, V. **Map** p251 H7.
Milan's leading rock venue occupies three floors, offering a selection of big-name gigs during the week and dancing on Fridays and Saturdays. The sounds vary according to the floor, and include electro, hip hop, rock, reggae and Latin music, depending on the weekend; check the website in advance.

Porta Romana & South

Lime Light

Via Castelbarco 11 (mobile 333 897 9299). Bus 79, 90, 91/tram 15. **Open** 11pm-4am Wed, Fri, Sat. Closed July, Aug. **Admission** €10-€15 (incl drink). **No credit cards. Map** p250 D9.

Suffering from a mild personality disorder, Lime Light seems to offer anything and everything. Not only is it a venue for live music, it also opens its doors to students on Wednesdays, and takes bookings for private parties. For cutting-edge music, you may want to head elsewhere, but for sweaty, lively crowds, it's a good bet.

Magazzini Generali
Via Pietrasanta 14 (02 539 3948/www.magazzini generali.it). Bus 79, 90, 91/tram 15. **Open** 11.30pm-4am Wed-Sat. Closed June-Aug. **Admission** free Wed; €15 Fri, Sat (incl drink). **Credit** MC, V. **Map** p251 F10.
With a capacity of around 1,000, Magazzini is a favourite for every type of live music, as well as popular club nights. Avoid Wednesdays unless you're after a very young student crowd; Thursdays and Fridays are mixture of house and techno upstairs, and 'dirty electro' in the room below, meeting point for Milan's hipster-intelligentsia. Saturdays are more commercial, with chart-topping classics.

Rocket
Via Pezzotti 52 (02 8950 3509/www.therocket.it). Bus 79, 90, 91/tram 15. **Open** 10pm-2am Mon-Sat. Closed Sun & Aug. **Admission** free. **No credit cards. Map** p250 D11.
More than five years after it opened, the small but ultra-cool Rocket is still fresh on everyone's lips. This DJ bar became popular thanks to a simple formula that's rare in Milan: entrance is free, the tunes are excellent (rock, electro, classic) and the bartender mixes great cocktails. Thursday nights are banging.

Sottomarino Giallo.
See p165.

Summer venues

Most of the action on summer nights is at the Idroscalo, a huge man-made lake near Linate airport (*see p147* **Milan's beach resort**). It's not the easiest place to get to by public transport, so make sure you keep enough cash for the taxi home. Right on the lake, Café Solaire and Le Jardin are two popular summer party places, with Le Jardin functioning as a summer version of historic gay club Plastic (*see p155*). Back in the city, Borgo del Tempo Perso is also a hopping spot, with DJs, drinks and dancing in its two garden areas, as well as inside. From Friday to Sunday it hosts Karma, which attracts some of the trendiest crowds.

In summer, the Navigli area is closed to traffic after 8.30pm, and canalside bars and cafés stay open until late. Bars in Brera, corso Como and Porta Ticinese also spill out on to the pavement, making the areas lively places in which to grab a cocktail, chat or observe.

Borgo del Tempo Perso/Karma
Via Fabio Massimo 36, East (02 569 4755/ www.borgodeltempoperso.net). Metro Porto di Mare. **Open** *May-Sept Dinner* 9.30-11.30pm Thur-Sat. *Club* 11.30pm-4am Thur-Sat; 8.30pm-2am Sun. *Oct-Apr* 8.30pm-4am Thur; 9.30pm-4am Fri, Sat; 8pm-2am Sun. **Admission** €10-€20 (incl drink). **Credit** DC, MC, V.

Café Solaire
Gate 7, Circonvallazione Idroscalo, Segrate (mobile 340 675 6096/www.beachsolaire.it). Bus 73, then walk. **Open** 9.30pm-4am Tue-Sat; 6.30pm-3am Sun. Closed Oct-Apr. **Admission** free Tue-Thur; €12-€20 (incl drink) Fri-Sun. **Credit** AmEx, DC, MC, V.

Le Jardin au Bord du Lac
Circonvallazione Idroscalo 51, Segrate (02 7020 8212/www.lejardinauborddulac.com). Bus 73, then walk. **Open** 10pm-4am Fri, Sat; 10pm-2am Sun. Closed Oct-Apr. **Admission** €10-€20 (incl drink). **Credit** MC, V.

Centri Sociali

See p164 **Sounds of the underground**.

Conchetta
Via Conchetta 18, South (02 8940 0302). Tram 3/bus 59, 71. **Open** Tue-Sun. **Admission** varies. **No credit cards. Map** p250 C10.

Leoncavallo
Via Watteau 7, North (02 670 5621/www.leon cavallo.org). Bus 43. **Open** Thur-Sun. **Admission** varies. **No credit cards.**

Pergola Move
Via Angelo della Pergola 5, North (02 6901 0129/ http://isole.ecn.org/pergolatribe). Metro Garibaldi/ tram 7, 11. **Open** 8pm-3am Thur-Sat. **Admission** varies. **No credit cards. Map** p248 D2.

Sport & Fitness

Warming up and cooling down.

With brioche for breakfast and pasta for lunch, how do the beautiful people stay so slim? The Lombard *paesani* may cock a snook at the exercise regimen of their urban cousins, but fitness is big business in Milan. Even jogging in the park is taken seriously, and has its own trendy pseudo-English name: *footing*.

Indoors, virtually every other imaginable way of getting fit, from dancing to spinning, judo, swimming, yoga, boxercise and squash, goes on at the city's many gyms. These are the places where moneyed Milanese come to burn off aperitifs and check out the talent – when they're not on the slopes or at the beach, that is.

Cycling

There are three main cycle paths in Milan, each passing historic sites and patches of natural beauty. The longest crosses the whole city, from the waterfalls of the Martesana canal in the north-east, along much of the canal's length, through Parco Sempione and Brera to Porta Genova in the south-west.

The paths along the Naviglio Pavese and the Naviglio Grande lead south to the towns of Pavia and Abbiategrasso. The former passes locks designed by da Vinci, but is a rough ride (you'll need a mountain bike); the latter is a smooth delight. Abbiategrasso, an hour away at racing speed, is quite bland, but the path runs on past verdant stretches with views of the Alps. A further 15 kilometres (9.5 miles) down the road, heading south-west, is the medieval town of Vigevano. For bike hire, *see p223*.

Football

Stadio Giuseppe Meazza, aka **San Siro**, is home to two of Italy's top teams, AC Milan and Inter Milan. It's one of the most illustrious grounds in Europe, and even on non-match days its museum and tour (*see p94*) can bring the 85,000-seat stadium to life.

AC Milan was established in 1899 by a group of British expats, who found themselves with few outlets for English sports in a cycling-mad city. So successful was the club that in 1908, the Italian Football Federation decided to exclude foreign players from the championship. The internationals on AC's roster formed their own club and called it Football Club Internazionale,

or simply Inter. Eventually, they won the right to compete in the championship, and kicked off a rivalry that stands to this day.

Once upon a time, team affiliations were split fairly neatly along political lines. From the 1950s until Silvio Berlusconi bought the nearly bankrupt AC in 1986 (*see p168* **Filthy rich football face-off**), its supporters were known as *cacciaviti* (screwdrivers), a reference to their blue-collar professions. In the tumultuous 1970s, the club represented the hard left, and the red of their red and black strip signalled their communist leanings. Inter, on the other hand – with regal blue-and-black stripes – has always been associated with the bourgeoisie; the Moratti family of oil barons has presided over the club for most of the 20th century.

The two teams face each other in the San Siro stadium twice a year, once in autumn and once in winter or spring. If you're lucky enough to get a ticket, turn up a good hour ahead of kickoff to secure your spot. Each team's *curva*, or end zone, is extremely raucous; and the safest places are away from the police, as they're the most popular target for missiles.

TICKETS
AC Milan vs Inter matches generally sell out well in advance. Tickets for forthcoming matches can be bought on the clubs' websites (www.acmilan.com, www.inter.it); extra tickets to AC Milan home games are sold at **Milan Point** (via San Gottardo 2, entrance in piazza XXIV Maggio, South, 02 8942 2711, closed Sun) or at 50 other addresses listed on the website. For Inter home games, try any branch of **Banca Popolare di Milano** (a central one is at via Meravigli 2, Centre, 02 8646 0598, www.bpm.it, closed Sat, Sun). Ticket prices start at €20; thereafter, the sky's the limit.

Stadio Giuseppe Meazza (San Siro)
Via Piccolomini 5, Sant'Ambrogio & West (02 404 2432/www.sansirotour.com). Metro Lotto/ tram 16.

Golf

The countryside around Milan has some of the loveliest golf courses in Italy; however, most require membership. The exception is **Golf Le Rovedine**, the only public course in Lombardy.

Filthy rich football face off

No trip to Milan could be considered complete without a visit to what the Italians call La Scala del Calcio – football's La Scala, the **San Siro** stadium (*see p167*). This massive 85,000-seater is home to the world's two most powerful clubs, AC Milan and FC Internazionale.

Commonly referred to as Milan and Inter, the squads have been bitter rivals since the dawn of Serie A; the city itself is split in two, *Interisti* versus *Milanisti*. One way to understand the two factions is by careful examination of the team presidents, Silvio Berlusconi and Massimo Moratti, each of whom embodies certain aspects of their team. Neither is camera-shy; each one is ever ready to allow a malicious slip of the tongue; and yet Berlusconi and Moratti are like chalk and cheese.

Massimo Moratti

The oil tycoon Massimo Moratti is known as a football gentleman, the scion of a powerful family with unlimited love for his team and an equally unlimited wallet for funding its transfers. Massimo is the son of Angelo Moratti, president of Inter during its 1960s golden age.

Moratti junior bought Inter in 1995, and made it his mission to restore his team to the glory days of his father's presidency. For his impulsiveness, he's the butt of endless jokes by AC Milan supporters: Moratti has bought dozens of players for far more than their real worth, and undersold others. Despite being less wealthy than Berlusconi, Moratti has spent slightly over €400 million during his years at the helm of Inter. (Only Chelsea's Roman Abramovich has spent more.)

Moratti's greatest strength is also his greatest weakness: he is his team's number one supporter. He often develops an almost familial relationship with many of his players, and is heartbroken to see them move on. A good representative of his sociological group, Moretti embodies the old-school *Interisti* – the well to do, educated middle and upper classes. After years of dignity and elegance, during which Inter has been only the city's number two team, it seems that Moratti's table-topping dream is becoming reality.

Silvio Berlusconi

As the Italians say, *se non ci fosse, non potresti inventarlo* – if he didn't exist, he'd be impossible to invent. A former cruise ship

crooner who has risen to the world's top 100 Rich List and been three-time Prime Minister of the Italian Republic, Berlusconi is a self-made real estate, publishing and TV magnate, as well as president of AC Milan.

After buying the struggling, working-class-backed AC Milan in 1986, *il Cavaliere* (as he's known) used his trademark mixture of suave charm and ruthless drive to lead Milan (with the help of master coaches like Sacchi, Ancelotti and current England manager Fabio Capello) to seven championships, five Champion's Leagues, three Club World Cups, and another 11 minor trophies – a bounty that has helped it become, in 2008, the club with the most international titles in the world.

However, when the summer 2006 *calciopoli* matchfixing scandal unearthed some dodgy dealing between AC Milan and the referees in the Italian Serie A, Inter rose to dominate the domestic league, winning three consecutive titles. Milan, despite winning a Champion's League in 2007, has lagged behind at home, and the *Milanisti* are grumbling.

Golf Le Rovedine

Via Karl Marx 18, Noverasco di Opera, South (02 5760 6420/www.rovedine.com). Tram 24 t hen bus 99. **Open** *Mar-Nov* 8am-8pm Tue-Sun. *Dec-Feb* 8am-6pm Tue-Sun. Closed 2wks Aug, 2wks Dec-Jan. **Rates** €40 Tue-Sat; €65 Sun. **Credit** AmEx, DC, MC, V.
This basic, par-72 course is 7km (4.5 miles) outside the city. It draws a crowd on good weather, in particular at the weekends, so if you decide to make the trip be sure to book ahead.

Gyms

In a city where what you look like can make or break a career, if not a life, it should come as little surprise that much of Milan's sport revolves around gyms, or *centri di benessere* (health and fitness centres). Facilities commonly include dance studios, sunbeds, nutritionists, pools, hairdressers, climbing walls and equipment stores. For tourists, however, they can be pricey and/or out of the way, so hotel gyms are often a better bet.

Downtown Palestre

Piazza Cavour 2, North (02 7601 1485/www. downtownpalestre.it). Metro Turati/bus 61, 94/ tram 1, 2, 20. **Open** 7am-midnight Mon-Fri; 10am-9pm Sat, Sun. Closed 2wks Aug. **Rates** €60/day; €200/mth. **Credit** AmEx, MC, V. **Map** p249 E5.
Downtown's clientele consists of the rich, the famous and the very beautiful. As well as a variety of classes, there are two floors of equipment, including treadmills and stairclimbers; a spa and beauty centre (02 7631 7233) offers all kinds of pampering. Note that the piazza Diaz branch closes an hour earlier. **Other locations**: piazza Diaz 6, Duomo & Centre (02 863 1181).

Tonic Club

Via Mestre 7, East (02 2641 0158/www.tonicnet.it), Metro Udine/bus 55, 75. **Open** 7am midnight Mon-Fri; 9am 7.30pm Sat, Sun. **Rates** €25/day. **Credit** MC, V.
Tonic is a national chain of gyms, based in large, industrial spaces and generally devoid of the glamour of the clubs closer to the centre. This location has four squash courts and racket rental, plus dance lessons, a climbing wall and martial arts training. **Other locations**: via Cassinis 23, South (02 5681 4740); via Giambellino 5, South (02 422 1537).

Skiing

Sloping off for a weekend on the mountains between December and April is a solid Milan tradition. The resort of **Bormio** offers a touch of class an hour north of Lago d'Iseo; more traditional **Madesimo** is 30 kilometres (20 miles) north of Lago di Como. Each has over 50 kilometres (30 miles) of runs.

Arts & Entertainment

Relax to the max

Pulled a muscle in the marathon? Need a post-shop pick-me-up? No sweat: one of Milan's spas will have a treatment for you.

The fashionable approach

Aveda-based **Lepri** (*see p171*) is a salon and spa owned by the gregarious Fabrizio Lepri, backstage manager for all Tom Ford events and one of the city's most sought-after stylists. Give your hair a boost at the hair spa (treatments from €20), or head downstairs for the rosemary and mint body wrap (1hr, €70).

Although it's billed as a 'tribute from the Italian jeweller to the world of luxury', there's nothing flashy about the cool, contemporary **Bulgari Hotel**. The spa (*see p171*), featuring subdued lighting effects and a stone and gold-mosaic swimming pool, is a serene, understated sanctuary. As you may expect, the prices match the setting: the new four-hand massage (1hr 25mins) costs €250. Or opt for one of the all-day treatments, which combine massage with pool use and lunch.

ESPA at Gianfranco Ferré (*see p171*) is a small but perfect spa inside a designer boutique. The black-and-gold pool overlooks the lawn of a walled garden. Jacuzzi, steam bath, mud treatments and facials are available. If you've been lugging around too many shopping bags, consider the back massage (55mins, €105). The spa stays open way after the shops close; just ring the bell after 7pm. Book ahead.

The steamy side

At **Hammam della Rosa** (*see p171*; pictured), you follow a circuit of varying temperatures, rooms and plunge pools. You start off relaxing in the tepidarium, a warm, mosaic-panelled room, before hitting the moist 45° heat of the caldarium. Stretch out on the beds, and you'll be vigorously scrubbed from head to toe (and then some). After a dip in the frigidarium, you'll be plied with sweets, tea and a ten-minute massage. Heaven? Awfully close.

Housed in a gorgeous palazzo built in 1908, the brand-new **Terme Milano** (*see p171*) have had various uses, including leisure centre for tram drivers and rocking disco bar. Now, the building has been restored to its former art deco glory, and kitted out with steambaths, saunas and open-air pools. A day pass (€35-€46) gives you access to all areas. The abundant buffet of fresh fruit and juices is included, and you can book additional treatments like the anti-stress massage (50mins, €56) at relatively reasonable rates. Slip into your swimsuit and dive in.

Bormio

The Valtellina region's classiest ski resort, Bormio (www.bormio.to) has a cute town centre and one of the most scenic positions in the entire valley. Bursting with hotels and restaurants, it also has four black runs, 11 red and ten blue, two chairlifts, 14 ski lifts and two cableways, cross-country tracks, and an outdoor ice-rink. Ski passes cost €29 per day.

Ski & boot hire: Celso Sport
Via Vallecetta 5 (0342 901 459/www.celsosport.it). **Open** 7.30am-8pm daily. **Rates** €19-€47/day. **Credit** AmEx, DC, MC, V.

Ski school: Scuola sci Contea di Bormio
via Btg Morbegno 13 (0342 911 605/www.scuola scibormio.it). **Open** 9am-5pm daily. Closed Apr-Nov. **Rates** €30-€35/hr. **Credit** MC, V.

Madesimo

A family-friendly resort near pretty Chiavenna, Madesimo (www.madesimo.com) has the notorious Canalone run, said to be Italy's hardest. It has two black runs, five red, four blue, seven chairlifts, seven ski lifts and three cableways. Ski passes cost €29-€32 per day.

Ski & boot hire: Olympic Sport
via dei Giacomi 3 (0342 54 330/www.olympic madesimo.it). **Open** 8.30am-7.30pm daily. **Rates** €32 per day. **Credit** AmEx, DC, MC, V.

Ski school: Scuola Italiana di Sci Madesimo
Via alla Fonte 4 (0343 53 049/www.scuolasci madesimo.org). **Open** 9am-6.30pm daily. Closed Apr-Nov. **Rates** €30-€35/hr. **Credit** MC, V.

Squash & tennis

Squash is popular in Milan: it's quick, played indoors and has a northern European feel. For outdoor tennis, the courts at the Tonic Club outlets at via Giambellino and via Cassinis (*see p169*) are among the best value in town.

Mediolanum Tennis
Via Vincenzo Monti 57/A, West (02 469 0405). Metro Pagano/tram 19, 27. **Open** 9am-11pm Mon-Fri; 9am-8pm Sat, Sun. **Rates** €16-€20/hr. **No credit cards. Map** p248 A5.
Mediolanum offers two tennis courts, covered or open-air according to season.

Vico Squash
Via GB Vico 38, West (02 4800 2762). Metro Sant'Agostino/bus 50, 94/tram 2, 14. **Open** 7am-11pm Mon, Wed; 8.30am-11pm Tue, Thur, Fri; 10am-9pm Sat, Sun. **Rates** €50/day; membership prices vary. **Credit** AmEx, MC, V. **Map** p250 B7.

With a dozen squash courts, Vico Squash is a good bet if you want to practise your smashes and get fit playing what is rapidly becoming the city's favourite new sport.

Spas

If all this talk of exercise is working up too much of a sweat and you'd really rather be pampered than perspiring, *see p170* **Relax to the max**.

Bulgari Hotel Spa
Via Privata Fratelli Gabba 7B, Centre (02 805 805 200/www.bulgarihotels.com). Metro Montenapoleone/tram 1, 2. **Open** 9am-11pm daily. **Credit** AmEx, DC, MC, V. **Map** p249 E5.

ESPA at Gianfranco Ferré
Via Sant'Andrea 15, Centre (02 7601 7526/www.gianfrancoferre.com/www.espaonline.com). Metro Montenapoleone or San Babila/bus 61, 94. **Open** 10am-10pm Tue-Fri; 10am-9pm Sat; 11am-8pm Sun. Closed 2wks Aug. **Credit** AmEx, DC, MC, V. **Map** p249 E5.

Hammam della Rosa
Viale Abruzzi 15, East (02 2941 1653/www.hammamdellarosa.com). Bus 92/tram 5, 23. **Open** *Women* 11.30am-11pm Tue-Thur; 11am-11pm Fri; 10.30am-9pm Sat; 10.30am-8pm Sun. *Men* 5-11pm Tue, Thur; 10.30am-2pm Sat, Sun. *Couples* 5-11pm Wed, Fri; 3-8pm Sat, Sun. Last entrance 2hrs before closing; reservations required. **Rates** €30-€140. **Credit** MC, V. **Map** P249 H4.

Lepri
Via Omenoni 2, Centre (02 659 5861/www.leprilss.it). Metro Duomo/tram 1. **Open** *Salon* 9am-7pm Mon-Sat. *Spa* 10.30am-7.30pm Mon-Sat. **Credit** AmEx, DC, MC, V. **Map** p252 E6.

Terme Milano
Piazza Medaglie d'Oro 2, South (02 5519 9367/www.termemilano.com). Metro Porta Romana/bus 62, 77/tram 9, 29, 30. **Open** 10am-10pm daily. **Rates** €35-€39 Mon-Fri; €46 Sat, Sun. **Credit** AmEx, MC, V. **Map** p251 F9.

Swimming pools

Although most private gyms have their own pools, many Milanese opt for a pay-as-you-swim plan. Public pools are much cheaper, though the open-access swimming schedules can be extremely complicated to work out. Remember your bathing cap: you won't be allowed in without one. Times below are for public swimming; at other times, pools are usually used for classes. The city's lidos (*see p172* **Take the plunge**) come into their own in the summer. Up-to-date information about all the pools listed can be found on www.milanosport.it.

Arts & Entertainment

Lido

Piazzale Lotto 15, West (02 392 791). Metro Lotto/bus 48, 90, 91, 199. **Open** *early June-early Sept* 10am-7pm Tue-Sun. **Rates** €5 Mon-Fri; €5.50 Sat, Sun; €40 11 sessions. **No credit cards.**
See below **Take the plunge**.

Piscina Argelati

Via Segantini 6, South (02 5810 0012). Bus 47. **Open** *early June-mid Aug* 10am-7pm daily. *Mid Aug-early Sept* 10am-7pm Mon, Wed-Sun. **Rates** €5 Mon-Fri; €5.50 Sat, Sun; €40 11 sessions. **No credit cards.**
See below **Take the plunge**.

Piscina Cozzi

Viale Tunisia 35, corner of via Antonio Zarotto, East (02 659 9703). Metro Porta Venezia or Repubblica/tram 1, 2, 5, 9, 11, 29, 30, 33. **Open** noon-11pm Mon; 7.30am-2.30pm Tue, Thur; 8.30am-4.30pm, 6-9.30pm Wed; 8.30am-4.30pm Fri; 10am-5.30pm Sat, Sun. **Rates** €4 Mon-Fri; €5.50 Sat, Sun; €40 11 sessions; €250 annual pass. **No credit cards. Map** p249 F4.
Built in 1934 with a grandiose Fascist exterior and a Soviet interior, and newly renovated in 2008, this is one of Milan's most popular pools: it's of Olympic size, but often crowded. Opening hours are extended during the hottest months.

Piscina Romano

Via Ampère 20, South (02 7060 0224). Bus 62, 90, 91, 93/tram 11, 23, 33. **Open** *early June-mid Aug* 10am-7pm daily. *Mid Aug-early Sept* 10am-7pm Mon, Tue, Thur-Sun. **Rates** €5 Mon-Fri; €5.50 Sat, Sun; €40 11 sessions. **No credit cards.**
See below **Take the plunge**.

Piscina Solari

Via Montevideo 20, West (02 469 5278). Metro Sant'Agostino/bus 50/tram 14, 29, 30. **Open** 7-9.45am, 11.30am-3.15pm Mon; 7-9.45am, 10.45am-3.15pm, 6.30-11.30pm Tue, Fri; 7-9.45am, 11.30am-3.15pm, 6.30-11.30pm Wed; 7-9.30am, noon-3.15pm Thur; 1-8pm Sat; 10am-7.30pm Sun; times may vary in summer. **Rates** €4 Mon-Fri; €5.50 Sat, Sun; €40 11 sessions. **No credit cards. Map** p250 A8.
This is one of the city's more modern-looking public pools, with tall windows looking over the park. There are few frills, and staff can be surly. Summer swimmers can use the pool's outdoor garden.

Yoga

Most gyms offer yoga courses as well as space for individuals to work through their own routines. Most have piles of exercise mats.

Istituto Kunpen Lama Gangchen

Via Marco Polo 13, North (02 2901 0263/www. kunpen.it). Metro Lotto/Bus 48, 90, 91, 199. **Open** times vary. **Rates** €15; €30 membership. **No credit cards. Map** p249 E4.
You can pay on the day at this Buddhist centre. Hatha and Asthanga classes take place on Monday and Friday at 7pm, with meditation on Mondays and Wednesdays at 1pm, and Thursdays at 10am.

Take the plunge

In the 1920s and '30s, private businesses and local government funnelled piles of lire into the construction of populist lidos throughout the city. Many of these still exist, and are used by residents to beat the intense summer heat with the same enthusiasm. Even if you're not in the city between June and August, keep your ear to the ground: all the spots listed here have been known to host exhibitions, furniture fair events (*see p29* **Tomorrow's world**) and concerts.

The city's first outdoor swimming pool was **Piscina Argelati** (*see above*), located in the *navigli* district. Although these days it's ringed by unattractive tower blocks, the three pools (including one for kids) are lively and spacious. Stick around until the evening for an *aperitivo* at on-site reggae bar Freeks: it's as near as Milan gets to the Caribbean.

Opened in 1931, the huge **Lido** (*see above*) is Milan's largest open-air pool. Created as a sport and amusement park, it was decked out with a pier, pontoons and Venetian street

lamps – but was, surprisingly, far less popular than anticipated. Milan's municipality bought it in 1936, and made it a sports-only complex: the result was a wild success. Sun loungers, waterslides and a beach volleyball area have been added over the years to up the holiday atmosphere. The grounds also have three gyms, two football grounds and four tennis courts.

The **Piscina Romano** (*see above*) is just half the size of the Lido. It was built in 1929, and designed by architect Luigi Secchi, who also designed the **Piscina Cozzi** (*see above*). Set near Città Studi, Milan's teeming university zone, the Romano is very popular with students; the proximity of a hopping bar area doesn't hurt either.

Finally, although the city's **Idroscalo** (*see p147* **Milan's beach resort**) was originally constructed to be a hydroplane landing strip, it soon developed into an out-of-town leisure centre; now it's packed with children's play areas, pedalos and three outdoor pools.

Theatre & Dance

You can take your hat off.

Theatre lovers will find the local scene to be underground and outlandish. Money troubles have forced some small groups into smaller productions, but fortunately the performances haven't suffered for it. Star actors, Rupert Everett included, are adding spice to the big stage scene, and out-of-work soap stars perform at the more 'lowbrow' theatres, which are still popular attractions for the Milanese.

Milanese theatre has produced some giants of its own over the years. Nobel prize winner Dario Fo, for example, is best known for the 1970 international smash hit *The Accidental Death of an Anarchist*, based on real events in the city; his works are regularly performed at the smaller theatres. The city's other theatre legend is the late, great Giorgio Strehler (1921-97), who is justly honoured with a theatre in his own name. A highly influential director, he is credited with, among other things, introducing the world to the works of the Venetian playwright Carlo Goldoni.

For non-Italian speakers, Milan's theatres offer a range of contemporary dance, musicals, live jazz and mime. **CRT Teatro Dell'Arte** has the Short Formats festival, and the **Teatro Smeraldo** hosts everything from ballet to rock bands. If you only have time to visit one venue, however, make it **La Scala** (*see p59*).

INFORMATION AND TICKETS

Individual theatres put on several productions during the course of the year. In London's West End or on Broadway, a show will run as long as it draws an audience; in Milan, it tends to run for a fortnight. Therefore, if you hear about a show that sounds appealing, you need to book pretty much immediately, or it will pass you by.

Milan theatres, like just about everything else in the city, come to a halt in the summer months. It's also worth remembering that Milan theatres are 'dark' on a Monday night; Sundays usually feature afternoon matinées and, in one or two cases, morning shows.

Until a few years ago, buying tickets for Milan theatre shows was far from straightforward. Audience members were expected to queue at the theatre box office at set times, several days ahead of the date in question, and as a result they would often spend as much time buying the tickets as watching the show. But most performances can now be booked over the phone using a credit card. Online booking at the larger theatres is a doddle, and the preferred online ticketing partners for each establishment are linked from their respective websites. Leading ones include **TicketOne** (www.ticketone.it), **Ticketweb** (www.ticketweb.it) and **Vivaticket** (www.vivaticket.it).

Should you be staying in Milan for a while, you might be interested in the **Invito a Teatro** scheme. For €68 you can choose eight shows to see in one season at 16 city theatres (including nine listed in this chapter, marked with the initials 'IT'). The pass goes on sale in October, and is available from the theatres themselves or from TicketOne in the Spazio Oberdan centre on viale Vittorio Veneto 2 (02 7740 6384).

Teatro Leonardo da Vinci. See p175.

Venues & companies

CRT

Teatro dell'Arte *Via Alemagna 6, West. Metro Cadorna/bus 61/tram 1, 19, 29, 30.* **Map** p248 B5.
CRT Salone *Via Dini 7, South. Metro Abbiategrasso/tram 3, 15.*

Teatro Smeraldo.

Both *02 8901 1644/www.teatrocrt.it.* **Season** mid Oct-mid June. **Open** *Box office* 10am-7pm Mon-Sat; 1hr before performances Sun. **Performances** *Teatro dell'Arte* 8.45pm Tue-Sun; 4pm Sun. *CRT Salone* 9pm Tue-Sat; 4pm Sun. **Tickets** €12-€18; €8-€12 reductions. IT. **Credit** MC, V.

This company, which was founded in the 1970s, has two locations. One is adjacent to the Palazzo dell'Arte, on the edge of Parco Sempione; the other, the CRT Salone, is on via Dini, on the south side of town. CRT stands for Centro di Ricerca per il Teatro (centre for theatre research), and it's considered to be Italy's leading forum for theatrical experimentation. Its programme combines contemporary drama, opera and classical theatre. Dance is also a feature: the Short Formats dance festival in October lines up over a dozen European companies.

Piccolo Theatre Group

Piccolo Teatro Strehler *Largo Greppi, North. Metro Lanza/bus 57/tram 3, 4, 12, 14, 20.* **Map** p248 D5.
Piccolo Teatro Grassi *Via Rovello 2, Centre. Metro Cordusio/bus 58/tram 1, 3, 5, 19, 20, 27.* **Map** p250 D6/p252 D6.
Both *02 7233 3222/www.piccoloteatro.org.* **Season** Sept-May. **Open** *Box office (Teatro Strehler)* 10am-6.45pm Mon-Sat; 1-6.30pm Sun. **Performances** 7.30pm Tue, Sat; 8.30pm Wed-Fri; 4pm Sun. **Tickets** €21.50-€38; €17-€22 reductions. IT. **Credit** AmEx, DC, MC, V.

Named in honour of the late director Giorgio Strehler, the Piccolo Teatro Strehler is generally acknowledged as the city's top venue. Its director, Luca Ronconi, is highly respected, and the fact that the theatre is publicly owned means that it is one of the very few to receive adequate funding. There are actually two theatres in regular use at the main site: the Teatro Strehler and the Teatro Studio, which looks like a smaller, red-brick version of London's National Theatre; the Piccolo Teatro Grassi is on via Rovello, a stone's throw from the Duomo. Recent large-scale productions have included *Moby Dick*, *Hamlet* and *Romeo and Juliet*.

Teatro Arsenale

Via Correnti 11, South (02 837 5896/www.teatro arsenale.org). Metro Sant'Ambrogio/bus 94/tram 2, 3, 20. **Season** Oct-June. **Open** *Box office* 6-8pm Tue-Fri; 4.30-8pm Sat. **Performances** 9.15pm Tue-Sat; 4.30pm Sun. **Tickets** €16; €12 reductions. IT. **Credit** MC, V. **Map** p250 C7/p252 C7.

This theatre is housed in a deconsecrated 13th-century church at the far end of via Torino. The company, directed by Annig Raimondi, tends to specialise in modern work, such as Beckett and Sartre, or older material by authors not generally known for theatre (such as Copi and Céline).

Teatro Carcano

Corso di Porta Romana 63, South (02 5518 1377/ www.teatrocarcano.com). Metro Crocetta/bus 77, 94/ tram 16. **Season** Oct-May. **Open** *Box office* 10am-6.30pm Mon; 10am-8pm Tue-Sat; 1-6.30pm Sun. **Performances** 8.30pm Tue-Sat; 3.30pm Sun. **Tickets** €25-€34; €13 reductions. IT. **Credit** MC, V. **Map** p251 E8.

This theatre opened its doors in 1803 and was subsequently the setting for the premieres of operas by Bellini and Donizetti. Not surprisingly, it tends to concentrate on theatre classics (Molière, Sophocles, Shakespeare, Pirandello) of high quality.

Teatro Ciak

Via Sangallo 33, East (02 7611 0093/www.teatro ciak.it). Bus 61, 90, 91, 93/tram 5. **Season** Sept-May. **Open** *Box office* 11am-5.30pm Mon-Fri. **Performances** 9pm Tue-Sun. **Tickets** €15-€35. **Credit** MC, V.

Leo Wachter, who organised the first Beatles concert in Italy, turned this cinema into a theatre in 1977. Today Ciak (which is the sound made by a clapperboard at the start of filming) works with two musical venues, Teatro Smeraldo and the Ventaglio Nazionale, and tends to concentrate on cabaret and comedy – most recently a spoof *Frankenstein* and a tribute to the cult film *Harold and Maud*.

Teatro dell'Elfo

Via Ciro Menotti 11, East (02 716 791/www.elfo. org). Bus 54, 61/tram 5, 11. **Season** Oct-June. **Open** *Box office* 2.30-7.30pm Mon; 11.30am-7.30pm Tue-Sat. **Tickets** €20 (€11 Tue); €13 reductions. IT. **No credit cards. Map** p249 H6.

This group was founded in 1973 by, among others, a young Gabriele Salvatores, who went on to direct movies such as the award-winning *Mediterraneo*. Teatridithalia Elfo has a reputation for non-traditional, hard-hitting theatre, with the odd Chekhov or Shakespeare thrown in. The troupe also performs in many of the city's other venues.

Teatro Franco Parenti

Via Pier Lombardo 14, South (02 5999 5206/www. teatrofrancoparenti.com). Bus 90, 91, 92/tram 16. **Season** Oct-late May. **Open** *Box office* 10am-7pm Mon-Fri; 10am-1pm, 2-7pm Sat & Sun. **Tickets** €25; €9-€12.50 reductions; €10 less than 6hrs before performance. **Performances** 9pm Tue-Sat; 4.30pm Sun. **Credit** MC, V.

As of the 2008 season, Teatro Franco Parenti is back in business at its historical headquarters on via Pier Lombardo. Director Andrée Ruth Shammah is renowned for tireless fund-raising and for producing a varied programme of quality: recently, lectures, dance, and works by Beckett and Thomas Bernhard.

Teatro Leonardo da Vinci

Via Ampère 1, at piazza Leonardo da Vinci, East (02 2668 1166/www.elfo.org). Metro Piola/bus 62, 90, 91/tram 11, 23. **Season** Oct-June. **Open** *Box office* 3.30-7.30pm Mon-Sat. **Tickets** €19 (€11 Tue); €9.50-€12 reductions. IT. **No credit cards.**

This is the home of the Quelli di Grock, an experimental theatre company established in 1976. One of its founders, Maurizio Nichetti, went on to become an acclaimed film director. The theatre concentrated on mime, clowns and dance, but it has recently gone in for reinterpretations of the classics, such as Molière, Goldoni, Beckett and Shakespeare. It also runs a theatre school (at another location) and hosts the Teatridithalia Elfo company (*see above*). *Photo p173.*

Teatro Litta

Corso Magenta 24, West (02 8645 4545/www.teatro litta.it). Metro Cadorna/bus 50, 54/tram 16, 18, 19, 24. **Season** mid Oct-June. **Open** *Box office* 2.30-7pm

Mon-Sat. **Performances** 8.30pm Tue-Sat; 4.30pm Sun. **Tickets** €18; €12 reductions. IT. **Credit** MC, V. **Map** p250 C6/p252 C6.

This theatre is housed in a splendid baroque building in an elegant part of Milan. The company, on the other hand, is young and endeavours to present the work of contemporary authors or rethink the classics; acclaimed recent productions included works by Dario Fo and Thackeray, for example. Young people's theatre regularly takes place here.

Teatro Manzoni

Via Manzoni 42, Centre (02 763 6901/www.teatro manzoni.it). Metro Montenapoleone/bus 61, 94/tram 1, 2, 20. **Season** Oct-May. **Open** *Box office* 10am-7pm Mon-Sat; 11am-5pm Sun. **Performances** 8.45pm Tue-Sat; 11am (concerts), 3.30pm Sun. **Tickets** €29-€34; €15 reductions. **Credit** MC, V. **Map** p249 E5.

This spectacular theatre is part of Silvio Berlusconi's vast media empire. The programme has more than a sprinkling of celebrities for an audience that is sometimes described as 'the bourgeoisie in fur coats'. Note the recent casting of Rupert Everett in Noël Coward's *Private Lives*.

Teatro Nuovo

Piazza San Babila, Centre (02 794 026/www.teatro nuovo.it). Metro San Babila/bus 54, 60, 73. **Season** Oct-Apr. **Open** *Box office* 10am-1pm, 2-6pm Tue-Fri; 10am-1pm Sat. **Performances** 8.45pm Tue-Sat; 4pm Sun. **Tickets** prices vary. **Credit** MC, V. **Map** p249 F6/p252 F6.

In spite of its central address, this theatre is hard to find, located downstairs among the shopping arcade colonnades at San Babila. The programme tends to feature comedies and musicals that are often vehicles for TV starlets, as well as dance and acrobatics.

Teatro Out Off

Via Mac Mahon 16, South (02 3453 2140/www. teatrooutoff.it). Tram 12, 14. **Season** Oct-early July. **Open** *Box office* 11am-1pm, 7-8.30pm Mon-Fri; 11am-1pm, 4-8.30pm Sat; 3-4pm Sun. **Performances** 8.45pm Tue-Sat; 4pm Sun. **Tickets** €16; €11 reductions. IT. **No credit cards. Map** p248 A2.

This company, which opened for business in 1976, moved to new premises (a converted cinema) in November 2004. Over the years it has acquired a reputation for serious theatre, with several works in the 2008 season by Henrik Ibsen.

Teatro Smeraldo

Piazza XXV Aprile 10, North (02 2900 6767/www. smeraldo.it). Metro Garibaldi or Moscova/bus 43/ tram 11, 29, 30, 33. **Season** Sept-May. **Open** *Box office* 11am-5.30pm Mon-Sat. **Performances** 8.45pm Tue-Sat; 4pm Sun. **Tickets** prices vary. **Credit** MC, V. **Map** p248 D4.

This 2,000-seater is one of the city's largest theatres, although it tends to concentrate on music and dance, rather than drama. The programme is eclectic, to say the least: things like Deep Purple coupled with a homage to Rudolph Nureyev.

Arts & Entertainment

novaimago.it

S.A.C.B.O. SpA
Via Aeroporto, 13 - 24050 Orio al Serio (BG)
+39 035 326323 - www.orioaeroporto.it

the short way...Dome

When you land in Milan Orio al Serio International Airport, you are at 45 km from Milan on a new four lanes highway. This means that in half an hour you'll be visiting the famous Duomo Cathedral.

Come to Orio, take the short way... Dome.

Orio al Serio
international
airport

Trips Out of Town

Lago di Garda. *See p209.*

Getting Started

All aboard for great lakes and historic hideaways.

Milan is blessed with one of Europe's biggest attractions right on its doorstep. Or five of the biggest, to be exact. Each of the region's great lakes has its own distinct character. The romantic speck of **Lago di Orta** in the west is a tranquil getaway; **Lago di Garda**'s family-friendly expanse in the east is great for hikers and extreme sports fanatics; **Lago di Como**, 30 minutes north of Milan, is hip and historic: tourists and local Milanese star-spot and soak up the sun on the often sandy shoreline. **Lago Maggiore** is arguably the region's most majestic lake, sheltering a string of Mediterranean-style fishing villages along its palm-lined coast; and relatively overlooked **Lago d'Iseo** is an Italian-only tourist spot with car-free towns and Europe's largest inland lake. One thing all these breathtakingly beautiful stretches of water have in common is their own balmy microclimate, far removed from fog-bound Milan.

Lombardy also boasts several towns that make ideal day-trip destinations. Majestically built high on a hill, **Bergamo** prides itself as a world apart: stressed-out Milanese come here to escape the city and to step back in time. **Monza**, meanwhile, is home to the famed racetrack, host of an annual F1 race. Packed with palazzi aplenty, it's surrounded by historic towns and swathes of natural parkland.

Getting around Lombardy

The end of each chapter has information about transport from Milan, by car or by public transport, and information on getting around the surrounding zone. The following overview may also be useful.

The Lombardy regional council's website has a journey planner (www.trasporti.regione.lombardia.it; in Italian), which is easy to use and works a treat. It has listings and timetables of all forms of public transport in the area.

Lago d'Iseo.

Regional bus services

Around 40 national bus services pass through Stazione Garibaldi. In general they serve destinations not covered by train services.

Regional rail services

Milan's largest train station, Stazione Centrale, serves most locations in Lombardy; many services also operate from the station at Porta Garibaldi. The private railway service Ferrovie Nord departs from Milan's Cadorna station to eastern Lake Maggiore and Como town.

Driving

Once you've exited Milan's *tangenziale* (ring road) at the relevant junction, the excellent *autostrade* (motorways) will lead you efficiently from A to B. You can pay for these toll roads with cash or at an automated credit card machine. Alternatively, there's a far-reaching and, on the whole, well-maintained network of *strade statali* (SS; state highways), which make for a more picturesque journey. *Strade provinciali* (SP; provincial roads) will provide some memorable driving.

For general driving information, *see p221.*

Eat slow

When a group of journalists in Piedmont learned in the mid-1980s that McDonald's was planning to set up shop in Rome's historic heart, they held an urgent meeting at their neighbourhood *osteria*. The result was a manifesto that promotes local, seasonal ingredients and counters 'the degrading effects of fast food'. The Slow Food movement was born.

The philosophy swept from one Italian region to another, taking hold with vigour in Milan and Lombardy. While fast food has been contributing to an overweight population as numerous as the under-nourished, Slow Food has embraced close to 90,000 members, from America to Asia. With the world's food supply under pressure, the movement's message may be more relevant now than ever before.

For a slow approach to eating in Italy, get your hands on a copy of the Slow Food bible, *Osterie d'Italia*, published yearly and available in most Milan book shops (*see p125*). It contains restaurant and shop listings, notes, menus and tours. You can also visit www.slowfood.com, or try the following pick of our Lombardy faves.

In Bergamo, grab a table in cosy **Al Donizetti** (*see p185*), or, if the sun's out, under the Renaissance-style arcade outside. Open all day, all night and all year, this well-stocked wine bar (more than 800 labels and counting) serves platters of salami and cheeses, as well as *casoncelli*, a Lombard pasta stuffed with ham, cheese, eggs and breadcrumbs. At the **Trattoria del Teatro** (*see p105*), osso bucco with polenta and *filetto dei fiera* (fillet steak with a slice of lemon) are lapped up by a faithful Bergamasco clientele. The sucker punch is the stinky trio of local cheeses.

On Lago di Garda, **La Contrada**'s Desenzano dining room (*see p210*) specialises in traditional northern Italian recipes. Try the duck salad starter, followed by the steak doused in Valpolicella's renowned Amarone wine. Further north, Gardone di Sopra's **Agli Angeli** (*see p213*) caters to classic Mediterranean tastes, with a seasonal menu that features goat's cheese and peppercorn parcels with pear chutney, or scallops on a thick tomato purée.

Trips Out of Town

Monza & Brianza

Petrol heads and pedal power.

As Milan mayor Letizia Moratti never ceases to repeat in front of the cameras, Milan's city limits encircle a metropolitan area almost as large as that of Los Angeles or New York – as if nearly ten million people living in a grey industrial sprawl were something to be proud of. To the naked eye, any towns on the edge of Milan seem to be a repetitive pattern of factory, industrial suburb and high-rise neighbourhoods.

North of Milan, however, is a welcome exception: hilly, temperate Brianza, with its charming regional capital town, Monza. Easily accessible, at the end of a major motorway that juts out from Milan's city centre, Brianza has leafy, sleepy hamlets, perfect for a relaxing day away from the rat race.

Monza

Once the jewel in the crown of the Lombard empire, Monza was a trade and commerce centre that rivalled Milan. Now a quaint, affluent town, it draws visitors principally for beautiful palazzi, gastronomic delights, a staggeringly huge park and the world-famous F1 racing track, the **Autodromo Nazionale Monza** (*see p181* **The fast and the furious**).

A rightful reward for the third-largest town in Lombardy, Monza will become the new capital of the national administrative unit of Monza & Brianza, which will come into effect in 2009. And, if Italian real estate developers are to be believed, Monza will also be connected to the city of Milan as the last stop of the new M5 metro line, which is being installed for Expo 2015 (*see p24* **Milan exposed**).

The magnificent **Duomo** (piazza Duomo, 039 389 420, closed Sat, Sun) and its stunning basilica offer a glimpse of the town's historic past. Boasting a Romanesque façade that was later decorated with stunning Gothic motifs, it includes two star attractions: the **Cappella di Teodolinda**, with its mannerist frescoes, and the historic Iron Crown of Lombardy, one of the most ancient European royal insignia, which was allegedly built around one of the iron nails used in the Crucifixion. The crown was used in the coronation ceremony of Charlemagne in 774, of Otto I the Great in 962, of Frederick Barbarossa in 1154, and of Napoleon in 1805. When you're ready for a break, hit the comfy

sofas at hip Tea Rose Café (piazza Duomo, 039 2356 0203) for a world-class cocktail and a plate of good (if pricey) antipasti, or choose from the extensive international tea menu.

The 13th-century town hall raised on arches, known as the **Arengario**, lends its medieval charm to the city, and the lesser churches, such as **Santa Maria in Strada** and the **San Pietro Martire**, are also worth a peek. Nearby, **Ospedale San Gerardino** sits in a quiet piazza (which doubles as a spill-out area for the charming Mulino a Vino wine bar, 039 384 180) a short distance from a pretty medieval bridge over the Lambro river. Europe's oldest working hospital has a breathtakingly serene courtyard, and the trendy Noble Lounge (039 3909 3290) restaurant shares its whitewashed walls, although none of its tranquillity.

No visit to Monza would be complete without a walk through the enormous **Parco di Monza**, one of the oldest and largest parks in Europe. It contains many attractions, including the famous Autodromo and the immense **Villa Reale** (viale Regina Margherita 2, 039 322 086, closed for refurbishment until 2009). Formerly the Archduke of Austria's hunting lodge, the Villa Reale was later used as the Savoys' summer retreat, until it was abandoned and subsequently donated to the town, after Umberto I's assassination nearby in 1900. En route from the city centre, you can join the many *Monzesi* who meet for a Campari in the shade at charming little Bar Balafüs, in Boschetti Reali's gardens – or rent a bike at the former farmhouse **Cascina Bastia**, near the park's main entrance.

Around Monza

Arcore, east of Monza, pulls in the crowds with its 18th-century **Villa Borromeo d'Adda** (039 60 171, www.villadarcore.com), whose beautiful grounds are open to the public. Nowadays its name is inevitably linked to that of neighbour Silvio Berlusconi, who lives in another, high-gated villa nearby. Although not open to the public, the Villa Borromeo does give a good idea of the lifestyle of the important Italian families during the Renaissance.

Despite being a thriving manufacturing centre, Vimercate has preserved much of its original charm. In the **Palazzo Trotti**, the

The fast and the furious

The **Autodromo Nazionale Monza** (Parco di Monza, 039 24 821, www.monzanet.it) is one of the world's most famous F1 circuits, and one of the fastest, most thrilling events in the global motor racing schedule. The long straights, the sweeping Curva Parabolica and the infamous chicane make for a nerve-racking race, for drivers and spectators alike.

Like many Italian institutions, its birth was linked to the constant rivalry between the *Bel Paese* and its neighbours to the west. If France's Automobile Club had a Grand Prix at Le Mans, why shouldn't the Italians have one too? And so, in 1922, a group of Italian speed freaks decided to mark the 25-year anniversary of the Milan Automobile Club by setting up a circuit at Monza.

Since then, the Autodromo has had more makeovers than a Hollywood star. Most frequent have been the safety improvements to limit the death toll. Between 1922 and 2000, 18 drivers and 41 spectators died in crashes; the most dramatic accident came in 1961, when Count Wolfgang von Trips' Ferrari collided with a Lotus belonging to Jim Clark, bounced into the crowd and killed 15 spectators. Safety regulations are much stricter than they were in the past, but the track is still known as the setting of one of the most accident-prone GPs on the circuit.

But the Autodromo is now so much more than the celebration of speed and progress that it was at its inception. It has evolved into a year-round attraction, with a schedule of events that caters to occasional drivers and professional daredevils alike. It's also the spiritual home of Team Ferrari, as well as a second home for its supporters, the *tifosi*, who know the track's ins and outs like a child knows his bedroom ceiling. The team's last home win came courtesy of Michael Schumacher in 2006, who capped off an extraordinary record of five wins in ten years at the circuit. The complex, set within a verdant park, boasts camping facilities, an Olympic swimming pool and a car museum.

town hall, an 18th-century fresco cycle fills 11 rooms. The basilica of **Santo Stefano** was built between the tenth and 11th centuries on earlier foundations. Along via Cavour, off the central piazza Roma, are several 15th-century palazzi and the little Romanesque **Oratorio di Sant'Antonio**, with frescoes from 1450. At the end of the street, the **Ponte di San Rocco**, built from recycled Roman remains, was part of the town's medieval fortifications.

North of Monza is **Biassono**. Its town hall, **Villa Verri**, is a perfect example of early 18th-century *barocchetto* architecture. Its **Museo Civico** (via San Martino 1, 039 220 1077, www.museobiassono.it) offers good archaeological and ethnographic reconstructions of Brianza farm life through the ages.

Getting there

By bus
ATM buses 723, 724 and 727 from Milan's Stazione Centrale, or 721, 820 and 821 from Sesto FS metro station, cover the short hop to Monza, Vimercate and other Brianza destinations.

By car
For Monza, take viale Zara out of Milan, which becomes viale Fulvio Testi (journey time 15mins-1hr, depending on traffic). From Monza, local roads are well signed for Biassono, Carate Brianza, Arcore, Oreno and Vimercate. Vimercate can also be reached via the A15 *autostrada*.

By train
Mainline trains for Monza leave Milan's Stazione Centrale or Porta Garibaldi every 15mins or so. Trains also leave hourly (every 30mins at rush hour) from both stations for Arcore, on the Milan–Sondrio line. Triuggio, headquarters for the Parco Lambro, is on the Sesto–Lecco line, with trains every hour.

Getting around
See p178 **Getting Started**.

Tourist information

Pro Monza (IAT)
Palazzo Comunale, piazza Carducci 2 (039 323 222/ www.comune.monza.mi.it). **Open** 9am-noon, 3-6pm Mon-Fri; 9am-noon Sat.

Trips Out of Town

Bergamo

A medieval festival of fine art and fabulous food.

The Venetians fortified this enchanting hilltop town, and the city's wealth, culture and unique cuisine have remained rich to this day. Now the *bergamaschi* have flung open their *palazzi* doors to reveal an unhurried retreat, blessed with fine architecture and an overwhelming array of art.

Bergamo's countless treasures fall into two areas. For intricate churches, belt-popping dining and a fleet of historical museums, hit the old **Città Alta** (Upper City). The modern **Città Bassa** (Lower City) has lashings of 19th-century chic and boasts parks, galleries and a good third of the city's ten or so museums. Just 30 minutes from Milan, it's the perfect antidote to the Lombard capital's stress and smog – although, with its own international airport ten minutes away, this medieval city proudly pulls in plenty of crowds of its own.

Sightseeing

Città Alta

A ride on Bergamo's wedge-shaped funicular from viale Vittorio Emanuelle II brings you up to the bustling **piazza Mercato delle Scarpe**. Follow the restaurant-lined via Gombito into the heart of Bergamo's enchanting old city, and turn up via Rocca to **piazza vecchia Museo Storico** (*see p186* **The Bergamo history project**). A former Venetian defensive bastion, La Rocca now houses one of five Città Alta historical museums accessible with a single €5 ticket, and boasts superb valley views from its grounds.

From via Gombito, narrow via San Pancrazio winds its way to another Bergamo history museum outpost in the old **convent of San Francesco** (*see p186* **The Bergamo history project**). At the intersection with via Lupo stands the **Torre Gombito** (035 399 111, visits by appointment), a defensive turret that dates back to the Guelph-Ghibelline struggles of the 12th century, and is newly open to the public.

Beyond the tower, via Gombito opens out into the lovely, spacious **piazza Vecchia**, which epitomises Bergamo at its finest. The beautiful bone-white buildings on the square's eastern side house the offices of the local university. On the south-western side of the square sits the magnificent **Palazzo della**

Ragione. Although currently under wraps until early 2009, the fresco-covered *sala superiore* inside usually serves as an impressive backdrop for various temporary exhibitions. Also here are Donato Bramante's *Tre Filosofi* frescoes (1477).

The neo-classical **Palazzo Nuovo** on the north-east of piazza Vecchia is home to the municipal archives and library. Towering nearly 53 metres (173 feet) above the square is another of the city's towers, the 12th-century **Torre Civica** (*see p186* **The Bergamo history project**).

Neighbouring **piazza Duomo** houses some of Bergamo's most captivating buildings: the Duomo, the basilica of Santa Maria Maggiore and the Cappella Colleoni.

The **Duomo** (035 210 223) is officially known as Cattedrale di Sant'Alessandro. Construction, to a design by Antonio 'Il Filarete' Averlino, started in 1459, on a spot previously occupied by an early Christian church. The project passed through the hands of several architects before the work was finally completed in 1886. Among the mostly 18th-century works surrounding the main altar is Giambattista Tiepolo's *Martyrdom of St John the Bishop*. The statue of Pope John XXIII at the Duomo's entrance is a reminder of the city's esteem for the 1950s *bergamasco* pope.

Next door to the Duomo is the equally impressive **Santa Maria Maggiore** (035 223 327). Construction, again atop the remains of an earlier church, began in 1157, and did not end until 1521. Each period of construction added something of beauty, from the presbytery (1187), to the baptistery (1350), to the new sacristy (late 15th century). The most stunning aspect of the church, however, is the series of wooden inlay works on the presbytery stalls. These exquisite 16th-century carvings, designed by Venetian artist Lorenzo Lotto, tell stories from the Old Testament; they also contain detailed comments in the form of alchemic symbols. The intricately frescoed roof counts among Bergamo's must-see sights.

The **Cappella Colleoni**, to the south-west of the square, was built by Venetian general Bartolomeo Colleoni. He had the old sacristy of Santa Maria Maggiore demolished to make way for his mausoleum, which was finished in 1475, a year after his death. Colleoni's tomb and that of his daughter Medea grace the chapel, as do frescoes (1733) by Gian Battista Tiepolo. On the gate outside the chapel, visitors looking for luck have rubbed the Colleoni coat of arms to a bright sheen. The coat of arms, it should be noted, bears three testicles – as did Colleoni, according to legend. Leading off the piazza is via Arena, home of the quirky **Museo Donizettiano** (*see p186* **The Bergamo history project**).

Beyond piazza Vecchia, via Gombito becomes via Bartolomeo Colleoni and leads to piazza Mascheroni, home to **La Cittadella**. Built in the 14th century to defend the Città Alta from attacks from the west, the citadel now plays host to a colourful Sunday craft market. Two

Città Alta.

museums are lodged in the city walls: the **Musico Civico di Scienze Naturali** (035 286 011, closed Mon), a taxidermy tour of the animal kingdom; and the highly recommended **Museo Archeologico** (035 242 839, closed Mon), which is packed with Roman, Renaissance and medieval artefacts. Rising above the square is the **Torre della Campanella**; built in 1355, this bell tower wasn't finished until the 19th century, hence the relatively modern-looking clock face.

Pass through piazza Cittadella and through the Porta Sant'Alessandro to Colle Aperto, an open space overlooking the foothills of the Alps. However pleasant, these views are nothing compared to the breathtaking sights to be had by catching Bergamo's second funicular line to **Il Castello San Viglio**, a former Venetian castle high above town. It's a pleasant 15-minute amble back down from the top, with picture-perfect views of the Città Bassa and Lombard plains way below.

Città Bassa

Bergamo's cultural riches are flaunted just as casually in the lower city. The high-end High Street that is via XX Settembre, studded with the likes of MaxMara and Marina Rinaldi, showcases a different side of the city's relative wealth.

Piazza Vittorio Veneto leads off this shopping paradise and forms the Città Bassa's centrepoint, alongside **Porta Nuova**, the city's main entrance from 1837 onwards. Further east is the **Santo Bartolomeo** church, which contains Lorenzo Lotto's *Madonna col Bambino e Santi* (1516). A block further is the imposing **Palazzo Viterbi**, host to a steady flow of temporary sculpture exhibitions, as well as the **Teatro Donizetti** theatre house.

Yet more art is on display on the palazzo-lined streets off via Pignolo. The **Museo Bernareggi** (closed Mon) has fine art and sculpture, and the **Galleria d'Arte Moderna**

Food fit for a pope

Look in the window of any *pasticceria* in Bergamo, and there'll be a round yellow cake topped with chocolate bits looking right back at you. These are *polenta e osei*, 'polenta and little birds'. They're made neither of polenta nor, thankfully, birds: instead, these little sponge cakes rolled in fondant icing are an affectionate tribute to the medieval dish of the same name that – you've guessed it – was exactly what its name suggests.

To the untrained eye, polenta looks like mash gone wrong; but the stodgy, savoury porridge has been eaten with passion for centuries. Traditionally it was the food of the poor, and over the centuries it has fed everyone from the Roman emperor's foot soldiers to the pope: polenta was the favourite dish of local-boy-made-good Pope John XXIII.

Made from spelt, millet and buckwheat – and, since the introduction of corn to Europe at the tail end of the Middle Ages, cornmeal – polenta was traditionally cooked over an open fire in a rounded copper pot (*paiolo*) – the copper to help distribute the heat, the rounded bottom to stop the food sticking. If the larder was empty, polenta was eaten on its own or, as was the case with that old Bergamo speciality, with grilled wild songbirds such as thrush. The lucky few ate it with game (furry and feathered kinds), and the grains were perfect for mopping up the meat's rich juices.

Though killing wild songbirds is somewhat frowned upon these days, polenta is still an intrinsic part of the Bergamo diet. In fact, the local speciality is held in such high esteem that in 1976 the Ordine dei Cavalieri della Polenta ('Order of the Knights of Polenta') was founded here. From running annual polenta festivals to devising new recipes, these apron-fronted polenta guardians are dedicated to 'upholding, defending, and promoting' the tasty mush.

Grilled, fried, boiled or baked, this staple is, undeniably, the most humble of foods. But served alongside succulent meats and sausages, or enriched with cheeses such as gorgonzola or branzi, it is a treat to sate the stomach and comfort the soul. The latter cheese takes its name from the town of Branzi 30 kilometres (20 miles) north of Bergamo, which hosts the annual Sagre della Polenta (polenta festival) every August.

---

e **Contemporanea** (closed Mon) is home to groundbreaking exhibitions, and a permanent collection including works from Enzo Cucchi and Vanessa Beecroft. Sadly, the 2,000 masterpieces in the prestigious **Accademia Carrara** are off limits until 2010, while a grand renovation project takes place.

Where to eat & drink

Bergamasco cuisine (*see p31*) is suited especially for those with hearty appetites. Starters focus on cold cuts, particularly homemade *salame* and *lardo*, creamy white slices of pork fat (it's better than it sounds), while main courses tend towards roasts and braised dishes, often served with polenta. The city is also home to some stunning *pasticcerie*.

Open all hours by the Piazza Mercato della Scarpe funicular, **Al Donizetti** (Via Gombito 17A, 035 242 661, average €25) serves up *salumeria* platters of prosciutto, *lardo* and salami, plus local cheeses with walnut and honey accompaniments. The historic **Antica Trattoria la Colombina** (Via Borgo Canale 12, 035 261 402, closed Mon, Tue & 2-3wks June-July, average €30) just outside the Città

Alta walls dishes up seriously traditional cuisine in its sun-dappled dining room. The *stinco al forno con polenta* (baked pork shank with polenta) will keep you going for a couple of days. **La Marianna** (Colle Aperto 2, 035 237 027, closed Mon & 2wks Jan, average €15) is pit stop par excellence. Grab a bellini sorbet, rose petal ice cream or warm *torta cioccolato* (chocolate tart) while sitting on the terrace overlooking the valley.

Open since 1956, **Da Mimmo** (Via Colleoni 17, 035 218 535, closed Tue, average €45) is more intricate and exciting than the other restaurants on Bergamo's main strip. The lunchtime *antipasti* buffet is great value, and there's a €60 evening *degustazione* menu for serious foodies. Very cheap and very cheerful, **Da Ornella** (Via Gombito 15, 035 232 736, closed Thur, average €25) is a *Bergamasco* restaurant popular with locals. The decor may be 30 years out of date, but the dishes, like *casoncelli alla Bergamesca* (meat and butter pasta pockets), are timeless. **Trattoria del Teatro** (Piazza Mascheroni 3, 035 238 862, closed Mon & 2 wks July, average €30) is a no nonsense restaurant with no English spoken and pretty abrupt service to boot. If you're brave enough to venture through the door you'll find the food absolutely divine.

Le Tris (Viale Vittorio Emanuele II 12, 035 217 037, closed Sun, average €35) in the Città Bassa is more *Milanese* than *Bergamasco* in both style and substance. Carpaccio of swordfish with pink pepper, and grilled *branzino* (seabass) with local vegetables are served up on the terrace or inside the chic black dining room.

Where to stay

Bergamo is blessed with an array of nicely priced, friendly hotels. In the Città Alta, the **Agnello d'Oro** (via Gombito 22, 035 249 883, www.agnellodoro.it, doubles €85) is as romantic as it gets: the building dates from the 16th century, and is laden with antiques; some of its 20 rooms have balconies over the square below. Across from the Cittadella, the upmarket **Hotel San Lorenzo** (piazza Mascheroni 9A, 035 237 383, www.hotelsanlorenzobg.it, doubles €128-€148) is modern and charming. **Il Sole** (via Colleoni 1, 035 218 238, www.ilsole bergamo.com, doubles €85), right on Piazza Vecchia, is well placed, but more low key.

For mod cons and a touch of flair in the Città Bassa, the modern **Mercure Palazzo Dolci** (viale Papa Giovanni XXIII 100, 035 227 411, doubles €120-€200) is an excellent bet.

Getting there

By air
For information about Bergamo's Orio al Serio airport, about 45km (28 miles) from Milan, *see p218*.

By bus
Autostradale buses (035 244 354, www.auto stradale.it) leave Milan's Stazione Porta Garibaldi for Bergamo every 30mins. Journey time is about 45mins.

By car
Take the A4 *autostrada* from Milan east towards Venice; exit at Bergamo.

By train
Services run from Milan's Stazione Centrale via Treviglio, and from Stazione Porta Garibaldi via Carnate. Of the two, the Carnate service is the more regular and has the added sightseeing advantage of crossing the Adda river over the dramatic Ponte di Paderno. Journey time is about 1hr.

Getting around

The buses in Bergamo are operated by ATB (035 364 211/www.atb.bergamo.it), as are the two funiculars in the city. Tickets (€1) must be bought before boarding. They are sold at tobacconists and some newsstands around town. *Giornaliero* tickets are also available for €3.50, which grant the bearer unlimited city centre and airport bus transport on the day of purchase.

Tourist information

IAT Città Alta
Via Gombito 13, Città Alta (035 242 226/ www.comune.bergamo.it). **Open** 9am-noon, 2-5.30pm daily.

IAT Città Bassa
Piazza Marconi 1, Città Bassa (035 210 204/ www.comune.bergamo.it). **Open** 9am-noon, 2-5.30pm daily.

The Bergamo history project

Five museums for the price of one? Bergamo's Fondazione nella Storia (www.bergamoestoria.it) has made several of the city's cultural highlights a lot more accessible by issuing a €5 pass, available at any of the five participating sights. All are closed on Mondays.

Visitors can take in the tale of modern-day Italy inside the two well-stocked historical museums, housed in the former **Convent of San Francesco** (piazza Mercato del Fieno 6) and in the **Rocco** (piazzale Brigata Legnano, 035 247 116). The latter is very touchy-feely: you can get close to Garibaldi's pistols, and stroke a bust of Napoleon Bonaparte.

The **Museo Donizettiano** (via Arena 9, 035 399 269) is tucked away on the first floor of

an evocative old palazzo. Just cross the courtyard and push your way in, even if the building does seem a bit deserted. Its wonderful collection of handwritten letters, harpsichords and opera posters highlighting the life of Bergamo-born composer Gaetano Donizetti (1797-1848) seems seldom visited; the only apparent nod to modernity is the fluorescent light above.

Piazza Vecchia has plenty of cafés to rest in after the lung-busting climb up the **Torre Civica** (035 247 116) lookout tower. Finally, down in the Città Bassa, the **Torre dei Cadui** clock tower on piazza Vittorio Veneto, inaugurated by Mussolini in 1924, can also be clambered up, providing five or more people are present.

Lago d'Orta

A petite Swallows and Amazons retreat.

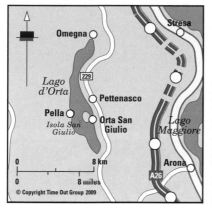

Lago d'Orta
229
Omegna
Stresa
Pettenasco
Pella
Isola San Giulio
Orta San Giulio
Lago Maggiore
Arona
A26
0   8 km
0   8 miles
© Copyright Time Out Group 2009

They say Lago d'Orta can make wishes come true. Looking out over this little piece of paradise, it would be hard to wish for anything else, except a few more days of holiday. Planned outings are soon discarded: many visitors become distracted by the stunning vistas. Few locals wear a watch. Set just west of Lago Maggiore, this small stretch of water (measuring just 18 square kilometres) has a lazy, magical air. Stroll along the shoreline paths, check the views from surrounding mountain summits, or just sip a sundowner in one of the picturesque squares. Fans of Italian design icon Alessi can visit the town of Omegna and pick up the latest kitchen lines direct from the factory (*see p189* **Alessi's cave**). The lake's one must is a boat trip to Orta's dreamy island of Isola San Giulio, dominated by an ancient abbey in the centre.

Orta San Giulio

Visitors to the medieval lakeside town of Orta San Giulio could be forgiven for thinking they have somehow stumbled onto a vintage movie set. Stone buildings adorned with the odd peeling hotel sign make up the main lakeside square of piazza Motta, seemingly unchanged for 80 years. A dramatic pathway sweeps uphill from here to the yellow-stained church of **Santa Maria Assunta** (1485). Crumbling villas stretch out from the town, and there's a shoreline walkway (via 11 Settembre

2001) that circumnavigates the peninsula. Back in the café-lined square, models are often found posing for photo shoots beneath the frescoes and *loggia* stilts of the 16th-century **Palazzo della Comunità** (the former town hall).

Perched above the town, in the wooded **Sacro Monte** nature reserve (0322 911 960, www.sacromonteorta.it), are 20 small Renaissance and Baroque chapels (1590-1785) containing 376 remarkably lifelike terracotta sculptures in tableaux depicting events from the life of St Francis of Assisi. A pleasant pilgrims' path (30 minutes) winds uphill from piazza Motta to the 17th-century **Chiesa di San Nicolao** and the Sacro Monte.

Where to stay, eat & shop

The luxurious **Villa Crespi** (via Fava 18, 0322 911 902, www.hotelvillacrespi.it, closed early Jan-Feb, doubles €190-€280; *photo p190*) is an over-the-top, carved Moorish villa on the road from the station. The villa's restaurant (closed Mon & lunch Tue, average €70) – under Michelin-starred Neapolitan chef Antonino Cannavacciuolo – is one of Italy's best.

Managed by the same family for over a century, **Hotel Orta** (piazza Motta, 0322 90 253, www.hotelorta.it, closed Nov-Easter, doubles €89-€115) sits on the main square. Its restaurant's panoramic terrace boasts fine views of the Isola San Giulio (average €30). The four-star **Hotel San Rocco** (via Gippini 11, 0322 911 977, www.hotelsanrocco.it, doubles €143-€288), set in a former 17th-century convent, offers swish lakeside rooms and fine dining (average €50). Speedos seem obligatory in its lakeside swimming pool.

On the town's oldest street, the 500-year-old wine bar **Al Boeuc** (via Bersani 28, mobile 339 584 0039, closed Tue Apr-Dec & Mon-Wed Jan-Mar, average €15) serves bruschette, local cheese and cold cuts, and over 350 wines. Order a cocktail (or one of their extravagant ice-cream sundaes) at **Bar Venus** (piazza Motta 50, 0322 90 362) and watch the sun set over the lake.

The cosy **Taverna Antico Agnello** (via Olina 18, 0322 90 259, closed Tue & Dec-Jan, average €40) serves modern takes on regional staples including rabbit, duck and venison. On a summer evening, the single balcony table for two has the best seats in town.

Isola San Giulio.

Finally, lovers of local crafts shouldn't miss **Penelope** (piazza Motta 26, 0322 905 600, www.penelope-orta.it), which specialises in hand-woven kitchen linens traditionally printed with antique wooden stamps and natural dyes.

Tourist information

Associazione Turistica Pro Loco

Via Bossi 11, Orta San Giulio (0322 90 155). **Open** 11am-1pm, 2-6pm Mon-Fri; 10am-1pm, 2-6pm Sat, Sun.

Distretto Turistico dei Laghi

Via Panoramica, Orta San Giulio (0322 905 614/ www.distrettolaghi.it). **Open** 9am-1pm, 2-6pm Wed-Sun.

Isola San Giulio

According to legend, St Julius (San Giulio) sailed to this island by floating on his cloak, then got down to banishing its multitude of snakes and dragons. Next, he established his 100th church, where he was eventually laid to rest. These days you can reach the enchanting island and its basilica (founded in 392) by mini-ferry (every 40 minutes, €2.50) or taxi boat (mobile 333 605 0288, €4) from piazza Motta at Orta San Giulio. From here you can also book a 30-minute tour of the lake with a stop on the island (€8), or, if you're feeling sporty, row yourself across (boat hire €10 per hour).

Inside the basilica, a black marble pulpit has rare Saxon-influenced carvings, and frescoes from many centuries battle for space around its walls. A circular pathway (via alla Basilica) runs around the island, past the cloistered Benedictine abbey and many romantic villas.

If you're here for St Julius's feast day, 31 January, rap on the convent door to get a bag of *pane San Giulio* (dried fruit, nut and chocolate bread) for a small donation. (This treat is for sale in mainland bakeries all year round.) There's no hotel on the island, but it is occasionally possible to stay at the **Mater Ecclesiae abbey** (via Basilica 5, 0322 905 010). You'll be expected to follow the monastic way of life, rising for dawn prayers at 4.50am. The island has just one hostelry, **Ristorante San Giulio** (via Basilica 4, 0322 90 234, www.orta.net/sangiulio). When it opens under new ownership in autumn 2008, it will retake the crown of Orta's most romantic restaurant.

Around the lake

Perched on the hill above Orta San Giulio, Vacciago di Ameno houses the **Collezione Calderara di Arte Contemporanea** (via

Alessi's cave

Away from its mystical monasteries and romantic alleyways, Lago d'Orta is home to a doyen of international design. Alessi (they of the Starck-designed, spindly legged juicer) set up shop near sleepy Omegna in 1921. The company employed cutting-edge designers hailing from as far afield as Australia and Japan, who have gone on to create over 22,000 pieces of inventive homeware for the firm. Some of these now reside in New York's MoMA and London's V&A.

Although only industry specialists can peek into Alessi's 'holy of holies' historical collection, mere mortals can revel in the company's huge factory shop. The entire Alessi range is on sale, from steel and leather champagne buckets to transparent plastic egg cups; there are special offers on seconds and end-of-line articles.

Alessi Outlet Store

Via Privata Alessi, Crusinallo di Omegna (0323 868 648/www.alessi.com). **Open** 9.30am-6pm Mon-Sat; 2.30-6.30pm Sun. **Credit** AmEx, DC, MC, V.

Bardelli 9, 0322 998 192, closed Mon mid May-mid Oct, open by appointment mid Oct-mid May). This museum was converted from a late 17th-century home by Antonio Calderara (1903-78), and of its 327 paintings and sculptures, 56 are by him. The impressive collection documents the international avant-garde from the 1950s and '60s, with an emphasis on kinetic art, geometric abstraction and visual poetry.

Pettenasco stands on the lake shore north of Orta. Its Romanesque church tower started life attached to the church of Sant'Audenzio, a pal of San Giulio and Pettenasco's town prefect in 300. The intricate woodwork for which the town was once famous is commemorated at the **Museo dell'Arte della Tornitura del Legno** (via Vittorio Veneto, 0323 89 622, closed Mon & Oct-May), which has tools, wooden items and machines from the town's old factories.

Named after the battle cry *Heu moenia!* ('Woe to you, walls!'), uttered by Julius Caesar before he ploughed through the defences of the city, **Omegna** was the site of heavy fighting in World War II. Today the town – the biggest on the lake – manufactures metal kitchenware. In the **Forum Omegna** cultural centre (parco Maulini 1, 0323 866 141, www.forumomegna. org, closed Sun morning), a museum documents

Trips Out of Town

the history of the area's industry. A gift shop sells new, discounted items by local brands Alessi, Bialetti, Calderoni and Lagostina.

Seven kilometres (4.5 miles) west and uphill from Omegna, **Quarna Sotto** enjoys great views of the lake, plus one of the area's wildest museums. Around the late 1800s, the town was famous around the world for its wood and metal wind instruments. The **Museo Etnografico** (via Roma, 0323 89 622, closed Mon & Oct-May) honours this tradition with graphic explanations of manufacturing methods; this lovingly curated gem also has displays on housing design, local costume and domestic arts, as well as a water mill.

From **Pella**, on the lake's western shore, a signposted road climbs uphill for ten kilometres (six miles) to the church of Madonna del Sasso. En route, the hamlet of **Artò** has antique wash-houses, sundials and a building adorned with a 16th-century fresco, and **Boleto** is a picture, with its cobbled lanes and church. At the top, the **Madonna del Sasso** church, built between 1730 and 1748, sits 638 metres (2,127 feet) above the lake on a granite outcrop. In thanks for a miracle, a successful local cobbler arranged for the bones of San Donato to be transferred here from the San Callisto catacombs in Rome. The holy skeleton, resting oddly on its side, lies in a transparent casket to the left of the altar. Most of the frescoes are the work of local artist

Lorenzo Peracino, and the painting above the pink, grey and black marble altar is the *Pietà* (1547) by Fermo Stella da Caravaggio.

Where to eat & stay

The **Hotel Panoramico Ristorante** in Boleto (via Frua 31, 0322 981 312, www.hotelpanora mico.it, closed Nov Mon-Thur and mid Jan-Mar, doubles €70-€85) has modest but comfortable rooms and a restaurant (average €30) with two outdoor terraces and unbeatable views over the lake. Beach lovers can head down to the lake's south-east corner, where **Camping Miami** (via Novara 69, 0322 998 444, €5 per person, €10 per tent) is located just over the road from the sunloungers and water sports at Spiaggia Miami (www.spiaggiamiami.com).

Tourist information

Ufficio Informazione Turistica Omegna
Piazza XXIV Aprile 17 (0323 61 930/www.distretto laghi.it). **Open** 9am-12.30pm, 2.30-5.30pm Mon-Fri; 9am-12.30pm Sat.

Getting there

By car
Take the motorway for the lakes (Ai Laghi). When it divides, head for Malpensa/Varese/Sesto Calende, then join the A26 in the direction of Gravellona Toce. Exit at Borgomanero, then follow the signs to Gozzano and Lago d'Orta.

By train
Mainline service from Stazione Centrale or Porta Garibaldi to Novara, then local service stopping at Orta/Miasino, Pettenasco and Omegna. Note: all stations except Omegna are on steep hills above the towns, 15-20mins walk from the lake. You can book a taxi with Servizi Lago d'Orta (mobile 338 986 4839).

Getting around

By boat
Navigazione Lago d'Orta (0322 844 862) runs a boat service around the lake, stopping at Orta, Isola San Giulio, Pettenasco, Gozzano and elsewhere (daily Easter-mid Oct; Sat, Sun in Oct, Nov; Sun only Jan-Easter). If you're coming by car, make for Pella or Omegna, where there's ample parking. A day ticket is €7.30 (no credit cards). Alternatively, book a tour in a water taxi from the Servizio Pubblico Motoscafi (mobile 333 605 0288) at Orta San Giulio.

By car
A car is essential for visiting the towns above the lake shore. Orta San Giulio's town centre is closed to traffic; cars must be left in the parking lots at the edge of town.

It's a hotel. **Villa Crespi**. *See p187*.

Lago Maggiore

The sun-blessed lakes at their best.

For many people touring the lakes, Maggiore is the major attraction. It's a perfect storm of rich history and sublime topography, a necklace of all too beautiful towns framed by sandy shores and vertiginous mountains, and with a balmy microclimate to boot. Cruising in the sunshine past one of the lake's lush islands evokes a 'died and gone to heaven' feeling.

Part of the majesty stems from the Visconti era: the family built several lakefront castles, later joined by the extravagant homes of the Borromeo dynasty that succeeded theirs. The three islands that bear the Borromeo name were where Napoleon rested his laurels after conquering northern Italy; the wily Corsican built the Simplon Pass soon after, which brought further riches to the lake. Finally, there are the fine establishments that accommodated Grand Tour veterans and the starlets of the belle époque. For the visitor today, it all means graceful hotels, lakeside promenades and manicured gardens of unrivalled elegance.

Maggiore is actually three lakes in one. The top fifth is Switzerland's sunniest corner, a setting for fun activities and great summer festivals. The little-visited Lombard side has cute villages, walks, churches and quiet corners waiting to be discovered. And Piedmont's long western stretch has town after town packed with pavement cafés, culture and restaurants to write home about.

The Piedmont shore

A trip down the Piedmont shore by ferry, train or even by bike is incredible. Each new turn exposes a villa, an island hotel or another red-roofed old town to explore. The lovely natural setting has drawn visitors from the Iron Age onwards, and the shore's only drawback is the summer throng around Maggiore's top sites.

At the southern tip of Lago Maggiore is **Arona**, a lively commercial town with a pretty, historic centre. San Carlo Borromeo was born here, and a 17th-century, 35-metre (117-foot) copper statue of the saintly local hero, built using the technique later employed to construct the Statue of Liberty, stands high on a hill two kilometres (1.2 miles) from the town (piazzale San Carlo, closed Mon-Fri Oct & Apr, Nov-Mar). Those with steely nerves can climb a narrow internal spiral staircase and ten-metre (32-foot)

vertical ladder to the statue's head, and peer at the lake through the saint's eyes.

A few kilometres north, the smaller town of **Meina** has some attractive private residences, although the odd derelict hotel and villa give the place a bankrupt aristocracy air. A dark event mars the serene town's history: in September 1943, Nazi troops shot 16 Jewish guests at a local hotel.

Above **Belgirate**'s tiny historic centre is the church of Santa Maria del Suffragio (closed Mon-Sat), lavishly adorned with frescoes by the school of Bernardino Luini, the local 16th-century artist.

Stresa stands magnificently on the Golfo Borromeo, which, with its islands, forms the heart of the lake. The town became famous after Dickens and Byron gave it rave reviews; Hemingway also set part of *A Farewell to Arms* here in the Grand Hotel Borromeo (*see p194* **Hemingway's haunts**). At the turn of the century, Stresa's grandiose hotels, refined attractions and casino rivalled those of Monte Carlo and the Venice Lido. **Villa Pallavicino** (Strada Statale 33, Località Stresa, 0323 30 501, www.parcozoopallavicino.it, closed Nov-Feb) has a vast English-style garden and a zoo. The town is also known for its season of summer classical concerts (www.stresafestival.eu).

The 1,491-metre-high (4,970-foot) summit of **Montagna Mottarone** can be reached by cable car (0323 302 95, www.stresa-mottarone.it, closed Dec-Feb) or a five-hour hike from Stresa. It becomes a ski resort in winter, and on a clear day you can enjoy a stunning view of the Alps, several lakes, and – on really exceptional days – as far as Milan and Turin. The cable car stops at the **Giardino Alpinia** (0323 302 95, www.giardinoalpinia.it, closed Nov-Mar), which boasts hundreds of alpine plant species; and it also offers a picture perfect view down onto the three **Isole Borromee** set a few hundred metres off Stresa's shore: Isola Bella, Isola Madre and Isola dei Pescatori. The regular ferries buzz past the mansions, gardens and vine-covered houses on each island: it's an unforgettable sight.

The Borromeo feudal lords took possession of these islands in the 16th century. **Isola Bella** was named in honour of Isabella d'Adda, whose husband Carlo Borromeo III began transforming the island in 1632. The island's baroque **Palazzo Borromeo** (0323 30 556, www.borromeoturismo.it, closed mid Oct-mid Mar), where Napoleon and Josephine slept after Napoleon's conquest of northern Italy, is a wonderfully gratuitous display of old money. Its stately Italian-style garden is stocked with albino peacocks. The 16th-century **Palazzo Borromeo** on **Isola Madre** (the largest of the three *isole*) has an 18th-century puppet theatre, and is surrounded by a magnificent English-style garden (0323 30 556, www.borromeoturismo.it, closed mid Oct-mid Mar). **Isola dei Pescatori** is the most enchanting of the three islands, and the most rewarding to explore on foot. It's a strip of narrow lanes, stray cats and whitewashed houses, ending in a park with benches and shady trees.

Beyond Stresa, **Baveno** is home to the tenth-century church of the saints Gervasio and Protasio; the octagonal baptistery dates from the fifth century. Some of the concerts in the town's opera festival (www.festivalgiordano.it) are held in the church early each July. The local pink marble is exported worldwide, and you can see the evidence of centuries of quarrying in the surrounding hills.

The reed thickets in the Riserva Naturale (nature reserve) at **Fondotoce** (0323 496 596, www.parchilagomaggiore.it) at the mouth of the Toce river are a nesting ground for many birds. Some of the hiking and bike trails here lead to the smaller Lago di Mergozzo. Marble used in the construction of Milan's Duomo was quarried nearby at Candoglia.

The provincial capital **Verbania** may look, on the map, like a single place, but is actually made up of several gorgeous towns a few kilometres apart. Peaceful **Pallanza** is renowned for its gardens, and has an attractive lakeside promenade overflowing with flowers. Open-air concerts are held all summer in the gardens of **Villa Giulia** (corso Sanitello 10, 0323 503 249) at the end of the promenade. It overlooks the privately owned islet San Giovanni Battista, where conductor Arturo Toscanini spent his holidays.

The garden at **Villa Taranto** (via Vittorio Veneto 111, 0323 556 667, www.villataranto.it, closed Nov-mid-Mar), between Pallanza and Intra, was laid out by captain Neil McEacharn, who bought the property in 1931. It contains over 20,000 species of plants, including giant Amazonian lilies and Japanese maples. **Intra** had a booming textile manufacturing industry in the 19th century, but the main reason to come here now is for the car ferry to Laveno on the Lombard shore.

One of Europe's largest wilderness areas, the **Parco Nazionale della Val Grande** stretches behind Verbania and is reached from the town of **Cicogna** in the hills above. Dozens of hiking and bike trails lead to meadows, gorges and peaks where chamois goats far outnumber hikers (information office: via Sanremigio 19, Pallanza, 0323 557 960, www.parcovalgrande.it, closed Sat, Sun).

On the way towards Switzerland, the Intra-Cannobio road is one of the lake's loveliest. Bordered by weathered stone walls, it winds along the shoreline, passing through quiet, genteel towns and offering views of ruined castles on tiny islands, and, across the water, the mountainsides of the sparsely inhabited eastern shore.

North of Intra is **Ghiffa**, one of the western shore's most peaceful villages. Here, the **Museo dell'Arte del Cappello** (corso Belvedere 279, 0323 59 209, www.comune.ghiffa.vb.it, closed Nov-Mar & Mon-Fri Apr-Oct) commemorates the once-thriving local felt hat industry. The **Riserva Naturale Sacro Monte della Santa Trinità** (information office at via Santissima Trinità 48, 0323 59 870, www.sacro monteghiffa.it, closed Sat, Sun), extending behind Ghiffa, has well-marked hiking trails.

Emerging from the waters off the shores of **Cannero Riviera** are the evocative ruins of the Malpaga castles, built on two rocky islets between the 13th and 15th centuries. At one time they were inhabited by pirates who plundered and pillaged the local towns.

The last stop before the Swiss border, **Cannobio**. Its palm trees and cacti are testament to the lake's balmy microclimate, and the architecture is a mix of Mediterranean and northern European. Nearby, the Orrido di Sant'Anna is a dramatic gorge plunging into dark depths and crossed by stone bridges. The 17th-century church of Sant'Anna (closed winter) sits perilously on one edge.

Where to eat

Arona's fine selection of restaurants includes **Osteria del Triass** (via Marconi 59, 0322 243 378, closed Tue & 2wks Nov-Dec, average €35) and **Café de la Sera** (lungolago Marconi 85, 0322 241 567, closed dinner & 2wks Jan-Feb, average €30), both with outdoor terraces and amazing, well-priced seafood.

Dining choices are plentiful in Stresa, and most of the restaurants in the town's centre are good. Particularly tasty pizzas and grilled lake fish come out of the wood-fired oven at **Taverna del Pappagallo** (via Principessa Margherita 46, 0323 30 411, closed Wed & mid Dec-Jan, average €30).

The pick of Pallanza's restaurants is the elegant **Milano** (corso Zanitello 2, 0323 556 816, closed dinner Mon, all Tue & Nov-Mar, average

€60), which serves classic French and Italian cuisine in its lakeside dining room. The busiest, and best, on the main square is **Bolongaro** (piazza Garibaldi 9, 0323 503 254, closed 25 Dec, average €25), a pizza and seafood specialist.

In Intra there are two aesthetically divine places on piazza Castello: for hunks of cheese and local wines hit **La Bottiglieria** (0323 516 579, closed Sun); and for hearty fare, try the jasmine-covered **Osteria del Castello** (no.9, 0323 516 579, closed Sun, average €35).

At Mergozzo, the central **Ristorante Vecchio Olmo** (piazza Cavour 2, 0323 80 335, closed Thur Oct-Apr & 2wks Feb, average €30) has a good value set menu and excellent fish and home-made pasta.

In Cannobio, **Lo Scalo** (piazza Vittorio Emanuele III 32, 0323 71 480, closed Mon, lunch Tue & 4wks Jan-Feb, average €45) serves meals made with fresh market produce plus local fish and crustaceans.

Where to stay

The **Hotel Atlantic** (corso della Repubblica 124, 0322 46 521, www.atlanticarona.com, doubles €120-€140) offers inexpensive 1950s chic by Arona's train station. Built on old money, Stresa has a collection of sumptuous belle époque hotels, including the **Grand Hotel des Iles Borromées** (corso Umberto I 67, 0323 938 938, www.borromees.it, closed 3wks mid Dec-Jan, doubles €265-€315), where Ernest Hemingway stayed. There's also the **Hotel Regina Palace** (corso Umberto I 33, 0323 936 936, closed 2wks Dec-Jan, doubles €128-€365), which was used as a location for Gina Lollobrigida's 1950 film *Miss Italia*.

For something different, **La Luna nel Porto** (Corso Italia 60, 0323 934 466, www.lalunanelporto.it, doubles €90-€150) is a cute villa with garden, divided into 12 two- to five-person apartments. Then there's the blissfully romantic **Hotel Verbano** (0323 30 408, www.hotelverbano.it, closed Nov-Feb, doubles €150-€180) on Isole Pescatori, the only hotel on the island. Half-board is available in their smart restaurant (average €50).

Pallanza's small **Albergo Villa Azalea** (salita San Remigio 4, 0323 556 692, www.albergovillaazalea.com, closed Nov-mid Mar, doubles €72-€79) is set high in the hills. On the waterfront, the **Aquadolce Hotel** (via Cietti 1, 0323 505 418, www.hotelaquadolce.it,

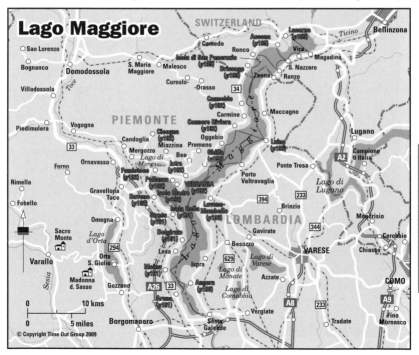

Hemingway's haunts

Ernest Hemingway was a thrill-seeker from an early age. He volunteered as an ambulance driver on Italy's Isonzo front at the age of 18, and after pulling into Milan's Garibaldi station on 7 June 1918, he was billeted close to the Austrian frontier and wounded by sniper fire a few weeks later. A semi-autobiographical narrative of these events appeared a decade later as *A Farewell to Arms*, a passionate, often funny, anti-war novel.

The story's wounded American volunteer, Lieutenant Frederic Henry, deserts from the collapsing front and convalesces at a mansion in Milan. This situation echoes the experience of the novelist, who lay up with shrapnel wounds at the Palazzo Anguissola

Antona Traversi at via Alessandro Manzoni 10, then a Red Cross Hospital, a stone's throw from Teatro la Scala. While recuperating – and smuggling bottles of Martini into the ward – Hemingway fell in love with an American nurse, Agnes von Kurowsky. Although she spurned him, her character was fictionalised as English nurse Catherine Barkley, who joined Frederic on the run to Stresa on Lago Maggiore.

Hemingway checked into the near-deserted Grand Hotel des Iles Borromeés (*see p193*) for a week in September 1918. It was the start of an enduring association with the hotel: he stayed there on and off until the 1950s, invariably in his favourite suite, room

106, overlooking the Isola Bella. In the book, the Italian military police come close to catching Lt Henry at the hotel, but the barman tips the couple off about their impending arrest. The penultimate chapter has them rowing by night across Lago Maggiore to the safe haven of the Swiss shore.

Although there are few actual Hemingway sights in Stresa, even non-guests can raise a glass of Martini in the Grand Hotel's piano bar. It's a much more rarefied atmosphere than that of Harry's Bar in Venice, another haunt of Hemingway pilgrims – and little wonder, as in the past 150 years the hotel has served guests as illustrious as Princess Margaret, David Niven and the Vanderbilts, people a lot more refined than Hemingway himself.

A Farewell to Arms was written in Paris in the late 1920s; Hemingway was the deserter this time, escaping the US during the prohibition period. Modern reprints of the 1929 novel that set old Ernest on the road to stardom are available from the Feltrinelli and Mondadori bookshops (*see p125*) in downtown Milan.

closed 4wks mid Jan-mid Feb, doubles €75-€110) is stocked with fine period furniture and has large rooms, some with balconies overlooking the lake. The **Grand Hotel Majestic** (via Vittorio Veneto 32, 0323 509 711, www.grandhotelmajestic.it, closed Oct, doubles €190-€360) is a delightful belle époque hotel with breathtaking views of the Isole Boromee. It also has a spa, gardens and an elegant 1920s vibe.

In the village of Bee in the hills behind Verbania, the **Chi Ghinn** (via Maggiore 21, 0323 56 326, www.chighinn.com, doubles from €80) has six homely rooms and a great restaurant (closed Tue, Wed Oct-Mar & early Jan-Feb, average €35) where local lake-caught delicacies such as crayfish are served.

Two of Cannobio's hotels stand out from the crowd. The family-run **Hotel Pironi** (via Marconi 35, 0323 70 624, www.pironihotel.it, closed mid Nov-mid Mar, doubles €130-€165) offers modern comforts in a former 15th-century monastery with frescoed ceilings. The **Hotel Cannobio** (piazza Vittorio Emanuele III, 0323 739 639, www.hotelcannobio.com, closed early Nov-Easter, doubles €130-€170) is equally beautiful, yet more refined; the rooms with tiny balconies on the lake are best.

A couple of kilometres south, the **Hotel del Lago** (via Nazionale 2, Carmine, 0323 70 595, www.enotecalago.com, closed Nov-Mar, doubles €100-€130) has ten rooms (most with a view over the lake), a private beach and a restaurant serving classic cuisine (average €50).

Tourist information

APT Arona
Piazza Duca d'Aosta (0322 243 601/www.comune. arona.no.it). **Open** 9.30am-12.30pm, 3-6pm Tue-Sat; 9.30am-12.30pm Sun.
As this guide went to press, the tourist office was closed for renovation, due to reopen in 2009. Until then, a temporary tourist office operates in the train station and at via San Carlo 2.

IAT Stresa
Piazza Marconi 16 (0323 30 150/www.comune. stresa.vb.it). **Open** *Apr-Oct* 10am-12.30pm, 3-6.30pm daily. *Nov-Mar* 10am-12.30pm, 3-6pm Mon-Sat.

IAT Verbania
Corso Zanitello 6-8 (0323 503 249/www.verbania-turismo.it). **Open** *Apr-Sept* 9am-1pm, 3-5.30pm daily. *Oct-Mar* 9am-1pm Mon-Fri, 3-5.30pm Mon, Tue, Thur.

Pro Loco IAT Cannobio
Viale Vittorio Veneto 4 (0323 71 212/www.pro cannobio.it). **Open** *Apr-Oct* 9am-noon, 4-7pm daily. *Nov-Mar* 9am-noon, 4-7pm Mon-Wed, Fri, Sat; 9am-noon Sun.

The Swiss shore

A faintly perceptible change occurs as you're waved across the Swiss border. The towns seem more orderly and the hills more alpine. As the country's warmest spot, Switzerland's lake zone is packed with activities, from scenic railways to speedboat hire and a series of internationally renowned festivals.

Brissago's reputation rests on its production of fine cigars. During the summer months, boats operated by Navigazione Lago Maggiore (*see p197*) serve the **Isole di Brissago**. The largest of these two islands, **Isola di San Pancrazio**, has a botanical garden (0041 91 791 4361, closed Nov-late Mar), and the other, **Isola di Sant'Apollinare**, is owned by a mystery businessman.

North-east of Brissago is the ancient fishing village of **Ascona**, which hosts an important jazz festival (end June-early July, www.jazz ascona.ch) and, from late August to October, classical music (www.settimane-musicali.ch).

Locarno, at the lake's northern tip, hosts a prestigious film fair (www.pardo.ch) every August. Most visitors are content to wander along the town's well-manicured lakeside promenade or putter about in a speedboat (SF48 per hour). For a more exhilarating ride there's a **cable car** (0041 91 735 3030/www.cardada.ch, closed Dec-Feb) running 1,000 metres up to a series of viewing platforms high in the Alps. The small **Pinacoteca** art gallery (0041 91 756 318, closed Mon) is inside the 17th-century Casa Rusca. To reach the art-filled **Madonna del Sasso** church, take the funicular or walk up the steep hill flanked by the Stations of the Cross.

Where to stay & eat

Although most of the area's action is in Locarno, family-run **Hotel Eden** (via Vamara 26, 0041 91 793 1255, www.hotel-eden-brissago.ch, closed Nov-mid Mar, doubles SF162-SF210) in Brissago is a pleasant option.

In Ascona, the **Hotel Luna** (via Buonamano 28, 0041 91 791 0161, www.hotel-luna.ch, closed Nov-Feb, doubles SF150-SF190) is family-run, ultra-friendly and quiet.

Breakfast is served on the outdoor sun terrace at Locarno's **Hotel du Lac** (via Ramogna 3, 0041 91 751 2921, www.du-lac-locarno.ch, closed Oct-Dec, doubles SF144-SF240), a small lakefront address with balconies galore. The 11 guestrooms of the **Millennium Hotel** (via Dogana Nuova 2, 0041 91 759 6767, www.millennium-hotel.ch, closed Jan-Mar, doubles SF180-SF280) come with Wi-Fi and great views. **Ristorante DiVino** (viale Verbano 13, 0041 91 759 1122,

Trips Out of Town

www.ristorantedivino.ch, average SF60) on
Locarno's waterfront promenade has heartier,
meatier cuisine than that served over the
border, plus a great selection of local cured
meats, cheeses and red wines. Nearby
Centenario (lungolago Motta 17, 0041 91
743 8822, closed Mon, Sun & Feb, average
SF90) is one of the most elegant spots in town.

Tourist information

Ente Turistico Lago Maggiore

*Via B Luini 3, Locarno (0041 91 791 0091/www.
maggiore.ch).* **Open** *Apr-Oct* 9am-6pm Mon-Fri;
10am-6pm Sat; 10am-5pm Sun. *Nov-Mar* 9am-noon,
1.30-5pm Mon-Sat.
The tourist office includes a bureau de change.

The Lombardy shore

For all its great rail and boat links, and a string
of pretty villages, few tourists visit Maggiore's
eastern shore. Those who do are in for a treat,
as there's a lot to explore, bags of afternoon
sunshine – and a complete lack of trinket shops.

   Angera's Rocca Borromeo (via alla Rocca,
0331 931 300, closed late Oct-mid Mar), a
fortress built in the 11th century and expanded
and fortified up until the 17th, dominates the
lake's southern stretches from its clifftop seat.
In Visconti hands from the 13th century, it
became Borromeo property in 1449. One wing
contains a rare cycle of 14th-century frescoes
by local Lombard artists; another houses a
collection of 17th-century dolls and children's
toys. The Borromeo wing features frescoes
taken from the family's palazzo in Milan.

   Laveno is a pleasant transport hub with two
train stations and ferries to Intra (*see p192*). Its
clutch of churches and quiet streets warrant a
mooch around. At weekends a cable car (0332
668 018) runs up Sasso del Ferro, a panoramic
plateau and hang-gliding launch point above
town. It's just a 12-kilometre (seven-mile) drive
from here to tiny Lago di Varese, a birder's
paradise beside the lake town of Azzate.

   It's possible to walk the six kilometres
(four miles) from Laveno to **Eremo di Santa
Caterina del Sasso Ballaro** (0332 647 172,
closed Mon-Fri Nov-Feb). This exquisite 12th-
century church is perched precipitously on the
rock face 18 metres (60 feet) above the water
near Leggiuno. Home to Dominican monks and
lavishly adorned with frescoes dating from the
14th century, the sanctuary has heartstopping
views across the lake. It can also be reached by
boat or 250-odd steep steps from the car park.

   Past the cute harbour of Caldè is **Luino**,
with its tranquil old town sprawling up the
hill; pedalos and speedboats (€35 per hour)

are available to hire. At the top is the church of
San Pietro, which has frescoes attributed to
Bernardino Luini and a Romanesque bell tower.

   The village of **Maccagno** is the last stop
before the Swiss-Lombard border. It has
the yellow **Santuario della Madonnina**
protruding into the lake to the south, and a
long beach to the north.

Where to stay & eat

In Angera, the cute **Hotel dei Tigli** (via
Paletta 20, 0331 930 836, www.hoteldeitigli.com,
closed 3wks Dec-Jan, doubles €120-€130) has
period furniture, a happy hour and Wi-Fi.

   At Laveno, just south of Mombello, the
Hotel Porticciolo (via Fortino 40, 0332
667 257, www.ilporticciolo.com, closed 2wks
Jan-Feb, 1wk Nov, doubles €140-€180) is a
charming spot with a fine restaurant (average
€50, closed Tue) serving up belly-busting set
menus. In town **Calianna** (via Tinelli 19, 0332
667 315, closed Jan, doubles €70-€80) has five
simple bedrooms. Downstairs, its restaurant
(closed Tue) is meaty, rustic and authentic. The
Hotel Moderno (via Garibaldi 15, 0332 668
373, closed Jan & Feb, www.meublemoderno.it,
doubles €70-€80), is an honest, cheap place.

   Luino's **Camin Hotel Luino** (viale Dante
35, 0332 530 118, www.caminhotelluino.com,
closed 5wks Dec-Jan, doubles €150-€180) is a
19th-century villa with a garden, decorated
with art deco furniture. A better food option
may be **Il Veliero** (via Amendola 12, 0332

closed Mon & 2wks Sept, average €50) however, an unassuming trattoria nearby. The first-floor dining terrace of the **AVAV Yacht Club** (viale Dante Alighieri 6, 0332 531 635, closed Mon, average €35) – not as posh as it sounds – is good for views and lake fish.

Tourist information

IAT Laveno-Mombello

Piazza d'Italia 7 (0332 668 785/www.laveno-online. it). **Open** 9.30am-1pm, 2.30-5pm Tue, Wed, Fri-Sun; 9.30am-1pm, 2.30-4pm Thur.

IAT Luino

Via Piero Chiara 1 (0332 530 019/www.comune. luino.va.it). **Open** *Easter-Sept* 9am-noon, 2-6pm daily. *Oct-Easter* 9am-noon, 2.30-6.30pm Mon-Sat.

Getting there

By boat

Navigazione Lago Maggiore (Italian side 0322 233 200, Swiss side 0041 917 516 140, www.navigazione laghi.it) operates boats and hydrofoils to most of the towns around the lake, including the Swiss side. Private water taxis can be hired at most ports.

By bus

Autoservizi Nerini (0323 552 172, www.safduemila. com) provides a twice-daily commuter bus service to the Piedmont shore from Porta Garibaldi. On the western shore, Trasporti Nerini (0323 552 172) runs a service between Arona and Verbania; VCO Trasporti (0323 518 711, www.vcoinbus.it) operates between Verbania to Brissago and Switzerland.

Autolinee Nicora e Baratelli (0332 668 056, www.sila.it) runs regular services between Luino and Laveno on the eastern shore.

On the Swiss side, FART Viaggi (0041 917 560 400, www.centovalli.ch) runs a regular service between Locarno and Brissago.

By car

The A8 motorway gets you from Milan to Sesto Calende. For towns on the lake's western (Piedmont) shores, take the A26 towards Gravellona Toce. The S33 skirts the lake to Fondotoce, where it becomes the S34 to Cannobio.

For the eastern shore, take the S629 to Laveno, then the S394, which skirts the lake, to Luino and beyond.

For Locarno, on the lake's Swiss side, take the A9 motorway from Milan to Como, switch to the A2 motorway to Bellinzona, and follow the signs. The road that runs along the lake is via Cantonale 13.

By train

For the western (Piedmont) shore, take the Domodossola service from Milan's Garibaldi station. This stops at Sesto Calende, Arona (journey time 1hr), Meina, Lesa, Belgirate, Stresa (1hr 30mins), Baveno, Verbania/Pallanza (1hr 40mins), Mergozzo and Candoglia. Express trains from the Stazione Centrale serve Arona (45mins) and Stresa (1hr).

For Laveno, take the Ferrovie Nord service from Cadorna station (journey time 1hr 30mins). Regular trains go to Luino, 15mins to the north.

For the Swiss shore, take the train to Domodossola from Milan's Stazione Centrale (1hr). Rail enthusiasts and lovers of rugged alpine landscapes will love the Centovalli (0041 091 756 0400, www.centovalli.ch), the 'hundred valleys' railway. This 1hr 40min ride over some 86 bridges is surely one of the finest mountain railway journeys anywhere in Europe.

Lago di Como

A day trip to stardom or a week off the beaten track.

Although Clooneymania has died down since gorgeous George bought a lakeside villa here in 2002, Lago di Como is still as A-list as St Tropez. Indeed, with the dramatic scenery and clement climate, it has been considered cool since Roman times. The deepest of the lakes, at over 400 metres (1,300 feet), it's also the most accessible. Just 30 minutes from downtown Milan, you can saunter through the streets of **Bellagio** and **Varenna** and be back in time for dinner; spend a little longer touring the sweeping shorelines, and you may not head back to the big city at all.

The original celebrity resident was Como-born Pliny the Younger (AD 62-112), who wrote ecstatically of the 'several villas' he possessed on the lake, explaining of one that 'you can quite simply cast your line out of the window without getting out of bed'. In AD 569, the Lombards decided they wanted a piece of the action and promptly took residence within the walls of **Como** town itself. In the 19th century, Stendhal, Rossini and Shelley all lodged at Villa Pliniana, and Verdi wrote much of *La Traviata* at Villa Margherita Ricordi. According to locals, President Kennedy romanced Marilyn Monroe in the area, and more recent visitors have included Madonna, a regular guest at Donatella Versace's Villa Le Fontanelle.

Lake Como, or Lario as it has been known since Roman times, extends in an inverted Y shape from the Alps in the north to surround the *triangolo lariano*, a mountainous triangular region, in the south. **Cólico** is at the northerly extreme, and the cities of Como and **Lecco**, some 50 kilometres (30 miles) away, are located at the other two ends. The three 'arms' come together to form the promontory of Bellagio.

Despite the fact that the lake has a 178-kilometre (106-mile) perimeter, it is never more than four and a half kilometres (three miles) wide, which creates a pleasing sense of intimacy. Moreover, each of the lake's 'arms' is different. The Como section is relatively narrow; the mountains behind are somewhat uniform, with plenty of little towns and grand villas along the shoreline. The Lecco branch is more rugged, the jagged edges of the Grigne range providing a strong contrast. The northern part features deep valleys and tall mountains, and is the most dramatic. The scenery is at its most spectacular in the central section of the

lake, around the triangle formed by Bellagio, **Menaggio** and Varenna.

The best time to come? It's a common belief in Italy that lakes in general, not just Como, are *tristi* (sad) from October to March. Make up your own mind, but it's worth noting that some hotels and restaurants may be closed during the winter months.

Como

Busy, industrialised and traffic-ridden: first impressions as you enter Como, the unofficial capital of the lake, can be disappointing. If you're arriving from Milan and this is your first experience of Italy's lakes, you might even suspect the whole thing's an elaborate wind-up. But once you reach the old town and sip your first coffee by the lake, the pieces will start to fall into place.

Como's architectural showstopper is its **Duomo** (piazza del Duomo, 031 265 244), a brilliant fusion of Romanesque, Gothic, Renaissance and baroque. Begun in 1396, it is unique as well as spectacularly beautiful. Its late-Gothic façade (1455-86) is even more striking for the fact that pride of place is given to two renowned pagans – the Plinies, Elder and Younger. Abutting the apse end of the Duomo, in piazza Verdi, stands the 19th-century **Teatro Sociale** (via Bellini 3, 031 270 170, www.teatrosocialecomo.it, closed Sun & Aug), its neo-classical façade adorned with six mighty Corinthian pillars. The theatre had its moment of glory at the end of World War II, when its opera season outshone Milan's – if only because La Scala had been badly damaged by bombs.

See the remaining stretches of Como's 12th-century walls along viale Battisti, running to the imposing **Porta Torre** gate (1192). A little off the beaten track, but worth the effort, is the **Museo Didattico della Seta** (via Castelnuovo 1, 031 303 180, www.museo setacomo.com, closed Mon, Sat, Sun), which brings the city's all-important silk industry to life.

On the lakeside by the ferry jetty, **piazza Cavour** is one of Como's most popular meeting points. Traffic and concrete embellishments mean it's not much to look at, but on a warm evening the place will be buzzing with locals on their *passaggiate*.

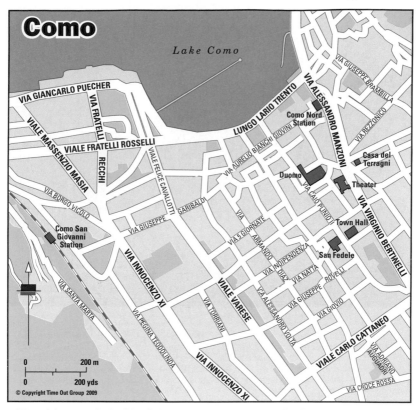

West of the square in the **Giardini Pubblici**, the neo-classical **Mausoleo Voltiano** (viale Marconi, 031 574 705, closed Mon) was erected in 1927 to mark the centenary of the death of Alessandro Volta, the Como-born physicist who invented the battery and gave his name to the volt – not to mention a score of piazzas around the lake. The museum contains some of his original instruments.

No trip to Como is complete without a visit to **Brunate**, the village 720 metres (2,400 feet) above Como town. The funicular railway (next to the Como Nord Lago railway station, www.funicolarecomo.it), will whizz you up there in just under seven minutes, saving you a 90-minute uphill slog. The five-kilometre pretty walk down is far more inviting.

Where to eat & drink

By general consensus, **Le Colonne** (piazza Mazzini 12, 031 266 166, average €25, closed Tue Oct-Mar), on a quiet piazza just back from the lake, serves the best pizza in Como – and

their creamy tagliatelle with lake fish (*al profumo del lago*) is a thing of wonder.

For the best *bresaola* in town, lunch with local artisans and owners Rosanna and Giuseppe at the rustic **Osteria Del Gallo** (via Vitani 16, 031 272591). The top dinner option is the **Ristorante Sociale** (via Rodare 6, 031 264 042, closed Tue, average €30), re-located in 2008 from its original address near the Teatro Sociale to an attractive former estate agent's near the lake. Its exquisite dishes include stunning risottos, a popular steak tartare and the spicy house creation, *penne Satanik*.

Deli, *enoteca* and lunchtime diner **Castiglioni** (via Cesare Cantu 9, 031 263 388, closed Sun) has a cute rear courtyard. For a touch of flair, try **La Colombetta** (via Diaz 40, 031 262 703, www.colombetta.it, average €90), housed in a former convent.

Friendly owner Federico at the **L'Angolo Divino** *enoteca* (via Diaz 69, 031 242 704) stocks his racks with decent, well-priced wine from all the major producing regions of Italy. He also offers a full lunch and dinner menu. For

Trips Out of Town

Messing about in boats **Lago di Como** style.

snacks to eat as you go, you could do a lot worse than nearby **Peach Pit** (via Diaz 41): take your pick of more than a dozen focaccia sandwiches at €2 a throw.

Hit the town on a Tuesday or Thursday morning, and you can pick up antiques, clothes and seasonal produce from the stalls and pavements along the old city walls.

Where to stay

Set in the main cluster of lakefront hotels, the four-star **Albergo Terminus** (lungo Lario Trieste 14, 03 329 111, www.hotel terminus-como.it, doubles €140-€270) has a grand Liberty design, and attracts a relatively mature crowd. Its new 16-room annex and two stunning apartments have a swish boutique feel and lake views throughout.

A relatively new hotel in a 17th-century building, the three-star, family-run **Albergo del Duca** (piazza Mazzini 12, 031 264 859, www.albergodelduca.it, doubles €100-€120) has justifiably become one of the old town's most popular addresses. Four of its nine rooms face on to a charming piazza, home to the excellent **Le Colonne** restaurant (*see p199*) run by the same couple.

Hotel Quarcino (salita Quarcino 4, 031 303 934, www.hotelquarcino.it, doubles €82) is a homely favourite in appealing proximity to

the lake – although whether the 7.30am wake-up call from the church bells next door is a curse or a blessing divides opinion. Outside the old town **Le Due Corti** (piazza Vittoria 12, 031 328 111, doubles €160) has been welcoming guests for over 150 years, and its bar is original. Exhibitionists can show off their water gymnastics in the plunge pool situated just metres from the breakfast terrace.

Next to the base of the Brunate Funicular, **Hotel Marco's** (via Coloniola 43, 031 303 628, www.hotelmarcos.it, doubles €150) is a clean, no-frills three-star address. Its attractive breakfast patio looks out over the water.

Tourist information

IAT Como

Piazza Cavour 17 (031 330 0128/www.lakecomo. com). **Open** *June-mid Sept* 9am-1pm, 2.30-6pm Mon-Sat; 9am-12.30pm Sun. *Mid Sept-May* 9am-1pm, 2.30-6pm Mon-Sat.

The western shore

Pretty and compact, **Cernobbio** is the first major stop on the commuter boat service. This town of magnificent villas and private boat jetties is dominated by **Villa d'Este**, often referred to as one of the world's great hotels. The villa became the focus of international attention in 2006, when Brad Pitt and Angelina Jolie were rumoured to be planning their wedding here. On the given day, the world's press, and the local mayor, turned up; the couple did not. Back in Cernobbio's real world, the promenade is attractive and has a lively Wednesday morning market.

Once you've taken a look around Cernobbio it's time to hop on the boat and head north for **Moltrasio**. In spring, the gorge which splits this small town in to two fills with a rapidly flowing torrent as the snow on the hills above melts. Moltrasio is home to the 18th-century **Villa Passalacqua** (www.thevillapassa lacqua.com), which has a beautiful Tuscan garden. Vincenzo Bellini wrote his opera *La Sonnambula* here between 1829 and 1833. Although it's closed to the public, it can be rented by the week, although you'll have to pay steeply for the musical history. Moltrasio boasts two other notable villas. **Villa Le Rose** was Winston Churchill's locale of choice for post-World War II R&R. Nearby **Villa Le Fontanelle** was acquired by the late Gianni Versace in 1977, and stars like Madonna, Princess Diana and Elton John were all guests at his frequent weekend glamour fests. The villa was sold for somewhere in the region of €32 million to Russian multi-millionaire Arkady Novikov in March 2008.

For many years the village of **Laglio**, just north of Moltrasio, was known primarily for the remains of a prehistoric bear found in the Grotta del Buco dell'Orso. That was BG (Before George). Then Mr Clooney bought **Villa Oleandra**, and the village became world-famous. To see George's house, cruise past on the boat. To see George himself, make for the nearest cinema.

Back in Moltrasio, take the fast ferry for Cólico and get off at the first stop, the little resort of **Argegno**. From here, a daily cable car (every 30 minutes) makes the journey up to **Pigra**, a lofty hamlet with superb views across the lake to **Isola Comacina** and the Bellagio promontory.

One man and his water taxi spend the day making the five-minute trip to and from the tiny port of **Sala Comacina** for Isola Comacina, the only island on the lake (031 821 955, mobile 335 707 4122, www.boatservices.it, no service Nov-Feb). There's a 50/50 chance you'll have to stand on the end of the pier to hail the boat from the other side, but tiny Isola Comacina, which houses a handful of ancient ruined churches, is well worth the trip. The island is just 600 metres (2,000 feet) long, 200 metres (650 feet) wide and two kilometres in circumference, and a walk around it is a short but surprisingly rugged pleasure.

LA TREMEZZINA

Awash with azaleas and dotted with luxurious villas, **La Tremezzina** is a gorgeous stretch of coast from **Lenno** to Menaggio. There are a few faded reminders of an age when British dowagers came to winter (and summer) here: an Anglican church (in Cadenabbia), a Victorian tearoom, and even a crazy golf course.

Lenno may have been the site of Commedia, one of Pliny the Younger's villas. Lenno's jetty is the departure point for boats to the picture-perfect **Villa del Balbianello** (*see p203* **Heavenly gardens**). The mansion was used in the Star Wars prequel *Attack of the Clones*, and was the villa where Daniel Craig's James Bond recuperated in *Casino Royale*.

In **Tremezzo**, the neo-classical **Villa Carlotta** (*see p203* **Heavenly gardens**) boasts sculptures by Antonio Canova and a massive, spectacular garden.

At **Cadenabbia**, the lake is at its widest. A foot and car ferry plies between here and Bellagio, and another car ferry goes to Varenna. Giuseppe Verdi composed much of *La Traviata* in **Villa Margherita Ricordi** (closed to the public, although apartments inside it can be privately rented) in the nearby hamlet of **Maiolica**.

Pretty pink-and-ochre Menaggio lacks the in-your-face charm of its opposite numbers Bellagio and Varenna, but is certainly worth a visit. Once a bustling commercial town and now an equally bustling resort, it boasts a ruined castle and lovely views across to the eastern shore. Menaggio is 12 kilometres (eight miles) from Lake Lugano, and keen walkers (with the emphasis on keen) might want to consider the hike up to **Monte Bregagno**, from which, on a very clear day, it's possible to see both lakes.

THE NORTHERN REACHES

Continuing north towards the peaks overlooking the Valchiavenna valley, you reach the Tre Pievi ('three parishes') of **Dongo**, **Gravedona** and **Sòrico**. Remembered as the place where Mussolini and his lover Clara Petacci were captured on 27 April 1945 as they headed for the Swiss border, Dongo was also the scene of violence in 1252, when St Peter Martyr was finished off with a hatchet by Cathar heretics.

A manufacturing town and popular water-sports centre, Gravedona was the most important of the Tre Pievi, and a key ally of medieval Milan – which is why it was razed by Como in the 12th century. The Romanesque church of **Santa Maria del Tiglio** (via Roma) is simple, severe and stunning. **Palazzo Gallio**, also known as Palazzo del Pero, was the second of the three houses commissioned by Tolomeo Gallio from Pellegrino Tibaldi (another was Villa d'Este; *see below*).

The fishing village of **Domaso** still produces a white wine mentioned by Pliny the Elder. It's also Lake Como's recognised windsurfing centre. In fortified Sòrico, tolls were extracted from travellers arriving on the lake's shores from Valchiavenna and Valtellina.

Where to eat

In Cernobbio, opt for the packed pizzeria at **Albergo Centrale** (*see below*, **Where to stay**). Above the town, in the hamlet of Piazza Santo Stefano, **Trattoria del Glicine** (via Paolo Carcano 1, 031 511 332, closed 2wks Jan, average €45) serves typical Mediterranean cuisine under a wisteria-covered pergola with a splendid view of the lake.

Further along the road between Cernobbio and Menaggio in Sala Comanesca, next to the Isola Comancina taxi pier, you'll come across the **Tirlindana** (0344 56 637, closed Wed Mar-Oct & Mon-Fri Nov-Feb, average €45), a pearl of a restaurant on the tiny cobbled piazza Matteotti; it's renowned for its delicious ravioli stuffed with lemon-flavoured cheese.

On the Isola Comacina, the owner of the **Locanda dell'Isola Comacina** (0344 55 083, www.comacina.it, closed Tue Mar-June, Sept & Oct, all Nov-Feb) has earned renown and a good income by limiting lunch and dinner to one option – the original 1947 five-course menu (€60). Every meal ends with said owner telling the story of the island and leading a toast of ceremonial local liqueur flambé, in order to combat an alleged curse.

For more rustic fare (car required), head for **Osteria del Giuanin** (via Sanctuario 8, 0344 55 241, average €35) in nearby Ossucio, which serves classic local cuisine, and during winter enthusiastically serves up steaming bowls of donkey stew.

In Tremezzo, book a day or two ahead during high season if you want to snag a lakeside table at the wonderful **La Darsena** (*see below* **Where to stay**). The sumptuous menu (average €50) includes lake fish *cannelloni* and the choice of over 20 different types of grappa.

Hotel restaurants line Menaggio's shore, whereas *trattorie* tend to hide away inland. **Hotel Bellavista** (via IV Novembre 21, 0344 32 166, www.hotel-bellavista.org, average €40) has a picture-perfect lakeside setting and a superb perch with almonds. The drawback is the constant panpipe music. The **Osteria Il Pozzo** (piazza Garibaldi, 0344 32 333, closed Wed, average €40) in a corner of the main piazza has a pretty courtyard, and a menu that includes roast kid and rabbit with *polenta*.

Locals go to **Pizzeria Lugano** (via Como 26, 0344 31 664, average €30) for the best pizzas, and newcomer **Ristorante Red Bay** (via Vittorio Emanuele 7, 0344 32 259, average €35), at the end of the Lungolago next to the mini golf, has the finest pizza/lake view combo.

Finally, for a romantic *aperitivo*, wander along the lakefront to **La Terrazza del Gabbiana** (Lungolago 25), where a handful of tables have snagged what is perhaps the best location in town – peaceful and right on the water's edge.

Where to stay

For unbeatable luxury and a chance to show off your latest designer threads, head to the exclusive **Villa d'Este** (viale Regina 40, Cernobbio, 031 34 81, www.villadeste.it, closed mid Nov-Feb, doubles from €750). If you're on a budget, you can still sip a *prosecco* in the bar and visit the hotel's heavenly gardens. A room at the family-run **Albergo Centrale** (via Regina 39, 031 511 411, www.albergo-centrale.com, doubles €115) just down the road is but a fraction of the price. The four-star **Regina Olga** opposite (via Regina 18, 031 510 171, www.hotelreginaolga.it, closed mid Nov-mid Feb, doubles €180-€280) caters for a business crowd. It's hardly swanky, but it does have 25 rooms with lake views and a fair-sized swimming pool.

In Moltrasio, the **Albergo Posta Ristorante** (piazza San Rocco 5, 031 290 444, www.hotel-posta.it, closed Jan & Feb, doubles €105-€155) is a popular and reliable bet, and Lenno's **San Giorgio** (via Regina 81, 0344 40 415, www.sangiorgiolenno.com, closed Oct-Mar, doubles €125-€145) is modest but pleasant, in a modern building with a garden.

Halfway between Como and Menaggio, the boutique hotel **Villa Belvedere** at Argegno (031 821 116, www.villabelvedere-argegno.it, doubles from €135) serves up tasty *pizzoccheri* on an attractive waterside terrace.

Tremezzo's **Hotel La Darsena** (via Regina 3, 0344 43 166, www.hotelladarsena.it, closed Jan & 1wk Feb, doubles €100-€180) is a good bargain, with its classical rooms with modern touches; and the splendid art nouveau **Grand Hotel Tremezzo Palace** (via Regina 8, 0344 42 491, www.grandhoteltremezzo.com, closed end Nov-end Feb, doubles €229-€880) is the town's luxury option, with spectacular views over the lake.

Menaggio's three-star **Hotel Du Lac** (via Mazzini 27, 0344 35 281, www.hoteldulac menaggio.it, doubles €140) is a little gem; for grand living, plump for the **Hotel Grand Victoria** (lungolago Castelli 7, 0344 32 003, www.grandhotelvictoria.it, closed Nov-Feb, doubles €130-€260). If you find yourself scraping around for a room, **Hotel Garni Corona** (largo Cavour 3, 0344 32 006, closed mid-Nov-Mar, €70-€95) is well located, if a touch tired, and has 21 basic rooms, ten with lake view.

Tourist information

IAT Cernobbio
Via Regina 23 (031 343 235). **Open** *May-Sept* 9am-1pm, 2.30-6pm Mon-Sat; 9am-12.30pm Sun.

IAT Menaggio
Piazza Garibaldi 3 (0344 32 924/www.menaggio. com). **Open** *Apr-Sept* 9am-12.30pm, 2.30-6pm Mon-Sat; 10am-4pm Sun. *Oct-Mar* 9am-12.30pm, 2.30-6pm Mon-Sat.

IAT Tremezzo
Via Regina 3 (0344 40 493/www.tremezzo.it). **Open** 9am-noon, 3.30-6.30pm Mon, Wed-Sun.

The eastern shore

Relatively few tourists sample the unhurried charms of Lake Como's mountainous eastern edge, which is all the more reason to meandering down the coast by road, rail or boat. There's village after village – especially the alluring Varenna – to mooch around.

From **Cólico**, a pretty, if average, port town at the far north-eastern end of the lake, it's a short hop down to **Piona**, where you can take a boat excursion to **Abbazia di Piona** (0341 940 331). This beautiful abbey is on a small promontory separating Lake Como proper from the strikingly green Laghetto di Piona. The

Heavenly gardens

The balmy microclimate of Lake Como has afforded splendid opportunities to gardeners and garden lovers over the centuries. One of the best is the garden of **Villa del Balbianello** (via Comoedia 8, 0344 56 110, www.fondo ambiente.it, closed mid Nov-mid Mar, Mon & Wed), located just south of Lenno. Built on a headland, a space that offered no scope for a formal Italian garden (or what the Italians call *un giardino all'inglese*), the gardens are what one might call site-specific: they interact with the lake and shoreline rather than follow any set design or concept. The fact that they are approached by water adds to the impact: visitors can feel what it was like to arrive as a guest of the original owners – among them Cardinal Durini, the families of Porro Lambertenghi and Arconati Visconti, and the explorer Count Guido Monzino. It was the latter who bequeathed Balbianello to the FAI (Fondo Ambiente Italiano), Italy's equivalent of Britain's National Trust, which used it as a backdrop in recent Star Wars and James Bond movies.

Renowned for its plane trees clipped into candle shapes, the garden follows a steep slope, where statues alternate with wisteria, and azaleas and rhododendrons provide exhilarating bursts of colour throughout the spring and early summer. Built in the 16th century and extended in the 18th, the villa itself can be visited by appointment only.

Rhododendrons are also very much in evidence among the 500-plus plant varieties in the 80,000 square metres (861,000

square feet) of garden at **Villa Carlotta** (via Regina 2, 0344 40 405, www.villacarlotta.it, closed Nov-mid-Mar), in Tremezzo. Named after princess Charlotte, who received it in 1843 as a wedding present from her mother, Princess Marianna of Nassau, the villa was built in neo-classical style in the early 1700s for the marquis Giorgio Clerici. Leading to the villa are five terraces, with stairs to either side; the geometric lines are softened by vines, climbing roses and trailing geraniums. The house contains many sculptures, including Antonio Canova's *Cupid and Psyche*.

Villa Melzi and Villa Serbelloni are two extra attractions for visitors to Bellagio. Although neither of the houses is open to the public, the gardens are exquisite and well worth seeing. **Villa Melzi** (lungolario Marconi, 031 950 204, www.giardinidivillamelzi.it, closed Nov-Mar) boasts a pretty Japanese garden and some splendid water lilies.

Open for guided tours twice a day, the 17th-century **Villa Serbelloni** (piazza della Chiesa, 031 951 555, www.bellagiolakecomo.com, closed Mon & Nov-Mar) stands high on the point above Bellagio's town centre – possibly on the site of Pliny the Younger's villa Tragedia (he had another villa called Commedia at Lenno; *see p201*). The trees in the gardens of Villa Serbelloni, added in the 19th century, are worth noting. Although they seem to blend effortlessly into the landscape, they were, in fact, among the first examples of magnolias, oleanders, palms and cedars ever planted in Italy.

Trips Out of Town

complex has a 13th-century cloister with Romanesque and Gothic columns, fragments of earlier frescoes lining its walls, and the abbey church of San Nicolao.

The Pioverna river thunders down the **Orrido di Bellano**, near the appealing village of **Bellano** itself. This gorge provides the driving force for the hydroelectricity that has long powered the area's textile industry. You can appreciate the force for yourself by braving the bridge suspended above the torrent (0341 821 124, www.comune. bellano.lc.it, closed Mon-Fri Nov-Feb).

The simple charms of **Varenna** are enough to relax even the most hectic and uptight of holidaymakers. The lakeside path from the boat terminal to the lakeside mansion **Villa Monastero** (0341 295 450, www.villamonastero.org, closed Dec-Mar) is the stuff that holiday brochures are made of. Adjacent is another lakeside spot steeped in history, the **Villa Cipressi** (*see below* **Where to stay & eat**), now a hotel; its spectacular gardens are a must.

A path leads from Varenna to the **Fiumelatte** ('river of milk'). This is Italy's shortest, most mysterious, and most predictable river. Its frothy, milk-white water rushes for all of 250 metres (833 feet) down the rockface and crashes into the lake from the end of March to the end of October each year – and then stops. Leonardo da Vinci climbed down to find out what happened to it the rest of the year, but neither he nor anyone else has ever discovered the secret. A 20-minute walk leads to the ruined **Castello di Vezio** (0341 814 911, www. castellodivezio.it, closed Dec-Mar), which boasts a splendid view of the lake. Then you can take the relatively short – but rather steep – set of steps (it takes about 20 minutes) back down to the centre of the town, and have a well-deserved drink in Varenna's pretty piazza.

Regular passenger ferries connect Varenna with Menaggio (*see p206*); a car ferry links it to Cadenabbia (*see p206*) and Bellagio (*see p206*).

Where to stay & eat

In Varenna, the **Hotel Villa Cipressi** (via IV Novembre 22, 0341 830 113, www.hotelvilla cipressi.it, closed Nov-Feb, doubles €125-€170) combines lakeside charm with 800 years of aristocratic history. Just as romantic is the 16-room **Hotel du Lac** (via del Prestino 4, 0341 830 238, www.albergodulac.com, closed mid Nov-mid Feb, doubles €145-€185), a restored 19th-century palazzo.

The **Royal Victoria** (piazza San Giorgio 5, 0341 815 111, www.royalvictoria.com, doubles €120-€210) has period furniture in its public

rooms and a lakeside swimming pool. Its main restaurant (closed Mon except in summer) serves upmarket Italian fare (average €35) as well as cheaper pizzas. **Vecchia Varenna** (contrada Scoscesa 14, 0341 830 793, www.vecchiavarenna.it, closed Mon & Jan, average €35) catches the last rays of sun and is a tad more experimental than most restaurants in town; the menu includes the likes of rabbit stuffed with prunes and baked guinea fowl.

Tourist information

Proloco Varenna
Via IV Novembre (0341 830 367/www.varenn aitaly.com). **Open** *Apr-Sept* 10am-12.30pm, 3-5pm Tue-Sat; 10am-12.30pm Sun. *Oct-Mar* 10am-5pm Sat.

Lecco, Bellagio & the southern shore

Full of pavement cafés and peaceful lakeside paths, **Lecco** is reminiscent of a pleasant town on the French Riviera. It has stood on key trading routes since ancient times, and is a good hub for travel by rail, boat and car. The town was an important link in the defences of Visconti-era Milan; Azzone Visconti built an eight-arch bridge (three more arches were added later on) over the River Adda in 1336. The bridge survives and still bears its maker's name.

But to most visitors, the city of Lecco signifies just one thing: the birthplace of Alessandro Manzoni (1785-1873), author of the novel that every Italian schoolchild loves to hate, *I Promessi Sposi* ('The Betrothed'). Central piazza Manzoni boasts an impressive statue of the town's most famous son, and **Villa Manzoni** (via Don Guanella 1, 0341 481 247, www.museilecco.org, closed Mon) houses a collection of his memorabilia and manuscripts. A block to the north, piazza Cermenati is the site of the basilica of **San Niccolò**, the city's cathedral.

Perched at the tip of the southern promontory, **Bellagio** is Lake Como's answer to St Tropez. Fine hotels dating from a more elegant age of tourism stand in a simply glorious setting, making the town ritzy and incurably cute at the same time. Among those who came and were enchanted were Liszt, Stendhal and Flaubert. Two villas provide the icing on the cake: **Villa Serbelloni** – crowning the hill where one of Pliny the Younger's villas may have stood – and **Villa Melzi**, a Napoleonic pile surrounded by lush gardens (for both, *see p203* **Heavenly gardens**).

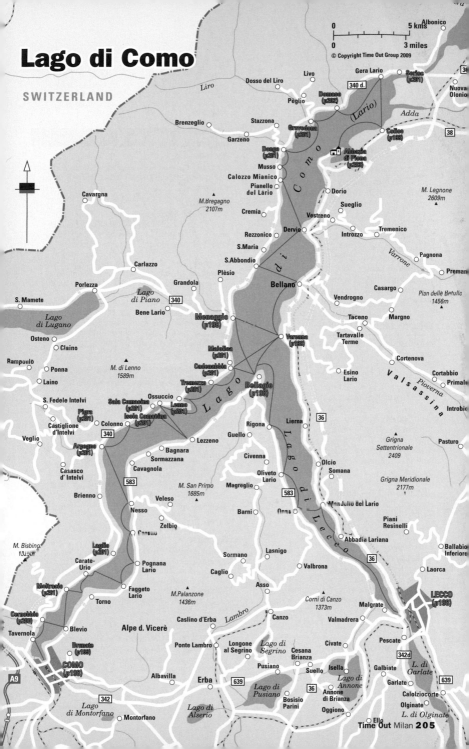

Lago di Como

SWITZERLAND

0   5 kms
0   3 miles
© Copyright Time Out Group 2009

Albonico
Sorico (p391)
Nuova Olonio
Gera Lario
Livo
Dosso del Liro
340 d.
Liro
Demasso (p392)
Pèglio
Brenzeglio
Stazzona
Garzeno
Gravedona (p391)
Adda
38
Celao (p393)
Abbadia di Piona (p393)
Dongo (p391)
Musso
Calozzo Mianico
Pianello del Lario
Dorio
M. Legnone 2609m
M.Bregagno 2107m
Cremia
Sueglio
Vestreno
Cavargna
Rezzonico
Dervio
Intrezzo
Tremenico
S.Maria
Premani
S.Abbondio
Varrone
Pagnona
Plèsio
Carlazzo
Grandola
Bellano
Casargo
Porlezza
Lago di Piano
340
Vendrogno
Pian delle Betulla 1456m
Margno
S. Mamete
Bene Lario
Menaggio (p198)
Taceno
Lago di Lugano
Tartavalle Terme
Varenna (p198)
Esino Lario
Cortenova
Cortabbio
Primali
Osteno
Claino
Malalca (p391)
Cadenabbia (p391)
Ramponio
Ponna
M. di Lenno 1589m
Tremezza (p391)
Introbio
Lago
Valsassina
Pioverna
Laino
Ossuccio
Lenno (p391)
Bellagio (p198)
S. Fedele Intelvi
Sala Comacina (p391)
Isola Comacina (p391)
Grigna Settentrionale 2409
Pasturo
Pigra (p391)
Colonno
Rigona
Lierna
36
Castiglione d'Intelvi
340
Lezzeno
Guello
Veglio
Arpegno (p391)
Bagnara
Civenna
Olcio
Somana
Grigna Meridionale 2177m
Sormazzana
Cavagnola
Oliveto Lario
Casasco d' Intelvi
583
M. San Primo 1685m
Magreglio
583
Brienno
Veleso
Barni
Onno
Mandello del Lario
Nesso
Piani Resinelli
M. Bisbino 1325m
Zelbio
Lasnigo
Abbadia Lariana
Ballabio Inferiore
Careno
Laglio (p391)
Sormano
Valbrona
Laorca
Carate-Urio
Pognana Lario
Caglio
Asso
36
Moltrasio (p391)
Faggeto Lario
M.Palanzone 1436m
Corni di Canzo 1373m
Malgrate
LECCO (p198)
Torno
Canzo
Valmadrera
Cernobbio (p390)
Blevio
Caslino d'Erba
Lambro
342d
Pescate
Tavernola
Alpe d. Vicerè
Ponte Lambro
Longone al Segrino
Lago di Segrino
Civate
Isella
L. di Garlate
Brunate (p193)
Cesana Brianza
639
COMO (p192)
Albavilla
Erba
Pusiano
Suello
Galbiate
Garlate
Calolziocorte
A9
639
Lago di Pusiano
36
Annone di Brianza
Olginate
342
Lago di Alserio
Bosisio Parini
Oggiono
L. di Olginate
Lago di Montorfano
Montorfano
Ello
Time Out Milan **205**

Where to eat

Cutting-edge cuisine in Lecco may seem like a contradiction in terms, but **Santa Lucia** (via Mascari 33, 0341 365 036, closed Mon, average €25) does its best to escape the ordinary: only the steak tartare escapes a balsamic drizzle and a flash in the wood-fired oven. For first-rate fish (at top prices), try **Al Porticciolo** (via Valsecchi 5-7, 0341 498 103, closed Mon, Tue, 2wks Jan & all Aug, average €60).

A dozen different trees cover the terrace of Bellagio's **Bilacus** (salita Serbelloni 32, 031 950 480, closed Mon, average €40), up a steep set of narrow stairs; its risottos are top-notch. In Bellagio's outskirts, towards Como, the family-run **Silvio** hotel and restaurant (via Carcano 12, 031 950 322, www.bellagio silvio.com, closed mid Nov-mid Dec, 6wks Jan-Feb, average €30) offers lake fish and beautiful views; it also has 21 rooms (doubles €70-€115), and rents upmarket apartments in town (www.bellagioapartments.it).

Where to stay

In Bellagio the well-appointed **Hotel du Lac** (piazza Mazzini 32, 031 950 320, www.bellagio hoteldulac.com, closed Nov-end Mar, doubles €160-€190) has been welcoming travellers for 150 years. Check out the owners' boutique hotel, **Hotel Bellagio** (salita Grande 6, 031 950 424, www.hotelbellagio.it, doubles €80-€160): nearly every room has a lake view, and there's also a small gym.

The **Hotel Metropole** (piazza Mazzini 1, 031 950 409, www.albergometropole.it, closed Jan-Feb, doubles €115-€150) boasts a rooftop sun terrace and a commanding central position. Half board is €15 extra; the restaurant has a lake view, lake fish and plenty of heavy northern Italian sauces. Facilities at the refined **Grand Hotel Villa Serbelloni** (via Roma 1, 031 950 216, www.villaserbelloni.com, closed Nov-Mar, doubles €375-€590) include indoor and outdoor pools, sauna and Turkish bath, as well as spectacular lake views. Non-guests can stop in for a €10 cup of Earl Grey in the ornate lounge where Churchill and JFK have sat.

The **Hotel Moderno** (piazza Diaz 5, 0314 286 519, doubles €70-€100) by the train station is typical of the less expensive hotels found in the city, with parquet floors and high ceilings.

Tourist information

APT Lecco
Via Nazario Sauro 6 (0341 295 720/www.turismo. provincia.lecco.it). **Open** *Mar-Oct* 9am-1pm, 2.30-6.30pm daily. *Nov-Feb* 9am-1pm, 2.30-5pm Mon-Sat.

IAT Bellagio
Piazza Mazzini – Pontile Imbarcadero (031 950 204/www.bellagiolakecomo.com). **Open** *Apr-Oct* 9am-12.30pm, 1-6.30pm Mon-Sat; 9.30am-noon, 1-2.30pm Sun. *Nov-Mar* 9am-noon, 3-6pm Mon, Wed-Sat.

Getting there

By car
For Como, take the A8 motorway west out of Milan and turn on to the A9 after Lainate. Take the SS36 for Lecco.

By train
Two railway companies serve Como. The state railways (www.ferroviedellostato.it) offer hourly services from Milan's Stazione Centrale on the Chiasso–Lugano route. This takes 30mins and comes into San Giovanni station; there's also an hourly service from Porta Garibaldi station. The Ferrovie Nord service departs every 30mins from Cadorna station for the more central Como Nord Lago station (journey time 1hr).

For Lecco, there's an hourly service from Porta Garibaldi (journey time around 1hr 15mins), and one train every hour or so (journey time 45mins) from Stazione Centrale. Services to Cólico from Stazione Centrale run every 90mins (journey time 1hr 30mins).

Getting around

By boat
Navigazione Lago di Como (via per Cernobbio 18, Como, 031 579 211, www.navigazionelaghi.it) operates ferry and hydrofoil services all year round. The boats run very frequently, and there are point-to-point commuter services to Tavernola, Cernobbio, Moltrasio, Torno and Urio at the southern end of the lake; Cólico at the lake's northern tip; and to intermediate towns such as Bellagio, Varenna, Cadenabbia and Menaggio. There are also some car-ferry services. Special tourist cruises are on offer in summer. If you're travelling between October and Easter, check the schedules on the website or on a tourist office handout, as services are often curtailed.

By bus
Buses run by SPT (031 247 111/www.sptlinea.it), among others, run round the lake from the Stazione Autolinee on Como's piazza Matteotti, departing twice an hour for Argegno (40mins), hourly for Menaggio and Bellagio (1hr), four times a day for Cólico (2hrs 20mins), and every 45 mins for Lecco (1hr).

By car
The SS340 and SP72 around the lake's shores are very scenic, but traffic is heavy, especially in summer and at weekends. Progress is quicker, if less picturesque, on the SS36, which follows the eastern shore of the lake. The minor roads up into the hill villages can be challenging, not least because they are favoured by motorcyclists and cyclists.

Lago d'Iseo

Crowd-free exploring on Europe's largest inland island.

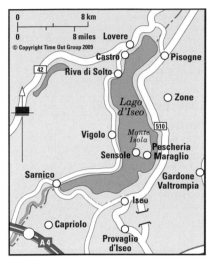

Little known outside Italy, Lago d'Iseo is nestled in the mountains between Bergamo and Brescia. Locals still refer to the lake by its Roman name, Lago Sebino, and the towns around it have a plentiful supply of towers, monasteries and castles that date from the past two millennia. It's the most tranquil of northern Italy's lakes: visitors are rewarded with uncrowded restaurants, clean Alpine air and little-used footpaths around the many sights.

The Bergamo shore

Sarnico, at the south-western tip of the lake, has been inhabited since prehistoric times. It's a popular spot for waterskiers and windsurfers, and home to the HQ of Riva yachts – the Rolls Royce of speedboats. On summer weekends the town packs out with campers visiting for supplies and *gelato*, but you can escape them in the winding streets of its medieval centre.

Towards the northern end of the lake, **Riva di Solto** has been an important harbour since Roman times. The 17-kilometre (ten-mile) Sebino Nature Walk starts here, and the sheer cliffs of Orrido di Zorzino are a short distance north; black marble from the nearby quarry was used to make the pillars of Venice's Basilica San Marco. **Castro** boasts a pretty

lakeside terrace, its atmosphere enhanced by a weighty bronze 'book' etched with Italian poet Montanari's description of the lake.

Lovere, in Lago d'Iseo's north-west corner, was historically important for its strategic position, guarding the passage from the lake to the textile-producing heart of the Valcamonica region. Three medieval towers rise above the café-lined *piazze* and elegant palazzi along the shore, the latter a mark of the prosperity the small town has enjoyed over the centuries. The imposing Accademia Tadini houses a fine selection of archaeological findings and Lombard paintings from the 15th century.

The Brescia shore

Across from Lovere sits **Pisogne**. Long known for its rich iron ore deposits, its once busy via Valeriana was the Roman road linking Brescia with Valcamonica. Today there's a relative lack of visitors, making it the perfect territory for a quiet stroll in the small medieval *borgo* behind the lake-front piazza del Mercato, with its 13th-century Torre del Vescovo.

From Marone, a narrow road (SP32) climbs through a series of hairpin turns to **Zone**, a hamlet surrounded by mountain peaks and offering glimpses of the lake. In Zone's small nature reserve, erosion has left bizarre boulders stranded on towering pinnacles; walking trails around them allow a closer look. At the entrance to the park, the isolated 15th-century church of San Giorgio is decorated with stunning frescoes.

Further south, **Iseo** is the lake's principal and most cosmopolitan town. Despite its focus on modern-day tourism, Iseo manages to retain a peculiar timelessness, thanks to its labyrinth of narrow alleys, the 12th-century Pieve di Sant'Andrea church and the 13th-century Castello Oldofredi. There's also a former Jewish ghetto area at the south end of the town, which is now filled with artisan shops and cafés, making the district ideal for wandering.

Monte Isola

The ferry from Sulzano to **Peschiera Maraglio** on Monte Isola only takes a few minutes, but carries visitors to a very different world. It's still famous for boat-building skills

Trips Out of Town

and handmade fishing nets. Besides Peschiera Maraglio, the gloriously car-free island is home to a number of other small, characterful villages. And yes, it is peaceful.

Take the lakeshore path, which runs the full nine kilometres (six miles) around the island, from Peschiera to **Sensole**, on the south-western corner, where the Mediterranean-style microclimate allows for olive cultivation. The quaintly traditional villages **Menzino**, **Sanchignano** and **Siviano** occupy the western coast, and two tiny islands, **Isola di Loreto** and **Isola di San Paolo**, stand off the northern and southern shores, respectively. The more adventurous can hike up to the 13th-century Madonna della Ceriola sanctuary at the top of the mountain (from Peschiera follow the signs for Senzano, then Cure), which offers unparalleled views of the lake.

Where to stay, eat & shop

In Iseo, **Il Volto** does a wonderful blend of haute cuisine and regional comfort food (via Mirolte 33, 030 981 462, closed all day Wed, Thur lunch, first 3wks July & 1wk Jan, average €50); or you might want to try the excellent *antipasto al lago*, based on the lake's fish, at

Al Porto (via Porto dei Pescatori 12, 030 989 014, closed Wed, average €35) in nearby Clusane. The 29-room **Romantik Relais Mirabella** (via Mirabella 34, 030 989 8051, www.relaismirabella.it, closed Nov-mid Mar, doubles €134-€164), also in Clusane, has lovely lake views and a swimming pool.

Outside Sale Marasino, family-run **Villa Kinzica** (via Provinciale 1, 030 982 0975, www.villakinzica.it, doubles €80-€140) is delightfully far from the lake's summer bustle. The excellent **Ristorante Uliveto** (030 986 7102, www.ristoranteuliveto.it, closed Oct-Mar Mon lunch, Sun dinner & 2wks Jan, average €35) is also here.

Tourist information

IAT Iseo

Lungolago Marconi 2C, Iseo (030 980 209/www. provincia.brescia.it/turismo). **Open** *Easter-Sept* 10am-12.30pm, 3.30-6.30pm daily. *Oct-Easter* 10am-12.30pm, 3-6pm Mon-Fri; 10am-12.30pm Sat.

Ufficio Turistico Alto Sebino (Lovere)

Piazza 13 Martiri, Lovere (035 962 178/www.apt. bergamo.it). **Open** *Easter-Sept* 9am-1pm, 2-5pm daily (until 6pm July & Aug). *Jan-Easter, Oct-mid Nov, Dec* 9am-noon, 2-5pm daily.

Getting there and around

By boat

Navigazione Lago d'Iseo runs ferries (035 971 483/ www.navigazionelagoiseo.it) up and down the lake (including stops at Monte Isola) every 1-2hrs, from around 7am to 6pm, although some stops are less frequently served. To visit Monte Isola, ferries depart from Sulzano for Pescheria every 15mins or so; ferries between Sale Marasino and Carzano run approximately every 20-30mins.

By bus

There are no buses from Milan directly to Lago d'Iseo. From Bergamo, Bergamo Trasporti (035 289 000/www.bergamoTrasporti.it) runs various services every 30mins to Lovere (journey time around 1hr 30mins) and Sarnico (journey time around 1hr).

By car

From Milan, take the A4 towards Brescia; exit at Grumello del Monte and follow signs for Lago d'Iseo.

By train

From Milan, take a train to Brescia (www.ferrovie dellostato.it), where there are frequent connecting trains to Iseo, Sulzano, Sale Marasino, Marone and Pisogne (www.lenord.it). Ticket prices vary; a day pass, valid for travel anywhere in the lake, is €11.20. On Sundays between June and September (daily in Aug), Navigazione Lago d'Iseo organises a 1hr tour around Monte Isola, Isola di San Paolo and Isola di Loreto, the lake's 'three pearls'.

Lago d'Iseo.

Lago di Garda

Go Mediterranean with palm trees, olive groves and bags of family fun.

Unlike fashionable Como or classy Maggiore, Lago di Garda has long since shrugged off its sophisticated, old-worldly veneer. These days, Italy's largest lake is the destination of choice for campers, kids and caravans, and as the summer days heat up, the families pour in. It's easy to see why. Surrounded by mountains rising sharply from the water's edge, it makes a laid-back, cooler alternative to the standard seaside holiday. The water is clean, and its depth (average 135 metres/443 feet) means it stays pleasantly fresh even in the hottest months. Surprisingly sandy beaches huddle at the southern end of the lake, and exhilarating mountain breezes around Limone sul Garda and Riva del Garda in the north create ideal conditions for wind- and kite-surfing.

If the thrills of water don't float your boat, have a look at the tiny, extremely picturesque towns that line the east and west shores of the lake. Many have their own medieval centres complete with fine Romanesque churches, and are often guarded by a miniature castle. Early 20th-century villas hug the lake's winding walkways, each more extravagant and ornate than the last. Citrus trees and palms give the area the feel of tropical paradise.

The southern shore

Nestled in Garda's south-western corner, **Desenzano del Garda** is the largest of the lakeside towns. Behind the quaint old port is the arcaded piazza Malvezzi, with its statue of St Angela, and the cathedral of Santa Maria Maddalena (open 9am-noon, 4-6pm daily). Inside the church is a striking *Last Supper* signed by Giambattista Tiepolo, although it is painted in a style more reminiscent of his son, Giandomenico, who may have restored *papà*'s work extensively. To the west, along via Crocefisso, are the remains of the fourth-century Villa Romana (no.22, 030 914 3547, closed Mon). Excavated in 1921, it has some fine mosaics.

Six kilometres (3.5 miles) to the east lies the lake's main tourist magnet: the medieval spa town of **Sirmione**, still pulling crowds with its healing thermal springs (*see p215* **Skin deep**). The historic old town at the peninsula's tip is protected by the supremely picturesque 13th-century **Rocca Scaligera** (piazza Castello, 030 916 468, closed Mon).

Also in Sirmione is the first-century **Grotte di Catullo** (piazza Orti Manara, 030 916 157,

closed Mon). Set among sloping olive groves at the tip of the peninsula, these ruins bear the name of the Roman poet Catullus, although it's more likely that such a colossal villa belonged to his wealthy family in Verona.

Peschiera del Garda, at the south-eastern corner of the lake, has a decidedly military feel to it. The town has been fortified since Roman times; in the 19th century the Austrians rebuilt and strengthened its 16th-century Venetian defences. It now houses a huge water purifying plant. Just to the north of the town is **Gardaland** (SS 249 Gardesana Orientale, Castelnuovo del Garda, Località Ronchi, 045 644 9777, www.gardaland.it, closed Nov-late Mar except school hols), Italy's answer to Disneyland. Over three million people each year visit its dinosaur islands, dolphinariums and (newly added) baby sharks in the aquarium. To the north lies the Canevaworld Resort, with Aquaparadise (www.aquaparadise.it), Europe's largest water park, and Movieland (www.movieland.it), an Italian take on Universal Studios. All play a part in generating the traffic that strangles the road system in high season.

Where to stay & eat

In Desenzano, the **Hotel Giardinetto** (viale Marconi 33, 030 914 1704, www.hotel-giardinetto.com, closed Mar, doubles €75-€93) is ideally situated between the train station and the lake; ask for a room with balcony. For Amarone-infused risotto and home-made desserts, head to **La Contrada** (via Bagatta 10-12, 030 914 2514, closed all Wed, lunch Thur & 2wks Nov, average €30; *see p179* **Eat slow**).

Albergo Grifone (via Bocchio 4, 030 916 014, closed Nov-Mar, doubles €67), in Sirmione, could be Lago di Garda's best bargain. Rooms are basic but all have a lake view; the hotel is located in the scenic old town behind the Rocca; and free parking is thrown in with the deal. The friendly **Osteria Al Torcol** (via San Salvatore 30, 030 990 4605, closed Wed & Jan, average €25) serves own-made pasta and hot and cold snacks. Just outside the city gates, **Erica** (viale Marconi 43, 030 916 141, closed Wed except July & Aug, and mid Dec-Jan, average €25) can seat the largest tour groups: its food, including perfect crispy pizzas, is tasty and fairly priced.

Tourist information

IAT Desenzano

Via Porto Vecchio 34 (030 914 1510/www.comune. desenzano.brescia.it). **Open** *June-Sept* 9am-12.30pm, 3-6pm Mon-Sat. *Oct-May* 9am-12.30pm, 3-6pm Mon-Fri; 9am-12.30pm Sat.

IAT Sirmione

Viale Marconi 8 (030 916 114/www.comune. sirmione.bs.it). **Open** *Easter-Oct* 9am-12.30pm, 3-6pm daily (12.30-3pm, the office is used by the Sirmione Hotel Association and is open to the public). *Nov-Easter* 9am-12.30pm, 3-6pm Mon-Fri; 9am-12.30pm Sat.

The western shore

The tropical palms and 18th-century villas, including those that belonged to Mussolini and poet Gabriele D'Annunzio, make Garda's rugged western shore one of the lake's most stunning stretches. The lakeside road leads north from Desenzano to **Salò** (known in Roman times as Salodium), set in a deep bay. The town's name is linked with the puppet republic set up here by the Nazis for Mussolini in 1943 (*see p216* **Benito's betrayal**); but Salò's other, happier, claim to fame is as the birthplace of Gasparo di Bertolotti, also known as Gasparo da Salò (1540-1609), who was one of the first great violin makers.

The fine art nouveau hotels (built in 1910) along the lake shore are mere pups compared to the many medieval and Renaissance palazzi in the centre of this important old town. In piazza del Duomo, the cathedral of the **Annunziata** has a Renaissance portal in its unfinished façade, and a splendid Venetian Gothic interior complete with gilded statues of saints, two paintings by Romanino and a polyptych by Paolo Veneziano. Around the cathedral is the oldest part of the town, with fine palazzi from the 15th to the 18th centuries lining the main street parallel to the lake.

Four kilometres (2.5 miles) further north is **Gardone Riviera**, which is made up of cosmopolitan hotels and holiday villas, including **Villa Alba**. This large neo-classical building, built in the 1880s as a mini-replica of the Parthenon for the Austrian emperor (he never used it), is now a conference centre.

Gardone's main attraction is the **Giardino Botanico Hruska** (via Roma 2, mobile 336 410 877, www.hellergarden.com, closed mid-Oct-mid-Mar), also known as the Heller Garden after the current owner, artist André Heller. Created in 1910 by Arturo Hruska, a dentist and naturalist, it has plants from every continent and climate, including magnolias, bamboo and orchids. The park is also dotted with installations by international artists, including Keith Haring and Roy Lichtenstein, and with Indian sculptures and Buddhist mandalas.

From Gardone there's a beautiful view of **Isola del Garda**. In the ninth century Charlemagne gave this island to Verona's archbishop (and later saint) Zeno; it remained in ecclesiastical hands until 1798. The extraordinary Venetian-Gothic-style villa (the largest on the lake) was built by the noble Borghese family between 1890 and 1903, and is still privately owned. Between June and September, Navigazione sul Lago di Garda (*see p216*) and the Borghese Cavazza family organise 15 ferry trips per week to the island, departing from various locations at the southern end of the lake. The steep ticket price (€27-€35) includes a guided tour of the island, gardens and parts of the villa, as well as sampling of local products and return transport (www.isoladelgarda.com).

On the hill above the Gardone Riviera is the old town of **Gardone di Sopra**, notable mostly as the site of the grandiose **Vittoriale degli Italiani** (via Vittoriale 22, 036 529 6511, www.vittoriale.it, villa interior closed Mon). This presumptuously named residence was the home of 19th-century poet, novelist, dramatist, man of action and grand poseur Gabriele D'Annunzio. Mussolini authorised the poet to turn the house into a national monument; it was one way for him to exert some kind of control over the only Italian capable of upstaging him. 'If you have a rotten tooth,' said *Il Duce* of the popular poet and hero, 'either you have it pulled out or you cover it with gold.'

Despite the patriotic name, the Vittoriale is essentially an extravagant monument to its owner, and no aspect of his character or achievements is uncelebrated. The interior, with its claustrophobia-inducing clutter, reveals D'Annunzio's numerous interests: music, literature, art, the Orient and – most of all – sex. Highlights include the spare bedroom, with the coffin in which D'Annunzio would meditate, and the dining room, which has an embalmed and bronzed pet tortoise that died from overeating. The grounds celebrate his more extrovert passions, from theatre (his most famous love affair was with actress Eleonora Duse) to bellicose heroics: where other people have gnomes, D'Annunzio planted the prow of the battleship *Puglia* to commemorate his quixotic attempt to 'liberate' the city of Fiume (now Rijeka) from Yugoslav rule. The **Museo della Guerra** (war museum; closed Wed), also on the grounds, celebrates D'Annunzio's more aggressive adventures: from the ceiling hangs the plane he used to fly over Vienna in 1918. Lastly, you can't miss his monstrous wedding-cake mausoleum. In July and August, the Vittoriale hosts outdoor concerts and opera.

Further north, **Toscolano-Maderno** is a resort with a great beach. Roman and Byzantine vestiges can be found in the 12th-century

The great lake outdoors

One of Lago di Garda's major tourist magnets is its superb selection of water sports. You can kitesurf, windsurf, waterski, wakeboard, sail, parasail, canoe, kayak or just rent a small motorboat and cruise. (Visit the Sirmione or Riva del Garda tourist offices to pick up lists of local operators.) But if you're more of a walker, or if ten minutes of waves make you go green, here's a summary of the area's other top outdoor pursuits.

You can taste your way from Lago di Garda to the Brenta Dolomites by following the northern **Strada del Vino e dei Sapori**,

the 'Road of Wine and Flavours'. Rather than a road per se, the term refers to the regional zones highlighting small local producers of traditional food and drink. See the website (www.gardadolomiti.it) for details of producers of olive oil, walnuts, *vin santo*, salami and spressa cheese, or contact the Association (info@gardadolomiti.it) for further information.

Alternatively, bird-watch in the **Alto Garda Bresciano park** (www.cm-parcoaltogarda. bs.it). The 38,000 hectares (94,000 acres) of parkland rise 1,976 metres (6,483 feet) from Toscolano Maderno, Gardone Riviera and Salò, on the Garda shoreline, to Monte Caplone. Pack binoculars to peer at golden eagles, kestrels, cuckoos, red kites and blackcaps, or coots and herring gulls on the lake's edges. Devoted birders can hike to the Alpine hut and observation post on Monte Spino, accessible by mule track only. Contact the Comunità Montana (0365 71 449) or the local tourist offices for further information.

If neither of the above appeals, hop on a bike and freewheel into the sunset. The topography around Lago di Garda changes dramatically between east and west and north and south, so be sure to match the landscape to your abilities. Bicycles are available to hire from **CTS** (piazza Einaudi 8, Desenzano del Garda, 030 914 2268) in Garda's south-west, and **Garda Bike Hotel** (via Veronello 2, Calmasino di Bardolino, 045 626 0126, www.gardabikehotel.it) in the south-east offers packages that include hotel stay, professional De Rosa bike rental and guided tours for all levels of ability.

Romanesque church of **Sant'Andrea** (piazza San Marco, open 8.30am-noon, 2.30-7pm daily), particularly in the pillar capitals, restored in 2008. The church is a miniature version of Verona's San Zeno Maggiore.

Bogliaco, the next village, is home to the grandiose 18th-century **Villa Bettoni** (closed to the public), its roof topped with eye-catching, life-sized mythological statues. The second largest villa on the lake, this was where the ministers of the Salò republic (*see p216* **Benito's betrayal**) would meet.

DH Lawrence lived in nearby **Gargnano** in 1912-13, where he completed *Sons and Lovers*. His collection of essays, *Twilight in Italy*, contains – amid reflections on Italian phallocentricity – some of the most evocative descriptions of the lake ever written. Along the Gardesana, the lakeside road, bare pillars that used to support protective greenhouse cover during the winter months now stand, as DH Lawrence fancifully put it, like 'ruined temples… forlorn in their colonnades and squares… as if they remained from some great race that had once worshipped here'. By the lake is **Palazzo Feltrinelli**, built in 1898-99 for a wealthy industrialist family. It's now a conference centre for Milan University, but in the Republic of Salò, this was Mussolini's administrative HQ. *Il Duce*'s private residence was in the larger **Villa Feltrinelli**, set in an expansive garden to the north of the town, and recently restored as a luxury hotel (*see below*).

Beyond Gargnano, the lake narrows and the mountains rise sheer out of the water. The Gardesana continues as a series of tunnels, used during World War II as bomb-proof factories.

A good 15 kilometres (10 miles) further north, and lined by a vast beach, **Limone sul Garda** has a small port and a medieval centre with steep, narrow streets and staircases. It's unclear whether the town's name derives from the Latin *limen* (border) or from its lemon plantations, which date back to the 13th century and are thought to have been the first in Europe.

Through yet more tunnels, **Riva del Garda** is the largest town in the northern half of the lake. It stands between Monte Brione to the east and the sheer cliffs of Monte Rocchetta to the west, which bring early dusk to the town. Riva was once a major port: from 1813 until 1918 it lay in Austrian territory, and saw fighting during World War I. The centre of the town is piazza III Novembre, with the city's imposing symbol, 13th-century **Torre Apponale** (piazza Catena, 0464 573 869, closed Nov-Feb). Climb the 165 steps to experience the advertised 'dizzying emotion', as well as the fine view over the lake. The square is also home to the 14th-century **Palazzo Pretorio** (not open to the public) and picturesque medieval porticoes. An archway beneath the Palazzo Pretorio leads to tiny piazza San Rocco, where the surviving apse of a church destroyed in World War I has been converted into an open-air chapel; the location of the original walls are marked on the piazza's pavement. Eastwards from piazza III Novembre is the moat-encircled **Rocca** (fortress), containing the **Museo Civico** (piazza Battisti 3, 0464 573 869, www.comune. rivadelgarda.tn.it/museo, closed Mon Mar-June & Sept-Nov, all Dec-Feb), with collections of archaeology and armour as well as temporary exhibitions by Italian artists. The more energetic can follow a zigzag path up to the **Bastione**, a cylindrical tower (212 metres/707 feet high) built by the Venetians in 1508, which commands spectacular views over the town.

Where to stay & eat

In Salò, the **Gallo Rosso** (vicolo Tomacelli 4, 0365 520 757, closed lunch Mon-Fri, dinner Tue & Wed, 1wk Jan & 1wk June, average €30)

serves excellent grilled fish. Near the cathedral is the **Hotel Duomo** (lungolago Zanardelli 63, 0365 21 026, www.hotelduomosalo.it, doubles €115-€195), with rooms that look out on to the lake or the duomo. **Agriturismo Conti Terzi** (via Panoramica 13, 0365 22 071, www.contiterzi.it, rates €32-€38 per person) is a farm about two kilometres (just over a mile) from the centre of Salò. Surrounded by cultivated olive groves, and with a splendid lake view, it offers basic accommodation for up to six guests.

In Gardone di Sopra, the restaurant **Agli Angeli** (piazza Garibaldi 2, 0365 20 832, www.agliangeli.com, closed Tue & mid Nov-Feb, average €30, *see p179* **Eat slow**) was recommended by Gabriele D'Annunzio to his friends as the place to eat (although he preferred to dine at home).

Built in 1892 and subsequently home to Mussolini, the **Villa Feltrinelli** (via Rimembranza 38-40, 0365 798 000, www. villafeltrinelli.com, closed Nov-Mar, suites €800-€2,400; *see p216* **Benito's betrayal**) in Gargnano has been all jazzed up to remove the taint of its Fascist associations, and is now an exclusive, adults-only getaway.

In Limone, the excellent family-run **Hotel Bellavista** by the lake (via Marconi 20, 0365 95 4001, www.bellavistalimone.eu, closed Nov-mid Mar, doubles €76-€90) has 12 rooms and a pretty garden.

In Riva del Garda, the **Ristorante Al Volt** (via Fiume 73, 0464 552 570, www.ristorante alvolt.com, closed Mon & mid Feb-mid Mar, average €40) serves excellent meals including specialities from the Trentino region. The **Grand Hotel Riva** (piazza Garibaldi 10, 0464 521 800, www.gardaresort.it, doubles €114-€205) is a large and comfortable hotel by the Rocca; its top-floor dining room commands panoramic views of the lake.

Tourist information

Consorzio Turistico Gargnano

Piazza Boldini 2 (0365 791 243/www.gargnanosul garda.com). Open Apr-Sept 9.30am-12.30pm, 2.30-4.30pm Mon, Tue, Fri, Sat; 9.30am-12.30pm Wed; 2.30-4.30pm Thur.

IAT Gardone Riviera

Corso Repubblica 8 (0365 20 347). Open June-mid Oct 9am-12.30pm, 3-6.30pm daily. *Mid Oct-May* 9am-12.30pm, 2.15-6pm Mon-Sat.

Ingarda Trentino Azienda per il Turismo, Riva del Garda

Largo Medaglio d'Oro (0464 554 444/www.garda trentino.it). Open Apr-Sept 9am-7pm daily. *Oct-Mar* 9am-7pm Mon-Sat.

The eastern shore

Medieval towns edge the northern half of the eastern shore, and campsites and amusement parks crowd most of its southern end. Poised on Garda's north-eastern corner is pretty **Torbole**, a historic town of considerbale strategic importance. In 1439 it witnessed the launch of 26 Venetian ships that had been hauled over the mountains for a surprise attack on the Milanese rulers, the Visconti.

Malcesine (15 kilometres/9.5 miles south) is arguably the eastern shore's most delightful stopover, especially notable for the **Castello Scaligero** (via Castello, 045 657 0499, closed Nov, Mon-Fri Feb-Mar). The castle was built, like many in the region, by Verona's ruling Della Scala family, from which the name *scaligero* derives. Situated on a craggy headland looming over the medieval quarter, the castle also has a small museum that holds sketches by Goethe. While drawing them in 1786, the poet was arrested for spying by a suspicious local.

For a blast of Alpine air, take a 15-minute cable car ride from Malcesine to the top of **Monte Baldo** (www.funiviedelbaldo.it, closed 2 wks Mar, mid Nov-mid Dec, €17 return), a popular ski resort in winter.

Further down the coast, in **Torri del Benaco**, are remnants of the ancient town walls and the 14th-century **Castello Scaligero** (viale Fratelli Lavanda 2, 045 629 6111, www.museodelcastelloditorridelbenaco.it, closed Nov-Mar); its *limonara*, or ancient lemon hothouse, is the only one on the lake still in operation. The church of **Santissima Trinità** (in the eponymous square) contains 15th-century frescoes, including a splendid Christ Pantocrator in gleaming floral garb.

In a deep bay in the shadow of Monte Garda, the town of **Garda** is home to a wide lakefront promenade and several notable Renaissance palazzi. (For more, take the sunny villa- and garden-lined path north along the curving shore towards **Punta San Vigilio**.) It was in a (now long-gone) castle on this hill in the tenth century that Queen Adelaide was imprisoned by Berengar II, after he had murdered her husband and she had refused to marry him (or his son Adalbert; sources are divided).

At the tip of the headland is a harbour with a tiny chapel dedicated to **San Vigilio**. From here, a path leads up to the 16th-century **Villa Guarienti-Brenzone**; it's privately owned, but a glimpse can be caught of its splendid formal gardens, much loved by Winston Churchill and Laurence Olivier, among others. On the far side of the promontory is the tiny **Baia delle Sirene**, which has a beach.

South of Garda, the waterside footpath is a pleasant and mostly pine-shaded walk as far as **Bardolino**. This small town, famed for its wine, is flanked by gardens leading to the lake, and has two fascinating churches. The tiny,

Rocca Scaligera. *See p209.*

Trips Out of Town

ninth-century **San Zeno** can be reached by turning eastwards off the Gardesana along the suburban-looking via San Zeno. **San Severo**, a well-preserved 12th-century building with a good campanile, contains notable 12th- and 14th-century frescoes.

In **Lazise** is another **Castello Scaligero**, now incorporated into the garden of a privately owned villa. South of here lie the theme park delights of the Canevaworld Resort and Gardaland (*see p210*).

Where to stay & eat

The 34-room **Hotel Gardesana** in Torri del Benaco (piazza Calderini 20, 045 722 5411, www.hotel-gardesana.com, closed Jan & Feb, doubles €100-€170) has a fine lakeside location; the list of former guests includes Winston Churchill and Maria Callas.

In Garda, away from the lake, **Stafolet** (via Poiano 9, 045 627 8939, closed Tue, average €25) does good grilled dishes and pizza. **Ancora** (via Manzoni 7, 045 725 5202, www.allancora.com, average €25) has laid-back local cuisine and hotel rooms upstairs. Near to Punta San Vigilio, **Locanda San Vigilio** (045 725 6688, www.locanda-sanvigilio.it, closed mid Nov-Mar, doubles €270-€375) spoils guests with antique furniture and exquisite luxury. A 15-minute stroll from the town centre, **Hotel Gardenia** (piazza Serenissima 12, 045 621

Skin deep

The area around Lago di Garda is renowned for its therapeutic *terme*, or thermal spas. Precious, mineral-enriched waters bubble up from hundreds of metres below the ground, packed chock-full of the magic ingredient sulphur, which sloughs off dead skin cells, leaving limbs polished and radiant. Sulphur encourages new skin cell production, reduces arterial pressure and the unattractive appearance of broken capillaries. It's also the source of that rather unpleasant eggy smell.

Medical benefits aside, sitting in warm bubbly waters is also thoroughly relaxing. Throw in a full-body mudpack and a massage or two, and you may feel tempted to make one of these centres the focal point of your holiday.

Aquaria (piazza Don Angelo Piatti, Sirmione, 030 916 044, www.termedi sirmione.com) is a play on the Italian words for water (*acqua*) and air (*aria*). It's set in Sirmione's picturesque old town, and offers everything from anti-cellulite mud masks to anti-age facials; if you're interested in these special treatments, be sure to book your sessions well in advance. You can also opt for an Aquaria day pass (€48), which gets you access to the thermal plunge pools, fitness centre and a lunch of salads and fruit juices.

Terme Virgilio & Terme Catullo (via Vittorio Alfieri & via Punta Staffalo, Sirmione, 030 990 4923, www.termedi sirmione.com, Catullo closed Nov-Mar) are part of a single co-operative, and their thermal baths are set aside for medical use. You'll need to book in advance: explain your ailments to one of the multilingual receptionists, and you'll get a private consultation with a doctor upon arrival. Most treatments last 12 days.

Parco Termale del Garda (Villa dei Cedri, piazza di Sopra 4, Colà di Lazise, 045 649 0382, www.villadeicedri.com) is set a short distance from Lago di Garda's south-east corner. This is a thermal lake that has over 5,000 square metres (54,000 square feet) of soothing waters at 37°C (98.6°F), a grotto with hydromassage jets, and therapeutic waterfalls. Daily entrance prices are lower than those on the lake (€21). Join the day-tripping Milan families, or book into one of the on-site apartments.

0882, www.hotelgardenia.it, closed Dec & Jan, doubles €88-€158) in Bardolino offers two swimming pools and views over the lake.

Tourist information

IAT Garda
Piazza Donatori di Sangue 1 (045 627 0384/www. tourism.verona.it). **Open** *Apr-Oct* 9am-7pm Mon-Sat; 10am-4pm Sun. *Nov-Mar* 9am-1pm, 3-6pm Mon-Fri; 9am-1pm Sat.

IAT Malcesine
Via Capitanato 8 (045 740 0044/www.malcesine piu.it). **Open** *Apr-Oct* 9am-7pm Mon-Sat; 10am-4pm Sun. *Nov-Mar* 9am-1pm, 3-6pm Tue, Thur; 9am-1pm Wed, Fri, Sat.

Getting there

By bus
The Brescia–Verona services run by SIA (030 44 061, 840 62 001, www.trasportibrescia.it) call at Desenzano (journey time 1hr), Sirmione (journey time 1hr 20mins) and Peschiera (journey time 1hr 30mins).

By car
The Milan–Venice A4 motorway has exits at Desenzano, Sirmione and Peschiera.

By train
Many trains on the Milan–Venice line from Stazione Centrale (www.trenitalia.it) stop at Desenzano, and some at Peschiera (journey time around 1hr 15mins and 1hr 30mins respectively).

Getting around

By boat
Hydrofoil and steamer services are frequent in the summer, connecting the most important points on the lake. All year round, a regular car ferry service (roughly every 40mins) runs between Toscolano-Maderno and Torri del Benaco. All boat services are operated by Navigazione sul Lago di Garda (030 914 9511, www.navigazionelaghi.it).

By bus
The southern shore (Desenzano, Sirmione, Peschiera) is served by buses from Brescia and Verona. SIA (030 44 061, 840 62 001, www.trasportibrescia.it) runs buses from Desenzano to Riva along the western shore; Verona's APT (045 805 7911, www.apt.vr.it) operates along the same route, and runs services from Lazise to Riva along the eastern shore.

By car
The road that skirts the lake is called the Gardesana. In summer, expect heavy traffic, particularly around the Gardaland amusement park (*see p210*).

Benito's betrayal

By the time northern Italy's Nazi occupiers installed Mussolini in Villa Feltrinelli in Gargnano (*see p213*), the Fascist leader had been humbled by events. Most of his Grand Council had voted to remove him from power on 25 July 1943, by which time Anglo-American forces were firmly installed in Sicily and cutting great swathes up the boot of Italy. The king had defected to the Allied side, and had had Mussolini imprisoned in a mountain stronghold in Abruzzo: it had taken an SS commando team to get him out and whisk him off to the north.

Il Duce's comeback took the vicious, squalid form of the Repubblica di Salò. Mussolini did not choose the place from which he was to 'govern' northern Italy for the next 18 months; he would have preferred to return to Rome for a bloody settling of accounts, but the pragmatic Germans put their feet down and kept him in the more easily controllable north. To ensure Mussolini was under no illusions that he was running anything other than a puppet administration, the Germans put ministries in lakeside towns and made it clear that everything – including

Mussolini's letters to his lover Clara Petacci, who had been housed in an ex-convent in Gargnano – was checked by the SS.

Holed up in Villa Feltrinelli, Mussolini was a pathetic parody of his former self. He drew up futile plans for the war effort, unwilling to admit the Nazis were now running the show. The Salò Republic's one memorable act was the trial and subsequent execution of five members of the Grand Council who had voted Mussolini out of office, including *il Duce*'s son-in-law, Galeazzo Ciano. Mussolini went to great lengths to pretend that the malevolence of others had prevented him from signing a pardon. When his daughter refused to believe him, he whinged that it was his 'destiny to be betrayed by everyone, including [his] own daughter'.

The beauty of the setting in which these events took place was of little consolation to Mussolini. 'Lakes are a compromise between river and sea,' he moaned, 'and I don't like compromises.' As it turned out, it was beside another lake – Como – that he was executed by partisans, before being strung up for all to see in Milan's piazza Loretto.

Directory

Features

Directory

Getting Around

Arriving & leaving

By air

Aeroporto di Malpensa

Milan's main airport (flight information 02 7485 2200, switchboard 02 74851, www.sea-aeroportimilano.it) is in Somma Lombarda, about 50km (32 miles) from the city centre. **Terminal 1** is for intercontinental, international and domestic flights. **Terminal 2** is for charter flights; it's also used by a few budget airlines.

Ferrovie Nord's **Malpensa Express** train (02 8511 4382, www.malpensaexpress.it) runs at 23 and 53 minutes past the hour from 6.53am to 9.53pm daily between Malpensa (Terminal 1) and Cadorna metro station (journey time 40mins), stopping at Bovisa/Politecnico, Saronno and Busto Arsizio. Tickets (€5.50-€11) can be bought at the Ferrovie Nord desks in the airport and at stations where the Malpensa Express stops, as well as all FN stations (they cost more if bought on the train), and must be stamped in the machines on the platform before boarding.

The train is replaced by a non-stop bus service (50mins) early mornings (4.20am and 5am from Cadorna, and 5.53am from Malpensa) and in the evenings (9-10.30pm from Cadorna, and 10pm-1.30am from Malpensa). A free shuttle bus runs every 15mins between Malpensa's two terminals.

Two bus services link Malpensa to Milan. The **Malpensa Bus Express** (02 240 7954) leaves every 30mins (6am-12.30am from Malpensa and 5.15am-9.15pm from Stazione Centrale) and takes 50 minutes. Tickets cost €2.75-€5.50 and are available in the arrivals terminals at the airport, in piazza Luigi di Savoia by Stazione Centrale, at the tourist office near the Duomo or on the bus. The service also stops at Terminal 2 and the new Fiera complex at Rho by request.

Malpensa Shuttle (0331 258 411, recorded information in English 02 5858 3185, www.malpensashuttle.it) services depart every 20mins (5.30am-12.15am from Terminal 1; 4.15am-11.15pm from Stazione Centrale) and take 50mins. Buses stop at the new Fiera on request. Tickets (€3.50-€7) can be bought in the airport arrivals halls, at most Stazione Centrale newsstands or on the bus. Malpensa Shuttle also runs ten shuttle bus services a day each way between Malpensa and Linate, with request stops at Terminal 2 (journey time 70mins). Tickets can be bought on the bus, and cost €5-€10.

A taxi (*see also p221*) from Malpensa to Milan has its fee fixed at €70; ask to make sure. Journey time is 45mins, more in rush hour. Use only official white taxis at the ranks.

Aeroporto di Linate

Milan's national airport (flight information 02 7485 2200, switchboard 02 74851, www.sea-aeroportimilano.it) is in Segrate, about 7km (4.5 miles) from the city centre. It handles domestic and continental flights.

There is no train service into Milan from Linate, but the excellent **ATM bus 73** leaves every ten minutes from Linate Airport and San Babila metro station. Travel time is around 25mins (40mins at rush hour). An ordinary €1 city bus ticket is valid for the airport service.

Starfly services (02 5858 7237) leave every 30mins (15mins at peak times) and link Linate airport and Stazione Centrale (5am-11.30pm from Linate; 5.40am-9.30pm from Stazione Centrale). Tickets cost €2-€4 and must be bought from the driver.

A taxi (*see also p221*) to or from Linate will cost €20-€25.

Aeroporto di Orio al Serio

Bergamo's airport (information 035 326 323, www.orioaeroporto.it) is in Orio al Serio, about 45km (28 miles) from Milan and 5km (three miles) from Bergamo. It handles national, international and budget airline flights. When Milan's airports are fog-bound, flights are often diverted here.

Trains leave regularly from Bergamo's station for Milan's Stazione Centrale or Garibaldi. Prices vary, depending on the train, from €3.50-€4; journey time is about 1hr. From the airport the **ATB bus 1C** (www.atb.bergamo.it) runs to the train station every 30mins, 5am-midnight (journey time 10mins), for €1.65. A taxi will cost you about €15.

Autostradale (information 02 7200 1304, www.autostradale.it) runs buses 4.30am-1am daily from Orio al Serio to the air terminal at Milan's Stazione Centrale; 4am-11.30pm in the other direction. Tickets can be bought on board and cost €4.45-€8.90 (three tickets €17.80).

Orioshuttle (035 319 366, www.orioshuttle.com) runs 4.50am-12.15am from Orio to Stazione Centrale; 4am-11.15pm in the other direction. The trip takes 1hr. Tickets are €4-€8 and can be bought on the bus, from the office at the station or from Orioshuttle staff at the airport. During trade fairs, Orioshuttle runs buses from the airport to FieraMilano in Rho.

Airlines

Alitalia 06 2222/www.alitalia.it.
BMIbaby +44 (0)871 224 0224/
www.bmibaby.com.
British Airways 199 712 266/
www.britishairways.com.
EasyJet 848 887 766/www.easyjet.com.
FlyBe +44 (0)1392 268529/
www.flybe.com.
Ryanair 899 678 910/www.ryanair.com.

By bus

Milan's central bus station is at metro stop Lampugnano (02 300 891), although some buses still pick up and drop off from piazza Freud in front of Stazione Garibaldi. A useful source of timetables is www. orariautobus.it, which also has links to coach companies that stop in Milan. Two companies that run international coaches are **Autostradale** (02 7200 1304, www.autostradale.it) and **Eurolines** (055 32 89 939, www.eurolines.it).

By train

International and long-distance train services arrive at and depart from Milan's Stazione Centrale. The station is a pickpocket's paradise, so keep a careful eye on your possessions. If you arrive late in the evening, it's advisable to take a taxi to your destination; the metro stops shortly after midnight (see p221). Note that Stazione Centrale is being refurbished and taxi ranks have recently been moved to the sides of the station. For information on buying train tickets, see p220.

Public transport

For transport map, see p256. The services operated by the **Azienda Trasporti Milanesi** (800 80 81 81/www.atm-mi.it) are the core of Milan's transport system, serving the inner-city rete urbana (urban network) and the Greater Milan area. ATM manages a network of three metropolitan railway lines and 120 tram, trolley bus and bus line. Public transport in Milan is fairly safe, even at night. Watch out for pickpockets in packed buses and subways.

In Milan

There are three underground (metro) lines. These are Linea 1, 2 and 3, aka red (rossa), green (verde) and yellow (gialla) lines. Stations are signposted with a red 'M'. A fourth service, the passante ferroviario urban railway, is shown in blue on transport maps and indicated by the letter 'R' above ground. As well as providing a link between metro stations inside the city, the passante serves outlying suburban areas, where it runs overground.

The city centre is circled by three concentric ring roads, each of which is served by public transport. Buses 50, 58, 61 and 94 travel portions of the inner ring, which passes close to the centre; trams 29 and 30 serve the middle ring; buses 90, 91 and 92 the outer ring road. Many trams cut across the city, intersecting the ring roads and continuing into outlying or suburban areas. One such is number 2, which runs from Stazione Centrale in the north through many of Milan's most famous tourist spots (via Manzoni, piazza della Scala, piazza Duomo, via Torino, corso Genova, corso Colombo) and ripa di Porta Ticinese in the south.

Metro trains run every 4-5mins, 6am-12.30am daily

(more frequently during rush hour); after 9pm, services run every 10-12mins until about 12.30am. After then, there are night buses, which replace metro lines 1 and 3 until about 2am. All ATM bus and tram services – except night services (see below) – also run between 6am and midnight daily, departing every 5-20mins. Doors for boarding are marked entrata; doors for alighting are marked uscita. Some new trams and buses require you to push a button to open the doors. If you wish to alight from a bus, make sure you have pushed one of the red buttons alerting the driver that the next stop is requested (fermata prenotata).

Each bus stop shows all stops made on the route, and a timetable for weekdays (feriali), Saturdays (sabato/ pre-festivi) and Sundays and holidays (domenica e festivi). Many stops have electronic signs showing how long you have to wait for your bus/tram. Timetables change for the summer, when Milan empties.

Radiobus (02 4803 4803, 1pm-2am daily) is a request-only bus service run by ATM. Call (up to three days ahead) to specify your route and the time you want to travel, and the bus will meet you at the most convenient stop. The service is rarely busy, and can feel like a private minibus (for a fraction of the cost of a taxi). Tickets are sold at all ATM sale points (€1.50) and on the bus (€3).

Night services

The three metro lines operate until 12.30am; buses then ply routes 1 and 3 until about 2am. There are also 55 night bus and tram routes, which run from 12.30am to 2.30am. There is no service between 2.30am and 6am.

Tourist services

See also p51 **Guided tours**. The hop-on, hop-off **CitySightseeing Milano** bus

(€20, 9.30am-7.30pm daily) is run by the tourist information centre in association with Zani Viaggi (02 867 131, www.zaniviaggi.it). Its two lines take in all the big sights. **Navigli Lombardi** (02 667 9131, www.navigilombardi.it) runs boat tours of the canal system (*see p86*).

Tickets & fares

Before boarding, you must buy an ATM ticket: at metro stations (6am-8pm at staffed desks, from ticket machines at other times), ATM points (Duomo, Loreto, Centrale, Romolo), *tabaccherie*, bars and most newsstands, as well as Lampugnano, Bisceglie and Famagosta station car parks. It's well to stock up, as tickets are hard to come by after 8pm, when most bars shut. If you're caught without a ticket, you will be fined.

The same tickets are valid on all ATM bus, tram and metro lines within the inner-city *rete urbana* (urban network). Travel to and through other zones requires appropriate tickets.

When you board a tram or bus, stamp tickets in the machines by the rear and/or front doors. Travelling without paying looks easy, but there are ticket inspectors around; if caught, you'll be fined €34.20 (or more) on the spot. In the metro, swipe your ticket in a machine as you go in and out.

A single ticket (**biglietto singolo**, €1) is valid for 75mins from when stamped; it can be used on unlimited ATM trams and buses on the *rete urbana* (inner-city network), plus one trip on the metro. This ticket is also valid on the *passante ferroviario* and on the urban sections of the Ferrovie Nord and Ferrovie dello Stato mainline railways.

An **abbonamento serale** (€1.80) can be used from 8pm to the end of the service.

An **abbonamento giornaliero** (€3) is valid for unlimited use for 24hrs on all transport in the *rete urbana*.

An **abbonamento bigiornaliero** (€5.50) is valid for 48hrs for unlimited use on all transport in the *rete urbana*.

The **settimanale** (€6.70) can be used for two trips of up to 75mins in one day, from Monday to Saturday. If one day is missed, the ticket can also be used on the Sunday.

A **carnet** (€9.20) is a strip worth ten tickets; it cannot be used by more than one person.

Armed with a passport-sized photo, you can buy a €10 magnetic pass that can be recharged with the following amounts:

An **abbonamento settimanale** (€9) is valid for seven days' unlimited use of all transport in the *rete urbana*.

An **abbonamento mensile** (€30) is valid for a month's unlimited use of all transport in the *rete urbana*, and entitles you to discounts on some concerts and exhibitions.

Public transport information

Information on routes, tickets and changes can be found at the ATM points in the metro stations at Duomo, Cadorna, Loreto, Centrale and Romolo (all 7.45am-7.15pm), by ringing freephone 800 808181 (also in English, 7.30am-7.30pm) or at www.atm-mi.it. You can buy a comprehensive city transport map at ATM points and most newsstands for €5.

Greater Milan services

ATM manages a Greater Milan fare system called **SITAM** (*Sistema Integrato Trasporti Area Milanese* or Milan Area Integrated Transport System). Many extra-urban transport operators with routes running into the city participate in this system. Beyond the *rete urbana* (*see p219*) are concentric coloured zones: yellow, green, red, blue, brown, orange, purple and grey. Fares depend on the number of zones travelled through.

Tickets

To travel from what Milanese call '*l'hinterland*' (the suburbs) to the city, or from one suburb to another, *biglietti interurbani* (inter-urban tickets) and *biglietti cumulativi* (combined tickets) are available. The former can be used exclusively on routes outside the *rete urbana* (or to travel from the city to the suburbs, and vice versa); the latter can be used in the suburbs and also on the urban network.

The **abbonamento 1 giorno cumulativo Area Grande** (€4.70-€8.65) is the most useful of the cumulative tickets, as it's valid for one day on all ATM routes and most inter-urban SITAM routes. There are special €4 return tickets (*biglietti andata e ritorno Rho Fiera*) between the city and FieraMilano in Rho.

Rail services

Milan's metropolitan rail network (*see above*) is heavily used. Regular bus/tram/metro tickets are valid on trains as far as the stations marked *limite tariffe urbana* (urban tariff limit) in red (*see map p256*).

For more information on train travel in the Lombardy region, *see p179* and also individual destinations in the **Trips Out of Town** section. The Lombardy Region's online guide (Italian only) is useful for planning journeys: www.trasporti.regione.lombardia.it.

Mainline train services are operated by state-run **Ferrovie dello Stato** (FS, aka Trenitalia) and private company **Ferrovie Nord**. Note that the main Stazione Centrale is undergoing refurbishment until 2010; keep abreast of temporary closures at www.grandistazioni.it.

FS (call centre) *892 021/06 6847 5475 (from abroad only).* **Open** 24hrs daily.
FS (disabled passengers) *199 303 060* **Open** 7am-9pm daily.
FS (lost & found) *02 6371 2667 (Stazione Centrale)/892 021 (national number).* **Open** 8.30am-4pm Mon-Fri/24hrs daily.

Train timetables & tickets

Train timetables can be bought at any newsstand. The easiest to read is *Nuovo Grippaudo Orario*, which includes all suburban train timetables, as well as boat schedules for Lake Maggiore, Como and Garda.

Train tickets can be bought at stations or travel agents with an FS sign, by credit card on 892 021 (24hrs, €0.54/min) or 06 6847 5475 (from abroad only), or on the FS website (www.trenitalia.com). The site is well organised and available in English, though making reservations and paying is a challenge. Children under 12 pay half fare; children under four travel free if they don't occupy a seat. There are also special deals for family bookings. For information on taking wheelchairs, *see p225*.

Train fares in Italy are much cheaper than in the UK, and various tariffs may be available on one route. Be aware that the cheaper the fare, the longer the train takes. However, do check timetables carefully – for short distances, an InterCity (IC) may be only slightly quicker than an *inter-regionale*. EuroCity (EC) or Eurostar (ES) cost more than the IC and are even faster. Reservations are essential on IC and ES trains.

Always stamp your train ticket – and any supplements – in the yellow machines by each platform before boarding the train. Eurostar and InterCity tickets do not have to be stamped, as their booking information is printed on them, but it's advisable to do so all the same.

Should you have to board a train without a ticket, get on at the front and find the conductor immediately. This way, you may only have to pay a €5 penalty, although the only acceptable excuse is if the ticket offices at the station are closed. If you wait for the ticket collector to come and find you, you'll be liable for a fine of €40.

Milan's main stations are listed below. For travel to other destinations in Lombardy, *see pp178-216* **Trips Out of Town**.

Stazione Centrale *Piazzale Duca D'Aosta, North.* **Map** p249 G3. Connects with metro lines 2 and 3.
Stazione di Cadorna (Ferrovie Nord) *Piazzale Cadorna, West.* **Map** p248 C6. Connects with metro lines 1 and 2 and the Malpensa Express.
Stazione Lambrate *Piazza Bottini, East.* Connects with metro line 2.
Stazione Porta Garibaldi *Piazza Freud, North.* **Map** p248 D3. Connects with metro line 2, the *passante ferroviario* and Milan's bus station.
Stazione Porta Genova *Piazza Porta Genova, South.* **Map** p250 B9. Connects with metro line 2.

Taxis

Licensed taxis are white and meter-operated. If a driver approaches you at the airport, Stazione Centrale or any of the major tourist spots muttering 'Taxi?', always refuse – he is likely to charge up to four times the standard rate.

Most of Milan's taxi drivers are honest; if, however, you suspect you're being ripped off, make a note of the driver's name and number from the metal plaque inside the car's rear door. The more openly you do this, the more likely you are to see the fare drop to its proper level. Report misdemeanours to the drivers' co-operative (the number is on the outside of each car) or, in serious cases, the police.

Fares & surcharges

When you pick up a taxi at a rank or hail one in the street, the meter should read zero. As you set off, it will indicate the minimum fare – €3.10 at time of writing – for the first 200 metres, after which the charge increases according to time and distance. Minimum fare on Sundays, public holidays and at night (9pm-6am) is €6.10.

Taxi ranks

Ranks are indicated by a white sign with 'Taxi' in black. In the centre there are ranks at largo Augusto, via Feltrami, piazzale Cadorna, largo Carrobbio, piazza Cavour, via Cordusio, piazza Duomo, piazza Fontana, via Gonzaga, corso Italia, via Manara, via Pisoni, via Santa Maria Segreta, via Mercato, via Francesco, corso Matteotti, via San Raffaele, via Spaderi, via Verri and via San Pietro all'Orto.

Phone cabs

To phone for a taxi, look under 'Taxi' in the phone book or dial one of the companies listed below. Give street and number, or name and location of a bar, club or restaurant where you wish to be picked up. You'll be given the taxi code (always a location and a number) and a time – for example, '*Como 69, tre minuti*' ('Como 69, in three minutes'). The meter will start from the moment the taxi sets off to pick you up. If you aim to use a taxi at rush hour, during a major event, or in bad weather, order well in advance.

Radio Taxi *02 8585*.
Taxi Blu *02 4040*.
Yellow Taxi *02 6969*.

Driving

Short-term visitors should have no trouble driving with their home licences, although if they are written in different scripts or less common languages, an international licence can be useful. Driving licences issued in other EU states are valid in Italy, and there is no legal obligation to convert them. Other licences must be converted after the owner has been resident in Italy for one year. Full details can be found on the

Directory

Automobile Club of Italy's website (ACI; www.aci.it).

Italy's system of points (*punti*) brings the country's road legislation in line with the rest of Europe. Traffic cops will deduct a certain number of points for infringements like speeding, jumping red lights and so on. You have 20 points to start with; when you lose them all, you must resit your driving test within 30 days, or your licence will be suspended.

Restricted areas

Large sections of the city centre are pedestrianised and closed to traffic at all times, unless you are a resident; the many signposts will direct you to the ring roads around the centre, making it difficult to reach the centre by car. If you do manage to slip into unauthorised areas, you may be fined and your car may be wheel-clamped if you park; you'll have to pay a fine and a charge to have the clamp removed. The best thing is to head for the *autosilos* (guarded car parks; *see below*) which, if not cheap, are at least safe. If you're in a hired car or have foreign plates and are stopped, mention the name of your hotel, and you'll probably be waved on.

Some Sundays are no-car days. These are heavily advertised beforehand, which is just as well, as they are rigidly enforced in the city centre. There are, however, exceptions for moving around outside the inner ring road.

The *corsie veloci* (fast lanes) that form the central parts of the ring roads are strictly for buses and taxis.

Breakdown services

It's advisable to join a national motoring organisation, such as the AA or RAC in Britain or the AAA in the US, before taking a car to Italy. These organisations have reciprocal arrangements with the Automobile Club d'Italia.

If you need extensive repairs and don't know a mechanic, pay a bit more and go to a manufacturer's official dealer, as reliable service at many garages depends on having built up a good client-mechanic relationship over several years. Dealers are listed in the *Pagine Gialle* (*www.paginegialle.it*) under 'Auto', along with specialist repairers such as *gommista* (tyres), *marmitte* (exhausts) and *carrozzerie* (bodywork and windscreens). The English-language *Yellow Pages*, available from most big bookshops, lists garages where English is spoken.

Automobile Club d'Italia (ACI)

Corso Venezia 43, East (02 77451/ 24hr emergency service 803 116/24hr traffic information 1518/www.acimi.it). Metro Palestro. **Open** 8.20am-1pm, 2-5.20pm Mon-Fri. **Map** p249 F6/ 252 F6.
The ACI has English-speaking staff. Members of associated organisations are entitled to free basic repairs, and to other services at preferential rates. This is still the best place to call in the event of a breakdown, even if you're not a member. You will be charged, but prices are generally reasonable.

Europ Assistance

Customer service 800 013 529/ 24hr assistance (non-members) 803 803/24hr assistance (members) 02 58241/www.europassistance.it. Via Albricci 2, Centre (02 5824 2424). Metro Missori/bus 54, 65/tram 12, 27. **Open** 9am-1pm, 2-6pm Mon-Fri. **Credit** AmEx, DC, MC, V. **Map** p251 E7/p252 E7.
Piazza Trento 8, South (02 583 841). Metro Lodi/bus 90, 91. **Open** 9am-1pm, 2-6pm Mon-Fri. **Credit** AmEx, DC, MC, V. **Map** p251 F10.
Europ Assistance has been offering a 24-hour breakdown service in Italy since 1968. Prices are reasonable, and staff speak good English.

Parking

Parking in Milan is a complete nightmare: it's best to leave your car in one of the 20-odd guarded car parks in the centre. Alternatively, use the **Sosta** Milano parking system, which operates in most of the city centre and Fiera: parking areas are marked on the road with blue lines; those with yellow lines are strictly for residents only. Buy tickets (€1.50/hr) at newsstands, *tabaccherie* (*see p232*), from some parking attendants or at the ATM points in Duomo and Cadorna, and scratch them to indicate the day and time. Leave the ticket visible on the dashboard. You can have a maximum of two hours. Parking is generally free after 8pm, except within the inner ring road (where €2 will get you five hours). Cars with disabled signs can park free within blue stripes.

Watch out for signs by entrances saying '*passo carrabile*' (access at all times), '*sosta vietata*' (no parking) and road signs denoting spaces reserved for handicapped drivers. The sign '*zona rimozione*' (tow-away area) means no parking and is valid for the whole street, or until you come to a tow-away sign with a red line through it. If a street or square that has no cars parked in it, you can assume it's a seriously enforced no-parking zone. Be aware of the weekly street cleaning that operates throughout Milan. Signposts along the road will tell you when that road and nearby streets are to be cleaned, and this means from midnight onwards of that day. If your car is found parked on the road at that time, expect a €35 fine. Avoid it by parking in neighbouring streets or on the pavement. In some areas, self-appointed *parcheggiatori* will look after your car for a small fee; although this practice is illegal, it's often worth coughing up to ensure your tyres remain intact.

Most of the car parks below lower their hourly rates after the first one to three hours.

Autosilo Diaz *Piazza Diaz, Centre (02 8646 0077). Metro Duomo or Missori/bus 54/tram 24.* **Open** 7am-2am daily. **Rates** €3/hr; €25/24hrs. **Credit** AmEx, DC, MC, V. **Map** p251 E7/p252 E7.

Garage Meravigli *Via Camperio 4, North (02 8646 1784). Metro Cairoli/bus 50, 58/tram 18.* **Open** 7am-midnight (entry until 7pm) Mon-Sat. **Rates** €5/hr; €31.20/24hrs. **Map** p248 D6/p252 D6.

Garage Zeus *Corso Europa 2, Centre (02 7602 2220). Metro San Babila/bus 54, 60, 73.* **Open** 24hrs daily. **Rates** €5/hr; €40/24hrs. **Map** p251 E7/p252 E7.

Mediolanum Parking *Largo Corsia dei Servi 15, Centre (02 7600 8467). Metro San Babila/bus 54.* **Open** 7am-1am daily. **Rates** €3/hr; €31/24 hrs.

Rinascente *Via Agnello, Centre (02 885 2419). Metro Duomo.* **Open** 7.30am-1.30am daily. **Rates** €3/hr; €72/24 hrs. **Credit** AmEx, DC, MC, V. **Map** p251 E6/p252 E6.

Car pounds

If you can't find your car, chances are it has been towed away. There's an information office staffed by police in via Beccaria 19, open 24hrs; ring it on 02 7727 0280 quoting your number plate, car model and where the car was last seen, and they'll tell you which car pound it has been taken to. It costs €62 to recover your car, on top of fines.

Fuel

Petrol stations sell regular petrol (*benzina*), unleaded petrol (*senza piombo* or *verde*) and diesel (*gasolio*). Liquid propane is GPL. Most stations offer full service on weekdays, but are often closed for lunch. At night and on Sundays, many have self-service pumps that accept €5, €10 or €20 notes in good condition. Most stations accept credit cards.

Car hire

To hire a car you must be over 21 (in some cases, 23) and have held a licence for at least a year. It's advisable to take out collision damage waiver and personal accident insurance on

top of basic third party cover. Companies that do not offer CDW are best avoided.

Avis

National bookings *(06 452 108 391/www.avisautonoleggio.it).* **Open** 24hrs daily.

Linate airport *(02 715 123).* **Open** 7am-midnight daily.

Malpensa airport *(02 585 8481).* **Open** 8am-midnight daily.

Piazza Diaz 6 *Centre (02 8901 0645). Metro Duomo/bus 54.* **Open** 8am-7pm Mon-Fri; 8am-2pm Sat. **Map** p251 E7/p252 E7.

Stazione Centrale *North (02 669 0280).* **Open** 8am-7pm Mon-Fri; 8am-2pm Sat. **Map** p249 G3.

All Credit AmEx, DC, MC, V.

Hertz

National bookings *(199 113 311/ www.hertz.it).* **Open** 8am-11pm daily.

Linate airport *02 7020 0256).* **Open** 7.30am-12.30am daily.

Malpensa airport *(02 5858 1312).* **Open** 7.30am-midnight daily.

Piazza Duca d'Aosta 9 *Stazione Centrale, North (02 6698 5151).* **Open** 8am-8pm Mon-Fri; 8am-2pm Sat, Sun. **Map** p249 G3.

Via Alcuino 16 *West (02 3360 3073). Metro Lotto/bus 48, 78.* **Open** 8am-7pm Mon-Fri; 8am-1pm Sat. **All** Credit AmEx, DC, MC, V.

Bicycles & motorbikes

Aggressive drivers, tram tracks and cobbled streets mean Milan is tough for cyclists. But, with the introduction of cycle paths and growing pedestrianisation, cycling is getting a little easier. The main paths are from the centre, north along via Melchiorre Gioia, south-east along Porta Romagna/corso Lodi, west along via Dezza and Monte Rosa, and south along the Navigli; there's also one in Parco Sempione. Be warned, however, that there are gaps in the paths where you'll have to brave the traffic.

Bikes are allowed on the metro after 8pm on weekdays; after 10am on Saturdays; and all day Sundays and holidays, and in August. There's an extra €1 charge and access is in the second, fifth and last

carriage of the train. Bikes can also be taken on all direct, regional and inter-regional trains for €3.50.

Ciclobby (02 6931 1624, www.ciclobby.it) organises bike tours on most weekends. The **Circolo Ricreativo Culturale Arci** (mobile 340 381 2708, www.arciquartiere. org) organises tours out of Milan every Sunday in spring and autumn (for members, occasionally in collaboration with Ciclobby).

Bike & motorbike hire

To hire a scooter or moped (*motorino*) you'll need a credit card, ID and a cash deposit. Helmets are required on all kinds of scooters, motorbikes or mopeds; the police enforce this rule strictly.

For bicycles, it's normally enough to leave ID; for mopeds up to 50cc, you need to be over 14; a driver's licence is needed for anything over 50cc.

AWS Bicimotor

Via Ponte Seveso 33, North (02 6707 2145/www.awsbici.com). Metro Centrale FS or Sondrio/bus 90, 91, 92/tram 2. **Open** 9am-1pm, 3-7pm Tue-Sat. **Rates** €11/24hrs; €2.60 per additional day; €100 deposit. **Credit** MC, V. **Map** p249 F2.
City, mountain and electric bike rental.

Biancoblu

Via Gallarate 33, West (02 308 2470/ www.biancoblu.com). Tram 14, 19, 33. **Open** 9am-12.30pm, 2.30-7pm Mon-Fri; 8-9am 6-8pm Sat; 8-10am 6-8pm Sun. **Rates** €26/day; €75 deposit. **Credit** AmEx, DC, MC, V.
Scooters and powerbikes for rent.

Cicli Rossignoli

Corso Garibaldi 65-71, North (02 804 960/www.rossignoli.it). Metro Moscova/bus 41, 43, 91/tram 3, 4. **Open** 2.30-7.30pm Mon; 9am-12.30pm, 2.30-7.30pm Tue-Sat. **Rates** €6/half day; €10/day; €18/wknd; €100 deposit. **Credit** MC, V. **Map** p248 D4.
City and mountain bikes.

Mototouring

Via del Ricordo 31, East (02 2720 1556/www.mototouring.com). Metro Crescenzago then bus 53. **Open** 9am-6pm Mon-Sat. **Rates** €35/day; €1,000 deposit. **Credit** AmEx, DC, MC, V.
Bikes, motorbikes and scooters.

Directory

Resources A-Z

Age restrictions

The age of consent is 14 for both gay and straight. Beer and wine can be bought at bars from the age of 16, spirits from 18. Cigarettes cannot be sold to under-16s. Anyone aged 14 or over can ride a moped or scooter of 50cc; no licence is needed (though this may change). You must be over 18 to drive and over 21 to hire a car.

Business

If you're setting up a business, visit the commercial section of your embassy or consulate (*see p226*). Personal contacts will smooth your way immensely: use them shamelessly.

American Chamber of Commerce *Via Cantù 1, Centre (02 869 0661/ www.amcham.it). Metro Cordusio or Duomo/bus 50/tram 19, 24, 27.* **Open** 9am-1pm, 2-6pm Mon-Fri. **Map** p250 D7/p252 D7.

British Chamber of Commerce *Via Dante 12, North (02 877 798/www.brit chamitaly.com). Metro Cairoli/bus 50/ tram 1, 24, 27.* **Open** 9am-1pm, 2-6pm Mon-Fri. **Map** p248 D6/p252 D6.

Business centres

Conservatorio 22 *Via Conservatorio 22, East (freephone 800 895 562/02 77 291/www.cogesta.eu). Metro San Babila/bus 54, 61.* **Open** 8.30am-9.30pm Mon-Fri; 9am-noon Sat. **Map** p251 F6/p252 F6.

Executive Service Network *Via Vincenzo Monti 8, West (freephone 800 938 373/02 467 121/www. executivenetwork.it). Metro Cadorna or Conciliazione/bus 61, 68/tram 1, 19, 27.* **Open** 7.30am-11pm Mon-Fri. **Map** p250 B6.

Tiempo Group *Via Giovanni da Udine 34, North (02 3809 3456/www.tiempo nord.it). Bus 40, 69/tram 14, 19, 33.* **Open** 8.30am-8pm Mon-Fri; 8.30am-12.30pm Sat.

Conventions & conferences

Business-oriented Milan has excellent conference facilities in all categories and locations.

The city hosts scores of trade fairs each year at the newer Fiera in Rho (*see p94*), and the odd fair at Fiera MilanoCity (*see p94*). Conferences can be held in magnificent historic buildings such as the Milan Chamber of Commerce's very central Palazzo Giureconsulti (piazza Mercanti 2, 02 8515 5873, www.palazzoaffari.it) or its equally delightful Palazzo Turati (via Meravigli 9B, 02 8518 5873, www.palazzo turati.it), or in the very modern Magna Pars (via Tortona 15, 02 8940 1384, www.magna pars.it), near the fashionable Navigli district. Also, most major hotels can host events.

If you don't wish to handle the practical details yourself, an agency will smooth the way for you. **Italcongressi** (www. italcongressi.com) can supply a lot of useful information on regional conference organisers.

AIM Group *Via Ripamonti 129 (02 566 011/www.aimgroup.eu).* **Easy Congress** *Via Console Flaminio 19 (02 2159 1024/ www.easycongress.net).* **PromoEst** *Via Buonarroti 2 (02 4391 2468/www.promoest.com).*

Couriers

International
DHL *199 199 345/www.dhl.it.* **Federal Express** *freephone 800 123 800/www.fedex.com/it.* **TNT/Rinaldi** *803 868/www.tntitaly.it.* **UPS** *freephone 800 877 877/ www.ups.com/it.*

Local
Shadow *02 8912 5505.*

Interpreters & translators

See *traduttori e interpreti* in the *Pagine Gialle* (*www.pagine gialle.it*). The conference organisers listed above can also arrange translation.

Communication Trend Italia *02 669 1338/ www.cti-communication.it.*

International Association of Conference Interpreters (AIIC) *+41 22 908 15 40/ www.aiic.net.* **Soget** *02 485 9141/www.soget.com*

Customs

Travellers arriving from other EU countries do not have to declare goods imported into or exported out of Italy for personal use, up to the following limits: 800 cigarettes or 200 cigars or 1kg tobacco; ten litres of alcoholic drinks (above 22 per cent); 90 litres of wine (including 60 litres of sparkling wine) and 110 litres of beer. Visitors are also allowed to carry up to €12,500 in cash.

For visitors arriving from non-EU countries, the following limits apply: 200 cigarettes or 100 small cigars or 50 cigars or 250g (8.8oz) of tobacco; one litre of spirits (over 22 per cent alcohol) or two litres of wine; 50g (1.76oz) of perfume or various goods up to the value of €175. Visitors are also allowed to carry up to €12,500 in cash.

Disabled

The best source of information is **AIAS** (Associazione Italiana Assistenza Spastici). Most literature (like their booklet *Milano Facile*) is in Italian, but the website has up-to-date information on Milan and Lombardy in English. You can send a specific request to aiasmi.vacanze@tiscalinet.it to receive information in English.

The city council operates a *sportello disabili* (disabled desk), where much helpful information is dispensed, although in Italian only. It can also provide a booklet in English, *Region of Lombardy Disability Advice Centre: Information and Services.*

AIAS Milano Onlus *02 330 2021/*
www.milanopertutti.it
Sportello disabili *Via Fabio Filzi 22,
North (02 6765 4740/sportello_disabili
@regione.lombardia.it).* Metro *Centrale
FS, Gioia or Repubblica/tram 2, 9, 33.*
Open 9am-5.30pm Mon-Thur; 9am-
1.30pm Fri. **Map** p249 F3.

Hotels & restaurants

AIAS (*see above*) keeps an list
of wheelchair-accessible hotels:
see the website for listings.

Few restaurants or bars are
fully accessible, though staff
will be more than willing to
help you at most of them. The
situation improves in summer,
when tables are placed outside.
AIAS lists accessible bars
and restaurants in all zones of
Milan – see under *Cerca locale*
at the *Banca dati accessibilità*
page of its website.

Sightseeing

Pavements in the centre are
narrow, and cobbled streets
are a challenge; but most street
corners have pram/wheelchair
ramps, and well-designed
ramps and lifts and disabled
toilets have been installed at
many of the city's museums.
Visit the AIAS website (*see
above*) for recommended routes
around the city for disabled
people, and accessibility to all
the city's points of interest.

Toilets

Although the law requires
all public facilities to have
disabled toilets, many of those
in old buildings have yet to
pay attention to the rules. The
more modern-looking the bar,
restaurant, convention facility
or museum, the more likely
it is to have appropriately
adapted its public facilities.

Transport

Some city transport services
are equipped for disabled
travellers. The Linea 3 metro
line is fully accessible by
elevators, but the older
lines 1 and 2 still have some
limitations; stations currently
fitted with lifts are:
Linea 1: Sesto Marelli,
Gorla, Loreto, Porta Venezia,
Palestro, San Babila, Cordusio,
Cairoli, Cadorna, Pagano,
Amendola Fiera, Lampugnano,
Bonola, Gambara, Bande
Nere, Inganni.
Linea 2: Romolo, Porta
Genova, Sant'Agostino,
Sant'Ambrogio, Cadorna,
Garibaldi FS, Gioia, Centrale
FS, Loreto, Piola, Lambrate,
Udine, Cascina Gobba.
Other stations have
wheelchair lifts fitted to the
stairs; ask the guard at the
ticket barrier for assistance.
For more information, call the
freephone number 800 808 181
or visit an ATM information
point (*see p220*). The evening
Radiobus service (*see p219*)
has lifts for wheelchairs and
spoken messages for the blind.
A number of the city's buses
and trams provide easy access
for disabled people.

In stations and airports, a
rubber strip along the floor
of passageways and corridors
helps orientate blind or
partially sighted people.

The Ferrovie dello Stato (*see
p220*) is slowly introducing
easy-access carriages. Trains
with wheelchair facilities are
indicated by a wheelchair
symbol on timetables. Many
medium- and long-distance
trains have a carriage
equipped to transport two
wheelchairs plus companion.
The **CAD Centro Assistenza
Disabili** (disabled assistance
assistenzaclientidisabili.mi@
trenitalia.it or 02 6707 0958
for Milan, or 0187 807 756
nationwide) at Centrale,
Cadorna or Garibaldi stations
will arrange help for boarding
or alighting from trains. Call
well in advance (minimum one
hour) to organise assistance in
Milan and other Italian cities.
For travel at night (10pm-6am),
call 12 hours ahead. For help
on international trains, the
request must be made two
days in advance. Details of
services for the disabled can be
found in *Services for Disabled
Passengers*, published by
Trenitalia and available from
the ticket offices at Stazione
Centrale. There's also a
nationwide disabled passenger
helpline (199 303 060).

Transport to Linate (bus
73) and Malpensa (Malpensa
Express) airports (*see p218*) is
wheelchair-friendly. Book taxis
in advance, specifying if you
need a car large enough to cope
with a wheelchair (*carrozzella*).
Alternatively, the following
services use small vans and
seating for up to eight; try to
book at least 48 hours ahead.

A.la.t.Ha *02 422 571/www.alatha.it.*
Open by appointment.
CTA *02 359 9360/ctagigli@virgilio.it.*
Open 7.30am-6pm Mon-Fri;
8am-noon Sat.
Missione Handicap *02 4229 0549/
coopsocmissionehandicap@virgilio.it.*
Open 7.30am-6pm Mon-Fri.

Wheelchair hire

Farmacie (pharmacies, *see
p227*) rent wheelchairs or
can direct you to specialised
wheelchair rental services.

Drugs

Italy's once lax drug laws were
toughened up by the previous
Berlusconi government in
2006. It is illegal to produce,
sell, distribute or deliver any
type of drug, either hard or
soft. If you are found holding
amounts considered to be for
personal use (for example, a
few grams of cannabis or half
a gram of cocaine), you will be
fined. Carry any more and you
risk a jail sentence. Sniffer
dogs are on watch at most
ports of entry into Italy.

Electricity

Most wiring systems run at
220V, which is compatible with
British-bought appliances.

Directory

With US 110V equipment you need a current transformer. A few systems in old buildings are 125V. Socket sizes, especially in older buildings, are not always standard, but two-pin adaptor plugs (*riduttori*) can be bought at any electrical shop (*elettricità*).

Embassies & consulates

For a full list of consulates, see *Consolati* in the *Pagine Gialle*.

Australia *Via Borgogna 2, Centre (02 777 041). Metro San Babila/bus 54, 60, 61, 73.* **Open** 9am-5pm Mon-Thur; 9am-4.15pm Fri. **Map** p249 F6/p252 F6.
South Africa *Vicolo San Giovanni sul Muro 4, Centre (02 885 8581). Metro Cairoli/tram 1, 16, 18, 19, 20.* **Open** 8.30am-4.45pm Mon-Fri. **Map** p248 D6/p252 D6.
UK *Via San Paolo 7, Centre (02 723 001). Metro Duomo or San Babila/bus 15, 60, 73/tram 1, 2, 20.* **Open** 9.15am-12.15pm, 2.30-4.30pm Mon-Fri. **Map** p251 E6/p252 E6.
US *Via Principe Amedeo 2-10, North (02 290 351). Metro Turati/tram 1, 2, 94.* **Open** 8.30am-4.30pm Mon-Fri. **Map** p249 E5.

Emergencies

See also below **Health**; *p230* **Money**; *p230* **Police**; *p231* **Safety & security**.

Thefts or losses should be reported immediately at the nearest police station (*see p230*). Report loss of your passport to your embassy or consulate (*see above*). Report loss of credit card or travellers' cheques immediately to your credit card supplier (*see p230*).

National emergency numbers

Ambulance *Ambulanza 118.*
Child helpline *114*
Fire service *Vigili del Fuoco 115.*
Police Carabinieri *(English helpline) 112; Polizia di Stato 113.*

Domestic emergencies

If you need to report a malfunction, these emergency lines are open 24 hours a day.

Electricity *AEM 02 2521; Enel 803500.*
Gas *AEM 02 5255.*
Telephone *Telecom Italia 187.*
Water *02 8477 2000.*

Gay & lesbian

For bars and nightlife, *see pp154-157* **Gay & Lesbian**.

Arcigay

Via Bezzecca 3, East (02 5412 2225/ helpline 02 5412 2227/www.arcigay milano.org). Bus 45, 66, 73/tram 27. **Open** 3.30-8pm Mon-Fri; 3.30-7.30pm Sun. Closed 1wk Aug, 1wk Dec. **Map** p251 H7.
Bologna-based Arcigay and Arcilesbica (*see below*), Italy's main gay and lesbian associations, are valuable sources of information. Arcigay runs an excellent website and helpline, and issues the Arcigay card (*see p154*), which is increasingly essential for getting into Milan's gay venues. The Milan office is open Sunday (3.30-7.30pm) to welcome new members and answer questions. There's a small library stocked with gay-related books, mags and videos.

Arcilesbica Zami

Via Bezzecca 4, South (www.arcilesbica. it/milano). Metro Bus 54, 73/tram 12. **Open** 9pm Tue (meetings); other times vary. **Map** p248 D4.
Although less active than Arcigay, this is Italy's main political organisation for lesbians. Its website has a calendar of events, from workshops to screenings. There's also a helpline (02 6311 8654, 7-9pm Thur).

Collettivi Donne Milanesi

Corso Garibaldi 91, North (02 2901 4027/www.women.it/cdm). Metro Moscova/bus 41, 43, 94/tram 3, 4, 12, 14. **Open** 4-7.30pm. **Map** p248 D4.
A lesbian group organising events, political evenings and film screenings in association with Arcigay.

Health

Emergency treatment, through the Italian health system, is available to all travellers. By law, hospital accident and emergency departments (*see below*) must treat emergency cases for free. Before travelling to Milan, EU citizens should obtain the **EHIC** (European Health Insurance Card), available in the UK from post offices, on 0845 605 0707 and at www.ehic.org.uk. This is

equivalent to the Lombardy *Carta Regionale dei Servizi* and lets you consult a national health service doctor free of charge.

Accident & emergency

Should you need urgent medical care, head to the *Pronto Soccorso* (casualty department) at one of the hospitals listed below, all of which offer 24hr emergency services. If your child needs emergency treatment, go to the casualty department of the Ospedale dei Bambini Vittore Buzzi or the Ospedale Maggiore.

Ospedale dei Bambini Vittore Buzzi

Via Castelvetro 32, North (02 331 9845). Bus 43, 57/tram 12, 14. **Map** p248 A3.
Obstetric as well as paediatric casualty departments.

Ospedale Fatebenefratelli

Corso Porta Nuova 23, North (02 63 631). Metro Turati/bus 41, 43. **Map** p249 E4.

Ospedale Maggiore di Milano Policlinico Mangiagalli e Regina Elena di Milano

Ospedale Maggiore *Via Francesco Sforza 28-35, South (switchboard 02 550 3501/paediatric 02 5799 2694/ 297). Metro Crocetta, Missori or San Babila/bus 60, 73, 77, 94/tram 12, 16, 23, 24, 27.* **Map** p251 E7.
Ospedale Mangiagalli *Via della Commenda 12, South (switchboard 02 550 3501). Metro Crocetta, Missori or San Babila/bus 60, 73, 77, 94/tram 12, 16, 23, 24, 27.* **Map** p251 F8.

Ospedale Niguarda

Piazza Ospedale Maggiore 3, North (02 64 441/poison centre 02 6610 1029 24hrs/www.ospedaleniguarda.it). Bus 5, 40, 51, 83/tram 4.
The Niguarda is renowned throughout Italy for its poison department.

Complementary medicine

A wide range of homeopathic remedies is available from pharmacies (*see p227*).

Contraception & abortion

Condoms (*preservativi*) are sold in supermarkets, or over the counter in pharmacies (*see below*). The contraceptive pill (*pillola anticoncezionale*) is available by prescription. The morning-after pill can be obtained at hospital casualty departments (*see p226*); the doctor on duty will write a prescription.

Abortion is available on financial hardship or health grounds, and legal only when performed in public hospitals.

Each district has a family-planning clinic (*consultorio familiare*), run by the health authority. EU citizens with an EHIC card (*see p226*) are entitled to use them, paying the same charges as locals. They're listed in the phone book under *Consultorio Familiare*; or visit www.asl.milano.it/DipAssi/consultorio.asp.

Gynaecological advice can also be had at the following clinics, or at the international health centres listed below.

AIED *Via Vitruvio 43, East (02 6671 4156/www.aiedmilano.com). Metro Lima/bus 60/tram 5, 33.* **Open** 9.30am-7pm Mon-Fri. **Map** p249 G3.
Centro Diagnostico Italiano *Via Saint Bon 20, West (02 483 171/www.cdi.it). Metro Inganni/bus 18, 49, 58, 67.* **Open** 8am-6pm Mon-Fri; 8am-noon Sat.

Dentists

Most dentists in Italy (see *Dentisti* in the *Pagine Gialle*) work privately; you can wait for months for an appointment in a public hospital. Treatment is not cheap, and may not be covered by your insurance. For dental emergencies, go to the hospital casualty departments listed above. Check with your consulate for health clinics where English-speaking dentists can help you. The English *Yellow Pages* (at www.englishyellowpages.it) lists English-speaking dentists.

Doctors

EU nationals with an EHIC card (*see p226*) can consult a national health service doctor free of charge. Drugs that he or she prescribes can be bought from chemists at prices set by the health ministry. If you need tests or specialist outpatient treatment, this will also be charged at fixed rates (known in Italian as '*il ticket*').

Non-EU nationals will be charged a small fee at the doctor's discretion.

Pharmacists (*see below*) are often useful sources of information: they can recommend local doctors and provide you with addresses of laboratories to have tests done.

Milan's long-established international health clinics have highly qualified medical staff, can do tests and also deal with emergency situations.

American International Medical Center (AIMC) *Via Mercalli 11, South (02 5831 9808/www.iht.it/aimc). Metro Crocetta or Missori/bus 94/tram 15.* **Open** 9am-6pm Mon-Fri. **Map** p251 E8.
International Health Centre *Galleria Strasburgo 3, Centre (02 7634 0720/www.ihc.it). Metro Duomo or San Babila/bus 61.* **Open** 9am-7pm Mon-Thu; 9am-6pm Fri. **Map** p252 F7.
Milan Clinic *Via Cerva 25, Centre (02 7601 6047/www.milanclinic.com). Metro San Babila/bus 60, 65, 73.* **Open** 7.30am-7.30pm Mon-Fri; 8am-1pm Sat. **Map** p252 F7.

Helplines & agencies

ALA
800 861 061/www.ulainrete.org. **Open** *Free helpline* 1-6pm Mon-Fri. *English operator* 1-6pm Mon. STD, HIV and AIDS helpline.

CADMI
02 5501 5519, www.cadmi.org. **Open** 2-6pm Tue-Thur. Sexual violence and rape helpline, and drop-in bureau. There is normally an English-speaking volunteer available.

Sexual violence first aid helpline
Ospedale Mangiagalli, via della Commenda 12 (02 5799 2489). **Open** *Hotline* 24hrs. *Drop-in centre* 9am-5pm Mon-Fri.

Hospitals

See p226 **Accident & emergency**.

Opticians

See p140.

Pharmacies & prescriptions

Pharmacies (*farmacie*, marked by a green cross) give informal medical advice for common ailments, and also make up prescriptions. Most also sell homeopathic medicines, and all will check your height/weight/blood pressure on request. Over-the-counter drugs such as aspirin are much costlier in Italy than in the UK or US. Anyone who needs regular medication should bring adequate supplies with them. Also, make sure you know the generic name of any medicines you need, since they may be marketed in Italy under different names.

Normal opening hours are 8.30am-12.30pm and 3.30-7.30pm Monday to Saturday. Outside these hours, a duty rota operates. Night service typically runs 8pm-8.30am. A list by the door of any pharmacy indicates the nearest open ones (also published in the paper); or you can call 800 801 185 to find the nearest open pharmacy. Duty pharmacies apply a surcharge of €3.87 per client (not per item) when the main shop is shut. The pharmacy at **Stazione Centrale** (North, 02 669 0735) is open 24 hours; **Carlo Erba** (piazza del Duomo 21, Centre, 02 8646 4832) is open 8pm-8.30am nightly, but closes for a few hours each day.

ID

You are required by law to carry photo ID with you at all times. You will be asked to

Directory

produce it if you are stopped by traffic police (who will demand your driving licence, which you must carry when you are in charge of a motor vehicle). You will also need ID when you check into a hotel or log in at a cyber café.

Insurance

See also p226 **Health** *and p230* **Police**.

EU nationals are entitled to medical care in Italy, provided they have an EHIC card (*see p226*). This will cover you for emergencies, but using it involves having to deal with the intricacies of the Italian state health system. For short-term visitors it may be better to take out private health insurance so you can choose your health care provider. Non-EU citizens should get private medical cover.

If you rent a vehicle, motorcycle or moped, it's worth paying the extra charge for full insurance cover and sign the collision damage waiver. *See p223* **Car hire**.

Internet & email

Most hotels in Milan have high-speed wireless (Wi-Fi) access, though you will usually be charged a daily rate for this (sometimes through a third party, though connection is usually simple, if not cheap). A growing number of cafés and bars have internet access, although not to the extent of many European business cities. The website Jiwire (www.jiwire.com) shows a map of Milan's paid and free Wi-Fi hotspots. Cybercafés are thin on the ground

Internet access

The following is a selection of internet spots throughout the city. Biblioteca Sormani (*see below*) and the Mediateca Santa Teresa offer free internet access.

FNAC *Via Torino, at via Palla 2, Centre (02 869 541). Metro Duomo/ tram 2, 3, 14.* **Open** 9am-8pm Mon-Sat; 10am-8pm Sun. **Rates** €3/hr; €2.50/hr with FNAC card. **Map** p252 D7.
Internet Enjoy *Alzaia Naviglio Pavese 2, South (02 835 7225). Metro Porta Genova/bus 59, 71/tram 9, 29, 30.* **Open** 10am-midnight Mon-Sat; 2pm-midnight Sun. **Rates** €3.20/hr. **Map** p250 C9.
Mediateca Santa Teresa *Via della Moscova 28, North (02 873 9781). Metro Moscova/bus 43, 94.* **Open** 10am-6pm Mon-Fri; 10am-1.45pm Sat. **Map** p249 F3.

Left luggage

Most hotels will look after your luggage for you for a few hours after you have checked out. The left luggage depot at Stazione Centrale (02 892 021) is open 24hrs, daily; the one at Malpensa airport Terminal 1 (02 5858 0298), 6am-10pm daily; at Linate airport (02 716 659), 7am-9.30pm daily.

Legal help

The first stop if you need legal help should always be your consulate (*see p226*). You may be directed to local law firms with English-speaking staff. Milan is also home to many associates of English and American law firms.

Libraries

Milan has some 40 public libraries, the most useful and central of which are listed below. Visit www.comune. milano.it/biblioteche for a full list. You'll need to show ID (such as a passport) to gain entry to most libraries.

Biblioteca del Conservatorio Giuseppe Verdi

Via Conservatorio 12, East (02 7621 10219/www.consmilano.it). Metro San Babila/bus 54, 61. **Open** 8am-7.30pm Mon-Fri; 8am-1pm Sat (book distribution 9am-noon, 3-6pm Mon-Fri; 9am-noon Sat). Closed July, Aug. **Map** p251 F6/p252 F6.
Attached to Milan's conservatory, this has a huge collection of music-related books and manuscripts.

Biblioteca Nazionale Braidense

Via Brera 28, North (02 8646 0907/ www.braidense.it). Metro Lanza or Montenapoleone/bus 61, 94/tram 1, 2, 3, 4, 12, 27. **Open** 8.30am-6.15pm Mon-Fri; 9am-1.45pm Sat. **Map** p248 D5/p252 D5.
The national library contains over a million books, plus manuscripts, periodicals, 19th-century prints and antique books. Consultation is free; only Lombardy residents can borrow.

Biblioteca Sormani

Corso di Porta Vittoria 6, South (freephone 800 880 066/02 8846 3397). Metro Missori or San Babila/bus 54, 60, 65, 73, 84, 94/tram 12, 23, 27. **Open** 9am-7.30pm Mon-Sat. Closed Aug. **Map** p251 F7/p252 F7.
Milan's central public library has over 600,000 works, including Stendhal's library, audio recordings and a great choice of daily papers. Entrance and consultation is free (over-14s only); only Lombardy residents can borrow.

English-language libraries

British Council

Via Manzoni 38, North (02 772 221/ www.britishcouncil.org). Metro Montenapoleone/bus 61/tram 1, 2, 20. **Open** 10am-5pm Mon-Thur. **Map** p250 D7/p252 D7.
A useful selection of English-language fiction and non-fiction, with British newspapers and periodicals. DVD rental covers British history to contemporary British humour.

CSSU (Centro di Studi sugli Stati Uniti)

Piazza Sant'Alessandro 1, Centre (02 5031 3593/users.unimi.it/cssu). Metro Missori/bus 15/tram 2, 3, 14. **Open** 10am-5pm Mon-Thur. **Map** p250 D7/p252 D7.
Housed in Milan's university, this library has a collection of over 10,000 English-language volumes, focusing on US literature, history and social and political issues. Consultation is free for everyone, but borrowing is confined to university staff and students.

Università Cattolica del Sacro Cuore

Largo Gemelli 1, West (freephone 800 209 902/02 72 341/Bibliopoint 02 7234 3849/www.unicatt.it). Metro Sant'Ambrogio/bus 50, 58, 94. **Open** 9am-8pm Mon-Fri. **Map** p250 C7.
A university library of over one million books, many in English. A free three-day pass is available from Bibliopoint, the office on the ground floor of the university's Gregorianum building.

Lost property

Ufficio Oggetti Rinvenuti

Via Friuli 30, South (02 8845 3900/ 08/09). Bus 91, 92/tram 16. **Open** 8.30am-4pm Mon-Fri. **Map** p251 H9.
You can search for lost items via Milan city council's lost property office (www.turismo.comune.milano.it) – see *Oggetti smarriti*, then *Oggetti rinvenuti*.

Ufficio Oggetti Smarriti Ferrovie dello Stato

Stazione Centrale, North (02 6371 2027). Metro Centrale FS/bus 60, 82, 169, 200/tram 2, 9, 29, 30, 33. **Open** 8.30am-4pm Mon-Fri. **Map** p249 G3.
Enter the station from piazza IV Novembre, and the lost property office is just across from the newsagents'. Anything lost on trains should eventually end up here.

Media

Magazines

With the naked female form draped across their covers, Italy's news magazines are not easily distinguishable from the large selection of soft porn on newsstands. *Panorama* and *L'Espresso* provide a generally high-standard round-up of the week's news; national daily *Corriere della Sera*'s Saturday colour supplement, *Io Donna*, is a meaty read and, despite the name, not just for women. For tabloid-style scandal, try *Gente* and *Oggi*, *Chi* or the execrable *Eva 3000*, *Novella 2000* and *Cronaca Vera*.

The biggest-selling title is *Famiglia Cristiana* – available from newsstands or most churches – which alternates Vatican line-toeing with Vatican-baiting, depending on relations between the Holy See and the idiosyncratic Paoline monks who produce it.

National daily newspapers

Italian newspapers can be frustrating: long, indigestible political stories with very little background explanation. That said, they are delightfully unsnobbish, and happily mix serious news, pieces by international commentators, and good, often surreal, crime and human-interest stories.

Sports coverage in the dailies is extensive and thorough, but if you're still not sated, there are the mass-circulation sports papers *Corriere dello Sport*, *Gazzetta dello Sport* and *Tuttosport*. Milan's businessmen are avid readers of the three big financial dailies, *Il Sole 24 Ore*, *Italia Oggi* and *MilanoFinanza*.

Corriere della Sera

www.corriere.it
To the centre of centre-left, Milan-based *Corriere della Sera* is good on crime and foreign news. It has a daily Milan section, which is useful for information on films and cultural events, strikes, roadworks and so on. Its *ViviMilano* supplement (Wednesday) has listings.

Il Giorno

www.ilgiorno.it
Owned by Silvio Berlusconi's family, *Il Giorno* is understandably pro-government – often to a nauseating (when not risible) extent.

La Repubblica

www.repubblica.it
This left-ish daily is good on the mafia and the Vatican, and produces the occasional business scoop. It has a Milan section and, on Thursdays, a weekly listings magazine, *TuttoMilano*.

La Stampa

www.lastampa.it
Part of the massive empire of Turin's Agnelli family, *La Stampa* has good (though inevitably pro-Agnelli) business reporting.

Local dailies

The free newspaper phenomenon hit Italy about five years ago. Milan has three: the first was *Metro*; *City* is published by *Corriere della Sera*; another is *Leggo*. All include brief news items.

Foreign press

The *Financial Times*, *Guardian*, *International Herald Tribune* (with *Italy Daily* supplement), *Wall Street Journal* and most British and European dailies can be found on the day of issue at central newsstands, along with weeklies such as *Newsweek*, *Time* and the *Economist*. For a selection of monthlies, visit **Mondadori** (*see p125*) and **La Feltrinelli** (*see p125*).

Comics

A surprising number of grown-up comics exist in Italy. *Dylan Dog* comics are set in London and feature a Rupert Everett lookalike who combats ghosts and spirits throughout the UK. You'll find people reading them everywhere and, if you are so inclined, they are a fun way to learn a bit of Italian.

Listings & small ads

Easy Milano

www.easymilano.it
Free fortnightly classified ads mag for the English-speaking community, distributed at consulates and expat meeting places in Milan.

Hello Milano

www.hellomilano.it
A free English monthly with event and exhibition listings, available from the tourist office (*see p233*).

The Informer

www.informer.it
Although not specifically Milanese, this long-established publication is based in Milan. It offers useful advice on dealing with red tape and a good small ads section. Worth reading if you're thinking of moving to Italy.

Secondamano

www.secondamano.it
The mother of all ad papers (in Italian). Includes ads for car, household and other second-hand sales, plus flat rents and shares. It's available daily at newsstands, and also has shops around the city where you can place adverts.

Urban

www.urbanmagazine.it
This free monthly publication (in Italian) provides listings of new bars and restaurants in Milan, as well as Rome, Turin, Florence, Naples and Bologna. Find it in racks outside the city's more trendy shops, restaurants and clubs.

Directory

Radio

The three state-owned stations, **RAI 1** (90.6FM), **RAI 2** (93.7FM) and **RAI 3** (99.4FM) play classical and light music, and feature endless chat shows and excellent news bulletins. If you can't stand jabbering DJs, try **LifeGate Radio** (105.1FM). For UK and US chart hits, interspersed with Italian tunes, try the following:

Kiss 97.6FM
Radio Capital 91.7FM
Radio DeeJay 107.0FM
Radio Milano 89.8FM
Radio Monte Carlo 105.3FM
Virgin 104.5FM

Television

Italy has six major networks, three of which are owned by state broadcaster RAI (RAI 1 being the most mainstream and RAI 3 the more 'radical'), and three belonging to Mediaset, owned by Silvio Berlusconi. Many smaller, local stations provide hours of compulsively awful channel-hopping fun. La7 stands out for its independent stance. The standard of news and current affairs slots varies, but most offer a breadth of coverage that makes British TV news look like a parish magazine. All channels dub programmes into Italian, but MTV often shows American sitcoms and other programmes in English with Italian subtitles, and the advent of Sky and digital terrestrial broadcasting means that many hotels (and homes) have better access to foreign channels, especially those running news.

Money

Italy's currency is the euro. There are banknotes of €5, €10, €20, €50, €100, €200 and €500, and coins worth €1 and €2 as well as 1, 2, 5, 10, 20 and 50 cents (c). Euros from any euro zone country are valid in Italy.

ATMs

Most banks and some post offices have 24-hour cashpoints (*bancomat*); the vast majority accept Visa, MasterCard and other cards.

Banking hours

Most banks are open 8.30am-1.30pm and 2.45-4.15pm Monday to Friday. Banks are closed on public holidays.

Bureaux de change

Commission rates vary greatly. Banks usually offer better exchange rates than private bureaux de change (*uffici di cambio*). Shun places displaying 'no commission' signs: the rate of exchange will almost certainly be bad. Main post offices (*see below*) also have exchange bureaux, but they don't accept travellers' cheques. Many city centre bank branches have automatic cash-exchange machines, which accept notes in most major currencies (in good condition). Take a passport or other ID whenever you deal with money, particularly to change travellers' cheques.

American Express *Via Larga 4, Centre (02 7210 4010). Metro Missori/bus 54/tram 12, 15, 27.* **Open** 9am-5.30pm Mon-Fri. **Map** p251 E7/p252 E7.

Credit cards

The Italians have a fondness for cash, but persuading them to take plastic has become easier in the last few years. Practically all hotels now accept at least some of the major credit cards. If your credit card has been lost or stolen, phone one of the emergency numbers listed below. All lines have English-speaking staff and are open 24 hours a day.

American Express *06 4290 4897 (see also above)/lost travellers' cheques 800 872 000.*

Diners Club *800 864 064.*
MasterCard *800 870 866.*
Visa *800 819 014.*

Tax

See also p234 **Working in Milan**. *For VAT rebates on goods purchased in Italy, see p122.*

Sales tax (IVA) is charged at varying rates on most goods and services, and is almost invariably quoted as an integral part of prices, though a few top-end hotels will quote prices without it. A tradesman will sometimes offer rates without it: the implication is that if you're willing to hand over cash and not demand a receipt in return, you'll pay around 20 per cent (ie the amount you would have spent on IVA) less than the real fee – but you and the tradesman risk hefty fines. You're legally required to keep a receipt from any purchase; you may have to show it to the Guardia di Finanza (customs and excise police) when you leave Italy.

Police

Polizia locale, the city police (rather like traffic wardens), deal with traffic and minor problems. They have a headquarters in via Beccaria 19 (Centre, 02 77 271). The main *polizia di stato* station, the **Questura Centrale**, is at via Fatebenefratelli 11 (North, 02 62 261). The addresses of others are listed in phone books under *Polizia* and *Carabinieri* respectively. Incidents can be reported to either force.

Postal services

For international and local courier services, *see p224*.

Italy's equivalent to first-class post, *posta prioritaria*, generally works well: it promises delivery within 24 hours in Italy, three days for

EU countries and four or five for the rest of the world. There's a 60c minimum cost for Italy, or 65c to the rest of Europe. This is the minimum price of a stamp for Europe.

Stamps are sold at post offices and *tabaccherie* only. Most post boxes are red and have two slots, one marked *Per la città* (for Milan), the other *Per tutte le altre destinazioni* (all other destinations).

The **CAI-Postacelere** service (available only at main post offices) costs more than *posta prioritaria* and delivers at the same speed, the only advantage being that you can track the progress of your letter on its website (www. poste.it) or by phone (803 160, 8am-8pm Mon-Sat). Registered mail (*raccomandata*), available only at post offices, has a €2.80 minimum cost in Italy and a €3.45 minimum cost in Europe.

There have been big changes in the management of the Italian post office system in the last few years, and this is reflected in the services they offer (fax, money transfers, banking facilities); for the traveller, the most important is that many now have longer opening hours (8am-7pm); the rest keep to the traditional 8am-2pm Monday to Friday, and 8.30am-noon on Saturday

and any day before a public holiday. Each post office displays a list of the nearest one open when it is closed.

For postal information of any kind, phone the central information office (803 160) or visit www.poste.it.

Posta Centrale *Piazza Cordusio 2 & Via Cordusio 4, Centre (02 7248 2126). Metro Cordusio/tram 2, 3, 4, 12, 14, 24, 27.* **Open** 8am-7pm Mon-Sat. **Map** p250 D6/p252 D6.
Ufficio Posta *Piazza Duca d'Aosta, North (02 669 2467). Metro Centrale FS/bus 90, 91, 92/tram 1, 5, 33.* **Open** 8am-7pm Mon-Sat. **Map** p249 F3. (This is the temporary address while Stazione Centrale undergoes renovation).

Religion

Anglican
All Saint's Church, via Solferino 17, North (02 655 2258). Metro Moscova/bus 43, 94. **Service** usually 7.15pm Wed; 10.30am Sun. **Map** p248 D4.

Catholic
San Carlo, piazza Santa Maria del Carmine 2, North (02 8646 3365). Metro Lanza/bus 57, 61/tram 3, 4, 12. **Service** (in English) 10.30am Sun. **Map** p248 D6/p252 D6.

Jewish
Central Synagogue, via Guastalla 19, East (02 551 2029). Bus 60, 77. **Service** times vary; call for details. **Map** p252 F7.

Methodist
Chiesa Evangelica Metodista di Milano, via Porro Lambertenghi 28, North (02 607 2631). Metro Garibaldi/bus 42, 51,

70, 83, 91, 92/tram 4, 11. **Service** (in English) 11.45 Sun; (bilingual English/Italian) 11am 1st Sun of mth.

Muslim
Centro Islamico di Milano e Lombardia, via Cassanese 3, Segrate (02 213 7080). Bus 73. **Service** times and locations vary; call for details.

Zen Buddhist
Via Agnesi 18, South (02 5830 6763/www.centroitalianozen.it). Metro Porta Romana/bus 62, 77, 90, 91, 92/tram 9, 24. **Service** times vary; call 6-7pm Wed for details. **Map** p251 F9.

Safety & security

Milan is, by and large, fairly safe. However, as in any large city, petty crime is a fact of life. Tourists who stand out as such are most susceptible to theft and pickpocketing. Pickpockets often work in pairs or groups, targeting tourist areas, public transport routes and the international arrival area of the airports. Everyone – and lone women especially – should be careful in Stazione Centrale, parks and Arco della Pace areas in the evenings.

A few basic precautions will greatly reduce a street thief's chances:

● Don't carry wallets in back pockets, particularly on buses. If you have a bag or camera with a long strap, wear it across your chest and not dangling from one shoulder.

● Keep bags closed, with your hand on them. Whenever you sit down, do not leave bags or coats on the ground or the back of a chair where you cannot see them.

● When walking down a street, hold cameras and bags on the side of you towards the wall, so you're less likely to become the prey of drive-by motorcycle thieves.

● If you see groups of ragged children brandishing pieces of cardboard, walk by quickly, holding on to your valuables. The cardboard is to confuse you while accomplices pick pockets or bags.

Travel advice

For up-to-date information on travel to a specific country – including the latest news on safety and security, health issues, local laws and customs – contact your home country government's department of foreign affairs. Most have websites packed with useful advice for would-be travellers

Australia
www.smartraveller.gov.au

Canada
www.voyage.gc.ca

New Zealand
www.mfat.govt.nz/travel

Republic of Ireland
http://foreignaffairs.gov.ie

UK
www.fco.gov.uk/travel

USA
http://travel.state.gov

Directory

If you're the victim of a crime, call the police helpline (*see p226*) or go to the nearest police station and say you want to report a *furto* (theft) or *scippo* (bag snatching). A *denuncia* (written statement) of the incident will be made for you. You will need this to make an insurance claim.

Smoking

The groups of people you find outside bars and restaurants will often consist of hardened smokers obeying Italy's rules on lighting up. Smoking is not permitted in any indoor public place, and this includes all bars, nightclubs and restaurants. The rule is strictly enforced, and you will incur a hefty fine if you disobey. For where to buy cigarettes, *see below* **Tobacconists**.

Study

Students staying in Italy for more than eight days need to get hold of a *permesso di soggiorno* (permit to stay; *see p234* **Residence permit**). This can be obtained at the Ufficio Stranieri at the police station (*questura*) at via Montebello 26 (North, 02 62 261). You'll need documents relating to your course, four passport photos, a *marca da bollo* for €14.62 and, if you come from outside the EU, an insurance policy to cover medical fees during your stay. If you are an EU citizen, your medical fees will be covered by your EHIC card (*see p226*).

Milan has a state university and polytechnic, a highly regarded language institute, two private universities, including the prestigious Bocconi, a fine art academy and a renowned music academy. Most run international programmes and have agreements with foreign universities. Consult university websites to see what's on offer. EU citizens have the same right

to study at Italian universities as Italian nationals; however, you will need to have your school diplomas translated and authenticated at the Italian consulate in your own country before presenting them to the *Ufficio Studenti Stranieri* (foreign students' department) of any university.

Outside Milan, there are also universities in Bergamo (www.unibg.it), Brescia (www.unibs.it), Pavia (www.unipv.it) and Castellanza (www.liuc.it). The Open University offers degree-level study programmes in English with tutors throughout Italy. Visit www.open.ac.uk or call 02 813 8048.

Accademia di Belle Arti di Brera *www.accademiadibrera.milano.it.*
Il Conservatorio di Milano *www.consmilano.it.*
Libera Università di Lingue e Comunicazione IULM *www.iulm.it.*
Politecnico di Milano *www.polimi.it/english.*
Universita' Cattolica del Sacro Cuore *www.unicatt.it.*
Università Commerciale Luigi Bocconi *www.uni-bocconi.it.*
Università degli Studi di Milano *www.unimi.it.*

Language schools

Look under *Scuole di lingua* in the *Yellow Pages* (www.englishyellowpages.it). The Società Dante Alighieri (02 669 2816, www.societadantealighieri.org) and Lingua Viva (02 2951 9972, www.linguaviva.it) are recommended for foreigners learning Italian.

Tobacconists

Tabaccherie or *tabaccai* (identified by a white T on a black or blue background) are the only places to buy tobacco products legally. They also sell stamps, phone cards and lottery tickets. Where a *tabaccheria* is located close to a tram, metro or bus stop, it may also sell transport tickets. If not, this duty may have fallen to the newsstand (*edicola*). Most *tabaccherie* keep proper

shop hours; many, however, are attached to bars or have external vending machines so you can satisfy your nicotine craving well into the night.

Telephones

Dialling & codes

Landline numbers in Milan begin with the area code 02, and this must be used whether you call from within or outside the city. Phone numbers within Milan generally have seven or eight digits, although some numbers (such as the central operator of a large firm) may have six or fewer.

All numbers beginning with 800 are freephone lines. For numbers beginning 199 (often for customer services or information), you will be charged a local rate from anywhere in the country. Be wary of calling any number that begins with 899 (often chatlines), as the cost can be as high as €2-€3 a minute and some have fixed rates of up to €15. These numbers can be called from within Italy only; some only function within one phone district.

Rates

Rates have tumbled since competition came to the phone system. The biggest Italian telephone company, Telecom Italia, charges about 20c a minute (45c for calls to mobiles), plus 44c when the caller picks up, for any call to Europe at any time of day. Local and inter-regional calls have off-peak prices from 6pm to 8am and all day Saturday, Sunday and bank holidays. Avoid using phones in hotels, as rates are extortionate.

Public phones

As the Italians are Europe's most enthusiastic mobile-phone users, it's not surprising the number of public phones has declined considerably in recent years. Some bars have pay phones, but if you need to make a long call go to the Telecom Italia phone centre in the Galleria Vittorio Emanuele II or one of many other cheap phone centres throughout the city. Most public phones only accept phone cards (*schede telefoniche*); a few also accept credit cards and cash. Phone cards are available from *tabaccherie* (*see above*) and some newsstands and bars. Note: they have expiry dates.

International calls

To make an international phone call from Italy, dial 00, then the country code: Australia 61; Canada 1; Republic of Ireland 353; New Zealand 64; South Africa 27; UK 44; US 1. Then dial the area code (for calls to the UK, omit the initial zero of the area code), then the number. To phone Milan from abroad, dial the international code (00 in the UK), then 39 for Italy and 02 for Milan, followed by the number.

Operator services

Use the operator to make a reverse charge (collect) call, to ask for a connection, or to ask for a wake-up call; in the latter case, an automatic message will ask you to dial in the time that you want your call – in four figures, using the 24hr clock – followed by your phone number.

Directory enquiries *892 892.*
Operator (also international) *170.*
Wake-up calls *4114.*

Mobile phones

Italian mobile phone numbers begin with 3. GSM phones operate on 900 and 1800 bands. Pre-paid mobile phones can be brought in any Tim, Tre, Vodaphone or Wind store, and

from most supermarkets. Pay-as-you-go SIM cards cost around €10; insert the chip into your own phone and you can dial out and receive calls at local Italian rates.

Fax

International faxes can be sent from the Posta in via Cordusio 4 (*see p231*), for around €2.50 per page. Otherwise, try *cartolerie* (stationers) or photocopying outlets; be aware that the cost may be higher.

Time

Italy is one hour ahead of London, six hours ahead of New York, eight behind Sydney. Clocks are moved forward by one hour in early spring and back in late autumn, as with other EU countries.

Tipping

Many of the larger restaurants now include a service charge of ten to 15 per cent. Tips are not expected in family-run restaurants, though a euro or two is appreciated. A cover charge (*coperto*) for the table and bread will automatically be added to your bill; check whether the service charge (*servizio*) is already included and calculate your tip based on any amounts already added and the quality of service. Ten per cent is considered generous. Taxi drivers will be happy if you round the fare up to the nearest whole euro.

Toilets

By law, Italian bars are obliged to let anyone use their toilets. Buying something will ensure the loo isn't 'out of order'. But don't go in expecting a bar's toilets to be clean or have toilet paper. There are toilets at or near most major tourist sites, some of the metro stations and Cadorna and Centrale railway

stations; most of these have attendants and you'll have to pay a small fee.

Tourist information

Friendly smiles, patience and printed information are rather thin on the ground in Milan's main tourist office by the Duomo; the office near piazza Castello is more helpful (and less busy). Their Welcome Card (€8) gets you discounts on selected sites and tours, and their publication *Milano Mese* has masses of information in English and Italian.

Tourist information
Piazza Duomo 19, Centre (02 7740 4343/www.visitamilano.it). Metro Duomo/tram 2, 3, 4, 13, 14, 24, 27. **Open** 8.45am-1pm, 2-6pm daily. **Map** p251 E7/p252 E7.

Tours

For guided tours, *see p51*.

Visas

EU nationals do not require a visa to visit Italy; neither do citizens of the US, Canada, Australia and New Zealand for stays of up to three months. For EU citizens, a passport or identity card valid for travel abroad is sufficient; all non-EU citizens must have full passports. All visitors should declare their presence to the police within eight days of arrival. If you're staying in a hotel, this will be done for you. If not, contact the Questura Centrale (main police station; *see p230*) for advice.

Water

There are public drinking fountains throughout Milan and in most cases the water is perfectly good to drink. If you have doubts, opt for bottled water. In bars, specify whether you want *acqua naturale* (still) or *gassata* (fizzy).

When to go

Climate

The low-lying Po valley is bound on the north by the Alps and the south-west by the Appennines, which keeps all that moisture firmly where it is – hence the notoriously thick fog that can bring traffic in the area around Milan to a halt. Winter in many parts of Lombardy can be bitter, with winds zipping down from the Alps. Milan, though, is almost wind-free, which makes it feel milder. Snow is uncommon. Spring can be rainy but is quite short, quickly turning to summer, which tends to be muggy and mosquito-ridden. If you are coming in July or August, ensure your hotel has air-conditioning. September is a very pleasant month in Milan, but rain may intrude in late October and November.

Public holidays

On public holidays (*giorni festivi*), banks and businesses are closed, although (with the exception of May Day, Assumption and Christmas Day) bars and restaurants and the shops in the city centre tend to stay open. Public transport is almost non-existent on 1 May and Christmas afternoon. Holidays falling on a Saturday or Sunday are not celebrated the following Monday; however, if a holiday falls on a Thursday or a Tuesday, many people will take the Friday/Monday off as well, a practice known as *fare il ponte* ('bridging') – but this doesn't mean offices are closed on these days.

Public holidays are: New Year's Day (*Capodanno*), 1 January; Epiphany (*Epifania*), 6 January; Easter Monday (*Pasquetta*); Liberation Day, 25 April; Labour Day, 1 May; Republic Day, 2 June; Feast of the Assumption (*Ferragosto*), 15 August; All Saints' (*Tutti Santi*), 1 November; Feast of Sant'Ambrogio (Milan's patron saint), 7 December; Immaculate Conception (*Festa dell'Immacolata*), 8 December; Christmas Day (*Natale*), 25 December; Boxing Day (*Santo Stefano*), 26 December.

Women

Foreign women will be the object of attention in Italy, no matter where they go. Most Italian men are attentive, interested and courteous. You are unlikely to encounter any aggressive behaviour, but avoid outlying areas and don't wander by yourself at night except in lively central zones. There are prostitutes and pushers in the area around Stazione Centrale after dark. They are unlikely to hassle you, but will make your late-night movements less than picturesque. A taxi (*see p221*) is a good idea if you're crossing the city late at night.

Working in Milan

Anyone looking to stay for longer periods in Milan for work is obliged to procure a series of forms and permits. EU citizens should have no problem getting the required documentation once they are in Italy, but non-EU citizens are strongly advised to enquire at their local Italian embassy or consulate before travelling. There are agencies that specialise in obtaining documents for you – for a price, of course (see *Pratiche e certificati – Agenzie* in the *Pagine Gialle*). An important address for all these tasks is the town hall:

Municipio di Milano

Via Larga 12, Centre (02 02 02). Metro Missori/bus 54, 199, 200/tram 12, 15, 23, 27. **Open** *Sept-mid June* 8.30am-3.30pm Mon-Fri. *Mid June-Aug* 8.30am-1pm, 2.30-3.30pm Mon-Fri. **Map** p251 E7/p252 E7.

Residence permit

If you're staying in Italy for longer than three months, you need a *permesso di soggiorno* ('permit to stay'), which is usually granted with little fuss to EU nationals. You should apply for one within eight days of arriving. Go to the Ufficio Stranieri at the police station (*questura*) at via Montebello 26 (North, 02 62 261) with four passport photos, a *marca da bollo* for €14.62 and, if you have one, a letter from your employer giving the reason for your stay. If you don't have such a letter you may be asked how you intend to support yourself. For non-EC nationals the procedure tends to be rather more rigorous.

Weather report

Month	Average temperature		Average rainfall	
	ºC	ºF	mm	in
January	3.5	38.3	65	2.6
February	5	41	50	2
March	9	48.2	75	3
April	13.5	56.3	95	3.7
May	18.5	65.3	120	4.7
June	22	71.6	85	3.4
July	24.5	76.1	75	3
August	24	75.2	85	3.4
September	19	66.2	100	4
October	14	57.2	115	4.5
November	9	48.2	85	3.4
December	4.5	40.1	60	2.4

Further Reference

Books

Classics

Catullus *Poems* Uncannily modern musings from Lake Garda's most famous Roman.
Pliny the Elder *Natural History* Observations of an old Como native.

Fiction

D'Annunzio, Gabriele *The Child of Pleasure* Autobiographical novel by a *bon viveur* and *grand poseur*.
Eco, Umberto *Foucault's Pendulum* Milan takes on a sinister air in this esoteric novel by the renowned author.
Fo, Dario *Accidental Death of an Anarchist* Darkly hilarious take on the fatal 'tumble' of an anarchist from a Milan police HQ window during an interrogation.
Hemingway, Ernest *A Farewell to Arms* Part of this love 'n' war epic is set in Milan and Lago di Maggiore.
Manzoni, Alessandro *I promessi sposi* (*The Betrothed*) The seminal Lombard novel, so ubiquitous you begin to wonder whether it isn't the only Lombard novel.

Non-fiction & travel

Burnett, Stanton H and Mantovani, Luca *The Italian Guillotine: Operation Clean Hands and the Overthrow of Italy's First Republic* A fine account of *Tangentopoli*, the scandal that brought Milan to its knees in the early 1990s, and its consequences.
Foot, John *Milan Since the Miracle: City, Culture and Identity* Intriguing study of the city's recent history and culture. *Calcio: A History of Italian Football* Recent study of the characters, scandals and great moments that have shaped the Italian game.
Grundy, Isobel *Lady Mary Wortley Montagu* This 18th-century English traveller spent many years in and around Lovere on Lake Garda.
Jones, Tobias *The Dark Heart of Italy* Exploration of modern-day Italian culture by British journalist.
Lawrence, DH *Twilight in Italy* Contains wonderful descriptions of Lake Garda.
Wharton, Edith *Italian Backgrounds* A refutation of the 'there's nothing to see in Milan' argument.

Film

L'Albero degli zoccoli (*The Tree of the Wooden Clogs*, Ermanno Olmi, 1978) This film about subsistence farming at the turn of the century was made with non-professional actors speaking in the *bergamasco* dialect.
Incantesimo Napoletano (Paolo Genovese & Luca Miniero, 1999) A Neapolitan girl rejects her heritage and embraces all things Milanese.
Miracle in Milan (*Miracolo a Milano*, Vittorio De Sica, 1950) A magical neo-realist tale about a young orphan who brings light to Milan's beggars.
A Month by the Lake (John Irvin, 1994) The beauty of Lake Como compensates for the turgid tug-of-love plot.
La Notte (Michelangelo Antonioni, 1961) The middle section of Antonioni's trilogy on bourgeois alienation, *La Notte* covers 24 hours in the breakdown of a 'typical' middle-class marriage.
1900 (Bernardo Bertolucci, 1976) This two-part epic on the conflict between fascism and communism was shot around Cremona.
Piso Pisello (Peter Del Monte, 1982) A Milan teenager becomes a father and decides to raise the child alone in this oddball comedy.
Riso Amaro (*Bitter Rice*, Giuseppe De Santis, 1948) Passion and exploitation among Lombardy's rice-paddy workers.
Rocco e i suoi fratelli (*Rocco and his Brothers*, Luchino Visconti, 1960) Five Sicilian brothers and their mother struggle to earn a living in industrial Milan.

Music

Verdi, Giuseppe (1813-1901) Lombard *per eccellenza*, Verdi gave many of his operas local themes or settings: *The Lombards at the First Crusade* (1843), *The Battle of Legnano* (1849) and *Rigoletto* (1851; set in Mantova). Many more reflect the tribulations of nations oppressed by foreign rulers, a sore point in Milan in Verdi's time.

Websites

www.beniculturali.it The cultural heritage ministry's site (Italian only) lists all state-owned museums, galleries, with details about temporary exhibitions.
www.cultura.regione.lombardia.it Information (Italian only) on every point of cultural interest in the Milan province and Lombardy region.
www.hellomilano.it Comprehensive English-language city guide.
www.infopoint.it Local transport information site (Italian only): type in departure point and destination and it will provide timetables.
www.milanotonight.it Italian-only site offering reader reviews of restaurants, bars and the like.

Vocabulary

Italians always appreciate attempts to speak their language, however faltering those attempts may be.

Note that there are two forms of address in the second person singular (you) in Italian: the formal *lei*, which should be used with strangers and older people; and the informal *tu*. The personal pronoun is usually omitted. Italian is pronounced as it is spelled.

Pronunciation

a – as in ask.
e – like a in age (closed e) or e in sell.
i – like ea in east.
o – as in hotel (closed o) or in hot.
u – as in boot.
In front of e and i, c and g sound like check and giraffe respectively. A c before a, o and u sounds as in cat; g before a, o and u sounds as in get. An h after any consonant makes it hard. Before a vowel, the h is silent.
gli sounds like lli in million.
gn sounds like ny in canyon.
qu sounds as in quick.
r is always rolled.
s has two sounds, as in soap or rose.
sc followed by e or i sounds like sh in shame.
sc followed by a, o or u sounds like sc in scout.
z can be sounded ts or dz.

Useful phrases

hello/goodbye (informal) – ciao
good morning – buon giorno
good evening – buona sera
good night – buona notte
please – per favore, per piacere
thank you – grazie
you're welcome – prego
excuse me, sorry – mi scusi (formal), scusa (informal)
I'm sorry, but… – mi dispiace, ma…
I don't speak Italian (very well) – non parlo (molto bene) l'italiano
I don't/didn't understand – non capisco/non ho capito
where's the toilet? – dov'è la toilette/il bagno? (toilets are sometimes marked 'servizi')
open – aperto
closed – chiuso
entrance – entrata/ingresso
exit – uscita
help! – aiuto!
there's a fire! – c'è un incendio!
I want a doctor/policeman – Voglio un dottore/poliziotto
Leave me alone, please – Mi lasci in pace

Times & timetables

could you tell me the time, please? – mi sa (*formal*)/sai (*informal*) dire l'ora, per favore?
it's x o'clock – sono le (…)
it's half past x – sono le (…) e mezza
when does it open? – a che ora apre?

Directions

(turn) left – (giri a) sinistra
(it's on the) right – è a destra
straight on – sempre diritto
where is…? – dov'è…?
could you show me the way to the Duomo? – mi potrebbe indicare la strada per il Duomo?
is it near/far? – è vicino/lontano?

Transport

bus – autobus
car – macchina
underground/subway – metro(politana)
coach – pullman
taxi – tassì, taxi
train – treno
tram – tram
plane – aereo
bus stop – fermata (d'autobus)
station – stazione
platform – binario
ticket/s – biglietto/biglietti
one way – solo andata
return – andata e ritorno
(I'd like) a ticket for – (vorrei) un biglietto per…
fine – multa
I'm sorry, I didn't know I had to stamp it – mi dispiace, non sapevo che lo dovevo timbrare

Communications

phone – telefono
stamp – francobollo
how much is a stamp for England/Australia/the United States? – quanto viene un francobollo per l'Inghilterra/l'Australia/gli Stati Uniti?
can I send a fax? – posso mandare un fax?
can I make a phone call? – posso fare una telefonata?
postcard – cartolina

Shopping

I'd like to try the blue sandals/black shoes/brown boots – vorrei provare i sandali blu/le scarpe nere/gli stivali marroni
do you have it/them in other colours? – ce l'ha in altri colori?
I take (shoe) size… – porto il numero…
I take (dress) size… – porto la taglia…
it's too loose/too tight/just right – mi sta largo/stretto/bene
can you give me a little more/less? – mi dia un po' di più/meno
100 grams of… – un etto di…
300 grams of… – tre etti di…
one kilo of… – un kilo/chilo di…
five kilos of… – cinque chili di…
a litre/two litres of… – un litro/due litri di…

Accommodation

a reservation – una prenotazione
I'd like to book a single/twin/double room – vorrei prenotare una camera singola/doppia/matrimoniale
I'd prefer a room with a bath/shower/window over the courtyard – preferirei una camera con vasca da bagno/doccia/finestra sul cortile
is service included? – è compreso il servizio?

Eating & drinking

I'd like to book a table for four at 8pm – vorrei prenotare un tavolo per quattro alle otto
I don't eat meat; what do you recommend? – non mangio carne; cosa mi consiglia?
this is lukewarm; can you heat it up? – è tiepido; lo può riscaldare?
this wine is corked; could you bring me another bottle? – questo vino sa di tappo; mi può portare un'altra bottiglia, per favore?
that was poor/good/(really) delicious – era mediocre/buono/(davvero) ottimo
the bill – il conto
is service included? – è incluso il servizio?
I think there's a mistake in this bill – credo che il conto sia sbagliato
See also p111 **On the menu**.

Days & nights

Monday – lunedì; **Tuesday** – martedì; **Wednesday** – mercoledì; **Thursday** – giovedì; **Friday** – venerdì; **Saturday** – sabato; **Sunday** – domenica; **yesterday** – ieri; **today** – oggi; **tomorrow** – domani; **morning** – mattina; **afternoon** – pomeriggio; **evening** – sera; **night** – notte; **weekend** – fine settimana or, more usually, weekend; **have a good weekend!** – buon fine settimana!

Numbers & money

0 zero; 1 uno; 2 due; 3 tre; 4 quattro; 5 cinque; 6 sei; 7 sette; 8 otto; 9 nove; 10 dieci; 11 undici; 12 dodici; 13 tredici; 14 quattordici; 15 quindici; 16 sedici; 17 diciasette; 18 diciotto; 19 diciannove; 20 venti; 30 trenta; 40 quaranta; 50 cinquanta; 60 sessanta; 70 settanta; 80 ottanta; 90 novanta; 100 cento; 200 duecento; **1,000** mille.
how much is it? – quanto costa?
do you take credit cards? – accettate carte di credito?
can I pay in pounds/dollars, with traveller's cheques? – posso pagare in sterline/dollari/con gli assegni di viaggio?

Index

Note: page numbers in **bold** indicate section(s) giving key information on a topic; *italics* indicate photographs.

ertisers' Index

...o the relevant pages for contact details

National border	-----
Province border	---
Motorway (*autostrada*)	===
Main road	
Lake/river/canal	
Place of interest	
Church	
Park	
Hospital/university	
Pedestrianised area	
Car park	P
Tourist information	i
Metro station	M

Maps

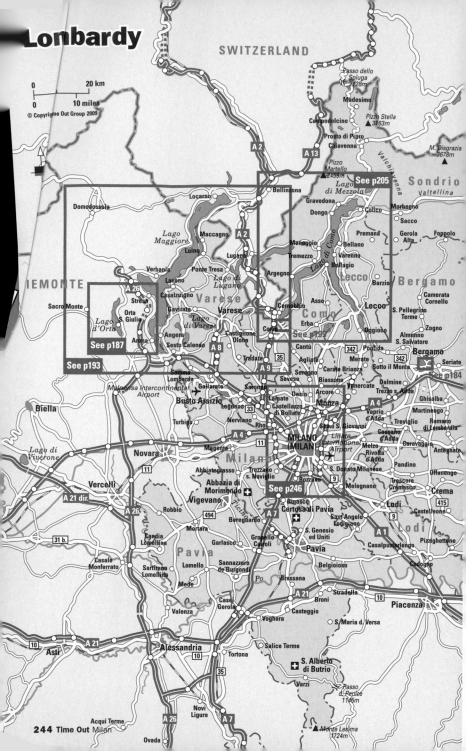

Lonbardy

0   20 km

0   10 miles

© Copyright Out Group 2009

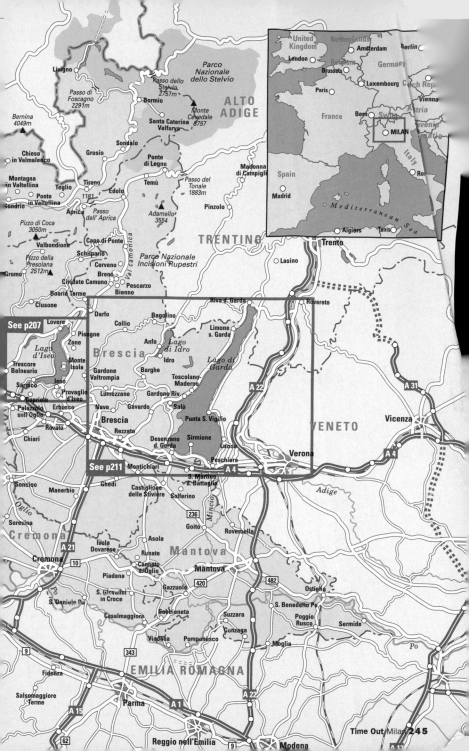

Greater Milan

© Copyright Time Out Group 2009

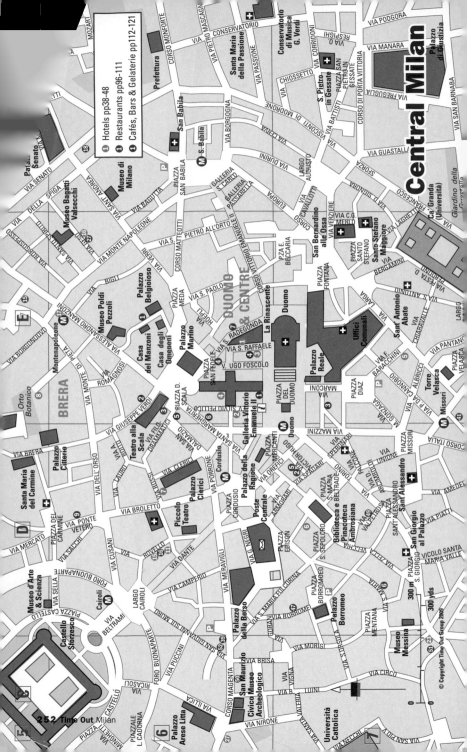

Central Milan

Palazzo di Giustizia

Ca' Granda (Università)

Giardino della

Legend:
🅗 Hotels pp38-48
🅡 Restaurants pp96-111
🅒 Cafés, Bars & Gelaterie pp112-121

BRERA

DUOMO & CENTRE

Orto Botanico

Castello Sforzesco

© Copyright Time Out Group 2009

Street Index

ATM Transport Map

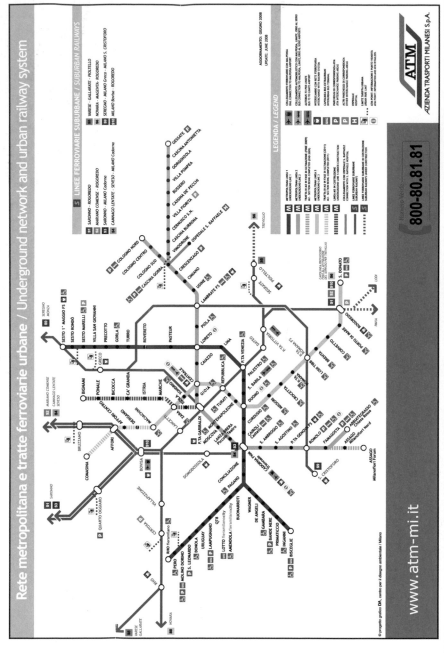